Digital Delirium

CultureTexts

Arthur and Marilouise Kroker   General Editors

CultureTexts is a series of creative explorations of the theory,
politics and culture of hypermodern society.

Titles

Digital Delirium

edited and introduced by
Arthur & Marilouise Kroker

St. Martin's Press
New York

Digital Delirium

St. Martin's Press
Scholarly and Reference Division
175 Fifth Avenue, New York, NY 10010

First published in the United States of America in 1997

Printed in Canada

ISBN 0-312-17237-0

Library of Congress Cataloging-in-Publication Data

Digital delirium / Arthur & Marilouise Kroker, editors.
　　p. cm.
　　Includes bibliographical references.
　　ISBN 0-312-17237-0 (paper)
　　1. Information and technology--Social aspects. 2. Information
technology--Social aspects--United States. 3. Information society.
4. Computers and civilization. I. Kroker, Arthur, 1945- .
II. Kroker, Marilouise.
HM221.D55 1997
303.48'34--dc21
　　　　　　　　　　　　　　　　　　　　　　　　　96-52858
　　　　　　　　　　　　　　　　　　　　　　　　　　　CIP

Contents

Net Politics

Memetic Flesh

Global Algorithm

Digital Delirium

Arthur and Marilouise Kroker

Speed Delirium

Fast Trip to Slow Suicide

Slow down for a fast trip on a slow ride to suicide. Gone through every fashion look in the video book: grunge, preppy, rapper, raver, extreme, street. Worn my Tommy, Ralph, and Calvin, A/X, XS, and all the rest. Eaten every fast food a million times. Heard every song. Seen every scene. God died, and sex is dead. No place to pierce. No body to hide. No drug to take. No word to read. No poetry to sing. It's a slow ride to suicide.

Slow Media

Image the world, but understand nothing.

The real can no longer keep up to the speed of the image. Reality shudders and collapses and fragments into the vortex of many different alternative realities: some cybernetic, some designer, some residual, some an outmoded stock of the vanishing real.

Today, things have speeded up to inertia.

Speed economy, but slow jobs. Speed images, but slow eyes. Speed finance, but slow morality. Speed sex, but slow desire. Speed globalization, but slow localization. Speed media, but slow communication. Speed talk, but no thought.

Image vectors entrap us, entrance us, and disappear us in an electronic labyrinth of the red sky night.

The Slow Mirror of Speed

we have not escaped and will never overcome the fatal destiny of the law of reversal... the faster the tech, the slower the speed of thought... the more accelerated the culture, the slower the rate of social change... the quicker the digital decomposition, the slower the political reflection... the more apparent the external speed, the more real the internal slowness... delirious speed and anxious slowness..a split reality... accelerating digital effects are neutralized by deaccelerating special human effects ... digital reality spins out of control, human reality slow-burns back to earth... speed bodies and slow vision... speed flesh and slow bones... speed web and slow riot... the slow mirror of speed

Body Delirium

It might be a slow ride to suicide but it's a fast trip to digital delirium.

Remember when you were a kid and you first heard the story that everyone was born with a double, a twin? If you were like us, you probably daydreamed about finding your double in a far off exotic land.

Recently, we were thinking about the childhood myth of finding your double while watching a French television documentary on twins. In particular, there was one set of female twins who talked evocatively about the constant 3-D mirror imaging of themselves, where every beauty and imperfection, every lump and line, was magnified one hundred times in stereoscopic imagery. Each twin was a living mirror to the other, with a biological need to see. A closed circle of two, always dressing the same, always sleeping in the same bed, always sharing the same lover, like a nerve connection between two bodies that could be one; even answering the phone with "It is us."

The twins talked with real emotion about the special pleasure that came with touching one another's skin, a pleasure they didn't experience with the same intensity when touching their own skin, and never when touching someone else. As they explained, touching one another's skin was like touching your own, only better.

Twinness was their being.

Sound familiar? Think about the most avant-garde of computer hackers wearing digital gear as part of the body apparatus, feeling a twinness with the machine — an overriding need not to be a machine but to be twinned with one. Digital twins with mirrored identities for a time when digital reality can be your twin, a long lost, but for that matter always desperately sought out electronic double in the digital vortex. Like those hackers at MIT's Media Lab involved in the "Body Net" project: actually externalizing the electro-magnetic field of the body only to better mirror themselves electronically with a digital Other. Not skin on skin, but skin on synthetics. Or those other extropians and futurists and uploaders who are determined to interface human flesh with digital reality — heads as passive terminals for virtual cellular telephones, hands embedded with electronic bank cards, DNA as a living computer matrix. It has always been assumed that computer hackers — cyberboys — have been motivated by a strong desire to dump human flesh, to mutate their skin, taking autistic shelter in an electronic homeland of their own creation.

But we don't think this is true, or, even if it is, it is certainly incomplete, and not complex enough to capture the mythical, even psychoanalytical processes, involved in inventing the digital future. In the same way that the French twins abandoned individual identity in favor of a life of the doubled Other, the digital uploader has found his double in the electronic womb. In the electronic mirror, digital and human reality have been twinned: the interface is complete between human and synthetic identity.

Or, as hackers involved in the Body Net project like to say: "It is us."

"Now We Are Alone in the Wires"

It's a Quake kind of day in San Francisco and we're taking our retrofitted bodies to an interactive art installation at Limn's, a cool 50s going on 2030 furniture store in SoMa, which in that perfect hybrid wave coming off the coast today doubles as cyber-city's hippest multimedia arts site.

"Dig It: Digital Art — The Next Generation" has been advertised as "art produced in the cyberstudios of Multimedia Gulch." One instal-

Graphic: brokenbot@construct.net

lation in particular immediately catches our attention. It's titled
brokenBot, and it's a perfect tech-trash counter-gradient digging its
way like a digital bur against the antiseptically confined rows of
computer art all around the white-on-white walled room. BrokenBot
is visual cybermayhem, a kind of mutating video/sound arcade from
hell. A series of amputated, flickering screens minus their cosmetic
housing are clumped at strange angles on a broken welded metal
table, thick rows of black wires snake out of what looks like the rusted
remains of an undersea diver's helmet, dirty fuse boxes blink on and
off randomly, dusty circuit boards thick with mud slither in space, a
wierdly out-of-place smell of black paint and gas fumes burns its way
into your lungs, and this whole end-of-millennium scene of media
debris for the time after communication is webbed together by violent images. Filmed executions — a shiver, shake and quiver — smell
the gas and feel the bolts of electricity as real bodies gasp for a last
breath, while bleeding out of the double-looped green and red/orange
screens. A perfect tabernacle for the burned-out flesh and cynical
nerves of the brokenBot body. In digital art, the next generation can

be tomorrow or could have been yesterday. BrokenBot mutates from a yesterday site to a tomorrow space. The accompanying text catches perfectly the spirit of terminal amputations:

> technology victim (eyes her) generational consumption. child torn to shreds digitized reprocessed marketed sold. breeds commercially viable product demographic. soviphobia pushes child from planet and back. now we are alone in the wires.

A few days later, we follow the trail of brokenBot to the cyber-home of its artistic creators, just down the street from the now abandoned original site of *Wired* magazine, which has taken flight with the chi-chi cocktail, jitterbugging, Hollywood glamor on my mind set to the twilight side of SoMa. It turns out that brokenBot was created by a brilliant group of artists from Construct, a breakout Web design company. Painters, architects, software designers, musicians, writers, 3D visionaries: Construct is a cyber-guild for the digital Renaissance.

We're talking to the artists/hackers, observing cold, shadowless images of impossible spatial perspectives, 3D flesh, and dark comic strip-like visual desert homages to the spirit of Max Ernst after the shockwave, when we smell the familiar brokenBot scent of black paint and gas fumes. So we check under the table, and sure enough, there's the debris from the brokenBot installation. A really perfect digital aesthetic: art as a broken mirror of life in the ruins of media debris. Digital figure one day, digital (junk) ground the next.

Life as brokenBot, alone in the wires.

Media Delirium

In the 90s, there is no medium, and there certainly is no message. We're living in the eclipse of the mass media. And why? Because a medium of communication implies reciprocity, exchange and a minimal degree of interaction. Mass media have never been about reciprocity, exchange, interaction, or even communication. They replace reciprocity with false simulation, exchange with the tyranny of information overload producing a numbed culture that shuts down for self-protection, interaction with a dense operational network subsituting polls and focus groups and high-intensity marketing warfare for genuine human solidarity, data for communication, and speed for meaning.

In the modern era, we were specialists, trapped in private identities. In the hypermodern era, identity goes public. It gets netted and webbed and digitally nested. Today, the hyperreal body, the hypermedia body, travels in exactly the way that McLuhan predicted: lighter than an astronaut, but at an accelerated speed. The Web is the digital mirror that reflects back to our nomadic bodies its fate as it is externalized in a world of artificial intelligence, recombinant genes, and spliced data streams. As the spectre that haunts the vanishing of mass media, the Web is our privileged window onto the 3d millennium.

A dream of pure operationality — transparent, fluid, circulating, a smooth semiurgy of data flows, digital reality is haunted by its own approaching catastrophe. Digital reality wants to impose the positive law of the Code, but human reality will not be denied. Human reality always contains a hidden, but powerful, reflex towards the rejection of the Code. A violent and primitive impulse of rejection that works less by open refusal than by excess, parody, and delirious intensity.

Digital Futures, Slow Suicide, 30 Cyber-Days in San Francisco, Net Politics, Memetic Flesh and the Global Algorithm: these are natural antibodies secreted by the cyber-body as ways of protecting itself against the sterility of dead digital codes. And ironically, digital reality requires this moment of excess for its very survival. But, as in ancient myth, by absorbing the anti-codes of Net reality, by drinking deeply of this song of slow suicide and delirious speed, digital reality only hastens its own disappearance.

Web Delirium

Severed Nets

There is another Net world: less visible, hidden from easy access, spiralling outwards in the digital archipelago like floating webs of glimmering vectors. Severed nets, populated by a global community of experimental media artists, techno-theorists, net activists, and android writers. Take a voyage on the free side of the Web, and you might just run across some of these wanderers. Like yesterday, when we received a cryptic note from Shu Lea Cheang asking for the URL for Taiwan Data Heaven, saying that it might provide a thread to memories of a lost homeland. When we wrote back saying that Taiwan Data Heaven (http://www.ctheory. com/) was cyber-fiction, she replied: "maybe not." And gave us a thread of her own to Elephant Cage Butterfly Locker (http://ec4.edu.u-ryukyu.ac.jp/radarweb/), a web site linking Tokyo, Okinawa, and the Internet in a thousand poles of repressed memory.

okinawa project

artist in residence: shu lea cheang
"Radarweb" site artists: sawad brooks + beth stryker

"Elephant Cage Butterfly Locker" project shifts sites among Okinawa, Tokyo and the Internet. A "Radarweb" is created tracing the remains of memory.

This project borrows the radar detect central Elephant Cage (nickname for US Sobe communications in Yomitan Village, Okinawa) as memo-data processing site.

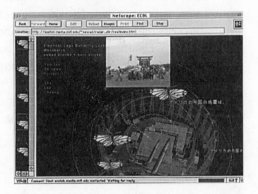

19.5% of Okinawa island is leased out to US military bases enforced by Japan's Central government. Okinawa is being developed as a subtropical resort complete with its own species of butterflies. Okinawa people believe that butterflies guide souls to heaven. Butterflies jamming; butterflies tracing memo-data.

As Nietzsche intimated, the Web has a skin and that skin has a memory: it's Elephant Cage Butterfly Locker. Reappropriating the visual iconography of the radar web installed by the US military in Okinawa, Elephant Cage Butterfly Locker tells the story of colonization suffered by Okinawans under the delirious pressure of the war machine. Stories of rapes and murders and official indifference and ecological genocide, Elephant Cage Butterfly Locker is a pole of resistance. Using the radar technology of the war machine against itself, this is one multimedia art project that transforms itself into a pole of memory: a Web butterfly "jamming, tracing memo-data."

www.ctheory.com

Digital Delirium is CTHEORY: a mutating web site and ascii listserv for bleeding together the critical edges of theory, technology and culture.

Everyday when the sun comes up over China Basin Landing in San Francisco, when cold digital winds blast the streets of Montréal, when guns and knives are silent for the moment in Sarajevo, and when pirate hackers band-talk from Amsterdam to Vienna and Bucharest, CTHEORY webs the globe, radiating back to its net readers a continuously updated media analysis. Theory from the academy without walls, where the very best cyber-philosophers today are standing on street corners in the middle of daily protests in Belgrade with wireless communication systems strapped to their heads rapping out an event-scene for instant transmission to a waiting CTHEORY global community.

A mutating theory-net: Jean Baudrillard vivisecting the 90s, Paul Virilio speaking about cyberwar, god and television, R.U. Sirius reflecting on how it's better to be inspired than wired, Slavoj Zizek meditating on the cultural politics of Japan and Slovenia, dispatches from hyperreal Serbia, event-scenes from the Zapatistas, reports from the virtual body wars of Los Angeles.

With CTHEORY, a new intellectual community is born in hyperreal mode. Sci-fi writer Bruce Sterling, mech poet John Nòto, extraordinary fiction writer Kathy Acker, pioneering electronic artist Lynn

Hershman Leeson, pulp theorist Sue Golding, and theory-fiction writers Stephen Pfohl and Lorenzo Miglioli levitate right off the page, writing cypherfunk, hyper-poems, philosophy, soliloquys, and librettos.

Siegfried Zielinski writes of ancient dreams and medieval cyber-art while computer programmers diagnose the star trekking of physics. Episcopalean priests stalk the UFO meme. Architects track the transphysical city. Hackers splice and rupture the cyber-delirium of Norbert Wiener. Others theorize the importance of "fonts and phrasing" as a new way of digital seeing, technologies of uselessness, whether Tokyo must be destroyed, or should we grow old with Negroponte? CTHEORY is a digital site where net games, panic quakes, and nanotech futures light up the darkening sky. An explosion of intellectual creativity — liquid and critical and diverse — announcing the surfacing of the Web as a new hypermedia of (dis)communication.

Refusing tech hype and rubbing theory against digital culture, CTHEORY brings together Silicon Valley engineers, electronic artists, nano-scientists, computer entrepreneurs, fiction writers, journalists, political, social and cultural theorists, Web Masters, and cyber-researchers in multimedia research institutes from Cologne and Tokyo to Paris, Milan and San Francisco. Moving between print and Web realities, *Digital Delirium* intensifies cyber-reality by allowing electronic writing to break the surface of print.

CTHEORY theorizes in, of, for, and sometimes against the Web, and reports back to the world in the cold type of *Digital Delirium*.

Cold print for a cool millennium.

Digital Renaissance

There is a new renaissance in the making: not medieval analog but hypermodern digital.

After the long sleep of modernism, the creative imagination dreams of coded castles in the air, opens its virtual eyes, and gets to work rewriting the digital world. Now, the future is flash-forwarded into the present: a convulsive recoding of digital reality where the essence of new codes is internalized, retheorised, mutated, and wetwired. Theory in the datastorm.

That's *Digital Delirium*: an upsurge of virtual writers who with every molecule, breath and synapse spark of cyber-imagination rethink life as it has never been known, but has been actually lived. Today, tech reality, like clonal engineering, genetic resequencing of DNA, copyrighting the human species, and tissue engineering, accelerates beyond tech ethics. Tech has taken a big hit on the central nervous system. But now, bunker time for the self-protection of the human species is over. The digital renaissance begins by retelling the story of life in the code exits of cloning, architecture, poetry, sci-fi, fiction, politics, robotic engineering, and science.

With vision, the androids flourish.

Acknowledgements

We would like to thank Michael Boyle for his invaluable help as listserv manager for CTHEORY as well as editorial assistant for *Digital Delirium*. His work has been indispensable for the project, and, in our estimation, Michael is a real model of a digital theorist, combining great craft knowledge of the Net with an intense commitment to the highest standards of intellectuality. CTHEORY's web site is made possible through the globally appreciated voluntary work of Carl Steadman, who links forward-edge digital knowledge with intellectual commitment.

Arthur Kroker's contribution to *Digital Delirium* was facilitated by a research grant from the Social Sciences and Humanities Research Council of Canada.

Going directly to the fabled origin of the so-called information highway, *Digital Delirium* writes the streets of San Francisco as a way of talking about the ambiguous legacy of wired culture.

Photo: Warren Padula

30 Cyber-Days in San Francisco

Arthur and Marilouise Kroker

Singing the Blues in Cyber-City

Chaos time. It's 6:30 p.m. on Market Street in San Francisco, just down the way from the Virgin Megastore. Business people are fleeing homeward, office towers are shutting down, security guards and cleaners are moving in, coffee shops and stores are locking up their doors, and smokers hurry by, lighting up first cigarettes since the afternoon break.

There are no street people in cyber-city, but there are plenty in SF. They might occupy different worlds, but when chaos time comes, when it's that dusky cusp between light and dark, between cyber-city at work and SF at evening play, sometimes, just sometimes, the two populations meet.

Like on the corner of Powell and Market, we hear a blast from the pre-MTV past. Hard drivin' 60s R&B tunes are being played by a guy who looks like Fats Domino and sounds like him too, putting down a heavy beat on a set of rusty blue drums, singing with a deep bass voice that puts into song the wail of America that has traveled from the plantations of the southern delta to the slaughterhouses of Chicago, and met futureshock in SF, this city at the end of the western continental migration of the body. He's got two sidemen, both sitting on speakers, the car battery for their electric guitars inside a white plastic garbage can.

A compact, wired guy steps up front and yells: "Just tell the story, brother, tell the story, tell the story, tell the story..." There was something about the music that just pumped the cynicism right out of the air. And it did tell the story. All of America was there: punks with torn Misfits and Fugazi T-shirts, a homeless white guy with an enormous hunting knife in an aluminum taped scabbard in his back pocket, somebody just to our side is drinking limegreen alcohol straight out of the bottle, a guy with a Cherokee Nation sweatshirt circles around the band, pulls a harmonica out of his pack and begins to play along, the shopping crowd carrying parcels from Macy's and Armani and GAP put their purchases down and listen, and, all the while, those gigantic posters from Virgin of k.d. lang and Tony Bennett look down on us from their multimillion dollar high-in-the-sky window perches.

But it doesn't really matter. Because for one twilight moment the American song is on the streets of SF, a kind of swirling charged-air energy vector that sweeps its way into your belly and your mind and your eyes, takes you suddenly to places sad and sorrowful and beautiful, and you stand there at this street scene, knowing that for one moment the continent has truly ended here, that it is the end of the road. Now, this is an old story that has been told again and again, in the founding myths of the country, in film, in music, in videos, in idle chatter, and sometimes even in writing. All the energies of the continental American migration are pushed up against the blue sheen of the Pacific. It's as if the massively shifting tectonic plates far under the ground with their eleven fault lines crisscrossing the Bay Area have their fleshly equivalent in the streets of cyber-city. And sometimes, just sometimes, the body plates rub up against the end of the continent just a bit too hard, all that pent-up, screwed down pressure inside the street bodies looks for an opening, an unstable fault line, and when it finds one, the result is a shuddering music quake. Like this dirt-poor outlaw street band. It has exited normal space, the space of SF that Jack Kerouac once described as a "police state." It's a kind of open fault line through which all the rage and the anger and the sorrow and the ecstasy of a street society at the end of the road, explodes out of rasping mouths and rusty drums and beat-up Fender guitars.

The R&B sound is a big rumble at the end of the continent, and so when the band flips into Otis Redding's *Dock of the Bay* with the words: "I left my home in Georgia… Headed for the Frisco Bay… Got nothing to live for 'cause nothin's been going my way," we can just feel the keening of the words inside our skin, and when Fats cuts the words down to the naked-edge line of "Nothin' to live for… Nothin' to live for… Nothin' to live for," which he rasps over and over again like a mantra of the dead, we know that we have mutated beyond music, and are present at a dirge, SF style: end of the continent, end of the road, end of the body, end of life, end of hope. It's just that moment when a song becomes lament, and the city streets are a dance of the dispossessed.

Sound crazy? Maybe. But everyone on that dusky corner, punks and grunge and rockers and homeless women and too-poor-to-be-just-down-and-out-guys and destroyed bodies and digital faces and panhandlers pleas and salaried smiles and AMA conventioneers straight out of the "internal medicine" show at the Hyatt just down the street, and alcoholics, and tourists and office workers — all the demented and the happy and the sad and the lonely and the tired and the frenzied and the dead — just everyone fell into a common magical spell. You could just see it register in body rhythms. Street people began to dance, sometimes fell down hard on their asses but clawed their way back up to air again, punks dropped the Misfits alien-zone stare for a brief moment, and even the tourist folks just couldn't leave, and just wouldn't leave, and just didn't leave. For one brief instant, we were listening to those silent tectonic plates shifting inside of our deep-down feelings, really hearing R&B on the hard luck streets of SF as the intense, ancient song of lament that it was always meant to be.

In the usual way of things, all this led to a no-time time and to a no-place place. The darkness came and the group of pilgrims on a dusky street corner in cyber-city dropped some quarters in the box and went their separate ways.

Red's Java House

Down on the San Francisco Bay along The Embarcadero, there is a place called Red's Java House. It's right across the wharf from the Jeremiah O'Brien, the last of the Liberty ships, and just down the way from a sidewalk plaque commemorating the "Lost Ghost Ship: Lydia." Lost, that is, because its remains have been buried forty feet beneath The Embarcadero, probably along with some tourists, since the last earthquake.

So it's a sunny day in California and we're sitting outside Red's Java House. The kind of place where the food is so bad and the bird shit's so heavy, it makes you want to puke. The longshoremen have fled long ago, and now it's been taken over by the khaki crowd and the Silicon set looking for a bit of True Grit. But not just techie bodies. Retro Hell's Angels are steady customers, a pickup truck for construction workers wheels in, complete with a bumper sticker that reads "Workers in the USA are best when they say Union Yes," guys with dreadlocks and Oakleys, bike messengers poured into data suits studded with digital comm-gear, ex-CEOs, from what the SoMa crowd calls "Multi-Media Gulch," slipstreaming their Chili Dogs and wondering whimsically where it all went wrong, a teal-haired woman in a blue leather US Highway 101 jacket, retired couples, and there's even some bunko artists in the corner cashing in their chips.

Red's Java House was really hopping that day: lunch-time crowd pigeon roosting, tooling Buds and vacuum-eating cheeseburgers. In the noonday sun, my body might be in San Francisco, but my thoughts are with the Germans. I'm reading Heidegger's essay on anxiety, looking, I suppose, for a philosophical encryption chip to the malaise of the hyper-media mind. And it's a curious thing. Heidegger says that anxiety is about confronting nothingness. I don't bother to think that one through, but feed Heidegger's insight directly to my stomach neurons, probably to get a quick take on what my eating intelligence has to say about the relationship between anxiety and nothingness.

Now crazy-ass seagulls, pure Clorox white, are circling in the air, cheeseburgers are being lazily chomped all around me, the Red's Java crowd is at that edge of late morning tiredness and lunch-time happiness, and I know, I just know, that

Heidegger is wrong. It's not nothingness that people are afraid of, at least the California crowd down on The Embarcadero, but just the opposite. What really hardwires the anxiety gene directly into the California cellular structure is not nothingness, but hyperactivity. Always having something to do like an ulcer-weight coming down heavy on your mind, and your body is rattled tight, and you can't walk except at a trot with face muscles pulled taut, and running shoes with your working clothes that you don't really want to wear, and you're on the run baby run treadmill at the high tech street level display-window gym speeding to nowhere; but time is money, appearance is everything, and you just can't afford to miss that nifty power walk up and down San Francisco Bay. Gogol's "dead souls" as 90s repressed young professionals. And not just the Silicon boys and girls either, but everybody in San Francisco has gotten into the act: the suits on Market Street put on hypermedia flesh to autodoc every morning at their cyber-work stations, homeless guys along the Bay do hard-edge military style calisthenics, complete with one-arm pushups with legs suspended three-feet off the air on park fencing, the Ferry building is a fast vector blast of cyber-muscle rolling in from the night-time dreamworld of Marin county, and there's not a word spoken here that's not a paean to promotional culture with a capital P. But then again, maybe Heidegger is right. Maybe the anxious self reaches pitch velocity running from nothingness, and really loving it.

Red's Java House is about as close to Heidegger's nothingness as you're going to get on this side of God's green acre. It's the kind of place where the Bay is on your mind, the sun is in your skin, and you're sitting there with a Bud and a cheeseburger and your cool shades tucked in tight. But your thoughts have drifted away to that quiet place we all have inside us where the horizon narrows down to a beautiful circle, where life and love and worries and just plain lunch-time eating vector together into a forget-me-not kind of day. If Heidegger could have just done some writing at Red's Java House, I'm pretty sure that he'd want to rethink nothingness. And why? Because in California, the hypermedia body has already blasted through to the other side of nothingness, to that crazy edge of end-of-the continent energy cut with a little earthquake hysteria, where what's really desirable is the panic anxiety that comes from riding the abyss, just between hyper-stress and flat-ass inertia. Lazy days are here again, I'm OK and so are you, as long as you're not in San Quentin. Hedonism, San Francisco style.

In California, nobody fears nothingness. It's what people eat for lunch, and in San Francisco they get it every day, for the price of a True Grit cheeseburger and a Bud at Red's Java House.

Digital Dustbowl: Squatting On the Dock of the Bay

In San Francisco, you don't have to look far to find the surplus class. Just go down to the old dry dock area, the one that used to hustle with all the sounds and sights of thousands of blue-collar workers repairing ships' conveyor lines, and you will suddenly find yourself exiting the glitzy world of SF gussying up for the millennium, and quick-time entering a surreal world of nomadic bodies and live-in campers squatting on the dock of the Bay. Every night when the sun goes down and the San Francisco cops come up, the squat comes alive with the survival tales of the surplus class living on the physical edge of technotopia, right in sight of the high finance, high-intensity money-spangled skyline with its Trans-America Masonic architecture.

It's a strange and surreal world of disappearances: disappeared ships, disappeared labor, disappeared communities. But in the squat, there's one thing that hasn't vanished, and that's memory. It's a real inter-zone of embedded memory, squatted by people with a story to tell of survivors living on the edge who have beat the odds, and who might be dumped into surplus flesh by the new technological elite — the virtual class — but who have learned new labor skills for the end-of-the-century: laboring, that is, to survive as the vanguard of the disappeared of America. This is what happens to Marx's "dead labor" when it starts to speak.

Take Jesus. He's a tough-ass, mean-thinking Puerto Rican organic intellectual married to a French Maoist. With a staccato way of thinking and a blue-collar way of talking, he puts into words the long-repressed story of the squat. And he's unflinching. "Don't give me that crap about the so-called War on Drugs. The White House is the biggest rock house in America." Or, "If you're poor and black in America, you ain't got no rights. When you're in the projects, the cops will bust down your door every night. In the projects, you're always living with your pants down." Or, "What are you going to say to a kid. Stay in school for chump change, when you could be a high roller starting up your own drug emporium on the street corner in front of your own home. In America, the kids that deal aren't getting drugs by themselves. We're talking here about a big distribution network: banks and cops and government."

And then there's the guy who calls himself the Desert Rat. A black leather cowboy hat pulled down over his eyes, with the strings pulled taut under his lip just above a full salt and pepper beard. He's been living in the squat for a few months, working out of the back of his truck as a car mechanic. He's reputed to be the best auto mechanic in a 50-mile radius of the city. The day we were there, a long line of Saabs and Corollas and Cherokees, straight from the Valley, were waiting in a long, snaking line to be diagnosed by the Desert Rat: delivering up their cars for final judgment — bad timing, burnt-out valves, shocks and struts, clutch and transmission problems, blown electrical fuses, shot computer circuitry, ignition failures, spitting, misfiring pistons. Now, most of the year, the Desert Rat spends his time walking barefoot in the Sonora Desert. He tells us his story sitting behind the wheel of his truck, drinking skim milk straight out of the carton, all the while listening to Jesus and nodding his head in assent. Then he adds: "I first came to SF in 68. Couldn't afford an apartment then, and sure can't afford one now."

This is a squat, California style: vehicle-oriented, perfectly nomadic, an interzone, where you can turn on the ignition, and leave at a moment's notice. In America, property is king, and nothing much has changed here. It could be a waterfront, picture window on the bay, suburb for the surplus class. Except it's not. It's got all the pain and the memory of people who have been pushed out of the system, and who have done the next best thing, becoming the lonely coyotes of the surplus class. Refusing service work, they are the last and best of the independent workers: living off the land, re-skilling their labor, prophets of the future of blue-collar work in the American digital dustbowl.

Remake Millennium

The 99 Year Phone Call

Did you see the clip on the news the other night about the so-called "crisis in the computer industry?" According to the hype, laid-back programmers in the 60s (probably under the influence of psychedelics) made a big coding error. Never suspecting that they were writing code for the millennium, they entered two-digit dates instead of four into the internal system-operating instructions of computers. This was thought to be a really groovy digital compression idea at the time. Until, that is, cyber-culture slammed into the vector wall of the Year 2000. As the TV doomsday anchor explained with smiling teeth: "Make a long-distance phone call one minute before the millennium and hang up one minute after, and receive for your two minute phone call a 99 year telephone bill." Unable to recognize the four digits in the 3d millennium, computers will do the next best thing. When in doubt, go remake and head straight back for the Year 1900 and do the 20th century (digitally) all over again. And it's kind of perfect. Just listen to all those bankers and computer CEO's who flash onto the screen, talking in earnest cyber-Red Scare terms about the "potential" 600 billion dollar cost to business to change a few digits, or the "I dunno, don't blame me" government spokesman who says that we're cyber-sunk as a nation: it's four digits or bust; or the insurance executives with worried faces who speak of changing 1.6 million dates in time for the millennium. But we're TV news scare-proofed. We know that this is all fake, that coding today is all auto-pilot stuff, that there is some hacker somewhere, probably inspired by this news report and with digital dreams galore of Netscape and Yahoo! in her mind, who is already putting down code to bring the lost in space cyber-millennium safely back to earth.

But maybe it's something else. Perhaps this news report doesn't have anything to do with money at all, but is a powerful metaphor for fear of the millennium.

Confronted by all the structural changes and seismic shifts brought on by the digital 90s, the fearful computer has an anxiety attack, quickly flipping from a cyber-aggressor of time to an historian of time past. Remake coding for a remake culture for a remake millennium. And why not? Computers have feelings too, and like a kitten that fails to make a jump, falls back to earth with a crash, and starts to lick itself furiously because it's embarrassed, computers sometimes go to ground in the past as a way of distracting attention from future fear. And so do we.

That's why it's the remake millennium. As the Year 2000 gets closer, the recycle cycle is more intense. Remake cinema, remake songs, remake music eras, remake Martini lunches and cocktail chatter, remake cigars, remake fashion, remake faces, remake politics, remake suburbia. The more things are front-loaded by future pressure, the more society reaches into the grab-bag of the past, and spews out lame remakes and flat-line memes and mutant recombinant images. Under the hyper-stress of a future of seismic shifts and radical structural changes and new technologies and new ways of digital understanding, culture retreats to the remake bunker. Not as McLuhan predicted when he said that old technologies have one last function as content for the invisible form of new technologies, but something much more politically perverse. The remake millennium is closer to Nietzsche's aphorism "Let the Dead Bury the Living." New technologies seem to entail a big drop in human creativity, and a vast increase in the pleasure of mass repetition. The "maggot man" is everywhere.

And it's killing us: 50s suburbs become the racially and class segregated privatized gated communities of the 90s; American rugged individualism comes back as Montana Freemen and private right-wing, gun-toting militias; First Amendment rights are recycled as libertarian squeals of total non-interference by government in private life; the 50s organization man disciplinary ideology returns under the mantra of "tough love". Frank Sinatra, the Beatles, Tony Bennett, Sgt. Bilko, Mod fashion, Bob Dole: 90s culture becomes a mortuary of the dead past and creepy images and resurrected effects and 3d generation TV series with TV hits as cinema blockbusters and repeat politics — recycled, recombined, reworked, respewed.

So, here's one more recycle. The TV report on the crisis in the computer industry said that the millennium "could be a big 0."

"Could be?" The remake millennium already is a "big 0." For remake culture, that's the point.

Yahoo! Capitalism

Yahoo! goes public and its share value zooms to $1.2 billion in a single day. Touted as one of the big "concept buys" of the 90s, Yahoo!, like Netscape before it, has no real value, only virtual value. And in the age of Web economy and digital production and multi-media culture and data infotainment and convergence among the vector giants of the new world of global telecommunications, the only value in play is virtual value. Psychological perception is everything: virtual value means that things have value only in relation to the speed of their own disappearance. No longer symbolic capital or scarcity capital, virtual value is about money in its purely mathematical stage as a global vector, gathering speed and momentum only in relation to the end of value itself.

And why? Because pan-capitalism has finally entered the age of virtual money. Exiting the society of consumption, refusing the reality constraints of information culture, and certainly leaving behind the scarcity values of industrial economy, pan-capitalism has gone over fully to the side of virtual exchange-value. Virtual exchange-value is time after money, when value goes supernova and in a final brilliant implosion breaks the referential link between value and production, code and solvency-principle, use-value and exchange-value. Time after money is neither about use nor exchange, but represents the end of utility and the eclipse of exchange. Today, economic vectors acquire value only to the extent that they implode beyond the inertial weight of use-value, and go terminal on the question of value in exchange. Vector economy — the post-production economy of time after money — is allergic to usefulness and hostile to exchange. Time after money wants only its own death. It wants to witness the disappearance of money into literature, to be present when pan-capitalism finally goes parodic, when capitalism becomes a satirist of its own exhaustion of value.

Consequently, the name Yahoo!. That's capitalism as the master of ceremonies at its own worldwide financial roast where the point is to reverse value, to praise by abuse, to honor by contempt, to affirm by the joke. Yahoo! capitalism, then, for a millennial culture where money is pure virtuality, pure disappearance, pure perception, pure speed, pure death, pure mockery.

In the digital economy of vectors and speeds and slownesses, things have determinate value only in relation to the end of value. We are also living in the twilight period of time after value. Beyond (popular) consciousness, beyond (strategic) control, beyond (modernist) rationality, time after value is understandable only in terms of the ancient language of alchemy where things are interesting only to the degree that they are chimerical and effervescent and liquid. Like Yahoo!, a "search engine," without real value for a society in search of the meaning of virtual value.

Triumphant in its victory over all the old referents, from consumption and information and production to scarcity value, pan-capitalism is confident enough to play a joke on itself, and perhaps on us. Reviving the medieval tradition of the court jester, it lets us into the vernacular secret of capitalism in its (post)-symbolic stage.

Yahoo! It's time after money.

ReBoot

Or, maybe it's the opposite. Perhaps virtual capitalism can't stand its own terminal speed, begins to shudder shock at its own future as a pure vector far from the comforting shore of consumption value, and, like everybody else in the convulsive 90s, panics at the digital wildness within. That would explain the magical attraction of the name Yahoo!. A "concept buy" alright for a panic capitalism that begins to clue in to its own terminal future in time after capitalism and heads for the security of the most ancient of all referents, for the library, for a "digital search engine," as a way of making (narrative) sense of it all.

Yahoo! for prospecting digital gold.

30 Smoke-Free Days in California

Zero Tolerance

I'm driving through the Sacramento Valley, listening to bible belt preachers on the radio cut with some patches of harp rap, thinking of Foucault in his Death Valley days, and smoking a Camel. Suddenly, a California State Trooper on his tech-customized Harley pops his flashing light and pulls me over. Fourteen antennas reaming from his Bladerunner helmet, no shades 'cause he's wearing contact lenses encrypted with the American flag, and with his left cheek tattooed, "It's all in the Good Book," the trooper pulls his sun-baked beef off the bike, stoops to wipe a speck of Interstate dust from his SM hi-top black leather boots, and steps over my rent-a-car with that peculiar "It's not just a good idea, it's the law" attitude.

I do an instant Catholic examination of (highway) conscience. Haven't broken the speed limit, my seat belt's tucked up tight to my belly, haven't been drinking for at least an hour, I've got no unconcealed weapons, my blood's drug-free and my mind is (pretty) pure, and unlike most of the teenage spirits and maybe some of the agri-business farmers in the Valley, I'm not sky-high on speed and whacked out on Prozac. I've got a cheery smile, an upright face, no cheesecake flesh, and a life-affirming attitude and I might be in the California midwest but I still believe in Life, Liberty and the pursuit of Techno-Culture, so help me God. But just to be sure, I reach in my pocket and pull out my rights: I've got a 1st amendment mouth, a 4th amendment vehicle, and a constitutional iron-clad guarantee to a zone of middle class white boy privacy.

Feeling pretty confident, I press down my window, and say: "What's the problem officer? I haven't been speeding."

He answers: "Speed's got nothing to do with it. Look what you're holding in your right hand."

So I say "Yeah," as I flick the ash from my Camel.

"Sir, there's zero tolerance for smoking in this town."

When I protest, "I'm just driving through," he hands me a $100 ticket and says: "I don't make the law — I just enforce it." And then, with just a little nod towards his Presbyterian past, he hands me a nicotine patch and smirks: "This should be enough to get you out of town."

Digital Angels: Timothy Leary in the Clouds

May 8, 1996

At the end of the evening, R.U. Sirius tells the story of his last trip to LA to visit Timothy Leary. Dying of cancer, Leary has already done death one better, passing over at hyper-speed to the beatific state as the guest of honor at a virtual wake for a virtual death. A kind of New Orleans auto-da-fe in advance for the wake Leary will never get to attend, his house is the daily scene of the greatest congregation of American writers and musicians and merry pranksters and spies and AI recombinants and hallucinogenic eyes and friends and foes and hangers-on and stars and unknowns and networkers and TV anchors and just-released-from-San-Quentin outlaws that this country has ever witnessed. Everybody has come to pay their virtual respects to one of California's most courageous, and certainly most creative, thinkers — to a spirit that passed over long ago to the side of the digital angels.

But not so fast! Gurgling away in the corner of Leary's bedroom is a state of the art 21st century full-body cryogenic unit, a beautiful bubbling vat of liquid nitrogen, accompanied by uniformed deep-freeze attendants ready on quick-time to snatch Leary's fading flesh away at the moment of death for the big cryo-heaven in the sky. Like Walt Disney before him, Leary is contemplating perpetual life on permanent reserve as a cryogenized icon, deep frozen, staring out with ice-blue nitrogen tinted eyes, liquid cooled for life in the 3d millennium. The twin cryo-heads of Disney and Leary: a perfect metaphor of America, united at last in virtual death.

Just before R.U. Sirius took his virtual leave from the virtual wake for the virtual death, Leary motioned to the cryo-unit in the corner, winked, and said: "Hey R.U. — want to be my roommate?"

June 4, 1996

In the end, Leary didn't have to bother with the cryo unit. And why? Because his image has already been frozen in time, preceding his virtual death with a precession of virtual memories. And if he could mutter "Why not?" at that fateful moment, that's because he was a real mystic, American style.

Out There Havin' Fun in the Warm California Sun

R. U. Sirius

California is the dissipating structure of analytic logic replaced by magick as mediated by engineering. Three feet off the ground and rising, the rest of the world rests its weary chin on our shores, gazing upwards. Critiquing. Swooning. Wishing it could come here to surf the silicon waves, fuck the silicone babes, or be swallowed up in some Mansonoid blood-red neon desert.

Reporters come and go. They find an adolescent 75-year-old philosopher king preparing to have his head cut off and preserved on ice. But before going, he would like you to know that "when the nervous system can be used at Einsteinian relativistic speeds, the passive limitations of the nervous system itself become apparent."

California is on the edge of a tremendous nervous breakthrough. Some of you are jealous.

European and eastern bohemians could never really embrace the psychedelic experience. It's not history that haunts them so much as the toilet training of classical education — the structures of credibility. California — INcredible home of Disneyland, Hollywood, Silicon Valley, and LSD culture hasn't merely UNmade history, it's flattened time. From our vantage point, we look forward as easily as we look backwards.

This doesn't necessarily make us nice or happy. It does tend to make us permissive, but it can be the permissiveness of a cowboy lynch mob that is mutating via some mix of tabloid vulgarity and mediated sophistication towards replicating the international outlaw occult recklessness personified by the weirdo freaks who surrounded Hitler in Germany.

But it doesn't have to be. From my time zone it's obvious that we are constructing the digital equivalent of the DMT experience. Soon, all of the information in the universe will be mainlined directly into your nervous system. Trust me on this. You have a choice. You can either become an information processing machine, or you can become an orgasm. In other words, *Wired* versus *Mondo 2000* — for all eternity.

The future, my cultured friends, is the direct interaction between the nervous system and the information system. The formerly interior terrain of thought and memory will be exteriorized. It will begin at our fingertips. Our experiences — far from being disembodied — will be one of direct bodily reception. The spinal chord/brain as antenna.

Don't be left behind. Here in California, there are many flavors of atavism to choose from. Look for the one that promises a breakthrough in the grey room. Nothing up our sleeves. No strings attached. This is what you've been waiting for.

STEP RIGHT UP. YOU CAN'T AFFORD TO MISS THIS!

The View from Butte, Montana

A Response to Red's Java House

Pat Munday

Walking the razor edge of hyperactivity, the SF post-moderns don't fear nothingness? They fear too much of too much? Then they move to Montana and give the state a bad name...

The view from here is a bit *contraire*. In old Butte, where the dust blows heavy with old smelter fallout, hyperactivity revolves around working 3 part-time minimum wage jobs to feed the kids, learning about the good life from watching prime-time TV, and trying to fill all your hunting tags by killing deer, elk, antelope, and moose. The nothingness creeps in. The nothingness is not like the cold feeling of the ground that creeps through your sleeping bag and into your bones on a 30 below night in the mountains. The cold ground is real. Even if you freeze to death, at least you know it's nature's eloquent way of reaching out to you. The abyss has no eloquence. It's a nothingness like the patches of blank screen that appear on your computer screen during a virus attack. Dead animals, beer, TV, and the fact that your boss is some high school kid don't fill no abyss.

The abyss, the nothingness, stems from the utter meaninglessness of your life. Being nice to some shmuck tourist who's paying for a bottle of pop with a credit card. Cheering for your kid who, even if he makes first-string offense, won't have any future. Watching some Californicator build a log mansion on the creek where your Dad used to take you fishing. You have little control and not many choices. Control? Tell the manager you think he should order more Coke and less Pepsi. Choice? Vote for the rich smooth-talking Democrat guy, or for the rich mean-spirited Republican guy.

I would guess even the hyperactive silicon info-geeks feel about the same way. What are they creating with their life? Do they have time after work to play catch with their sons, or teach their daughters to two-step? Is the only difference between them and marginally employed Montanans that they are filling the hole in their life with a red Porsche and a trophy wife instead of an old Wagoneer and a .270 Winchester? Unfortunately, they all want to vacation in Montana, in August, when it seldom snows.

Maybe the Unabomber was right: "It would be better to dump the whole stinking system and take the consequences." The Unabomber was mostly talk. He didn't do as much harm as the LA Freeway on a good day. And if we believe evolution, a human individual, even one who sends bombs in the mail, is just another stochastic factor, no more purposeful than an avalanche or a hungry grizzly. Now that really pulls me back from the abyss, the thought that human nature is just another random and meaningless Darwinian maze-way.

How about Zen? We're just part of nature, bobbing along on the watercourse way, so go with the flow... But then there are those who insist on building logjams (or log mansions) in the very spot nature leads me, graphite flyrod in hand. Hmmm, no political solution to be had there.

Al Borgmann (he's a philosophy professor in Missoula, but that's OK; Missoula isn't much further from Montana than Butte) believes the essential problem lies with the impotence of liberalism. Liberals refuse to make judgments on what constitutes the good life. So, without a goal, we board the train, criticize one another, and argue about where we have went wrong in the past. Meanwhile, the train pushes on, further blurring our sense of place, disrupting connections with community, and accelerating our mental pace, so that it becomes more and more difficult to hop off.

Have a nice day.

Digital Futures

Following the thread of leading cyber-thinkers, *Digital Delirium* interviews R.U. Sirius, Paul Virilio, Jean Baudrillard, and Slavoj Zizek, and includes a major state of the digital union address by sci-fi writer, Bruce Sterling.

It's Better to be Inspired than Wired

An Interview with R.U. Sirius

Jon Lebkowsky

Clown Prince of the Digital Counterculture

The evolution of a bohemian, technohip subculture within the vibrant and elastic digital culture of today was mediated by two important events. One was the opening of the Internet. The other was the appearance of *Mondo 2000*.

The early Internet derived much of its ambiance from a strange hybrid of 60s counterculture and 80s libertarianism. *Mondo 2000*, a glossy periodical that evolved from an earlier neopsychedelic zine, incorporated this sociopolitical sensibility and blended it with their own peculiar sense of post-punk irreverence, drugged-up pranksterism, and high style. The result was a new cultural trend, or at least the media-generated illusion of one.

It was 1989. Computers were seen as tools of High Geekdom. *Mondo*, however, portrayed the new technology as sexy, hip, and powerfully subversive. And as Captain Picard might say, they made it so.

It was Bart Nagel's unique computer-enhanced graphic style that pushed *Mondo 2K* over the top, making it something of a phenomenon in the early 90s. However, the real meat was in the cheerfully irreverent exploration of nascent technoculture and the evolving computer underground from the perspectives of the writers/editors, whose handles were R.U. Sirius, St. Jude, and Queen Mu. Besides displaying strangeness and charm, early *Mondo* was the only popular representation of the hacker ethic, described by author Andrew Ross as "libertarian and crypto-anarchist in its right-to-know principles and its advocacy of decentralized knowl-edge. [It] asserts the basic right of users to free access to all information. It is a principled attempt, in other words, to challenge the tendency to use technology to form information elites." [*Technoculture* 116]

Despite being non-technical, *Mondo 2000*'s original Editor-in-Chief, the iconoclastic prankster R.U. Sirius, saw clearly the broad implications of the hacker ethic and incorporated it into his bag of tricks. He began hanging out on the WELL, at that time a little-known Bay Area conferencing system that attracted writers, hackers, artists, poets, and publishers from all over the world. He started a topic on *Mondo 2000* in the Hacking conference on the WELL, which evolved into the once-vibrant, now defunct Mondo 2000 conference.

In 1993, Sirius split from *Mondo 2000*. Since then, he's contributed his increasingly acerbic scribblings to publications ranging from *ARTFORUM International* to *Wired* to *Esquire* Japan. In 1994, he recorded an unreleased album called *IOU Babe* for Trent Reznor's Nothing Records with his conceptual-art rock band MV Inc. (formerly called Mondo Vanilli). He has also co-authored two books with St. Jude, *Cyberpunk Handbook: the Real Cyberpunk Fakebook* (Random House), and *How to Mutate and Take Over the World* (Ballantine).

As this interview was completed, Sirius told me about his new website, called "The Mutate Project", that includes a public forum on "how to conduct a guerrilla war against the censorship of the Internet... and other stuff." However sirius this may sound, you can bet it's always somewhat tongue-in-chic.

Mondo to the Core

Lebkowski: Did *Mondo 2000* just cycle out? Or do you think, in a perfect world, you could've held the cultural edge and continued to produce quality content?

R.U. Sirius: Mondo had its moment on the tip of the wave. But I think that a certain combination of our editors and art people could have launched the truly corrosive assault on computer and media culture that was implicit in *Mondo* at its best. I think it's silly to chase the edge. It's much more interesting to explode it... as well as the mainstream. It's better to be inspired than wired.

Lebkowski: When you're associated with the neophile fringe there's that expectation that you'll always be remaking reality, though. Finding the next frontier...

RU: Right. But I don't worry so much about the "neophile fringe" or the cult of newness, believe it or not. I'm more interested in passion and philosophy, sex and subversion... you know... those old-fashioned values. This macho sort of posturing about being the fastest, most technohip, way-ahead person around gets really tiresome. It was sort of funny to me as the *Mondo 2000* thing got going that some people really thought that I should feel ashamed because I'm not an authentic hacker. Really, who gives a fuck? I'm not an auto mechanic either. I just feel compelled to do various forms of communication and make art about the things that intrigue me.

Lebkowski: It seems that *Mondo* tried to be digital culture while at the same time slam dunking it.

RU: Yes! My book *How To Mutate & Take Over the World* does that also. *HTM&TOW* is both the next stage and my personal kiss off to the so-called cyberculture.

We were always horribly ambiguous. Even our hortatory, wild-eyed, faux-utopian opening statement from the first issue (which, incidentally, the academic types insist on keeping in circulation as proof of our naïveté), was more an exercise in poetic extravagance then something to live and die by. So I rode the Virtual Reality hype and the smart drugs hype, but I also made a lot of cynical statements about them. Throughout the early 90s, I repeated the line "I'd rather watch Ren and Stimpy on caffeine than experience virtual reality on smart drugs" in all my lectures and interviews, to try to detach from excessive identification with disappointing infant technologies. It's a very true statement, by the way. But ironic distance also quickly becomes banal… and that spells exhaustion. Let's not talk about exhaustion. What can you say, really?

Lebkowski: There have been many rumors about your reasons for splitting from *Mondo* in 1993. What's the real, unexpurgated story?

RU: I split primarily because I wasn't the one at the controls, and I could feel the thing spinning out of control and couldn't do anything about it.

Unless you were inside *Mondo*, you couldn't possibly understand what it was like. Read *Alice In Wonderland* and the collected works of Kafka as though they were instruction manuals for how to succeed in business, for starters. I'm not interested in magnifying the details though. I love everybody involved.

You know, only an absolute nut would have supported and helped to create *Mondo 2000* when it started in 1989 so what the hell. And I'm a complete lunatic myself so I can only be thankful. I've always been through the looking glass.

Cyberpunk: Threat, Menace, or Marketing Concept?

Lebkowski: Speaking of the past, let's talk about the c-word. *Mondo 2000* was a focus of a superficial "movement" that called itself cyberpunk, after the literary genre. But like *Mondo*, it seems to be gasping for breath. The sf writers who were reluctantly responsible for the meme seem kind of relieved. But you released a book called *The Cyberpunk Handbook* in 95. What's your take?

RU: Bruce Sterling didn't want to have anything to do with it when we interviewed him back in 89. He said he was "taking down the neon sign."

All labels are just conveniences and anybody who takes them too seriously is a fool. But the compulsive need to jettison a label might just be one aspect of taking it too seriously. Does the label help you to communicate a certain aesthetic or a set of generally held beliefs and attitudes? Are you searching for a new label just because somebody told you that it wasn't hip to use this one anymore?

I'm terribly trendy myself. I'm easily pressured by the tyranny of hip. So I had resolutely forsworn against the use of "cyber" in any form. But then I was offered a mercenary opportunity by Random House to assault the cyberpunk concept — in other words to help write a book called *The Cyberpunk Handbook*. It was their idea. I wanted to get the advance for the book and then change the title, but by the time we got the advance, Jude had written a whole bunch of great stuff about cyberpunks. And you know, fuck 'em if they can't take a joke.

Lebkowski: Cyberpunk was really just a marketing term from the word go.

RU: Art movements usually are. Gibson, Sterling and company saw an opportunity to market a genre, which is how you move product in a dense media culture. People need the various classifications and subclassifications to know where to go, because there's too much stuff. The cool thing about the cyberpunk genre is that it's been pretty elastic. Pat Cadigan, Rudy Rucker, *Mondo 2000*, ravers, SRL, underground hackers, Gibson, Leary… it provided a pretty big tent for people to hawk their wares from.

Lebkowski: But cyberpunk seems to be dying now as a marketing concept. We thought we were in on the ground floor and, next thing we knew, we were buried under the basement — coopted by a larger commercial mainstream. The big question seems to be whether the Internet will become completely corporatized. And if it does, will there be alternative channels?

RU: Well, it's a legal matter now. A heavily censored net will make any sort of alternativeness difficult. But there's no easy division. Push comes to shove, the media corps have to sell our pre-packaged little revolts-into-style for us because there's a consumer demand that isn't going to go away. Things are too unsatisfactory and people need to spit it up. Or, in other words, the corporate sponsors will want to put their little logos on everything.

Lebkowski: A favorite example being William S. Burroughs in a Nike ad.

RU: You said it! Would I do a Nike ad? I would! And does that weaken my stance? It does!

Lebkowski: And do you care?

RU: I don't! Really, heroism is a spectator sport. Fuck spectators. Anybody who doesn't factor a need to pay rent and to have pleasures into whatever expectations they have of anybody else can go to fuck. I hate expectations of any kind.

Lebkowski: Subversion never completely succeeds but neither does the attempt to squash it.

RU: Subversion by its nature parisitizes whatever it attempts to subvert. But subversion isn't really subversive any more. I mean, you can do the most outrageous shit, and people's ability to react is just flattened. The greatest hope for subversives is William Bennett and the Christian Coalition and all that. They are trying their best to make subversion subversive again… god bless 'em!

Trapped in a World He Never Made

Lebkowski: You seem to be into paradox. Leading cyberculture while slamming it, practicing raw capitalism while critiquing it in the process. This paradox seems to run through much of the culture jamming stuff.

RU: Well, anybody who doesn't believe that we're trapped hasn't taken a good look around. We're trapped in a sort of mutating multinational corporate oligarchy that's not about to go away. We're trapped by the limitations of our species. We're trapped in time. At the same time identity, politics, and ethics have long turned liquid. It seems that what we have, at least among the sort of hip technophile population, is an experimental attitude. An experimental attitude is one of not knowing, otherwise it's not really experimental.

Also, most people try so hard to put their best face forward, right? I mean, if you're writing a righteous political statement on Monday and you're hyping your ass and talking to the lawyers on Tuesday, you're not going to emphasize Tuesday. You're not going to emphasize your own corruption. Except I tend to, because the deal is what's real. If I can make one claim, it's that I'm the most anti-purist motherfucker around.

Lebkowski: I was talking to former FCC commissioner Nicholas Johnson at a party last night. He was talking about the corporate monopolization of media. If five major corporations control all but the tiniest media channels, then they control the flow of information. In an information economy, that's the flow of life. That's why the corporate/government interests want to control the Internet. To them, it's just one of the several media distribution channels. Zines and pirate media may continue to exist, but they're nothing against the corporate powers.

RU: There's some complicated dynamics there, between corporate interests, government interests, popular interests, and individual liberties that aren't so easily sorted out, but I'll say this from my little corner of the universe. If you have laws against "obscenity" and "indecency" in an open channel like the net, you've effectively silenced the non-mainstream, non-conforming voice because, sooner or later, this is the medium where it all converges. That's not some kind of *Wired*-style technophilia, that's just a fact of life. Sooner or later it all converges around an extension of telephony. Now, corporate media is a tremendous sponsor of alternativeness, but they can survive without it. Or they can pressure artists to tone it down. So it's the independents who are going to be crushed by this, as usual.

However, the net is a terrific environment for guerrilla warfare. It's a great jungle in which to hide and from which to make attacks. And your attacks are by nature communicative. That's what a big chunk of *HTM&TOW* is about.

Lebkowski: I think that effective "guerrilla actions" in a mediated environment will have terrific subtlety. Have you any examples of this kind of poetic terrorism from your own work?

RU: I hope that *HTM&TOW* is the answer to that question. One idea we propagate is that media hackers have to be really fucking great entertainers. That's the key. When you pirate television time, for instance, it should be such a fun thing that people are waiting at their VCRs for the next one.

I remember having an underground paper in high school. As soon as the Principal announced over the loudspeaker that kids weren't allowed to have it, everybody wanted one. As soon as the kids saw that it was playful and funny, they wanted the next one. Of course, adults tend to view anything that isn't dull with suspicion, which is a problem.

Bigger than Satan? R.U. Sirius for Anti-Newt!

Lebkowski: You clearly embrace a lot of contradictions. But what is it that you hope to accomplish? Is there, in any sense, a positive project?

RU: The R.U. Sirius project has always been largely about re-energizing the forgotten "ideology" of the 60s revolt, primarily the notion of post-scarcity liberation. I hesitate in tying myself to the 60s mast, but we're not talking Paul McCartney or George McGovern here.

OK... post-scarcity was basically a premature post-industrial vision of a cybernetic culture in which alienated labor and scarcity was all but eliminated by technology. This had an enormous influence, sometimes explicit and sometimes subterranean. If you go back and investigate the writings of the Yippies, the Diggers, Daniel Cohn-Bendit, who led a near revolution in France in 1968, and various other political radicals, the ones that didn't get absorbed into old fashioned Marx-Leninism, you find this theme over and over again. The machines of loving grace.

This isn't utopian, by the way. I'm anti-utopian. I don't believe in totalizing philosophies or perfectly happy endings. But it could be helluva lot better than it is now.

Lebkowski: This is like [anarchist subculture figure] Bob Black's vision of ludic society.

RU: Actually we're in a very perverted version of a ludic society, in the sense that what's driving technological evolution is shifting from warfare to information, communications, and entertainment... better games, greater bandwidth, film projects the size of military invasions and entertainment corporations the size of medium nation states.

Lebkowski: An extension of the Japanese postwar economy.

RU: Yes. Big business with everybody so seriously dedicated to play that they never get a chance to...

Lebkowski: Play is work.

RU: Right. In so many ways, our society explicitly strives to be the direct opposite of the ideal. It's pretty funny. On the other hand, this speed-of-light hell-on-wheels that we're living in seems to make for a lot of creative energy. There's something to be said for the stress that makes us all want to kill each other and make really cool web pages.

Lebkowski: Notions like the end of work and scarcity are very obscure right now. Why do you think they're relevant?

RU: All you have to do is look at the situation to realize that it's the only relevant political position for anybody who isn't rich. As the result of automation and internationalization, the economic power of ordinary people, which used to reside in the "working class," has completely disappeared — which, incidentally, is why a lot of people have little reason to be thrilled by the relative democratization of media communications that *Wired* and *Mondo* have touted. Also, the virtual economy has overwhelmed the "real" economy of goods and services... at the cutting edge of capitalism, you're in a pure "transacting" economy of derivatives, currency exchanges, options and so forth that has displaced economics. Networked electronic trading is very much its own unique ecology. "Money" is being made not in the investing itself but on the abstraction of the transacting of conceptual wealth. Tremendous profits can be conjured from the consensual hallucination that a transaction that doesn't necessarily have to happen might accumulate (for example) interest at a later date.

The important thing here is that not only doesn't capitalism require as many workers, it doesn't require as many consumers. An economy that trades in pure abstraction is self-sufficient. It can satisfy itself building hallucinatory fortunes that can be cashed in for ownership of property and advanced techno-toys for your wired elite. It's all just bits and bytes really. It's a trick. But it conflates nicely with the logic of late capitalism which is to eliminate that which is superfluous, in other words the formerly working class people who are no longer needed as workers or consumers. That's what downsizing is about... killing the poor. This is not even a slight exaggeration. This is exactly the trajectory of late capitalism, and specifically of the Republican revolution.

Anyway, grant me that we're in a situation where workers are increasingly superfluous. I don't have the figures on hand, but some extraordinary percentage of those people who are employed work for temp agencies. Hazel Henderson told me that 60% of the American people are either unemployable, unemployed, working temp, or working without benefits or job security. A week after she said that, I saw Labor Secretary Robert Reich on television saying more or less the same thing, but the figure was 70%. But a recent poll shows that something like 95% identify themselves as middle class. Hah! They're not middle class.

What you actually have, in vaguely Marxist terminology, is an enormous lumpenproletariat. In other words, non-working or barely-working poor. I mean, this is the most oppressed country in the Western world according to all kinds of statistics. The Reagan Revolution turned the average American into a citizen of the third world. And here comes Newtie to finish the job.

People identify with the middle class though... they're temp workers with televisions, cd players, and hip clothes and hairstyles.

The only alternative to a world of human refuse, serfs and slaves abandoned by an increasingly self-sufficient corporate cyber/media oligarchy is a revolution of this lumpenproletariat (the formerly working class), based not in neo-Luddite refusal but in desire, a desire to live. Which means that the essentials should be given away free, unconditionally. This notion is of course completely in opposition to the current political discourse, and probably goes against every instinct in, say, the average *Wired* reader's brain. I'd like them to just think of me as the anti-Newt.

Cyberculture (a meme that I'm at least partly responsible for generating, incidentally) has emerged as a gleeful apologist for this kill-the-poor trajectory of the Republican revolution. You find it all over *Wired* — this mix of chaos theory and biological modeling that is somehow interpreted as scientific proof of the need to devolve and decentralize the social welfare state while also deregulating and empowering the powerful, autocratic, multinational corporations. You've basically got the breakdown of nation states into global economies simultaneous with the atomization of individuals or their balkanization into disconnected sub-groups, because digital technology conflates space while decentralizing communication and attention. The result is a clear playing field for a mutating corporate oligarchy, which is what we have. I mean, people think it's really liberating because the old industrial ruling class has been liquefied and it's possible for young players to amass extraordinary instant dynasties. But it's savage and inhuman. Maybe the wired elite think that's hip. But then don't go around crying about crime in the streets or pretending to be concerned with ethics.

It's particularly sad and poignant for me to witness how comfortably the subcultural contempt for the normal, the hunger for novelty and change, and the basic anarchistic temperament that was at the core of *Mondo 2000* fits the hip, smug, boundary-breaking, fast-moving, no-time-for-social-niceties world of your wired mega-corporate info/comm/media players. You can find our dirty finger-prints, our rhetoric, all over their advertising style. The joke's on me.

Lebkowski: Clearly there's a fragmentation of community and dissolution of soul. We all sort of slid into it as cyberfoo was co-opted and the Internet was transformed into digital Las Vagueness, but what are you going to do? Do you have a political agenda or a performance agenda?

RU: My main agenda is to explode constricting illusions, whether it's bourgeois propriety, expectation, shame over sexuality, or the money system. Also, in Freudian terms, I'm at war with the cultural superego in favor of the disencumberment of the libido, the id, and the ego... definitely in that order — which connects me to the surrealist and dadaist traditions. Anyway, I don't acknowledge any separation between a political agenda, a performance agenda, a pop agenda, a theoretical agenda, a radical agenda, a survival agenda, a sexual agenda...

My activities right now include getting attention for the book *How To Mutate & Take Over the World*, which I believe is an actual act of sabotage against the plans of big media/technology business, for reasons that aren't immediately obvious. The book announces itself as an act of sabotage on the surface, and fails as that, again on the surface. Wait and see how it unfolds.

At the same time, I believe that I'm finally prepared to give expression to a complete alternative, revolutionary philosophy for the next decade. I'm prepared to deal with both deconstructions and visionary alternatives regarding the money system, cyborgization, virtualization, media, violence and violent media and art, censorship, uncertainty, extropianism or the transcendence of ordinary life, sociobiology, race, gender, sexuality, drugs, individualism and community. I'm ready to put forth a digital age politic that embraces the goals of both liberalism and libertarianism. I believe this will come together with the help of collaborators over the next year or two, and will be presented on The Mutate Project web page.

Nobody has exploded the meaning of the money system or really produced a visionary sociopolitical agenda for a post-industrial economy. It can be done. And I'll do it, with some help.

You know, I see all these media and software people making and spending millions and millions of dollars, and all of these millions of dollars being pissed away on mediocre films, mediocre magazines, peabrained rock bands, stupid web sites — it makes me sick. Give me one million fucking dollars and I'll bring you major cultural and political change within four years. The few people who really know about *Mondo 2000* and what we did with very tiny resources will know that I'm being megalomaniacal but I may be right, everybody else will think I'm just being megalomaniacal. But I've grown a lot since *Mondo 2000*. Get me behind the wheel of another vehicle and *Wired* will be eating my dust. I want to be bigger than Satan.

Unstable Networks

Bruce Sterling

The commentary at cyberspace events often comes from a surprisingly wide area of the political and social spectrum, especially considering that most of the principals dress alike, look alike, and all use the same machinery. Still, the widely various people who speak at events like this have a bedrock of agreement. They will all declare that these are unprecedented and revolutionary times for computer communications, and that the decisions we make right now are going to drastically affect society for dozens, if not hundreds, of years to come.

And there's a lot of home truth in that assessment. We really have been involved in a revolutionary epoch — during the past seven years the status quo has taken a terrible battering, not just in the world of computation, but across the board, economically, politically, socially. There is a level of instability loose at the end of the 20th century that has not been around since at least 1945. Computer communications is one of most powerful, most influential, and least stable areas in the new world disorder.

However, it seems to me that finally, now, in the summer of 1996, we may have attained a comparative breathing-space. The flash-bulb of cyber-novelty has begun to fade from the retina of the public eye.

The bloom of apparently unlimited possibility has receded a bit. We've begun to get a grip on our dumbfounded wonder. This process may be disillusioning, but one needn't feel cynical about it. It's not a cause for despair. That's the lovely thing about unlimited possibility and its down-and-dirty interaction with the human condition.

There you are, you see — facing the marvellous unknown — all those possibilities. And, being human, you just have to make one little decision. Take one little action — just to show that you can, really. And there's a reaction to that action, and that's gratifying, so you take another step. Then another, and another, and another, and pretty soon you've got kids and a mortgage. You're committed. That's life.

We've managed to take some very important and very consequential actions in the past seven years. They may not have been wise actions, but we're not wise; we're just blundering about and doing the best we can. And what was the upshot? Basically, we've bet the farm on the digital imperative.

In the year 1996, everything aspires to the condition of software. Art, politics, music, money, words-in-a-row, even sex wants to be digital and on a network. Everything aspires to the nebulous and liquid quality of moving digital information. We're getting used to this prospect in 1996. We can spare ourselves the exhilarating sense of hysteria that this new reality provokes. We should seize this chance to get a little mental oxygen. We'll need it.

The year 1996 is nicely poised between the world-shattering events of 1989 and the onrushing specter of the year 2000. The planet is still visibly recovering from 1989, the year the cold war ended, and maybe the first year in which computer networks came creeping out of technical obscurity to seriously menace the status quo. Unless I miss my guess, the year 2000 will also be a truly extraordinary historical moment. The year 2000 will be an excellent opportunity to deny and dispose of the deeply repugnant twentieth century. In the year 2000 there will be a general erasing of the memory banks, a bitter scorn for the hopelessly outdated, a firm and somewhat frantic rejection of a great deal of cultural baggage. Like most New Year's Parties, it'll feel so good that none of us will be able to resist. In the year 2000, we'll all be engaged in a general frenzy of bright-eyed denial.

So there's not much point in raising the black flag and rushing the barricades in 1996. That's always a natural temptation, but we might be better advised to gather our wits and save some strength. Anything that we decide is electronic gospel right now will simply be kicked out of court in 2001. So even though we are all computer enthusiasts here, just for once let's try not to get completely worked up. There's sure to be plenty of time and reason for panic later.

Because now, in 1996, we really have an Information Society. We used to talk about having an information society, and dream ardently of living in one, and now we've actually got one. In 1989 it was still theory and vaporware, but this is 1996, and we're in bed with it. We have to watch it eat crackers, we have to launder its sheets.

Now that we've got it, what can we say about it? The very first fact to bear in mind about our Information Society is that this too shall pass.

We live in the Information Age now, but there are people walking around in this city who have lived through the Aviation Age, the Radio Age, the Thousand-Year Reich, the Atomic Age, the Space Age, the New Age, the Aquarian Age, not to mention the sexual revolution and the epoch of New Soviet Man. And trust me, a lot of these geezers and geezerettes are going to outlive the Information Age as well. In the old days history used to leave people behind, but now the pace of innovation is so savage that individual human beings can leave history behind. This "age" stuff comes pretty cheap to us nowadays. We postmodern types can burn out an age in ten years.

There's nothing more grotesquely temporary than a computer. I, personally, have two perfectly functional Apples and an Atari in a storeroom. I have no idea what to do with these computers. They cost me a great deal of money. Learning to use them was very complex and tiresome. It seemed like a very hip and groovy idea at the time, but now those high-tech gizmos are utterly obsolete and worthless. If I leave them on the sidewalk outside my house, together with the software and the manuals, nobody will bother to bend over and pick them up.

I moved house recently. This caused me to make a trip to the Austin city landfill. Austin has a very nice landfill actually, it's manned by well-meaning Green enthusiasts who are working hard to recycle anything usable. When I went there last month I discovered a heap of junked computers that was two stories high. Dead monitors, dead keyboards, dead CPUs, dead modems. The junk people in my home town get a stack that size once a week.

I had to pay some close attention to that mighty heap of dead computers. It had all the sinister lure of the elephants' graveyard. Most of those computers looked like they were in perfect working order. The really ominous part of the stack was the really quite large percentage of discarded junk that was still in the shrinkwrap. Never been used, and already extinct.

Sometimes I talk to audiences who aren't computer enthusiasts like you, people who are deeply and genuinely intimidated by computers. I urge them not to worry too much. I urge them to think of a computer as something like a dragonfly. Yes, a dragonfly can do many impressive things that no human being can do, such as hover in midair and eat gnats. And yes, a dragonfly might even bite you. But you see, a dragonfly is a very temporary thing. In the height of summer, there will be whole clouds of them up there, sunlight glinting off their diaphanous wings, just flitting by, eating those gnats.

But then the winter will come. And the snow will pile high. And every one of those lovely dragonflies will be cold, and stiff, and dead. But you — you'll be cozied up in your bathrobe and bunny slippers, sipping hot chocolate and reading Danielle Steel novels.

Gordon Moore says that a computer generation lasts about eighteen months. He says that computer chips double in power every eighteen months, roughly speaking. That means that a computer in 2010 is about 150 times as powerful as a computer in 1990. Roughly speaking. I had a computer in 1990. With any kind of luck I'll probably be around in 2010, and I rather imagine I'll have a computer then, too. So exactly how impressed am I supposed to get about a 1996 computer? It's maybe five percent of the computer I'll eventually be using. That's like comparing a matchbox car to a Rolls Royce.

Even paperback books have a far longer lifespan than computers. It's a humble thing, a book, but the interface doesn't change and they don't need software upgrades and new operating systems. A five dollar paperback book will dance on the grave of a five thousand dollar computer.

Nothing that is real is absolute. In anything real there is good news and there's bad news. The Information Society has become a reality. There's good news, ladies and gentlemen, and there's bad news. The good news is, the digital revolution is over. The digits won hands down. Casualties were low, considering. We now live in the early days of the digital provisional government.

The bad news is that the provisional government is inherently unstable. Its powerbase is a giant virtual castle made of bits. Bits of sand.

It's a very mixed bag, the information age. Don't get me wrong; I love living here. Like a lot of my generation, I grew up more or less expecting nuclear armageddon, and with that prospect off the front burner, life for me is a carnival. In the Information Age, every day's an adventure. I'm never bored.

The Information Age has many stellar virtues. It is market driven and extremely innovative. It's high-tech, hip and fast on its feet. People who work in this field are deeply opportunistic and will seize on the slightest chance at daylight.

The bad news is, if you survive every day by agile broken-field running it's easy to lose sight of your goals. In fact, you can forget the very concept of goals; you can run incredibly hard every day just to remain in the same place.

The Information Society has basically forfeited any democratic control over its own destiny. No one's opinion is ever asked, nobody is ever polled. If we'd been asked to vote in a digital revolution, it almost certainly would never have happened. We were never offered that chance, it never occurred to us to ask for it or take it. Our lives have been turned upside down by a series of obscure technical events that transpired in a nearly perfect political vacuum. The moral idea of informed consent was never raised. Weird homemade machinery that was full of bugs and never worked very well burst out of garages in California and destroyed the modern capitalist order. That's the story, basically. Like it or lump it.

There are vast fortunes to be made overnight in the Information Society. It's the hottest economic game on the planet. Vast fortunes can be lost just as quickly. Worse yet, there's no good safe place to store your loot if you make a pile and decide to jump off the jampacked no-brakes information bus. Thanks to computers, the stock market and bond market and currency markets are aswarm with sophisticated capital instruments that have created a seething global casino economy. There's more money in the thrash of leverage, futures and derivatives than there is in rational capitalist investment. In an Information Society, even oil companies want to act like Hollywood.

Thanks to modems, cellphones, cell-faxes, laptops, beepers and satellite dishes, we're never out of touch. I can read my email (which I happen to store in San Francisco) whenever I'm in Vancouver. The bad news is that, yes, I can read my email in Vancouver. I *could* be doing great British Columbia-type things instead: having the BC sushi roll, shopping in Chinatown, spiking the old growth forest. But I'll deny myself those harmless, life-enhancing amusements, because I feel compelled to mind my business and read my email.

There might be some kind of urgent message from a publisher in Italy. I've had publishers in Italy for years now, but they never, ever sent me urgent messages, because they used to know full well that it was useless. Now they can reach me fast and cheap and by golly, they expect to reach me and they expect a response. Can't neglect that email. It's got global reach! I might get fanmail from some cypherpunk in Finland. Some teenage hacker in Abu Dhabi wants me to tell him how to break into Saudi mainframes, so he can get his hands chopped off by the authorities. I'm never out of touch. I'm never allowed to be, because there's no place left to hide.

When I'm not changing diapers, I fancy myself quite the hip globetrotter Information Age kind of guy. That's because I have friends in Prague. People in Prague are very friendly, they have a lovely town and a unique culture. They're also very hospitable, and it's a good thing, because since 1990 or so they've been getting about 80 million people a year through that city.

This influence of rampant globalization is hitting a little country which was deepfrozen behind the Iron Curtain for forty years. The Web throws down its virtual threading all over the world, and what does this do to indigenous cultures? I don't think there's a lot of use in mincing words here. I think it's pretty clear that the Information Society engulfs and devours the little unique places.

It's wonderful to visit Prague, but if you're a citizen of the Information Society, you can't touch that place without denting it. Every quiet and hidden place in the world bears our fingerprints now. As the seasoned travel writer Pico Iyer likes to put it, it's Video Night in Katmandu.

For me this situation is great. Basically, I live and breathe and thrive through cultural imperialism. I have four books out in Denmark this year. You see, I got interviewed by some stranger over the Internet, and it turned out he worked for a major newspaper in Copenhagen. Suddenly and quite without my own intention, I became rather well-known in Denmark. This October I'm flying to Copenhagen to do my one-man corporate multinational thing.

I'll be an American science fiction writer living it up in Denmark. How many Danish science fiction writers do I know? Zero. I know they must exist, so I hope I'll meet some. For me to get published in their country — it's easy, it's something I can do by accident. For a Danish science fiction writer to get published in my country — they'd have better luck trying to ooze face-first through a one-way mirror.

Is the Internet really a many-to-many, egalitarian network? Is a guy with a modem in Copenhagen or Montreal really on the same level as a guy with a modem in Austin or San Francisco? I'd like to think that is the case. Although it clearly isn't.

Personally, I like to talk to remote strangers on the Internet. I always go out of my way to reply politely to these odd characters around the planet with their unlikely Internet addresses and their entertainingly broken English — English which, by the way, is always a million times better than my French, my Russian, my Czech, my Danish, or my Japanese.

The good news is that I can chat with distant strangers. The bad news is that while I'm on the Internet, I'm not chatting to my next door neighbor. I'm not going to any neighborhood rallies, I'm not throwing parties for local friends, I'm not babysitting other people's kids. It may be that I'm not even talking to my own children, who are off in the living room being raised by Nintendo. Sure, I can trade digital video clips with hackers in Borneo over World Wide Web, but for all I know my next-door neighbor is a serial killer with an icebox full of his acquaintances.

Is this a *pernicious* aspect of the Information Society? Well, how will we know? Who can tell? Who's keeping track? Suppose it *were* pernicious — how would they stop me? Are the police supposed to unplug and confiscate my modem, tell me to go to the local Rotary Club and stop typing messages to people in Djakarta and Vladivostok? By what right?

There's always something new in cyberspace circles. It's unfailingly entertaining, you've got to give it that. There's a scandal a week, sometimes two. I wrote a nonfiction true-crime book about one of these cyberspace scandals once — it took me a year and a half to do it. I could write a similar book once every week if there were fifty-two of me.

Let's just dip our fingertips into this brimming cornucopia of digital bounty, shall we? Government abuse of confidential files. Software piracy on pirate bulletin boards. Canadian judicial gag rules on cases flouted by people on the Internet. The CIA, the NSA trolling the Internet for anything they might find useful. The French secret service bribing and supplying money to the Chaos Computer Club. Cryptography scandals, just no end to those; crypto has more scandals and screw-ups and bonehead moves than a 24 hour festival of the Three Stooges.

Oceans of money sloshing around. Telephone companies buying cable companies, software companies buying cellphone companies, computer companies buying parts of the radio spectrum. Internet startups offering voice phone software, telephone companies offering Internet hookups. Software patents, algorithm patents. Computer search and seizure practice. Spamming scandals, virus scandals. Poisoned JAVA applets — bad applets — rotten applets.

I've watched this stuff going on for years now. A pattern is emerging. It's amazing how little is ever decided, how little there is to show at the end of the day. Everything is temporary, all band-aids and toothpicks. Every once in a while there's a solemn edict from on high, something like America's Communications Decency Act, a ridiculous gesture with absolutely no connection to reality. Quite often some small and innocent person is inconvenienced, insulted or even crushed by the blind mechanisms of the powers-that-be, but that changes nothing. Events that might become case law or policy are treated merely as traffic accidents on the Internet. "What, they arrested him? Too bad! What, they might arrest me too? Ha ha ha! Forget it!"

People who like computers are really smart. They're bright, imaginative and inventive people. They also work hard, they are quick studies and they tend to have quite a lot of money and to deploy it with gusto and relish. Despite these manifest virtues, these bright, inventive computer people are some of the worst organizers in the world. They can't organize a bridge party without wanting to change the cards half-way for a colorful graphic-intensive Tarot deck. Everybody wants to be the symbolic analyst, nobody wants to empty the ashtrays and make the hors d'oeuvres. They're hungry all right, but they don't want to fill the sink, roll up sleeves and do the dishes. Too slow, too dirty, too analog. Can't we just order Chinese take-out and have it faxed in?

Instability is the congenital disorder of the lords of the Information Society. It's their version of the mark of Cain. Even the pathetic brainwashed victims of corrupt Christian televangelists can out-organize computer people. They don't want to build their own system, fill the potholes and root out the sewers. They want to hack the old system overnight and scamper off with unearned rewards. That's why Ross Perot, a textbook case of a megalomaniacal computer tycoon, thinks he can make himself President by skipping any actual political career and making gestures on a TV talk show.

Computer activists react in deep existential horror at the thought of political scutwork, patiently testifying to subcommittees, lobbying legislators. Actual politics is beneath them. They want to sit down at the console, hit alt-control-F2 and have a law come out. The price of liberty is said to be eternal vigilance — but that's a pretty steep price, isn't it? Can't we just automate this eternal vigilance thing? Maybe we can just install lots of 24-hour networked videocams.

The Information Society is not at all a friendly environment for the knight in gray flannel armor, the loyal employee, Mr. Cog, the Organization Man. This guy is dwindling like the bison, because we can't be bothered to support him and yet we still want his territory. We don't want to guarantee this guy anything, because we probably won't be around ourselves when he needs us. We Information Age types lack the patience for actual corporations, so we prefer nice, flimsy, gilded-pasteboard virtual corporations. In virtual corporations, there are no corporate power pyramids and no lines of accountability. That's exactly *why* people like virtual corporations in the Information Society — amazing stuff happens and huge sums change hands, and yet no one can be held responsible. Your average high-tech start-up is one of those decentralized, empowered, Third Wave organizations. Something like a mafia. Not the old-fashioned mafia where people swore loyalty till death, though. No, it's new and postmodern, like the Russian Mafia.

It's the Silicon Valley ethos. People in Silicon Valley prefer to work for a company for two years and then bail. They don't want to creep up dull and tiresome corporate ladders. I don't blame 'em, because I sure never did it, but they have developed a hack for this. They place their bets on a bunch of different start-ups, and then have one hit big and dump a load of cash in their laps. The idea of being morally, fiscally and socially responsible for your professional activities over a twenty or thirty year period is completely anathema to Silicon Valley people, to electronic frontier people. They really do have a frontier mentality — a brave, optimistic, can-do, strip-mining, clear-cutting mentality. They don't eat what they kill.

People as bright as really bright computer people just can't stand to do boring things for a long boring time. They fear and despise concepts like political party discipline, institutions, armies.

That's why the Internet is not at all like an army. An army is a vast machine for forcing somebody's unwilling flesh into the meatgrinder. It gets results by forcing results with blood and discipline and bayonets. The internet is a vast machine for finding somebody else to write your term paper for you. It gets results by mechanically sifting through enormous heaps of useless gibberish. You pay your money and you take your choice.

The Internet is out of control. No one is responsible for it. This is its most charming aspect. It's that sense of wizardry, that dionysian quality, the spontaneous way it accretes, the way it spreads on the wind all over the place, much like bread mold. People really enjoying watching phenomena that are out of control, especially when they're at a safe distance, like behind the glass of a computer screen. It's a fine spectacle, a truly noble spectacle, a 105% genuine vision thing, one of the very few aspects of contemporary society which isn't transparently motivated by bald greed

and ruthless opportunism. People lean on the Net and believe in it with a conviction all the stronger because there is so little else left for them to believe in. They
don't mind that it's out of control, when the things that are in control are commonly bent to such sordid ends.

Of course, *living* in a way which is genuinely out of control is a rather
different business. People like to *be* out of control for, like, the space of a Mardi
Gras weekend. After that they want a back rub and some money. They start looking
around for their house shoes. If they can't find them they start getting anxious. And
justly so.

People in the Information Society are adaptable and fast on their feet. They're
all road warriors with laptops. They don't need a big clunky ranch house with a
white picket fence; they're living out of the back of a Ferrari. Which is very cool.
Unless your grandmother loses her ranch house because the entire economy has
downsized and devolved into a viral mess. Then your grandmother decides that she
has to move into the back seat of the Ferrari with you. Then you and your fleet-
footed highly wired lifestyle look a tad less cozy. It becomes a tad hard to tell the
jetsetters from the gypsies in that situation.

All this free-floating anxiety you've been feeling suddenly comes home to
roost. Who's logging those frequent-flyer miles, and who's merely homeless? It's
great to cut fine distinctions between the keyboard punching virtual class and the
rust-belt lumpenproletariat, but a real no-kidding aristocracy has a host of ways to
tell Us from Them. The Information Age doesn't have that, it moves too fast for
elegant manners. In the Information Age, you can be a physicist with four post-
docs and still drive a cab. It's market-driven this and market driven that, market-
driven dog and market-driven cat. In the Information Society, the invisible hand of
the market isn't a human hand. It never was, but now its nature is obvious. It's some
kind of spastically twitching titanium-coated manipulator.

In the Information Society we like to believe that knowledge is power.
Because it is, sort of kind of. On alternate Tuesdays, maybe. People like to say that
the so-called knowledge found on the Internet is empowering to the individual. Is it
really?

Let's try a thought experiment. Let's imagine you have a brain tumor. You're
in big trouble, but luckily, you're on the Internet. You could try to find a brain
surgeon in your home town, but why risk this old-fashioned, limited, parochial
solution? Instead, you do an Alta Vista search for the term "brain surgeon." Sure
enough, you get an Internet entrepreneur. You go to an IRC channel to have a chat
with this guy.

"So, can you tell me a little about your qualifications?"

"Sure! I've memorized the Brain Surgery Frequently Asked Questions list. I
always read netnews from alt.brain.surgery. I've ftp'd and gophered hundreds of files
about human brains. Plus, I have fifteen CD-ROMS about brain surgery. In fact,
I've even put on a headset and goggles and performed virtual brain surgery, rehears-
ing the procedures hundreds of times in computer simulations. Plus, I work cheap!
No union! When can you come on down to the lab?"

"So you're not an actual MD, then?"

"Sure I got a degree, I've got a nice printout diploma from Dr. Benway's Online College of Virtual Medical Knowledge. It's based in a website in Grenada. I downloaded and read every one of the lessons, so you don't need to worry. Software engineers don't have licenses, politicians don't have licenses, journalists don't have licenses either, and those are all important knowledge-based professions, so I don't see why you need to get all fussy about cutting people's heads open. This is the Information Age, and thanks to the Internet I possess all the photos and words and documents that any doctor has. Why should I go through a a lot of tiresome pro forma nonsense before I hang up my shingle? Let's do business."

"How about the Hippocratic Oath?"

"Look, that documentation is over two thousand years old. Get up to date, pal. Your pathetic nationalist government may not approve of our healthcare methods up there in stuffy socialist Canada, but not everybody has your health system. Here in the Turks and Caicos Islands everything we do is perfectly legal."

There's a word for people who can learn all the buzzwords of medicine without getting a diploma, serving an internship, or joining a professional medical association. We call these people "quacks." Quacks are a very interesting class of people. They're inventive and clever and make a lot of money. They've always made a lot of money, but with the free flow of specialized information on the Internet, incredible new vistas open up for quacks. I haven't seen many of these vistas fully exploited yet, but I rather expect to.

Information Society people may not be quacks exactly, but they sure do wear a lot of hats. I know people personally who are CD-ROM designers and software entrepreneurs and system administrators and security consultants and conference organizers, and that's all in one week. They are clever, inventive people who are quick studies and can brush up on the jargon of several widely different occupations and convince their clients that they are genuinely skilled and experienced.

If you do that in the world of computers it's called access to information and self-guided education, but if you try it in law or medicine or civil engineering you are best described as a "charlatan." The Information Age may be the golden age of charlatanry.

This is the way that system-cracking hackers act, the way that hackers learn things. When system cracker people use convincing language to get people to give them access that they really shouldn't have, they call that practice "social engineering." It's very powerful and very corrosive.

Hackers are very evangelical about liberating other people's secrets. It's a core myth of the era. There have been several Hollywood movies that hinge on gallant Robin Hood hackers breaking into a system and finding out some terrible and important secret. The baddies try to grab them and shut them up, but in the last reel the hackers always blow the hidden information all over the network and it ends up in the New York Times or CNN. End of story.

It's a beautiful idea really, one of the central romantic myths of the Information Age. No one can shut up the heroic hacker dissidents, and the bad guys always crumble and scamper off like whipped dogs when the truth comes out. A beautiful myth. I've been following the hack-phreak scene for years now, hoping that someday, just once, something like that would actually happen. Some hacker kid breaks into the sinister corporate mainframe and he finds and distributes the secret and hideous data files that prove that rich guys in suits are deliberately poisoning us with dioxin. Or maybe they've got the aliens from the Roswell incident or just a few of the 47 guys who shot John Kennedy. If a hacker really did something like that would make up for a lot of annoyances.

Never happens. Never ever. Actually, horrible secrets come up all the time, but they're usually found out by journalists and cops. And even that finishes up with a happy ending about one time in twenty. Does the free flow of information on the Internet help? I wonder. I do know of one revelatory scandal that broke on the Internet, the Pentium chip bug. I don't think I've ever seen an example of people on the Internet unearthing and distributing a real-world non-computer-based scandal.

Something really embarrassing. The truth comes in over the modems and governments fall. Maybe that'll happen someday. I don't think it's happening now.

Let me give you what seems to me to be a swell real-world example of this. I think this story is the single weirdest story I've ever heard over the Internet.

This story has been happening in the country of Slovakia over the past year. Slovakia used to be the right half of Czechoslovakia, but the Czech Republic ended up in the hands of Vaclav Havel, and the Slovak Republic ended up in the pockets of a gentleman named Vladimir Meciar. Meciar became Prime Minister of his new little republic, but he got into a nasty power-struggle with Slovakia's President, a guy named Michal Kovac. Kovac and Meciar were from different parties and they just didn't get along.

Well, President Michal Kovac has a son named Michal Kovac Jr., and this younger man was involved in some shady business deals in Austria. Meciar knew this, he was making a big deal of it. Nothing much was happening there though, his son's financial scandal wasn't destroying Kovac politically.

So last August eight guys jump Michal Kovac Jr. in his Mercedes limo. First they handcuff him, then they put a black hood on him, then they beat him up, then they torture him with electric shocks, then they force him to guzzle half a liter of whiskey so he gets completely plastered. Then they bundle the president's son into his own Mercedes limo, and they drive him across the border into Austria. Then they dump him and leave.

So the Austrian cops, all surprised, find the son of the President of Slovakia dead drunk in his car. So they arrest him and take him to the hospital to patch up his wounds.

So after a while the Austrian cops figure it's kind of embarrassing to have the Slovak President's son in the slammer, especially under these circumstances with the electric shocks and all. It's sort of as if Hillary Clinton had been beaten up and dumped in Canada and accused of shady dealing in Arkansas real estate. I mean, maybe you Canadians would have your suspicions about Hillary, but I figure you would probably want to give her back pronto. So the Austrians let Kovak Jr. go back to Slovakia. He goes back plenty mad.

Well, the Slovaks get a cop to investigate this kidnapping, but the cop gets fired right away. You see, the cop swiftly discovered that these kidnappers were members of the Slovak Intelligence Service, which is a secret police agency in the pocket of the Prime Minister. Another cop took the job, he found out the same thing, and he got fired too. The head of the Slovak Intelligence Service arranged both of these firings. He complained that the police were being too rough on his secret police agents and endangering national security.

This is all a true story, ladies and gentlemen. I'm not embroidering this, in fact I'm sparing you some of the real *Prisoner of Zenda* elements because they're too melodramatic even for a science fiction writer. The scandal is looking pretty bad for the Prime Minister at this point, so he gets some of his allies in the Parliament to accuse the President of high treason.

That doesn't work out. The treason impeachment trial doesn't get off the ground, because the Prime Minister hasn't figured out how to swing votes in his own parliament. And also because the President himself has actually done anything.

At this point one of the original kidnappers becomes disgusted. He's a secret policeman and a torturer, but he just can't take it any more. He goes to the press and confesses everything. He testifies repeatedly, to the newspapers, to the radio, to the cops, that the head of the secret service was on the radio personally directing the whole affair.

Prime Minister Meciar and his secret police boss loudly deny this. They swiftly come up with an alternate story. They declare that the President's son kidnapped himself, tortured himself with electrodes, and dumped himself in Austria dead drunk, just to make the Prime Minister look bad.

Secret police agents then find the family of this guy whose confessed to the kidnapping, and they start beating them up. Later the guy's best friend is blown up by a car bomb. When the autopsy is performed the coroner finds a bullet in the dead man's stomach. The Prime Minister's stooges claim that the car blew up by accident and the bullets was an accidental bullet in the stomach that came from the victim's own gun when it accidentally went off in the terrific heat from the car's accidentally blowing up, and that it's terribly shocking and even libellous to allege that this was a political murder.

The President's out of patience now. The President openly accuses the secret police of kidnapping his son, so the head of the secret police sues him for libel. He also sues the local newspaper for saying the same thing, and then he sues a priest who presided over the blown-up guy's funeral. The Prime Minister puts yet another stooge on TV who claims that the president's son rigged the whole thing.

Then the Slovak Parliament gets into the act. They've got an independent commission which has been investigating. Got some results too — the committee gives out the names of the eight kidnappers and the cars they were driving and exactly how they went about kidnapping the President's son.

And I'm watching this whole thing take place, week by week, day by day, in amazed fascination. Because I'm on a couple of central European Internet mailing lists.

There's even a tasty phone phreak angle in this, because at one point some-body taps the phone calls coming out of the limo of the chief of secret police, and the chief spook is laughing evilly at the investigators and calling them a bunch of idiots who'll never prove anything. They got the tape and they play it on the radio. The secret policeman says the tape is forged. He refuses to resign. He's still in power right now.

Now — if having the truth splashed across the Internet was enough to bring down a government, wouldn't this do it? This looks like a pretty whacking good scandal to me. It's quite a story, it's too weird even for Hollywood. It's got kidnap-pers and electrodes and carbombs and secret policemen and embezzlement and thugs and politicians. At the risk of being sued for libel by angry Slovak authorities, I would have to conclude that the country's highest officials are — well, let's just say they're strongly implicated. So is the Prime Minister going to resign? Do the decent thing? Skulk off in shame? Bow to public opinion, roused to righteous fury by these unsavory revelations?

Of course not! He's simply gonna brazen it out in the broad light of day. People from outside Slovakia will simply be ignored, and troublesome people inside Slovakia will be sued, pursued, beaten up, zapped with electrodes and dumped in Austria if not blown sky high. The Prime Minister is like a wolverine with his foot nailed to a board. Except that it's not his foot, and that's not a board, and it's not a big bloody nail, and anybody who says different had better be real careful around an ignition key.

You shall know the truth and the truth will make you free, right? Sunlight is the best disinfectant. Well, maybe.

We might learn a lot of truth about a lot of things off the Internet, or at least access a lot of data about a lot of weird junk, but does that mean that evil vanishes? Is our technology really a panacea for our bad politics? I don't see how. We can't wave a floppy disk like a bag of garlic and expect every vampire in history to vanish.

Isn't it far more likely that we'll get the Internet that we deserve? Cyberspace isn't a world all its own like Jupiter or Pluto, it's a funhouse mirror of the society that breeds it. Like most mirrors it shows whatever it's given: on any day, that's mostly human banality. Cyberspace is not a fairy realm of magical transformations. It's a realm of transformations all right, but since human beings aren't magical fairies you can pretty well scratch the magic and the fairy parts.

Sometimes computers really are empowering. On the days when they're new, and the days when they really work, which are pretty much contradictory times, actually. When computers do work, it's the power to be your best. It's also the power to be your worst, which doesn't get quite so much publicity in the ads. But you know, a power that was only the power to do good would not be power at all. Real power is a genuine trial. Real power is a grave responsibility and a grave temptation which often causes people to go mad. Technical power is power. When you deal with power you have to fear the consequence of a bad decision before you can find any satisfaction in a good one. Real power means real decisions, real action with real consequence. If that weren't true then we would be puppets devoid of will, permanent children always spared temptation by machinery in the role of the adults.

It saddens me to say these things, because it goes so much against my nature. I'm a science fiction writer. People pay me to dream stuff up. People have to have their dreams; without vision, the people perish.

It's not that fabulous possibilities aren't real. They are real. In the cold objective eye of eternity, everyone who has ever flown across the Atlantic has done something just as marvelous as Lindbergh did. Lucky Lindy was met by cheering crowds who heralded the mighty dawn of the new age of flight. But if you were met by cheering crowds on the far side of the Atlantic when you flew to France in 1996, this would not be good. You would not be pleased to see that their sense of wonder about the act of flight was still intact. You wouldn't congratulate the French on their lack of disillusionment. On the contrary, you would know full well that something had gone terribly wrong with the human beings who were witnessing this event. It would be a sign of psychopathic disruption, a society stuck in an infinite loop, jaws always agape, learning nothing, experiencing nothing.

We shouldn't blame ourselves when the wonder fades, much less blame our machinery. Instead, we should come to appreciate the way that human beings give ideas their substance. We can take fantastic abstractions and personify them, make them real. We're not disembodied intellects; that was a powerful dream of the last millennium, but a new millennium is at hand now, and our machines can play that dismal role for us. Infinity and eternity are not our problems.

Science fiction writers say a lot of silly things, but H.G. Wells once said a very wise thing. "If anything is possible, then nothing is interesting." It's not the center of ideas that are interesting, these bloodless Platonic concepts of bogus purity and lifeless rigid order. It's the living, seething mess out there, where actions have consequences, where the street finds its own uses for things. That is our arena. And it's up to us, not just to imagine it, but to inhabit it. Not just to admire it and make gestures, but to judge it and take action.

The future is unwritten.

Global Debt and Parallel Universe

Jean Baudrillard

An electronic billboard in Times Square displays the American public debt, an astronomical figure of some thousands of billions of dollars which increases at a rate of $20,000 a second. Another electronic billboard at the Beaubourg Center in Paris displays the thousands of seconds until the year 2000. The latter figure is that of time, which gradually diminishes. The former figure is that of money, which increases at a sky-rocketing speed. The latter is a countdown to second zero. The former, on the contrary, extends to infinity. Yet, at least in the imaginary, both of them evoke a catastrophe: the vanishing of time at Beaubourg; the passing of the debt into an exponential mode and the possibility of a financial crash in Times Square.

In fact, the debt will never be paid. No debt will ever be paid. The final counts will never take place. If time is counted [*si le temps nous est compté*], the missing money is beyond counting [*au-délà de toute comptabilité*]. The United States is already virtually unable to pay, but this will have no consequence whatsoever. There will be no judgment day for this virtual bankruptcy. It is simple enough to enter an exponential or virtual mode to become free of any responsibility, since there is no reference any more, no referential world to serve as a measuring norm.

The disappearance of the referential universe is a brand new phenomenon. When one looks at the billboard on Broadway, with its flying figures, one has the impression that the debt takes off to reach the stratosphere. This is simply the figure in light years of a galaxy that vanishes in the cosmos. The speed of liberation of the debt is just like one of earth's satellites. That's exactly what it is: the debt circulates on its own orbit, with its own trajectory made up of capital, which, from now on, is free of any economic contingency and moves about in a parallel universe (the acceleration of capital has exonerated money of its involvements with the everyday universe of production, value and utility). It is not even an orbital universe: it is rather ex-orbital, ex-centered, ex-centric, with only a very faint probability that, one day, it might rejoin ours. That's why no debt will ever be paid. At most, it can be bought over at a bargain price to later be placed back on a debt market (public debt, national debt, global debt) where it will have become a currency of exchange. Since there is no likely settlement date, the debt has an incalculable [*inestimable*] value. As long as it hangs like that over our heads with no reference whatsoever, it also serves as our only guarantee against time. Unlike the countdown which signifies the end of time, an indefinitely deferred debt is the guarantee that even time is inexhaustible… And we really need a virtual time insurance since our future is about to dissipate in real time.

Clearing the debt, settling the accounts, cancelling the payments by the Third World… Don't even think about it! We only live because of this imbalance, of the proliferation and the promise of infinity created by the debt. The global or planetary debt has, of course, no meaning in the classical terms of stock or credit. But it acts as our true collective credit line, a symbolic credit system whereby people, corporations, nations are attached to one another by default. People are tied to each other (this goes for the banks too) by means of their virtual bankruptcy, just as accomplices are tied by their crime. Everyone is certain to exist for the other in the shadow of an unamendable and insolvable debt for, as of today, the total amount of the global debt is much larger than the total amount of available capital. Thus, the debt no longer has any meaning but to unite all civilized beings to a same destiny served on credit. A similar thing takes place with nuclear weapons whose global capacity is much bigger than what is needed to destroy the entire planet. Yet, it remains as a way of uniting all of humankind to a same destiny marked by threat and deterrence.

At least, it is easier now to understand why the Americans are so eager to advertise their domestic debt in such a spectacular manner. The Times Square initiative is designed to make the state feel guilty about the way it runs the country, and intended to warn the citizens about the imminent collapse of the financial and public spheres. But, of course, the exorbitant figure deprives the billboard of any meaning (even figures have lost their credit line). In fact, this is nothing more than a gigantic advertising campaign and, by the way, this is why the neon "billboard" is made to look like a triumphant stock exchange quotation that has gone over the top. And people stare at it, fascinated by the spectacle of a world performance (in the meantime, people rarely look at the numerical time clock at Beaubourg to witness the gradual ending of this century). People are collectively in the same situation as that Russian test pilot who, until the very last second, was able to see his airplane drop and crash on the video system of his Tupolev jet. Did he have the ultimate reflex to look at the image before dying? He could have imagined his last living moments in virtual reality. Did the image survive the pilot, even for a tenth of a second, or vice versa? Does virtual reality live on after the catastrophe of the real world?

Our true artificial satellites are the global debt, the flows of capital, and the nuclear loads that circle around the earth in an orbital dance. As pure artifacts, with a sidereal velocity and an instantaneous capacity of reversal, they have found their true place. This place is even more extraordinary than the Stock Exchange, banks, or nuclear stockpiles: it is that of the orbit, where they rise and set like artificial suns.

Some of the most recent of these exponentially developing parallel worlds are the Internet and the many worldwide webs of information. Each day, in real time, the irresistible growth (or outgrowth perhaps) of information could be measured there, with numbers representing the millions of people and the billions of operations that they cover. Information now expands to such an extent that it no longer has anything to do with gaining knowledge. Information's immense potential will never be redeemed and it will never be able to achieve its finality. It's just like the debt. Information is just as insolvable as the debt and we'll never be able to get rid of it. Collecting data, accumulating and transporting information all over the world are the same thing as compiling an unpayable debt. And here too, since proliferating information is larger than the needs and capacities of any individual, and of the human species in general, it has no other meaning but that of binding humankind to a destiny of cerebral automation and mental underdevelopment. It is clear that if a small dose of information reduces ignorance, a massive dose of artificial intelligence can only reinforce the belief that our natural intelligence is deficient. The worst thing that can happen to an individual is to know too much and, thus, to fall beyond knowledge. It is exactly the same thing with responsibility and emotional capacity. The perpetual intimation of the media in terms of violence, suffering, and catastrophe, far from exalting some sort of collective solidarity, only demonstrates our real impotence and drives us to panic and resentment.

Caught in their autonomous and exponential logic, all these parallel worlds are like time bombs. It is more obvious with nuclear weapons, but it is also true of the debt and capital flows. The smallest intrusion of these worlds into ours, the least noticeable encounter between their orbits and ours, would immediately disrupt the fragile equilibrium of our exchanges and economies. This would (or will) be the same with the total liberation of information, which could transform us into free radicals desperately searching for our molecules in a scanty cyberspace.

Reason would probably insist that we include these worlds into our homogeneous universe: nuclear weapons would have a peaceful use, all the debts would be erased, all the flows of capital would be reinvested in terms of social well-being, and information would contribute to knowledge. This is, no doubt, a dangerous utopia. Let these worlds remain parallel to ours, let their threats hang up in the air: their ex-centricity is what protects us. For, no matter how parallel and ex-centric they may be, they are in fact ours. We are the ones who created them and placed them beyond our reach, as an ersatz of transcendence. We are the ones who placed them on their orbits as some sort of catastrophic imaginaries. And it is perhaps better this way. Our society was once solidified by a utopia of progress. It now exists because of a catastrophic imaginary.

Translated by François Debrix.
Originally published as "Dette mondiale et univers
parallèle" in Liberation, *Paris, January 15,*
1996.

Cyberwar, God and Television

An Interview with Paul Virilio

Louise Wilson

Beneath Mirabeau bridge flows the Seine
And our love
Must I remember
Joy followed always after rain
Let night come sound the hour
Time draws in I remain

> *Extract from* Mirabeau Bridge *by Guillaume*
> *Apollinaire, quoted by Paul Virilio at the beginning of*
> *the interview.*

Louise Wilson: First of all, I'd like to say that I approach your work as a visual artist.

Paul Virilio: But, I always write with images. I cannot write a book if I don't have images.

I believe that philosophy is part of literature, and not the reverse. Writing is not possible without images. Yet, images don't have to be descriptive; they can be concepts, and Deleuze and I often discuss this point. Concepts are mental images.

Wilson: In the text *The Museum of Accidents*, you write about the problem of positivism facing a museology of science, and the need for "the science of an anti-science museum."

Virilio: In *The Museum of Accidents*, I say at the end of the article that television is the actual museum. In the beginning, I say: a museum of accidents is needed, and the reader imagines a building with accidents inside. But at the end, I say: no, this museum already exists, it's television.

This is more than a metaphor: the cinema was certainly an art, but television can't be, because it is the museum of accidents. In other words, its art is to be the site where all accidents happen. But that's its only art.

Wilson: So in talking about the simulation industry and its function to "expose the accident in order not to be exposed to it," could you say more about that in its relationship to television?

Virilio: One exposes the accident in order not to be exposed to the accident. It's an inversion. There is a French expression that says: to be exposed to an accident, to cross a street without looking at the cars means exposing oneself to be run over. This is more than a play with words, it's fundamental. For instance, when a painter exhibits his work, one says: he exposes his work. Similarly, when we cross the street, we expose ourselves to a car accident.

And television exposes the world to the accident. The world is exposed to accidents through television. The editor of the *New York Times* was recently interviewed in *Le Nouvel Observateur*, and he said something that I really agree with: television is a media of crisis, which means that television is a media of accidents. Television can only destroy. In this respect, and even though he was a friend of mine, I believe that McLuhan was completely wrong (in his idyllic view of television).

Wilson: But surely the commodification of the accident happened before television through simulation?

Virilio: To start with, the simulator is an object in itself, which is different from televison and leads to cyberspace. The US Air Force flight simulator — the first sophisticated simulators were created by the US Air Force — has been used in order to save gas on real flights by training pilots on the ground. Thus there is a cyberspace vision: one doesn't fly in real space, one creates a poor cyberspace, with headphones, etc... it is a different logic. In a way, the simulator is closer to cyberspace than televison. It creates a different world. So, of course, the simulator quickly became a simulator of accidents, but not only that: it started simulating actual flight hours, and these hours have been counted as real hours to evaluate the experience of pilots. Simulated flight hours and real flight hours became equivalent, and this was cyberspace, not the accident but something else, or rather the accident of reality. What is accidented is reality. Virtuality will destroy reality. So, it's some kind of accident, but an accident of a very different nature.

The accident is not the accident. For instance, if I let this glass fall, is it an accident? No, it's the reality of the glass that is accidented, not the glass itself. The glass is certainly broken and no longer exists, but with a flight simulator, what is accidented is the reality of the glass, and not the glass itself: what is accidented is the reality of the whole world. Cyberspace is an accident of the real. Virtual reality is the accident of reality itself.

Wilson: But then simulation doesn't really pretend to be the glass?

Virilio: This is a little hard to explain. We have a sense of reality which is sustained by a physical sensation. Right now, I am holding a bottle: this is reality. With a data glove, I could hold a virtual bottle. Cybersex is similar: it is an accident of sexual reality, perhaps the most extraordinary accident, but still an accident. I would be tempted to say: the accident is shifting. It no longer occurs in matter, but in light or in images. A Cyberspace is a light-show. Thus, the accident is in light, not in matter. The creation of a virtual image is a form of accident. This explains why virtual reality is a cosmic accident. It's the accident of the real.

I disagree with my friend Baudrillard on the subject of simulation. To the word simulation, I prefer the one substitution. This is a real glass, this is no simulation. When I hold a virtual glass with a data glove, this is no simulation, but substitution. Here lies the big difference between Baudrillard and myself: I don't believe in simulationism, I believe that the word is already old-fashioned. As I see it, new technologies are substituting a virtual reality for an actual reality. And this is more than a phase: it's a definite change. We are entering a world where there won't be one but two realities, just like we have two eyes or hear bass and treble tones, just like we now have stereoscopy and stereophony: there will be two realities: the actual, and the virtual. Thus there is no simulation, but substitution. Reality has become symmetrical. The splitting of reality in two parts is a considerable event which goes far beyond simulation.

Wilson: What about early cinema as a primitive form of this, when people left the cinema in fright?

Virilio: Unlike Serge Daney or Deleuze, I think that cinema and television have nothing in common. There is a breaking point between photography and cinema on the one hand and television and virtual reality on the other hand. The simulator is the stage in-between television and virtual reality, a moment, a phase. The simulator is a moment that leads to cyberspace, that is to say, to the process because of which we now have two bottles instead of one. I might not see this virtual bottle, but I can feel it. It is settled within reality. This explains why the word virtual reality is more important than the word cyberspace, which is more poetic. As far as gender is concerned, there are now two men and two women, real and virtual. People make fun of cybersex, but it's really something to take into account: it is a drama, a split of the human being! The human being can now be changed into some kind of spectrum or ghost who has sex at a distance. That is really scary because what used to be the most intimate and the most important relationship to reality is being split. This is no simulation but the coexistence of two separate worlds. One day the virtual world might win over the real world.

These new technologies try to make virtual reality more powerful than actual reality, which is the true accident. The day when virtual reality becomes more powerful than reality will be the day of the big accident. Mankind never experienced such an extraordinary accident.

Wilson: What is your own feeling about that?

Virilio: I'm not scared, just interested.

This is drama. Art is drama. Any relationship to art is also a relationship to death. Creation exists only in regard to destruction. Creation is against destruction. You cannot dissociate birth from death, creation from destruction, good from evil. Thus any art is a form of drama standing between the two extreme poles of birth and death, just like life is drama. This is not sad, because to be alive means to be mortal, to pass through. And art is alive because it is mortal. Except that now, art has become more than painting, sculpture or music: art is more than Van Gogh painting a landscape or Wagner composing an opera. The whole of reality itself has become the object of art. To someone like Zurbaran, who paints still lifes, lemons and pears are the objects of art. But to the electronics engineer who works on the technologies of virtual reality, the whole reality has become the object of art, with a possibility to substitute the virtual with the real.

Wilson: Is there a transcendence of the body?

Virilio: That is difficult to say. First, what is under consideration is not only the body itself, but the environment of the body as well. The notion of transcendence is a complex one, but it is true that there is something divine in this new technology. The research on cyberspace is a quest for God. To be God. To be here and there. For example, when I say: "I'm looking at you, I can see you", that means: "I can see you because I can't see what is behind you: I see you through the frame I am drawing. I can't see inside you". If I could see you from beneath or from behind, I would be God. I can see you because my back and my sides are blind. One can't even imagine what it would be like to see inside people.

The technologies of virtual reality are attempting to make us see from beneath, from inside, from behind... as if we were God. I am a Christian, and even though I know we are talking about metaphysics and not about religion, I must say that cyberspace is acting like God and deals with the idea of God who is, sees and hears everything.

Wilson: What will happen when virtual reality takes the upper hand?

Virilio: It already has. If you look at the Gulf War or new military technologies, they are moving towards cyberwars. Most video-technologies and technologies of simulation have been used for war. For example, video was created after the Second World War in order to radio-control planes and aircraft carriers. Thus video came with the war. It took twenty years before it became a means of expression for artists. Similarly, television was first conceived to be used as some kind of telescope, not for broadcasting. Originally, Sworkin, the inventor of television, wanted to settle cameras on rockets so that it would be possible to watch the sky.

Wilson: So it was only by a matter of degrees that the Gulf War became the "virtual war"? It was live broadcasting that really effected this change?

Virilio: The high level of the technologies used during the Gulf War makes this conflict quite unique, but the very process of de-realization of the war started in 1945. War occured in Kuwait, but it also occured on the screens of the entire world. The site of defeat or victory was not the ground, but the screen. (I wrote a book called Desert Screen on the Gulf War.) Thus it becomes obvious that television is a media of crisis, a museum of accidents.

Wilson: This must surely result in some psychic crisis?

Virilio: It is as if I was to take my eye, to throw it away, and still be able to see. Video is originally a de-corporation, a disqualification of the sensorial organs which are replaced by machines... The eye and the hand are replaced by the data glove, the body is replaced by a data suit, sex is replaced by cybersex. All the qualities of the body are transferred to the machine. This is a subject I discuss in my last book, The Art of The Engine.

We haven't adjusted yet, we are forgetting our body, we are losing it. This is an accident of the body, a de-corporation. The body is torn and disintegrated.

Wilson: With the Gulf War, there was such incomprehension because it was so removed.

Virilio: The Gulf War was the first "live" war. World War Two was a world war in space. It spread from Europe to Japan, to the Soviet Union, etc. World War Two was quite different from World War One which was geographically limited to Europe. But in the case of the Gulf War, we are dealing with a war which is extremely local in space, but global in time, since it is the first "live" war. And to those, like my friend Baudrillard, who say that this war did not actually occur, I reply: this war may not have occurred in the actual global space, but it did occur in global time. And this thanks to CNN and The Pentagon. This is a new form of war, and all future wars, all future accidents will be live wars and live accidents.

Wilson: How will this removal affect people?

Virilio: Firstly, a de-realization, the accident of the real. It's not one, two, hundreds or thousands of people who are being killed, but the whole reality itself. In a way, everybody is wounded from the wound of the real. This phenomenon is similar to madness. The mad person is wounded by his or her distorted relationship to the real. Imagine that all of a sudden I am convinced that I am Napoleon: I am no longer Virilio, but Napoleon. My reality is wounded. Virtual reality leads to a similar de-realization. However, it no longer works only at the scale of individuals, as in madness, but at the scale of the world.

By the way, this might sound like drama, but it is not the end of the world: it is both sad and happy, nasty and kind. It is a lot of contradictory things at the same time. And it is complex.

Wilson: How can we address this loss?

Virilio: The true problem with virtual reality is that orientation is no longer possible. We have lost our points of reference to orient ourselves. The de-realized man is a disoriented man. In my last book, *The Art of The Engine*, I conclude by pointing at a recent American discovery, the GPS (Global Positioning System) which is the second watch. The first watch tells you what time it is, the second one tells you where you are. If I had a GPS, I could know where this table stands in relation to the whole world, with an amazing precision, thanks to satellites. This is extraordinary: in the 15th century, we invented the first watch, and now we have invented the GPS to know where we are.

When you find yourself in the middle of virtual reality, you don't know where you are, but with this machine, you can know. This watch has been used for ships and not only can it tell you where you are, but also it can tell others where you are: it works in the two ways. The question you're asking is really interesting. For one can't even know what it means to be lost in reality. For instance, it is easy to know whether you are lost or not in the Sahara desert, but to be lost in reality! This is much more complex! Since there are two realities, how can we say where we are? We are far away from simulation, we have reached substitution! I believe this is, all in the same time, a fantastic, a very scary and an extraordinary world.

Wilson: But to return to this question of transcendance…

Virilio: All in all, I believe that this divine dimension raises the question of transcendance, that is to say the question of the Judeo-Christian God for instance. People agree to say that it is rationality and science which have eliminated what is called magic and religion. But ultimately, the ironic outcome of this techno-scientific development is a renewed need for the idea of God. Many people question their religious identity today, not necessarily by thinking of converting to Judaism or to Islam: it's just that technologies seriously challenge the status of the human being. All technologies converge toward the same spot, they all lead to a Deus ex Machina, a machine-God. In a way, technologies have negated the transcendental God in order to invent the machine-God. However, these two gods raise similar questions.

As you can see, we are still within the museum of accidents. That's a huge, cosmic accident, and television, which made reality explode, is part of it. I agree with what Einstein used to say about the three bombs: there are three bombs. The first one is the atomic bomb, which disintegrates reality, the second one is the digital or computer bomb, which destroys the principle of reality itself — not the actual object — and rebuilds it, and finally the third bomb is the demographic one. Some experts have found out that in five thousand years from now, the weight of the population will be heavier than the weight of the planet. That means that humanity will constitute a planet of its own!

Wilson: Do you always separate the body from technology?

Virilio: No. The body is extremely important to me, because it is a planet. For instance, if you compare Earth and an astronomer, you will see that the man is a planet. There is a very interesting Jewish proverb that says: "If you save one man, you save the world: That's a reverse version of the idea of the Messiah: one man can save the world, but to save a man is to save the world. The world and man are identical. This is why racism is the most stupid thing in the world.

You are a universe, and so am I; we are four universes here. And there are millions of others around us. Thus the body is not simply the combination of dance, muscles, body-building, strength and sex: it is a universe. What brought me to Christianity is Incarnation, not Ressurection. Because Man is God, and God is Man, the world is nothing but the world of Man — or Woman. So, to separate mind from body doesn't make any sense. To a materialist, matter is essential: a stone is a stone, a mountain is a mountain, water is water and earth is earth. As far as I am concerned, I am a materialist of the body, which means that the body is the basis of all my work.

To me, dance is an extraordinary thing, more extraordinary than most people usually think. Dance preceded writing, speaking and music. When mute people speak their body language, it is true speaking rather than handicap, this is the first word and the first writing. Thus to me, the body is fundamental. The body, and the territory of course, for there cannot be an animal body without a territorial body: three bodies are grafted over each other: the territorial body — the planet, the social body — the couple — and the animal body — you and me. And technology splits this unity, leaving us without a sense of where we are. This, too, is de-realization. There is a buddhist proverb which I like a lot. It says: "Everybody deserves mercy". That means that every body is holy. This is to answer the body question.

Technologies first equipped the territorial body with bridges, aqueducts, railways, highways, airports, etc... Now that the most powerful technologies are becoming tiny — microtechnologies — all technologies can invade the body. These micro-machines will feed the body. Research is being conducted in order to create additional memory for instance. For the time being, technologies are colonizing our body through implants. We started with human implants, but research leads us to microtechnological implants.

The territorial body has been polluted by roads, elevators, etc. Similarly, our animal body starts being polluted. Ecology no longer deals with water, flora, wildlife and air only. It deals with the body itself as well. It is comparable with an invasion: technology is invading our body because of miniaturisation. [Referring to the interviewer's microphone] Next time you come you won't even ask — you'll just throw a bit of dust on the table!

There is a great science-fiction short story, it's too bad I can't remember the name of its author, in which a camera has been invented which can be carried by flakes of snow. Cameras are inseminated into artificial snow which is dropped by planes, and when the snow falls, there are eyes everywhere. There is no blind spot left.

Wilson: But what shall we dream of when everything becomes visible?

Virilio: We'll dream of being blind. This is the art of the engine. Art used to be painting, sculpture, music, etc, but now, all technology has become art. Of course, this form of art is still very primitive, but it is slowly replacing reality. This is what I call the art of the engine. For instance, when I take the TGV (*Train a Grande Vitesse*) in France, I love watching the landscape: this landscape, as well as works by Picasso or Klee, is art. The engine makes the art of the engine. Wim Wenders made road movies, but what is the engine of a road movie? It's a car, like in Paris, Texas. Dromoscopy. Now all we have to do to enter the realm of art is to take a car. Many engines made History.

Wilson: Finally to return to the accident! Is it possible to see the body itself as a simulator? (Within medical aerospace research, for example, the body's own accident, that of motion sickness, can be eradicated.)

Virilio: The body has a dimension of simulation. The learning process, for instance: when one learns how to drive a car or a van, once in the van, one feels completely lost. But then, once you have learnt how to drive, the whole van is in your body. It is integrated into your body. Another example: a man who pilots a Jumbo Jet will ultimately feel that the Boeing is entering his body. But what is going on now, or should happen in one or two generations, is the disintegration of the world. Real time 'live' technologies, cyberreality, will permit the incorporation of the world within oneself. One will be able to read the entire world, just like during the Gulf War. And I will have become the world. The body of the world and my body will be one. Once again, this is a divine vision; and this is what the military are looking for. Earth is already being integrated into the Pentagon, and the man in the Pentagon is already piloting the world war — or the Gulf War — as if he were a captain whose huge boat would have become his own body. Thus the body simulates the relationship to the world.

Wilson: Are you suggesting the human body will disappear in all senses of the word?

Virilio: We haven't reached that point yet: what I have described is the end, or a vision of the end. What will prevail is this will to reduce the world to the point where one could possess it. All military technologies reduce the world to nothing. And since military technologies are advanced technologies, what they actually sketch today is the future of the civil realm. But this, too, is an accident.

When I was a young soldier, I was asked to drive a huge van while I had never driven a car. Here I am, driving through a German village (this takes place during the occupation) and there was this painter who had settled his ladder on the side of the street. I thought that my big van was going to crash his ladder. That didn't happen. I just passed through.

Vivisecting the 90s
An Interview with Jean Baudrillard

Caroline Bayard and Graham Knight

Caroline Bayard and Graham Knight: Your relation to McLuhan is interesting, the more so since few critics have analysed it, although they have often commented on it. What is the role of the strong presence of the visual, so real in your texts, in relation to the notion of distance, or of obscenity, and in relation to irony as distance? It is clear that the visual would be necessary to separate and distance an imaginary on which sense is founded. But how does one treat the question of the differentiation of image and sound, the latter being a much more supple, fluid, floating medium than the former?

Jean Baudrillard: I have some difficulty replying to this question because sound, the sphere of sound, the acoustic sphere, audio, is really more alien to me than the visual. It is true there is a *feeling* [word spoken in English] about the visual, or rather for the image and the concept itself, whereas sound is less familiar to me. I have less perception, less analytic perception, of this aspect. That is not to say that I would not make a distinction between noise and sound, but ultimately, in terms of this ambient world's hyperreality, this noosphere, I see it much more as a visualization of the world rather than its hypersonorization.

What can I say about the difference between the two? I have the impression that cutting across the world of McLuhan — he too is very much oriented to the visual, of course, in spite of the fact that he was, I believe, a musician — there is a small problem, which is that the different sensorial, perceptual registers tend, in this media noosphere, to conflate, to fuse together into a kind of depolarization of sensory domains. We speak quite rightly today of the audio-visual; we couple them together in some sort, some kind of amalgam or "patchwork". Perhaps I am led to view space in this way by my lesser sensitivity to the acoustic, but it seems to me that everything is summed up in a logistic which integrates all the perceptual domains in a way even more undifferentiated than before. Everything is now received in a manner that is indistinct, virtually indistinct, in fact.

The virtual is the kind of concept that is a bit cosmopolitan, if one can call it that; or postmodern, I do not know. In that respect, it is not about the gaze but the visual, it is not about the acoustic, but the audio. Besides, for McLuhan in fact, everything is ultimately reduced to the tactile. Tactility is really that register of sense which is of the order of contact, not of physical or sensual contact of course, but a sort of communication contact where, right now in fact, there is a short-circuit between receiver and sender. I mean directly in individual perception, not only in the world of the media but in our bodily way of living, there is a form of indistinction, of amalgamation, of indifferentiation where all the perceptions arrive en bloc and are reduced to a tactile ambiance. In the latter there would be a lesser differentiation of registers, a lesser singularity of the gaze, a lesser singularity of sound, of music.

So, that is all one can say. That said, within this state of affairs of course there is perhaps still a way to master the tactile world. I think that McLuhan himself thought so in every way; he thought that there really was a strategy of the tactile world, and that it is not just any one. It is not at all a question of saying that it is insignificant, but simply that it is more undifferentiated.

Bayard/Knight: I remember what you wrote about Westmoreland and Coppola in *Simulacres*, but re-reading your text some thirteen years later, I wonder whether the real question may not be somewhere else. If, quite simply, neither one (Westmoreland), nor the other (Coppola), had the last word because there is no such thing as the last word, because history continues, just as stories do and our history may be just this, a long rewriting process, prolonged *ad infinitum*, strewn with glosses/counter-glosses. With John Johnston, on the other hand (in Gane, 161), you read History as the re-actualisation of a past in which we all are accusers and defenders, as well as complicitous. Later, in *Cool Memories II*, you interpret it as a stoic temptation, that of a Marcus-Aurelius, neither resigned, nor hurried in his late Antiquity, waiting by the sea. Are all of those two facets a reflection of your sensitivity? Which of the three is closer to you presently?

Baudrillard: I am not a historian. I do not have an historical perception of events. But I would say that I have a mystical reading of them and that history for me, would be a long narrative which I tend to mythologize. Curiously, I am going back here to an interesting hypothesis, that of an English naturalist of the 19th century, called Philip Henry Gosse, who was a paleolontologist and archeologist. He was studying fossils found in geological sediments and his hypothesis, as he was a Christian and a reader of the Bible, was that creation had taken place ex-nihilo and the world created as such five thousand years before his time. Thus God had created at once fossils, geological sediments, exactly as they were in the 18th century, and he had created them as simulacra, as a *trompe-l'oeil* in order to provide humanity — which might have been traumatized by such a brutal creation — with a history, hence a past. Therefore God would have provided human beings with a retrospective past by creating fossils and geological sediments. And he would have created them as such, with utmost exactitude so that people may study them scientifically, although their past had thus been invented. This brings me specifically to Russell's paradox, which suggests that the world as such could have been created yesterday, and everything in it could be interpreted as retrospective simulation. Of course, this is a paradox, but for myself I would tend to use such a paradox. This where one ends up in a real or hyper-real situation, that of the history of historical narratives, of historiography which do pose a historical question about the re-invention of past history through the historian's discourse, a discourse which, by definition is a re-construction. In a way, that reconstruction is also necessarily artificial.

The tendency today is not to regress, but to go back to the those moments which preceded that history, as if it were taking us backward, a process which allows questions as cruel as: "Did the Holocaust actually take place, did gas chambers really exist?" One question, latent within our contemporary imagination, is its incapacity really to understand history, to capture its responsibility, its finality and therefore to ask such a query which is absurd, but which constitutes the ultimate test about a past event. Did it actually take place? What proof do we have about it?

Of course we have a multitude of objective, real proofs, but what does one do with historical reality in a system which itself has become virtual?

As for history, well I cannot situate it within a realistic framework, nor can I integrate it within a moral, or even political, reference system. There may be a philosophical moral of history, but I do not know what my position would be on that score. It would have to be one of undecidability about what history is. As history today enters into the same domain of indeterminate, undefined interpretations or into the principle of indeterminacy. And this not only applies to the past, but also to the future as well as to the present. At the moment, we live in a sort of uninterrupted time, especially as we move towards the crystallisation of time in each instant, as we keep losing our sense of any objective reference. I do not want to defend history, I only observe a series of problems.

Bayard/Knight: I might be tempted to say that your simultaneously ironic and perspicacious scrutiny of the social and political effects of simulation has been your gift to the end of this century. What made such a scrutiny vulnerable, for some, has not been the epistemological fallibility upon which it grounded itself (as that could be as a demonstration of humility coming from the end of an empire, assuming such is the case with the western world), but rather, it has been your refusal to recognize that CNN, the Murdochs and Maxwells of this world, dead or alive, do exert a remarkable control over the images which our eyes look at day after day, whatever those media empires' powerlessness to resolve even our most insignificant problems be. Yes this did puzzle a number of us. While I do recognize that our referents have been transformed by these images' interaction, I have enormous difficulty to admit that reference itself could have sunk below the horizon of our collective anomie. Bodies are killed, entire cities, or small towns and communities disappear, between Sarajevo and southern Iraq. No one denies the simulation effect which our information networks rely upon, but it is your denial of reality, of personal experience initiated by those simulations which disturbs me. Had you been in Baghdad in February 1991, or in Sarajevo these past two years, might you not have hesitated before casting reference into the dustbin of history?

Baudrillard: Yes, I would not be irresponsible enough to claim an extra-territorial position. When I speak, I do so from a given place. I do have roots. Obviously, all radicals do. I have mine, but those are not ideological references.

Sarajevo, since you are talking about it, reminds me of a media incident, precisely. Bernard-Henri Levy went there to do a TV programme during one of the worst bombings and he interviewed a woman, a librarian, who spoke to him and said: "I wish Baudrillard were here to see what transparency really is." Well, she was doing me a great honour, remembering what I have written about the transparency of evil, the trans-apparition of evil, specifically in a universe which pretends to be a New World Order whence evil, at least theoretically, has been eliminated. She felt this was a further illustration of what I have written about the transparency of evil. Let us talk about this. Such a perspective may arouse a certain misunderstanding. One finds oneself within the virtuality of goodness, of positivity, whereas, on the contrary, within such a system evil transpires everywhere. And that is the trans-apparition of evil. Evil is not that through which one sees, but that which sees through everything, which goes through, transpires through Good, as well. And at that specific time, one notices a perverse conversion of all positive effects, of all political constructions which finally, through some perverse and magical effect, become evil. So that, ultimately, all of those events taking place in Central Europe, the liberation of these countries, Yugoslavia, Bosnia, Sarajevo, are a terrifying demonstration of this catastrophic, recurrent scheme wherein evil takes place. And I do not understand evil as suffering, as pain. I define it, rather, as negativity, as the diabolical nature of things when they are reversed into their opposite, so that they never reach their finality, nor even go beyond it and thus become, at that specific time, monstrous. A good part of monstrosity, in our banality, is just that: all phenomena become extreme. Because of the media, our scientific means, our knowhow, progress all take an uncontrollable, inhuman dimension. Evil, for me is just that form.

I do not interpret it on the level of experienced pain, in which case I have nothing to say, any more than anybody else, except from a moral viewpoint, but I do not want to consider that. I interpret it not by bracketing it off, but by relativizing it. And I can only write while doing this in my own life. But I do not want to be more specific. There is a logic about writing, about thought, about philosophizing, yes, a stoic logic in that sense. One cannot add pathos, a subjective dimension, nor a collective sense of things to the vision one may have of the world, as well as of nature. Although, of course, when I say this I am quite aware that such a position is provocative, paradoxical and ultimately unacceptable. I do understand people's anger against such a position. And it is also true that of all this does not leave me indifferent. One can participate physically and morally in collective grief and since we are talking about this, I also believe that it is a Stoic's duty, if there is one, not to sublimate, not to abstract, not to distance oneself, but to say: such is the rule of the game and this is how I play it. To maintain this ultimate ironic possibility may be the essence of grief, the obsession of grief, the therapeutic obsession to dispose of evil, but those may not constitute the last word of history. I cannot say much more about it although I do recognize that such a position exposes itself to very serious charges.

Bayard/Knight: The question which comes most easily to mind, in line with what Caroline [Bayard] was asking you, relates to what I would call "the morning after."

To offer one's eye may well be seductive, overlooking the physical discomfort of the initial moment, but what happens the next day when one finds oneself blind in one eye? Is not the choice obvious between the suffering of seduction and eternal infirmity? Bodies do obliterate other losses.

Baudrillard: Stories do not have a day after; they are made to be used up. There too, if you take things literally that becomes unacceptable. Ultimately, right, one is in the realm of cruelty, in a certain sense. And what now could happen the next day if not vengeance? In every respect sacrifice has no final end in that sense. It has no day after, in the sense that it has no end since it reproduces itself. Each extends it. In every way, we know well enough that it is a little game, like money that one wins or loses in a game. Money won in a game does not leave the game. It must be burnt up, consumed like that, in the game. And it seems to be the same thing in a system of gift-giving, of sacrifice, where there is no day after, no point at which one would settle accounts. No point at which one would say: "So, I have been robbed. I am the loser. I have been sacrificed and I must avenge myself." No, one keeps on playing. One can perhaps reply to your question "what happens the day after?" by saying that at that point one rips out the other eye, and solves the problem!

Bayard/Knight: How is the concept of strategy used? It is implicit that it connotes a form of subjectivity, and yet it is used in such a way that subjectivity is undermined, or placed in a context where it is made volatile or fragile. Moreover, strategy being originally a military metaphor, to what extent does it retain today martial connotations which complicate its sense even more?

Baudrillard: Yes, there I agree with you. The term "strategy" represents an opportunity because it is apt. It is a nice term. It has form, it speaks to the imaginary. It has a form of mastery and, at the same time, it is deployed within space. But it no longer means anything great in my opinion, because, for there to be a strategy, there has to be a subject of the strategy, someone who has a will, a representation of the outcome. There has to be a finality. If the strategy has to become logistically chancy, it is no longer a strategy properly speaking. Thus, one can still use this term in a metaphorical sense perhaps, but it has certainly lost its military reference, and perhaps even its reference to a finality.

When I use it in the expression "fatal strategies", it is clear that it no longer has any finality in itself. It is a type of fatal process, a process in which there is certainly no more subject, no more subjectivity. Fatal strategy for me is a strategy of the object. Which means nothing, to be sure! How could an object have a strategy? It would be absurd. But all the same, I like to apply things that are paradoxical. I also speak of objective illusion. Illusion, if it is contrary to a truth principle, cannot be based on objectivity. But I like to bring these two terms together all the same to create a clash between them. Thus fatal strategy is, effectively, an expression which describes a process, a reversibility that is in the order of things, and this is, at the moment, truly delirious, fatal. We are all inside it, but we are nevertheless a vectorial element of the thing, though not in the sense of subjects. At this point it has to be said that this supposes such relativity in the subject-object relation that it is that which becomes fatal.

We witness the loss of subjectivity on the one hand, and the intervention of the object itself in the game in a fatal, decisive and determinant way. And the fact that it is no longer the subject that possesses things when, properly speaking, there is only a strategy of the subject, the fact of speaking of the strategy of objects is a paradox, a kind of metaphorical transfer of things. But, as discourse itself is so grounded in subjectivity in this sense, we do not have an objective discourse available in the sense I intend it, which has nothing to do with scientificity, but which would be the discourse of the object. Well, we do not have it. What we have is the event itself, the flow of the world itself, and there is, if not a strategy, at least a rule of the game. Regardless, I think that there is a rule. But I am not the one who is going to say that. It is truly unreadable; it is a secret. But somewhere there is a logic in the unfolding of things, even if it is a crazy logic. Let us call it strategy. Why not! It is, all the same, the way that the discourse of sense tries to describe non-sense. But clearly, one will always remain between the two. There will not be any objectivity there in the scientific sense of the term. That is not possible.

Bayard/Knight: It seems clear at this point that a younger generation of philosophers, such as Luc Ferry, Alain Renaut, of social critics, such as Michel Maffesoli, or even of less young ones, such as Alain Touraine (*Retour de l'acteur*, 1988, trans. *The Return of the Actor*, 1990; Edgar Morin, *Pour un nouveau commencement*, 1991), have focused on the return of this same subject. Certainly not in the same terms as their humanist predecessors, or their foundationalist ones, but upon the subject nevertheless, let us leave it undefined for the moment... I found it quite striking that in your *Cool Memories* (1987), you began to sketch some of his/her defining features ("What has been exuberantly demolished is being reconstructed sadly"). Except that, in this particular case, sadness is yours only and the authors mentioned above do not appear to share your grief. Are you interpreting their efforts as a self-delusional journey? Or alternatively, are you interpreting them as a curious ecological process and a re-cycling temptation for the end of a century: a bit of postmodernity, a sprinkle of liberalism, a dab of Kantian ethics with, at the end, a solid dose of optimism while facing the grief of the rest of the world? Maffesoli and Ferry are notably more optimistic than their elders, Morin and Touraine are more prudent. What is your position upon this so-called return of the subject?

Baudrillard: In Maffesoli's case, you are dealing with a very specific subject, since the latter is inscribing his position within a form of tribality. To me it looks like a tribal resurgence in which the subject has become the expression of a specificity, of a singularity. One observes a tribality and a singularity conjoined, in a way. For myself, I am inclined to think that such tendencies are not residual, but represent an elaboration upon or around vestigial elements which may well be alive, which function as the scattered fragments of a totality, a globality capable, in spite of everything, to organize the world and the subject as the convenor of that world. This subject had created a form of philosophy, of the "becoming-subject" of the world. We do not need to invoke Hegel here, but all the same, his texts signalled a certain power, specifically a conceptual power, and as everyone knows it does not exist today. My view is that what you are describing today is a form of reparation, that we all are involved in such reparations today, in the S.O.S. subject, or in the S.O.S. subjectivity [The term S.O.S has recently been used in the context of social and political activism, e.g., S.O.S. Racisme, an organisation founded by Harlem Desir concerned with combatting racism against non-European immigrants has mobilized considerable attention -transl]. Such a subject, moreover, does not appear to be a divided one, a really alienated one drawing all of its energies from its alienation, but, rather a reconstituted one, a re-synthesized one within which you cannot discern this pull, this divisiveness with all the consequences they entail upon symbolic and imaginary levels. Such a subject is the standard figure, robot of a reconstituted subject trying to recoup its residual vestiges, or whatever is left of them. It could be an ecological subject, and then one would witness the ecology of the subject, the saving of the subject, since it is quite evident that it has been threatened by a very simple evidence and symptom: the disappearance of its object. If it did not die purely and simply, this subject as well as that which it pretended to objectify, to master, now presently escapes it just as its position of power, of mastery, escapes it too. That subject is not even supposed to know, to be able to believe in anything, it cannot even believe in itself. And among those who reactivate this subject, who turn it into an actor, even those people know that it has lost its integrity as a subject, its conviction to adhere to its own effort to change the world. It does not believe in it anymore; it pretends to, it is a form of strategy, a posthumous strategy. That subject is a survivor and one witnesses the survival of the subject or the revival of the subject. Of course it is all about subjectivity, as it is in the interest of all those disciplines right now, sociology, psychology, philosophy to save their subject. Then it might be the case that, given the disappearance of this active subject and its passive counterpart, one presently witnesses the effects of a subject which attempts to reconstitute around itself the elements of a willpower, of a vision of the world. I really do not believe this. But this being said, there might be an effect of re-innovation, of renovation after a long period of philosophical, or maybe structuralist destructuring of the subject. It is not mine, but that does not matter. It may also be possible that we are observing a pendulum effect, the weighing scales tilting one way since in the history of ideas one could witness an internal phenomenon, a reactional one, vis-à-vis the history of the world. Because in fact it appears that the subject is only a vanishing point at the moment, to such an extent that it may have reached its fading point and what you are describing may only be a resurgence in the philosophical world. I certainly do not look upon it as a credible phenomenon, not for myself in any case.

Bayard/Knight: Sometime in France, after the socialist victory of 1980, I noticed a very healthy reaction on your part, on that of Lyotard as well (*The Intellectual's Grave*), when you both stressed that intellectuals should not speak in anyone's name, except in their own. But such were the times in the early eighties when the Left finally had access to power there. It is also clear that you did express such discomfort in your interview with Shevtsova (Gane, 79). Nevertheless, some fourteen years later, British and American intellectuals such as Tony Judt and Susan Sontag have enunciated interesting reminders to French intellectuals. They have done so without any moralizing intent, but firmly. Since you were mentioned let us talk about the latter. Sontag, in particular, enunciated discomfort about the French intelligentsia, on the line of fire if you wish, in Sarajevo where she produced the first act of *Waiting for Godot*. This otherness which she invoked was a humble, physical choice, a presence which did not force itself, did not operate in a grandiloquent manner, *à la* Glucksmann so to speak (he descended upon the burning city for a few hours, just to explain while quoting you, that wars are made, won, or lost on TV). Sontag, with her defiance, is determined to return to that city, to produce this play with actors who want to live, to survive, to play, even if they occasionally need to lie down on the floor as they are too tired, too hungry or too ragged. "Because I want to finish that play, I had to be there with them" says she. In 1993, it probably is a desperate choice, a form of refusal against the worn-out pragmatism of Vance and Owen, an act deprived of any illusions about our collective cowardice and yet essential to remind a blind Europe it should minimally come out of its anomie if it wants Bosnia to survive.

The questions I would like to ask you are the following: first, the realist abjection you were mentioning in *The Illusion of the End*, rather than an insistence upon actual interventions, may well be the acceptance of an inevitability which does not cost us anything and leaves us prostrated as couch potatoes in front of our screens. Then if people such as Sontag were not doing what they're doing, who would do it? How do you define the role of individuals, be it water-engineers, intellectuals, pall-bearers, writers or surgeons in those micro-spaces which presently constellate our planet?

Baudrillard: I would like to agree with you. I would love it if there were the simple possibility to finish off this pain. Because if, when one does what Sontag does, it is with no illusion whatsoever, beyond any objective, independent from any goal, any result, to save, to save what? Whatever it is, a form of conscience, pride, a sort of: "I do it in spite of everything," then I can see that. And it is a heroic act, in the sense that heroism has always been without illusions. Real heroes are always in that sense tragic. They do not exactly foresee the result of their actions. But that is the same thing, one cannot be heroic alone. In that sense I am almost collectivistic. To me, an act does not have meaning by itself, except in an absurd context. Maybe suicide does, maybe in fact what we are looking at here is a form of suicide. I am not sure. But for a choice such as Sontag's to be meaningful, even if it is without illusion, it has to have repercussions upon other consciences, and especially within the conscience of those to whom it is destined, such as the people from Bosnia, or the others.

And this is where the clockwork breaks down, because the absorption of all this, by the resonance of the sounding board on which it falls, as it is completely perturbed, falsified, mediatised, this anticipated absorption, through the precession of whatever you do, that is what distresses me. I understand one doing it anyway, to save one's own illusions, the illusion of one's will. But is it meaningful to do it? If there is no intellectual world operating as a sounding board, one which would be in solidarity with such an act and which would be capable of extracting a meaning from it, why do it? If one cannot create repercussions, reverberations for such an act, to bring it back within history, so that it was an event, then there is no point in doing it. In that sense I would be extremely, not opportunistic, but realistic, it is realpolitik I would invoke and suggest that if one does this, chooses to do this, it has to be an event. Not that it should be important, but it should create a rupture within the information continuum. Did it, or did it not, create a rupture? Everything hinges upon this. Otherwise it is hard to assess it as a rupture. Of course, one may entertain the idea that if everyone does one's bit, all of this will produce a primitive accumulation of courage, actions and will ultimately produce an event. But today I do not believe it. Now we are, as Paul Virilio has put it, living in real time, and real time means fatality. Actions have no antecedent, even when they refer to other revolutionary periods, they do not have any finality, even in a long term context, as no one knows where this is coming from and it all happens within real time. And such a real time manages to set it all up in a state of total ephemerality. Susan Sontag's act is limited. It cannot operate incognito, it is automatically mediatised, that is for sure. This in itself does not represent a radical objection, but it points out a tendency. Information is not what it used to be a long time ago. In the past, something would take place, then one would know it had taken place, then others would hear about it. Now, one knows everything before it has even taken place, and incidentally, it does not even have the time to take place. Mediatisation is a precession, you could call it the precession of simulacra within time. One is in a world where, in order to respond to a reality, to the importance of things, one needs to be far ahead, in an extreme way, one would need to precede the precession itself, to anticipate those simulacra, otherwise the clockwork, the system will be present before we are there. The simulacra will be ahead of us everywhere.

This was the situation of the Prague student and his double. His double was always there before him. Whenever he would go and meet someone for a duel for instance, the other had come before him, his adversary had been killed. So there was no reason for him to exist. We now live in such a system. Can one move forward? In a global situation, one is held hostage, complicitous even with such a situation. Such is the effect of the Stockholm syndrome: within such events, victims and executioners become in some way complicitous. It is monstrous, but real. Between the hostage and hostage-takers a form of complicity establishes itself.

In order to be able to have a bearing upon that immediate event, which is already devoid of its meaning, one would need to be far ahead of the game, in a state of extraordinary anticipation. One can try to do so, through one's intellect, or one's writing, although today it is remarkably harder to do so in practical terms. Sontag's gesture, and this is not a value judgment, or a judgment on her courage, because there was a real virtue in doing what she did, but virtues are something else. Strategically, if one uses that word, then there I would be more cynical. There is division of labour that should be respected. Even if there are any intellectuals left — and I am not sure I am one of them, even if I appear to share in such a life, appear to share a specific discourse — I do not share in that complicity of intellectuals who perceive themselves as responsible for something, as privileged with a sort of conscience-radicalness that used to be the privilege of intellectuals and now has moved on to another space. Subjects such as Susan Sontag cannot intervene anymore, even symbolically, but once again this is not a prognosis or diagnosis.

Bayard/Knight: Would it be possible to say that the hyperreal is a state where there is too much reality and not enough ideology? Have we become ideological paupers? Not in the sense that we still believe in it, in fact rather the opposite, in the sense that it used to be our alibi, our excuse on the terrain of subjective irony, something in fact in which not to believe. Interestingly, it has even become difficult to be cynical these days!

Baudrillard: Yes, it is true, since in every respect nobody believes in it any longer. And there lies the problem, when nobody believes in it any more. And not only in relation to ideology, but to indifference as well. Indifference was a fantastic quality, something almost stoical. It was very good to be indifferent in a world which was not, where there were differences, conflicts. So this kind of indifference, of a strategy of indifference, created a privileged situation. But in a world that has become completely indifferent what would it serve? It would be necessary to become different again in order to differentiate oneself from a world which has, objectively, become indifferent. That history is very pernicious.

It is the same thing for art with its power of illusion. What does this become in a world which itself ends up being totally illusory, even random? It becomes very difficult to find a form of intervention like that. So ideology… yes, the world is now so totally ideologized where everything passes through the narrative of ideology that it no longer serves any purpose to have any. Out of that follows the situation, the transcendence if you like, of ideology which actually, in fact, no longer exists.

I had an experience with simulation and the simulacrum. Nowadays I have had enough of it — 20 years of it, or almost, is enough! Something interesting happened to me recently on this subject, in relation to Japan. There was an erudite Japanese man who had come to interview me, and I asked him why for a number of years he had been translating my books — I had not received any word of it. I had been translated there several times before, and I had been told at that time "Ah, simulation and the simulacrum! In Japan you are an important spokesman." So I asked him why I no longer heard about readers' reactions and he told me, "But it is very simple, very simple you know. Simulation and the simulacrum have been realized. You were quite right: the world has become yours… and so we no longer have any need of you. You have disappeared. You have been volatilized in reality, or in the realization of hyperreality. It is over. In terms of theory, we no longer need you, and there is no longer a need to defend your theories." That is the paradox of utopia made real; it clearly makes every utopian dimension perfectly useless.

So I do not know if that answers your question, but ideology seems to me now to be so old a word that in some respects I do not even like to talk about it. In short, if it were true what Marx said, that it is the effect of a reaction of the super-structure on the infrastructure, a mode that reflects the conflictual relation of superstructure and infrastructure… but clearly one can no longer give it a funda-mental interpretation today except to produce a referential discourse which itself no longer has the effect of a real clash in the reality of the infrastructure, but is the legacy of a conceptual discourse that is already archaic/ancient. It becomes a kind of ideological zombie of itself, an artefact of itself. But then, without knowing it because everybody eventually takes up the language of ideology, everybody ideologizes things, it becomes our anchor.

As for me, I believe deeply that no one truly believes in it any longer at all. But it will always be there, and that is still the role, unfortunately, of the intellectual class, the political-intellectual class, which maintains the fiction of ideological discourse. Everyone pretends all the same to consume it since otherwise there would be panic. But at a profound level all this has no more credibility. This is what makes everything suddenly collapse, some day or other. It is a collapse that takes place because for a long time there has no longer been any credible basis to the thing at all. We have always wondered why, in the East, everything happened so fast without, apparently, any possible foreshadowing of the collapse. Well, it is simply that everything had been completely devitalized for a long time, and the discourse was no longer anything more than a parody of itself. Eventually, a reality that is only a parody of itself will cave in without resistance. There is not even any need to give it a push. Moreover, this new type of event is interesting, arising effectively out of indifference and no longer out of a will to action but out of a long inertia which has sapped the system. And then sooner or later, it implodes.

Bayard/Knight: Given the allusions to the Manichean nature of your strategy, irony is a rather isolated term here. It functions well with parody, but the latter hardly appears in your texts. Why not? Is it because the contradiction between them is already contained within irony?

Baudrillard: You say parody does not appear very much? Though I like the term well enough, parody is still perhaps a little too theatrical, too specular, in spite of everything. The parodic still has a certain power. It is true that I use the term irony a lot more, and what is more, I do not use it in the subjective sense any more. It is no longer subjective or romantic irony, nor humour in that sense. Rather it is a form of irony that is pataphysical, but objective. Before, it was subjective irony. It was to some extent connected to critique, to a critical, romantic, negative point of view, to a form of disillusion. The new irony seems to me rather to be an excess of positivity, of reality. And that is why I call it pataphysical because pataphysics, Alfred Jarry's *Ubu*, is precisely that. It is the too full, the too much of itself, it is an absolute, total over-awareness, positivity without fault. Ubu's big gut will clearly explode one day. And that is metaphysical irony, the irony of our world, and it is related to a kind of protuberance and excrescence of the system. It is no longer ridiculous in the classic theatrical sense, it is pataphysical. Ubu swallowed his own superego.

Everything is at the same time untouchable and non-existent, and that is the irony of non-existence, of insignificance. It is more radical than the Other. The Other was still, and that, moreover, is what gave it beauty and charm, complicity in the object, whereas irony now pertains to events themselves. The events in the East, where all of a sudden, at a time when one could have believed in the fall of capital, we witness the fall of communism. And that seems to be an ironic event to me, perfectly unforeseeable, and nevertheless dependent on a fantastic logic. It is that irony, rather, that I would insist on now. But it is difficult to thematize because it no longer lends itself to laughter, nor even to a smile really! Perhaps there is an object somewhere that smiles, but we do not know it.

Bayard/Knight: There are times when you almost speak as an Albigiensis.

Baudrillard: An Albigiensis, yes a Manichean. Certainly Manichean in *The Transparency of Evil.*

Bayard/Knight: There is a paradox which captures my attention in all this. On the one hand I hear a certain Albigiensianism, which sooner or later is read as a form of prophetic interpretation, it could be Jeremiah in the Old Testament, or even Job on his garbage heap, in other occasions you almost sound as Ecclesiastes. The paradox, for me, hinges around the fact that while I know you feel a perfect repulsion for moralistic rigorism, is it possible to behave as a prophet, especially as accurately as you have sometimes turned out to do, without being also a rigorous moralist?

Baudrillard: Rigorous… yes, to an extent that is a quality, although rigourism is a flaw, rigour, an extreme rigour is a strength. I would be in favour of extreme rigour. Radicalism is also a form of rigour as well. A rigourous logic seems to be necessary. Pity, mercy towards reality are not exactly my choice. I would rather go in the opposite direction. And, in a way, that is true, this could be perceived as a prophetic moralism. Prophetic… well, I am not sure, I guess one can extrapolate. I, in a way, love to extrapolate, take an idea to its utmost limit, to its extreme. Is this being prophetic? Sometimes, it happens to be right, but not necessarily. I do remember that someone had tried to make a inventory of all the inane comments I had made, well maybe not inane, but at least illusory and they had found quite a few. It was a newspaper which had done this, I think it was the *Globe-Hebdo*, or some such publication. In a way, it provided me with some publicity for things which had indeed taken place. But I had not uttered those prophecies out of a moralistic sense, although I am not sure whether I am devoid of it, I might have inherited some from my ancestors, who were peasants. So that my rigour would be of such a kind. It might come from a sense of repulsion, rather than moralism. Indeed I may be moral in the sense that everything I describe, I do from a sort of distance, cynicism, objectivity, from a paradoxical stance also. I do entertain deep repulsions, simultaneously with some attractions. Of course morals are being sustained by resentments and repulsions. And I must confess that I do feel an objective repulsion towards a number of things. In order to describe something you need to be nasty, to be propelled by the energy of repulsion. The Beaubourg architecture, the Beaubourg aesthetics aroused that in me and I described them with a degree of loathsomeness. But ultimately, when one ends up giving the object its monstrous dimension, its scale, or scope strikes you. And in order to find them or to express them, you need to absorb this object and identify with it as well as reject it, violently even. Writing also comes from that locus. It is an acting-out, as we were saying yesterday. Morals also reprove, reject, forbid although I am not certain that the analogy holds the same primitive reference, that the primitive scene would be the same.

Bayard/Knight: If you had to describe yourself, today, in a quick shot, would you describe yourself as *The Accidental Tourist* of the end of this century: little luggage, few illusions and gifted with that psychic stoicism the end of a millennium leaves us with at dawn?

Baudrillard: Tourist… well that is not very positive. I guess a form of speculation, a capacity for crossing, traversing yes. A tourist goes through, demonstrates a certain transversality, no doubt, goes to the end of things, or around them. If going around an object or looking at it from multiple viewpoints, defines the tourist, yes that is true. But there is also the fact that tourists avoid, let off, abandon a number of belongings and I did strive to do that. Why? because I probably was the happy owner of valuable gear and I tried to get rid of it. I tried not to refer to all of the history of ideas, philosophy even, to all of that richness I admired the most. Somewhere they are still close to me, but I did try not to make references to them, I chose to forsake them, to abandon objects, that is true. Did I try to create a power vacuum? I do not know whether the term tourist has that meaning, but it invokes a comparable mobility, the absence of primitive, or secondary accumulations, that is me. I tried to avoid accumulations, rather than lean towards expanding. I am not a gambler, not a spendthrift, but one needs to be able to sacrifice in order to re-create a vacuum, and not the other way around, that is clear.

Bayard/Knight: I was thinking about *The Accidental Tourist*, when asking you this question, as in *Cool Memories* you delineate beautiful meanders around the subject of exile, which you describe as a wonderful and comfortable structure, marked by unreality and the end of the world. Have you been looking for those as fragments to be reached outside of a France filled with greyness and chagrined undecisiveness?

Baudrillard: Exile, yes of course. I am quite aware that I operate from a prejudiced position against nationalism, from one which is anti-nationalist, or even anti-cultural. Somewhere within me there is a distancing away from what is closer to the bone, for that which is closer to one's own culture, one's country, family is that from which one cannot escape. Such a promiscuousness I perceive as dangerous and therefore I have always tried to distance myself from it, sometimes with some partiality about what is the closest to me. And yet, I do value intimacy, roots, ancestry. It is maybe because I have those roots within me that I can afford to become the perfect cosmopolitan since I know I will always have that form, that substance which solidity confers upon oneself and that I will never lose those elements. Therefore I never look upon the world as a lost object and I can afford to loose sight of it, especially that which is closer to me, territory or country. That is true as far as France is concerned, where I have always had an anti-cultural preju-dice, clearly I have never forgiven culture, it contains too many unacceptable elements and the world becomes increasingly unacceptable because it "culturalizes" itself at full-speed. Everything has now turned into culture and it has even become very difficult to go beyond one's own culture since one finds it everywhere. There will even be a moment when one will not be able to find any deserts. Deserts are a metaphor for disappearing objects, evanescence beyond culture. Now that they have become increasingly culturalized they are virtually impossible to find.

Patagonia has become a new frontier, absence as much as the locus of absence, have become extremely difficult to access. The real danger, that is true, is to end up wallowing in an obsessional negativity vis-à-vis the others' culture and the rest of the world. And it is true that I have developed my own biased distance, but I think it is better that way, rather than the other way around.

Bayard/Knight: In the interviews you have given, from Paris to Australia via California, you often speak of the cinema, of the plastic arts, architecture, painting. What place do the other four senses occupy in your life — taste, smell, touch, hearing?

Baudrillard: Ah, we have almost come back to the opening question! How shall I put it? I have not had any musical culture, or acculturation to music, practically none. These are things which later on, in adulthood, you definitely miss. As for painting, the situation was a little bit autodidactic, but ultimately there I know where this is all coming from. Cinema much more because I really was a bit of a cinema fan at a certain point in my life, while I am much less so today because I no longer happen to find myself there and no longer see what it is any more, that is true. And then lastly architecture? Yes, that much more so because of friends in architecture, because of a milieu I knew well, though not through any initial intervention on my part. And so, then, I have finished up with photography which was and still is exactly a register which is completely intimate and profound for me. Not a profoundness of substance, but perhaps on the surface, though very intense all the same. I have not practised it for very long, perhaps a dozen years, which makes photography as intense for me as writing, though in a completely different way. Yet perhaps it has given me pleasures even more intense than writing.

Is it a relationship with an image, and can you call it an image? It is perhaps for me something else. It is more magical than the real thing. It is the object that, right from the start, has deeply intrigued and obsessed me. I began with the object, after that perhaps the Object with a capital letter, or even the metaphysical object which can be anything one wishes, then perhaps the object as radical otherness, like radical exoticism. For me, the photographic image is a little bit like that, and that is different from cinema. I am not the only one to think that the photographic image is superior to the cinematic image because cinema, in relation to photography, is a loss in terms of illusion, the power of illusion. Of course, it is a progression, an objective one if you like, but like all progress it can very well be precisely, objectively, a loss. Cinema itself, right inside its practice, has lost the force of illusion. It has lost it through colour, by all the improvements that have been made which have, in fact, always seems highly problematic to me. So the photographic image restores a sort of absolute moment. What Barthes says about it is very nice, though perhaps too nice. I have not really thought about it. It is a raw element, evidently, and I try to keep it that way, harsh, and to practise it harshly, a dimension I recognize quite willingly. For the other senses, even art and painting, I have never been involved in them except at a remove, and rather episodically. I have never really addressed things from that point of view, although sometimes I have found myself involved in these spaces in spite of myself, with New York artists and the simulationists. And that was an extremely ambiguous adventure. I found myself taken in there like a referent, a referential hostage. I was badly treated. One minute I found myself praised to the skies, and then cut down maliciously. Fine, none of that was my doing. It was an unwitting destiny.

Choice, desire, investments, these would be in the area of the image, effectively, in the domain of the image, and more precisely in that of photography. I cannot really explain why; it is where I have found a sort of, not of alternative but of a total alternation with writing. Not to have anything but writing makes you really an intellectual, even if you do not like it all the same. Writing is, nonetheless, related more to discourse while photography can be done with a total singularity that is external, alien. Of course there is still a danger there that people end up identifying you as a photographer anyway, and then you find yourself co-opted once again. But for the moment, things are still O.K.!

This interview was conducted in French and translated into English by Professors Caroline Bayard and Graham Knight.

Civil Society, Fanaticism, and Digital Reality
An Interview with Slavoj Zizek

Geert Lovink

Geert Lovink: Let's speak about the role of intellectuals. Before 1989, there was a strange relationship among intellectuals and those in power in Eastern Europe. Both bureaucrats and dissidents had some sort of relationship with politics. Even now, this is partly the case. In Western Europe this phenomenon disappeared and it is hard to see any relationship or even dialogue. What should be the role of intellectuals?

Slavoj Zizek: Partially this is true. For me what was partially so attractive, so sympathetic about real socialism, despite being a corrupt, cynical system, was the belief in the power of the spoken word. Some twenty years ago, I was editor of a small art-theoretical journal with a circulation of 3,400. Once we published a small, obscure poem, incomprehensibly modern, but between the lines there was a dissident message. If the power would have ignored the poem, nothing would have happened. But there was an extraordinary session of the Central Committee. Okay, this is repression, but what I like about it is that the communist power took the potential, detonating force of the spoken word very seriously. They were always interested in arguing with intellectuals. Let's take an artist like Tarkovski, who was half dissident. He was half allowed to work, even if they suppressed some of his films. They were impressed, they bothered. Fredric Jameson made a nice point about this: we are only now becoming aware that what we liked about East-European dissidents like Havel is only possible within a socialist system.

   Our influence, beginning in the mid-eighties, was at that time incredibly large, especially the philosophers, sociologists, literary theoreticians. But this was a very limited conjunction. Now there is the pure ignorance of the regime, which is simply not interested in ideological questions. I feel sorry for those countries in which writers nowadays play an important role. Take Serbia, where this nationalist madness was fabricated by writers. Even in Slovenia it's the same with the nationalist writers, although they do not have much influence.

Lovink: But you are involved in politics yourself, up until this moment. There are a lot of controversies in Ljubljiana about your involvement in the governing party and the fact that you write speeches for them.

Zizek: There is a messianic complex with intellectuals in Eastern Europe. Nothing against it, but it becomes extremely dangerous in Slovenia when this messianic vision of intellectuals is combined with a vulgar anti-Americanism, which is a very popular political attitude of right wingers. America for them means no national solidarity, filthy liberalism, multi-culturalism, individualism, the market. They are afraid of a pluralistic democracy and there is a proto-fascistic potential in it. This combination of nationalist writers, whose obsession is how to retain national identity, and an anti-capitalist right-wing movement is very dangerous.

I did something for which I lost almost all my friends, what no good leftist ever does: I fully supported the ruling party in Slovenia. For this all my leftist friends hate me and of course the whole right wing. What the liberal democratic party did was a miracle. Five years ago we were the remainder of the new social movements, like feminist and ecological groups. At that time everybody thought that we would be vanishing mediators. We made some slyly corrupted, but good moves and now we are the strongest party. I think it was our party that saved Slovenia from the fate of the other former Yugoslav republics, where they have the one-party model. Either right wing like in Croatia or left wing like in Serbia, which hegemonised in the name of the national interest. With us it's a really diverse, pluralist scene, open towards foreigners (of course, there are some critical cases). But the changes of a genuine pluralist society are not yet lost.

It's typical that this position triggers an enormous hatred against me. Slovene media absolutely ignore me, there is never an article about me. On the other hand, if some nationalist poet publishes a small poem in some obscure Austrian journal, it's a big success in Slovenia. I am rather perceived as some dark, ominous, plotting, political manipulator, a role I enjoy immensely and like very much.

Lovink: You have not become cynical about the current power struggles you are involved in?

Zizek: You do not hear me not saying that it is so disgusting. It's a simple, professional choice. Now politics is becoming business-as-usual in Slovenia. It's no longer that once a week you write a heroic article and you are a hero. It means intrigues and meetings. I simply had to choose. Do I do serious theory or politics? What I hate most are the beautiful souls of the left wing who complain about their losses, that everything is corrupted, where are the good old days of the original, left-wing dissidence? No, you must accept the rules of the game. Svetlana Slapzak [from Belgrade, now Ljubljana – GL] and the group around her present themselves as marginalised victims. But her groups control two departments and the most powerful publishing house. They get the most money from the ministry of science. And via the Soros Foundation they are selling the story of being surrounded by nationalism.

Let's take me. I was blocked from the university before; I was only teaching abroad, in France and in America. I never taught at any university in Slovenia, I am absolutely alone, without any research assistant. They just give me enough money in order to survive. My answer to Svetlana Slapzak would be: why did she become a Slovenian citizen? Her very position is a contradiction of what she says. In a state of less than 2 million we offered 100,000 non-Slovenians permanent citizenship, against terrible nationalistic resistance. There were no dirty tricks involved, like a test if you knew Slovenian. We are still in an intermediate stage. When a new political logic imposes itself, the *Sittlichkeit*, the unwritten rules are still unsure, people are still searching for a model. The question is: will we become just another small, stupid, nationalistic state or maintain this elementary, pluralistic opening? And all compromises are worth it for this goal.

Lovink: What is your view on the work of the Soros Foundation and the concept of an "open society"?

Zizek: If you look into my heart, you'll see I am an old-fashioned left winger. In the short term I support it, but I don't have Popper notions about it. Soros is doing good work in the field of education, refugees and keeping the theoretical and social sciences' spirit alive. These countries are not only impoverished, but the sphere of social sciences is hegemonised by Heideggerian nationalists. But the Soros people have this ethic of the bad state vs. good, civic, independent structures. But sorry, in Slovenia I am for the state and against civil society! In Slovenia, civil society is equal to the right wingers. In America, after the Oklahoma bombing, they suddenly discovered that madmen are everywhere. Civil society is not this nice, social movement, but a network of moral majority, conservative and nationalist pressure groups, against abortion, religious education in schools. A real pressure from below.

For me the open society means something very practical: the unwritten rules of the political space. For example, if you oppose the present government or the hegemonic party, are you then still accepted or is there an unwritten, unspoken stigma that you are a half-nationalist traitor and so on? Up to what extent can you make a career without making political compromises? I don't have any fundamental hopes in a socialist revolution or whatever. We have several big crises coming: the ecological, the developed against the underdeveloped world and the loss of the sense of reality in the face of all the rapid changes. I don't underestimate the social impact of the loss of stability. Is the frame of liberal capitalism able to solve this antago-nism? Unfortunately my answer is no. Here I am the old-fashioned left-wing pessimist. I think that ghettoisation, like half of L.A., is far stronger than the Marxist class struggle. At least both workers and capitalists still participated in legality and the state, whereas liberal capitalism simply doesn't integrate the new ghettoes. Liberal democracy has no answer to these problems.

A lot of times, this Soros approach of openness indulges in its own species of covered racism. Recently at a conference in Amsterdam, Press Now asked whether it was possible to find a universal language so that intellectuals from various parts of the former Yugoslavia could start a dialogue. I find this cliché extremely dangerous, because it comes from an idea of the Balkans as the phantasmatic space of national-istic madness. This phantasy is very well manipulated and expressed in some popular works of art, like Kusturica's film *Underground*. He said himself, in *Cahiers du cinéma*, that in the Balkans, war is a natural phenomenon, nobody knows when it will emerge, it just comes, it's in our genes. This naturalisation of the Balkans into an apolitical, primordial theatre of passions is cliché and I find it very suspicious. I would like to quote Hegel here: "The true evil is an attitude which perceives evil everywhere." I am very suspicious about this apparent multi-cultural, neutral, liberal attitude, which only sees nationalistic madness around itself. It posits itself in a witness role. The post-Yugoslav war is strictly the result of European cultural dynamics. We don't need this simplistic liberal deploring of "why don't people speak to each other?" Nobody is doing power analysis.

A common western cliché is the so-called complexity of the Balkans. This specifically allows the west to maintain its position as an excluded observer. What you should do is what I call a phenomenological *réduction à l'envers*. You should not try to understand it. Like TV, the funny effect when you disconnect the voice, you only have these stupid gestures. Cut off the meaning and then you'll get the pure power battle. The Balkans are a symptom of Europe in the sense that it embodies all that is wrong in the light of the utopian notion of the European Community itself. What is the dream? A kind of neutral, purely technocratic Brussels bureaucracy. They project their mirror image on the Balkans. What they both have in common is the exclusion of the proper political antagonisms.

Lovink: The campaign in Holland, Press Now, supports so-called independent media in the former Yugoslavia. One of its premises is the idea that the war started with propaganda from above through state-controlled media. Seeing that any western intervention already came too late, it states that, for example, through independent media, one could work on a long term solution. Do you agree with this analysis?

Zizek: Up to a point I agree with this, but I have always been in favour of military intervention from the west. Around 1992, with a little bit of pressure, the war would have been over. But they missed the moment. Now, with the shift of balance and the stronger Russia, this is no longer possible. At that time, Croatians and Slovenians were in favour of independence, and the Bosnians were much more ambiguous and they are paying the price for it. The Bosnians didn't want to prepare for war, they were slower, more careful and that's why they are now so mad at the west. There was no protection of Bosnia for the Yugoslav army, despite all the guarantees. And then, after the attack, the west suddenly started talking about ethnic struggles, all sides must be guilty, and primordial passions.

I don't cry too much for Yugoslavia. The moment Milosevic took over and annexed Kosovo and Vojvodina, the balance of power shifted. There was the choice between a more federal Yugoslavia and a new, centralist one. Do not overestimate the role of the media in the late eighties. Media were allowed to play this role in order for local communist bureaucracies to survive. The key to the Yugoslav crisis is Milosevic's strategy to maintain the power of the old nomenclatura by raking up this national question. The media did their dirty work. It was horrible to watch day by day the stories in Slovenia about Serbs raping us and in Serbia about Albanians raping them. All the news was filtered through this poisoning hatred, from everyday crime to economics. But that was not the origin of the conflict. That was the calculation from the power elite to maintain power.

If you define independence in terms of not being supported or controlled by the state, then the worst right wing weekly is a independent medium and should be supported by Soros. I do admit that in Serbia and Croatia there is absolute control over the media. What they allow are really small, marginalised media. Impartial, independent information can help a lot, but don't expect too much of it.

Lovink: In your speech during the Ars Electronica conference, you emphasised the fact that after a phase of introduction, the seduction of the new media will be over and so will "virtual sex." So the desire to be wired will be over soon?

Zizek: The so-called "virtual communities" are not such a great revolution as it might appear. What impresses me is the extent to which these virtual phenomena retroactively enable us to discover to what extent our self has always been virtual. Even the most physical self experience has a symbolic, virtual element in it. For example playing sex games. What fascinates me is that the possibility of satisfaction already counts as an actual satisfaction. A lot of my friends used to play sex games on Minitel in France. They told me that the point is not really to meet a person, not even to masturbate, but that just typing your phantasies is the fascination itself. In the symbolic order the potentiality already gives actual satisfaction. In psycho-analytic theory the notion of symbolic castration is often misunderstood. The threat of castration as to its effects, acts as a castration. Or in power relations, where the potential authority forms the actual threat. Take Margaret Thatcher. Her point was that if you don't rely on state support but on your individual resources, luck is around the corner. The majority didn't believe this, they knew very well that most of them would remain poor. But it was enough to be in a position where they might succeed.

The idea that you were able to do something, but didn't, gives you more satisfaction than actually doing it. In Italy, it is said to be very popular during the sexual act that a woman tells a man some dirty phantasies. It is not enough that you are actually doing it, you need some phantasmatic, virtual support. "You are good, but yesterday I fucked another one and he was better..." What interests me are the so-called sado-masochistic, ritualised, sexual practices. You never go to the end, you just repeat a certain foreplay. Virtual in the sense that you announce it, but never do it. Some write a contract. Even when you are doing it, you never lose control, all the time you behave as the director of your own game. What fascinates me is this *Spaltung*, this gap in order to remain a certain distance. This distance, far from spoiling enjoyment, makes it even more intense. Here I see great possibilities for the VR stuff.

In the computer I see virtuality, in the sense of symbolic fiction, collapsing. This notion has a long tradition. In Bentham's Panopticon we find virtuality at its purest. You never know if somebody is there in the centre. If you knew someone was there, it would have been less horrifying. Now's it's just an "utterly dark spot," as Bentham calls it. If someone is following you and you're not sure, it is more horrible than if you know that there is somebody. A radical uncertainty.

Lovink: You are famous for your film analyses. But can you imagine also using examples from computer networks, analyzing the storyline of a CD-ROM or use television material?

Zizek: The British Film Institute proposed to me to choose my own six, seven films and to do a couple of lectures there, since I use so many film examples. They came up with the idea to do a CD-ROM, because I write in the same manner: click here, go there, use this fragment, that story or scene. My books are already failed CD-ROMs, as someone told me. But because of copyright, it is extremely difficult to realise and dirty capitalism will destroy this plan. Don't they realise that if you use an excerpt of theirs, you create propaganda for them? But it is my dream to do something like this. In my favorite book, *Tarrying with the Negative*, I use some fragments of Hitchcock. How nice it would be to have it included in the text. But concerning film, I am indeed rather conservative. At this moment I am working on the theme of the role of music in cinema. The idea is that in the mid-thirties, when the classical Hollywood code was established, it was strictly Wagnerian, pure accompanying music, radical underscoring, determining your subjective perspective. It's a classical case of a conservative revolution. As Wagner said about his *Gesamtkunstwerk*: "if we allow music to develop by itself, it will become atonal and inimitable."

What I also study are the soundtracks in the films of Lynch and Altman and the shift from the landscape to the soundscape. With Altman and Dolby stereo, you no longer need the soundtrack as a general frame, as if you have inconsistent fragments. The unity is no longer established at the visual level. I want to connect this with Altman's *Short Cuts*, with its series of faiths, contingently hitting each other. Very Deleuzean: global nonsense where contingent encounters produce local effects of sense in order to understand what subjective in our late capitalist society means. Or let's take Lynch's biggest failure, *Dune*. Did you notice the use of multiple inner monologues? Reality is something very fragile for Lynch. If you get too close to it you discover Leni Riefenstahl. I am not interested in direct content analysis, but the kind of purely formal changes in how we relate to the physicality of the film and the shifts in the notions of subjectivity. Of course all of this is done in a kindly anti-Derridian swing. For us, it is the sound that is the traumatic point, the cry or even the song. The point where you lose your unity and the ways the self-enjoying voice always gets controlled. What interests me at the political level is how the discourse machinery, in order to function, has to rely on the obscene voice. What appears to be a carnivalesque subversion, this eruption of obscene freedom, really serves the power. But these are my B-productions, if you want to put it in Hollywood terms. The A-production of the last two years was a book on Schelling that I just finished.

Lovink: We recently celebrated the centenary of cinema. What's the condition of current film theory? What will come after the critical, semiological and gender approaches? Is it still useful to see film as a unity or should we surf through the media, like the users do and use a variety of sources?

Zizek: Fredric Jameson has already made this point. What goes on in cinema is determined by what happens in other media. Concerning theory, there are a lot of others, the whole domain of cultural criticism in America is basically cinema theory. What attracts me, is the axis between gaze and voice and nowhere will you find this tension better than in cinema. This still is for me the principal axis. Cinema is for me a kind of condensation. On the one hand you have the problem of voice, on the other the narrativisation.

The only change I can think of is that up until twenty years ago, going to the cinema was a totally different social experience. It was a Saturday or Sunday afternoon, and this changed. But what still appears in ordinary commercial films is the shift in the notion of subjectivity. You can detect what goes on at the profoundest, most radical level of our symbolic identities and how we experience ourselves. Cinema is still the easiest way. Like for Freud, dreams were the royal way to the unconscious.

Maybe I am part of a nostalgic movement. Nowadays, because of all these new media, cinema is in a crisis. It has become popular as a nostalgic medium. And what is modern film theory really about? Its ultimate objects are nostalgic films from the thirties and forties. It is as if you need the theory in order to enjoy them. It's incredible how even Marxists enjoy this game. They have seen every film, I'm not joking. It's not only this paternalising notion that it is good to use examples from cinema. I would still claim that there is an inherent logic of the theory itself, as if there is a privileged relationship, like the role literature played in the nineteenth century.

Lovink: You have been to Japan. What's your opinion on the technological culture in that country?

Zizek: First I must say that I don't have my own positive theory about Japan. What I do have, as every western intellectual, are the myths of reference. There is the old, right wing image of the Samurai code, fighting to death, the absolute, ethical Japan. Then there is the leftist image, from Eisenstein: the semiotic Japan. The empty signs, no western metaphysics of presence. It's a no less phantasmatic Japan than the first one. We know that Eisenstein for his montage of attractions used Japanese ideograms.

Then there is Bertolt Brecht as an exception. He took over elements like sacrifice and authority and put them in a left-wing context. Here in the west, Brecht was seen as someone introducing a fanatic Eastern morality. But now there's in *Suhrkamp Verlag* a detailed edition of his "Jasager" and his "Lernstacke." They discovered that all those moments the western critics perceived as remainders of this imperial and sacrificing Japan were indeed edited by Brecht. What they perceived as Japanese was Brecht.

Then there is the capitalist Japan and its different stages. There is the myth of non-original Japan taking over, but developing better: Philips for the rich and Sony for the poor. Twenty years later this was of course the other way round. Then there is the Kojèvian Japan. First, for Kojève the end of history was Russia and America, the realisation of the French Revolution. Then he noticed that something was missing. He found the answer in Japan, in the little surplus. If everything only functions, as in America, you would kill yourself. In the snobbism, drinking tea in a nice way, he found that life still had a meaning.

But there is another Japan, the psycho-analytic. For the multi-culturalist approach, the almost standard example is Japan and its way of *Verneinung*, saying no. There are thirty ways to say no. You say no to your wife in one way, no to a child in another way. There is not one negation. There is a small Lacanian volume, *La chose japonaise*. They elaborate the borrowing of other languages, all these ambiguities. Didn't Lacan say that Japanese do not have an unconscious?

For the west, Japan is the ambiguous Other: at the same time it fascinates you and repels you. Let's not forget the psychological cliché of Japan: you smile, but you never know if it is sincere or if you are mocking us – the idea of Japan as the impenetrable Other. This ambiguous politeness. What do they really want? There's also the idea of the Japanese as the ersatz Jews for the Americans. The Japanese governments together with two or three mega companies, plotting. All this spleen, this palette of phantasies, is Japan for us. But what surprised me is that authors, whom I considered strictly European, are widely read in Japan, as for example George Lukacs.

Then there is a Japan, loved by those who criticise our western, decadent way of liberal democracy and who look for a model that would combine the dynamics of capitalism, while maintaining some firm traditional structure of authority. And again, it can work both ways. What I like about phantasies is that they are always ambiguous. You can turn it in a negative way, Japanese pretending to play capitalism, while in reality what you have is conspiracy and authority. On the positive side you see that there is a capitalism possible with moral values.

What I liked there, in restaurants and subway stations, is the absence of English. You don't have this self-humiliating, disgusting, pleasing attitude. It's up to the foreigners to find their way out. I liked tremendously those automatic vending machines. Did you see *The Shining*, based on Stephen King's novel? This is America at its worst. Three people, a family, in a big hotel and still the space is too small for them and they start killing each other. In Japan, even when it is very crowded, you don't feel the pressure, even if you are physically close. The art of ignoring. In the New York subway, even when it's half full, you would have this horrifying experience of the absolute proximity of the Other. What I liked about the Foucault conference in Tokyo I attended was that one would expect the Japanese to apply Foucault to their own notions. But all the Japanese interventions were about Flaubert. They didn't accept this anthropological game of playing idiots for you. No, they tried to beat us at our own game. We know Flaubert better than you.

Every nation in Europe has this fanaticism, conceiving itself as the true, primordial nation. The Serbian myth, for example, is that they are the first nation of the world. The Croatians consider themselves as primordial Aryans. The Slovenians are not really Slavs, but pretend to be of Etrurian origin. It would be nice to find a nation that accepts the fact of being the second and not the first. This might be a part of the Japanese identity, if you look at the way they borrow languages.

I recently read a book on Kurosawa. It is said that *Rashomon* was seen in the early fifties as the big discovery of the Eastern spirit. But in Japan it was perceived as way too western. My favorite Japanese film is *Sansho* by Michoguchi because it offers itself for a nice, Lacanian reading, the problem of the lost mother, the mother's voice reaching the son, etc. This is the Japanese advantage over America when the mother's voice tries to reach the son. In America one would get madness, like Hitchcock's *Psycho*, but in Japan you get a normal family.

The Balkans is now a region where the west is projecting its own phantasies, like Japan. And again, this can be very contradictory. The film *Rising Sun* ambiguously suggests that there is a Japanese plot to take over and buy Hollywood. The idea is that they do not just want our factories, our land, they even want our dreams. Behind this there's the notion of thought control. It's the old Marxist notion of buying the whole chain, from the hardware to the movie theatres. What interests me in Japan is that it is a good argument against the vulgar, pseudo-Marxist evolutionary notion that you have to go through certain evolutionary stages. Japan proves that you can make a direct short circuit. You retain certain elements of the old hierarchical superstructure and combine it very nicely with the most effective version of capitalism it pretends to be. It's a good experience in non-anthropocentrism. It's a mystery for western sociologists who say that you need Protestant ethics for good capitalism.

What I see in Japan, and maybe this is my own myth, is that behind all these notions of politeness, snobbism etc. the Japanese are well aware that something which may appear superficial and unnecessary has a much deeper structural function. A western approach would be: who needs this? But a totally ridiculous thing at a deeper level might play a stabilizing function we are not aware of. Everybody laughs at the English monarchy, but you'll never know.

There is another notion that is popular now amongst American sociologists; civilizations of guilt versus civilizations of shame. The Jews and their inner guilt and the Greeks with their culture of shame. The usual cliché now is that Japan is the ultimate civilization of shame. What I despise in America is the studio actors logic, as if there is something good in self expression: do not be oppressed, open yourself, even if you shout and kick the others, everything in order to express and liberate yourself. This is a stupid idea, that behind the mask there is some truth. In Japan, and I hope that this is not only a myth, even if something is merely an appearance, politeness is not simply insincere. There is a difference between saying "Hello, how are you?" and the New York taxi drivers who swear at you. Surfaces do matter. If you disturb the surfaces you may lose a lot more than you think. You shouldn't play with rituals. Masks are never simply mere masks. Perhaps that's why Brecht became close to Japan. He also liked this notion that there is nothing really liberating in this typical western gesture of stealing the masks and showing the true face. What you discover is something absolutely disgusting. Let's maintain the appearances, that's my own phantasy of Japan.

Panic Quake Servers

Frank Lantz

Author's Note: Quake is id software's much-anticipated follow-up to Doom, the most successful computer game of all time. Addictive, immersive, and hyperviolent, Quake has already established itself as the ultimate productivity black hole. Now, across the network, puzzled system administrators are discovering more and more machines that have been transformed into secret servers dedicated to managing the shadow traffic of non-stop multiplayer deathmatches.

> *Quake is just one step toward the future, but I think it has a good shot at spawning a pretty complicated online, networked universe.*
>
> Michael Abrash, id programmer

Panic Quake Servers are the avant-garde of a parasite nervous system grafting itself onto the corporate backbone. Bandwidth scavengers hosting the endless recombinant congregations of vapourwar.

Forget virtual reality and cyberspace. The ultimate synthesis of architecture and cinema is already being coded up around you. Forget about soaring over gleaming spires of data in a weightless universe of pure information. Quakespace is claustrophobic, scatological, pre-pubescent, and very, very dangerous.

And forget about leaving the meat behind: Panic Quake is nothing *but* bodies. Bodies splattered, pulverized and exploded. The body fragged and multiplied, becoming pure speed in a point-to-point network of ammunition flows and tactical lust. All-sucking, all-spewing, the Quakebody is projectile and target, monster and hero, author and interface, key, switch, and trap. It is the body with nothing but organs, irrupting and transmitting, and always forever the barricaded global variable in an infinite cascade of light-speed calculations: surface, perspective, and line of sight – the baroque codes for subjectivity in the digital space of deathmatch culture.

Captain Kirk Was Never the Original

Alan Shapiro

In its prevalent forms, the cottage consumer industry of *Star Trek* is a classic virtuality of identification where the viewers' senses of self, otherness, and reality are blurred by the contemplation of iconic spectacles. The fanatic relationship to media objects and fetishized paraphernalia is a partial, transitional realization of the reign of simulacra, effected at this stage in the logic of the model and its serial differentiation. After the original *Star Trek* series came the animated series, then *The Next Generation*, six original series movies, one inter-generational movie, *Deep Space Nine*, *Voyager*, and now *The Next Generation* movie (*First Contact*) and the current 30th anniversary festivities. It is an endless cloned succession, a lineal, self-evolving pataphysics of re-worked plots, trans-species Federation officers, sentimental cyborgs, humanoid hyperlife, engineering re-stabilizations following perturbations, non-Möbius time travel, and warp drive accelerations beyond the speed of light.

But this unceasing serial commodification or anabolic self-replication always sustains itself through reverent reference to the original referent — the pantheonic first generation of Captain James T. Kirk, graduate of Starfleet Academy, First and Science Officer $@&# (unpronounceable) Spock, Chief Medical Officer Dr. Leonard "Bones" McCoy, Scott, Uhura, Chekov, Sulu, Chapel, and Rand. *But Captain Kirk was never the original.* Attention, red alert, all hailing channels being jammed, switching to sub-space frequency, and repeating: William Shatner/James T. Kirk was not the original Captain of the Starship Enterprise.

In the pilot broadcast for the first *Star Trek* series, entitled "The Cage" (aired on February 1, 1965), the Enterprise (NCC-1701A, prototype model), with Captain Christopher Pike (Jeffrey Hunter) in command, answers a mysterious distress call from long-lost Federation settlers believed to have crashed on the planet Talos IV. The distress call turns out to have been fabricated by the super-intelligent beings of Talos to lure Pike and two of his most attractive female crew members into a zoo-like captivity. After Captain Kirk replaced Captain Pike for the eventual prime-time series, the footage from "The Cage" was re-edited into a two-part episode called "The Menagerie" (stardates 3012.4 and 3012.5). The keepers of the *menagerie* are so scientifically advanced that they are *all brain* — they have lost the capabilities to experience sensory and tactile reality, to feel or emote, and to stroke the physical world. They seek to benignly imprison two humans (a male and a female), cut them loose in a high-tech digitized parallel-processed virtual

Disneyland, and start grooving vicariously on the sensations and emotions. The Talosians have collected biological specimens from around the galaxy in their zoo, but the two humans will be their premium ticket to a virtual reality lust-fest.

Aside from hints about its von Neumann architecture, the underlying algorithms and class inheritances of the *menagerie*'s virtuality engine are not specified. We can assume a ring zero concentric clustering saltation, descendent from early artificial life programs. Captain Pike and his holographic computer-generated ideal woman can live out any scenario which is found in the dream-reservoir in Pike's head (Pike rejects the two female officers in favor of the gentle hologram as his companion). Any childhood memory, sexual fantasy, "historical" time and place, folklore, fairy tale, vision of home, or galaxial adventure can be "brought to life" by the *menagerie*'s virtual reality neural network and wetware. The ideal woman is synthesized from a reading of Captain Pike's libidinal unconscious worked upon the ruined body of an Earth woman who, as a young girl years ago, was the sole survivor of the crash of the Federation settlers' spaceship. The scarred, now fully-grown woman appears beautiful to Captain Pike through trick photochronography. For her part, she has been raised in the zoo by the Talosians and has never seen a *real man* before Pike.

In the story of Captain Pike, a much later and conclusive stage in the accomplishment of simulacra is invoked. Beyond *Star Trek*'s predominant virtuality of virtuous identification is the virtuality of the unconditional worship of simulacra, a final stage exemplified by digital media's synthesis of synthetic three-dimensional video and the jacked-in nervous system. Having completed the pilot episode, the producers of *Star Trek* must have realized that they had given birth to a Captain whose precocious engagement with virtual reality already disqualified him from serving as the model for a sequelized succession of media commodities. The successful media product model has as prerequisite a mythical moment of transcendent creativity which clears the way for the emergence of a new spectacle object. The spectacle object (celebrity, consumer gadget, media property) then enters the panoply of fetishes among which we shop in our efforts to find an identity "niche" and dubiously distinguish ourselves from others. The model serves as lightning rod for ambivalent collective projections, allowing each individual to feel unique at the very moment when all consumers of that same niche are imitating the same elevated pattern.

But the fully achieved simulacra of virtual reality threaten the stability and profitability of this system of differences. This is why Captain Pike, who was too far ahead of his time, had to be shunted aside in favor of the valorous Captain Kirk. The binary oppositions of compartmentalized analytical thought which uphold the progress of the media and computer industries (the dualities between original and copy, mind and body, model and series, real and virtual, reality and information) begin to break down in the era of consummated virtuality in favor of a perpetual Möbius strip which appears at all points to have two sides but really has one. The dichotomy between computer applications which belong to the official category of virtual reality software and the rest of computer applications is a prime example of such increasingly precarious binary oppositions in the computer industry. In the first type of virtual reality application (the official product category), a purposive activity, such as piloting an airplane or meeting a new girlfriend, is simulated both by providing sensory information to the user that mimics the real activity, and by handling changes in perceptual angles caused by the user's moves through the cyberspace.[1] In the second type of virtual reality application (not recognized as such by the computer industry), a familiar human activity such as driving in the country or eating dinner at a restaurant is organized as a virtual machine by the increased information that is brought to bear upon it. Claude Shannon, one of the original Captains of Computer Science, defined information as the "reduction of uncertainty." These familiar activities which become the domain of software applications were previously "hotbeds of uncertainty" needing to be brought under control by a wallet-sized or car computer. At some point there will no longer be any difference between the three-dimensional digital video images displayed outside the window of the cockpit flight simulator and the three-dimensional digital video images of sunny landscapes projected outside the passenger window by the car computer as I drive through the country on a rainy afternoon. Once we arrive at this point of convergence between the named virtual simulation of a remote, normally inaccessible activity (like exploring the surface of Mars or meeting a new girlfriend) and the unnamed virtual simulation of a familiar, accessible human activity (like eating in a restaurant or meeting a new girlfriend), then both types of software application have elaborated their object to the point where the elaborations join together in the same completed and perfected simulacra. What was previously called information and what was called reality become as alike as the two sides of the Möbius strip. The assumption that information is a science which is "useful" to a separate, intact object called reality ignores the ascendence of the seamless, uninterrupted network interface (between "knowing" and object) and its transfiguring sway. A fully accomplished virtual network, such as the one which beckoned Captain Pike, endangers the primacy of the model and the powerful dissemination of its aura in the perpetual substitutions and re-arrangements of the series. The logic of the charismatic media model and its propagated array of serial distinctions was essential in supporting the illusion of the uniqueness and individuality of each consumer of shared media spectacles. The displacement of this system by immersive or neural-direct fusion with spectral, holographic environments portends a potentially reversible endpoint to the history of images and simulacra.

In the zoo on Talos IV, Captain Pike is at first as valorous as Captain Kirk eventually will be. Although he participates for a while, Pike is not seduced for long by the virtual reality goodies proffered by the Talosians. His freedom and ontological grounding in reality are more precious to him than fated reunions with loved ones and pets from his childhood. His sworn duty to "get back to his ship" is more important than saving the woman of his dreams from monsters in a Gothic castle. A polymorphous perverse prisoner is still a prisoner, and Pike has nothing but contempt for his over-cerebrated sedentary voyeuristic captors. He summons all his cunning, exhorting himself to figure out a way to escape.

Captain Pike discovers a bug in the Talosians' system, a flaw in their security software. They have not accounted in their human resources package for the emotion of raw hatred. When Pike concentrates all his feelings on his hatred of the Talosians, the processor-generated force field which surrounds Pike's cage breaks down. Pike is able to dart out of the cage and ring his hands around the Talosian leader's neck. After this outburst of hatred, the Talosians are only too happy to let Captain Pike go. They admit that they underestimated the human species' aversion to confinement. They have now discovered that humans are capable of extreme phenomena, such as radical passions towards others, and extreme phenomena were not considered in the object-oriented design of their software. In most cases, proper software engineering directs that reality is a bug to be fixed in the next release. But a radical passion like hatred necessitates more than a version patch. To the Talosians, this vehement human potentiality is like a rogue virus which threatens to bring down their entire planetary network.

Captain Pike is reunited with the Enterprise crew and Talos IV is classified as an off-limits planet which all Federation ships are prohibited from going near. But eleven years later, Captain Pike is involved in a terrible, disastrous accident, a fiery explosion, and he is left nearly dead. His body, aside from a brutally scarred face, is destroyed, and his consciousness or soul is transferred into a stationary box or "housing unit" without prosthetics. His only means of communication is using the simplest digital code of beeping once for "yes" and twice for "no". Faced with this reduced, diminutive existence, Captain Pike is reminded of the virtual paradise offered by the Talosians where he can be "able-bodied" once again. He now wishes to return to the *menagerie*. But by this time, Captain Kirk has taken command of the Enterprise, and Kirk sees it as his duty to enforce the injunction against visiting Talos IV. Mr. $@&# Spock, Pike's loyal First Officer from eleven years back, commandeers the ship without Captain Kirk's knowledge (placing his own career at risk) and brings the homuncular Pike back to the zoo planet.[2] Mr. $@&# Spock, the half-human, half-Alan Turing logician, is the only officer to serve under the Captainships of both Pike and Kirk. For the autistic and quasi-comatose Talosians, eleven years was just a nanoinstant, and they are waiting to greet Pike with as much revelry as their atrophied funny bones can muster.

Star Trek has never been considered by science fiction critics for its "secondary current" of virtual reality themes. But from "The Menagerie" to "All Our Yester-days" to the pivotal role of the (downtime) holodeck in *The Next Generation* to the *Deep Space Nine* "Shadow Play" villagers, *Star Trek* is replete with polysemous "texts" about the last stage of simulacra and virtuality. This minor key throughout the *Star Trek* opus can be seen as the lingering symbolic influence of the brief reign of Captain Pike. According to self-anointed "postmodern" media critics like Scott Bukatman and Walter McDougall, *Star Trek* is too heroically individualist to be much valued as a "text." Unlike the cyberpunk canon of William Gibson, *Blade Runner, et al.* which Bukatman celebrates, *Star Trek* fails to address or extol the terminal identity, body electronic, fractal geography, subject-decentering, ontology-shattering themes and transmigrations of the digital age. For these postmodern critics, the recurring effect of *Star Trek* is to reconfirm the television or movie viewers' belief "that we can subsume our individualism into the rationality of systems yet retain our humanity still." The popularity of *Star Trek* is attributed to our delight in the "human qualities of Captain Kirk," which "are always victorious over the very technological mega-systems that make [his] adventures possible."[3] It may be correct that Captain Kirk's outwitting of evil empires and evil computers through use of logical paradox and human foible reinforces traditional post-Enlightenment (Captains of Industry) subjectivity. But what Kirk's antics are always debunking are the computer's pretentions to artificial intelligence. Kirk gets it on in a metaphoric three-dimensional chess match against super-computers like Landru ("The Return of the Archons"), Nomad ("The Changeling"), Vaal ("The Apple"), and the Daystrom-clone ("The Ultimate Computer"). These voice-enabled computers all seek to rise above their programming and *think* for themselves, but they always lack that certain little human *je ne sais quoi*. The Pentagon could have saved billions on futile artificial intelligence research if it had watched these early *Star Trek* episodes. But, as Bill Gates and Kevin Kelly (those amiable prophets of the wired world and the interactive network) remind us, artificial intelligence was always a detour, and never the destination, of the computer.[4] It was the complex-systems side of cybernetics, not the artificial intelligence side, which would lead to the true destiny of the computer: virtual reality.

One of Marshall McLuhan's discursive descendants has recently said that the effects of television on the world and how we see it were *invisible* until McLuhan "pointed out TV."[5] One of the obstacles to *seeing virtuality* today, and the grave dangers which loom through its mist, is that we believe in an enterprise called science — the epistemology, methodology, and applications of which have supposedly ushered in a grand and eternal age of progress and wizardry. We have constructed a pantheon of original scientific heroes, whose heroism derives from their original acts of having been the first to investigate the physical objects of the world independent from any prejudicial system of interpretation. We neglect to scrutinize what really happened at the primal anthropological scene of the beginnings of scientific method and the first Captains of science. At the back end of the chronology, we have been equally remiss in failing to observe that the privileging of the autonomy of the physical object was a phase which came to an end in the mid-twentieth century, at the time of the invention of the virtuality engine known as the computer and the new "sciences" of information and bio-cybernetic complex systems.

According to Bill Gates, we will soon work, learn, make friends, shop, explore cultures, and be entertained from the privacy of our homes and without leaving our armchairs. On the post-Web Internet, which Gates calls the interactive network, we will enter into total immersion cyber-environments via our high-bandwidth connections. This penetration to the other side of the screen is but the latest step in the civilizational project of creating a second, doubled, substitute world — a movement from reality to virtuality. The *virtuality syndrome* arose as a consequence of the scientific revolutions which caused humanity to feel its insignificance and transience in contrast to the permanent and consequential status of the objective, natural world. Other cultures had dealt with human death in an integrated way through symbolic rituals and sacrifice, and with the cosmos through the mediation of mythology, but it was our destiny to face down the harsh *reality principles* of mortality and an external world of permanent, inexorable, *superior* laws. Confronted with this severity, we felt anxiety and ultimately developed an *immortality* neurosis or virtuality syndrome to manage our distress. To match the permanence of the "laws of nature," we devised our own project of step-by-step constructing a media permanence which we would then eventually jump into. The immortality neurosis is exhibited in the new American business of customers having their heads preserved after death so they can someday have their consciousnesses revived and transferred into robotic bodies when science has reached that stage of progress. But the immortality or virtuality syndrome is also manifest in the interactive networks and in all of the mass media in their earlier, transitional forms.

Anteceding the legend of the original heroic scientists is the seminal, primal scene of the initial stirrings in "tribal" societies of the *gaze on the autonomous object*. This was the transformation from a symbolic, *intimate* relationship to the object to an operational, percipient one discussed, for example, by Bataille in *Theory of Religion*. This neglected transmutational scene resembles the unexamined "text" which antecedes the legend of the original heroic Captain Kirk: the primal scene of the virtuality decisions of Captain Christopher Pike.

For Captain Pike, the appeal of virtuality is relative. Compared with the able-bodied, open-spaced conditions of vitality, mobility, and irreducible language, virtual reality is a sham. It is a spurious and pale facsimile of life, and Pike will have no truck with it. But compared to the degraded conditions of immobility and digital inarticulateness (reduced to the unravelled binary code of communication) virtual reality is preferred. From the standpoint of spatial, quadriplegic, and semantic incapacitation, *and only from this standpoint*, virtual reality is accepted and embraced. As long as Captain Pike has a body, he is not seduced to make the leap beyond the screen to the full achievement of simulacra. Once he no longer has a body, he is ready to put on his data body suit, goggles, and glove. At the dawn of Kirk's term as Captain, and the seminal confusion of his status as original or copy, we have a powerful statement about the new interactive networks. It is only from the position of an already debased spatial immobility and urban hyperconcentration that we are prepared to embrace the doubled, substitute world of virtuality. Fellow homunculi, *where do you want to go today?*[6]

So Pike, the true first-born, was whisked away into virtual reality and replaced by the changeling Kirk. There was, of course, another way forward for Captain Pike, but the screenwriters of "The Menagerie" were unfortunately ignorant of the basics of writing operating systems software drivers for peripheral devices. Since Pike's bio-rehabilitation programmers had succeeded in resuscitating at least one controllable nerve impulse from his consciousness, and connecting the discrete signals of this impulse across the synaptic gap to an output device (the beeping for "yes" or "no"), further layers of software to drive more sophisticated output devices and sound cards would certainly be possible. From the single binary registering of a 0 or a 1, an entire operational language (a full digital communication) can be devised. One merely has to enumerate and combine varied sequences of 0s and 1s as discrete identifiers in an infinitely permutated system. The only drawback would be that Pike's consciousness itself would always remain at the level of the lowest machine language, forced to perpetually master and *will* the lengthy binary sequences in order to express himself. He would literally be the machine and its finally awakened artificial intelligence.

Another episode of the original *Star Trek* series, "All Our Yesterdays," presents us with a beautiful, succinct metaphor for the scientific revolution and the virtuality syndrome. Captain Kirk, Mr. $@&# Spock, and Dr. McCoy beam down to the planet Sarpeidon, which belongs to a solar system the sun of which is about to explode as a supernova. The planet's political leaders and chief scientists have known of this impending catastrophic event for a long time and have diligently implemented a digital survival plan. After the sun goes supernova, the planet will become permanently uninhabitable, but the inhabitants will not be faced with their deaths. The planet's entire new media resources have been mobilized into the construction of a vast library and computer administered by technicians. The library does not contain books, but rather tapes in canisters which store the virtual content of all occurrences in the planet's history. In the waning days before the supernova catastrophe, each inhabitant selects his favorite historical time from the library's vast archives, has a technician retrieve and insert the chosen tape into an input device, and passes through a portal from which he or she can never return again. Any attempt to return will result in instant death, since the subject's genetic code has been altered for adaptation to the destination historical period. The *time portal* is the focal point of the library, and through it each inhabitant makes a definitive exit from the planet's dying reality. At the very last moment before the supernova explosion, the principal technician inserts his personal tape and heads off to the most exclusive virtual history theme park.

The heliocentric discoveries of Copernicus and Galileo ignited a kind of metaphoric supernova explosion. The Copernican model of the sun-earth relation-ship, which challenged and replaced the geocentric universe of Ptolemy, was not accepted for centuries due to the anxiety about our status in the cosmos which it provoked. Humans, created in God's image, were no longer the center of the universe. The sun does not revolve around the earth as was previously believed; the earth revolves around the sun. With Copernicus, the sun expanded and the virtual-ity syndrome was given an anti-gravitational boost. Physical reality and its classical laws (which only operate until you approach light speed, or the hyperbolic speed of the media and computers) were elevated to a sovereign, more permanent status in relation to mortals. On Sarpeidon ("All Our Yesterdays") the course of the virtuality syndrome is played out at accelerated speed. The original physical reality of Sarpeidon is wiped out by the supernova of its sun. But a second, substitute, cloned reality has been preserved for the planet's inhabitants thanks to the virtuality engine of digital technology. The Sarpeidonians can *go anywhere they want to go* — on a one-way ticket.

For the cool experimenters in jacked-in data-suited subject-decentering terminal identity like Scott Bukatman, or the writers of cyborg manifestoes like Donna Haraway, *Star Trek* is a conventional media industry which never stops showing the same old reruns of gendered and immune system "tropes" like military hardware, space adventures, and extra-terrestrial invaders.[7] But *Star Trek* is an ordinary screen, and like Bukowski's ordinary madness, it is ironically and seductively reversible. It may even be one of the "texts" which, in its minor key, is pointing the way towards that ultimate reversibility of things that is set in motion at the moment when reality and information reach the point of their final (and fatal) inter-changeability.[8] One must read *Star Trek* against *Star Trek*. As in other ordinary screens, like Fox Football or video poker or Windows 97, the apparently dominant "window" has been "re-sized"; it has been turned oblique or spun diagonally into the background with respect to the physical screen, making room for other, less ideologically stable, "windows." We can no longer presume that viewers see a univocal screen or hear only the monotonic drone of an idiot box. The enduring popularity of *Star Trek* may indicate a fascination and engagement by the mass of viewers with motifs of their own disappearing reality.

Notes

1. In Japan, a multimedia CD-ROM application called "Heartthrob Memorial" recently sold more than a million copies and spawned a nationwide industry of virtual girl love worship. The interactive program re-writes the (mis)adventures of a young male student who was often rejected during his high school years by girls whom he fancied. The product was developed by a programmer who says that he wanted to undo his own memories of rejection. See Andrew Pollack, "Japan's Newest Heartthrobs are Sexy, Talented and Virtual" in *The New York Times*, November 25, 1996. Reality can be simulated, but it can also be made to turn out differently from how it did the first time. These "official virtual reality" software applications are informational machines, either for simulation or daydreamlike transformation.

2. An homunculus is a miniature body believed by some early medical theorists to be contained in spermatozoon, or a graphical projection on the cerebral cortex which depicts parts of the body under voluntary motoric control. In Philip K. Dick's science fiction novel *Dr. Bloodmoney* (1965), the homunculus is a (former) quadriplegic who, in a post-apocalypse society, goes from a state of disability to one of hyperability (leapfrogging normal humans) after being equipped with special government-supplied prosthetics.

3. Walter A. McDougall, *The Heavens and the Earth: A Political History of the Space Age*. New York: Basic Books, 1985; p. 449. Scott Bukatman, *Terminal Identity: The Virtual Subject in Post-Modern Science Fiction*. Durham: Duke University Press, 1993. The quotation is from McDougall, cited by Bukatman.

4. "Although I believe that eventually there will be programs that will re-create some elements of human intelligence, I don't think it's likely to happen in my lifetime... So far every prediction about major advances in artificial intelligence has proved to be overly optimistic... progress in artificial intelligence research is ... incredibly slow." Bill Gates, *The Road Ahead*. London: Penguin, 1996; pp. 289-290. Kelly describes the field of artificial intelligence as being "stillborn," and having failed "to produce usefulness." Kevin Kelly, *Out of Control: The New Biology of Machines, Social Systems, and the Economic World*. New York: Addison-Wesley, 1994; p. 453.

5. "What Would McLuhan Say?", interview with Derrick de Kerckhove, in *Wired*, October 1996, p. 149.

6. "*Where do you want to go today?*" is a Microsoft advertising slogan, recently superceded in Europe by the "*what a wonderful world*" campaign.

7. Donna J. Haraway, *Simians, Cyborgs, and Women: The Reinvention of Nature*. New York: Routledge, 1991; pp. 204-205.

8. "What we must do is think this unconditional realization of the world, which is at the same time its unconditional simulacrum. What we lack most is a conceptualization of the completion of reality." Jean Baudrillard, *The Perfect Crime* (translated by Chris Turner). London: Verso, 1996; p. 65.

The 90s began with a blast of techno-utopianism, but it will end with slow suicide in the surplus streets. Net politics is the story of the 90s as a radically split reality: surplus class and virtual class, surplus flesh and virtual flesh, separate and digitally unequal.

Infobahn Blues

Robert Adrian X

Since American Vice-President Al Gore made his famous speech in California a few years ago, it has become impossible to scan any news medium without finding at least one reference to the "Information Superhighway". The Information Super-highway metaphor — specially tailored for Mr. Gore's California audience — is so brilliantly simplistic it seems to have blown the mind of every media editor in the Western Hemisphere. With an Information Superhighway you just plug in your modem and roll your data out onto the ramp and into the dataflow where it zips along the freeway until it hits the appropriate off-ramp. Finding data is the same — it's all nice straight data-lanes with on and off ramps and well-banked curves. You pick your way through the interchanges — just like L.A. commuting only much more comfortable. The Superhighway metaphor does not threaten the status quo or challenge the prevailing ideologies as did "Cyberspace," that other, earlier, name for the net coined by William Gibson and Bruce Sterling. Cyberspace has no highways or interchanges or even directions, it is just a vast universe of connections in a multi-dimensional data-field. You can get lost in Cyberspace, it is dark and threat-ening and infested with spikey-haired hackers with dirty fingernails and shabby hardware. Cyberspace is infinite, chaotic and scary while Mr. Gore's Superhighway is finite, linear and very familiar — at least to suburban Americans, who are, after all, his constituents. The Infobahn is driven by folks just like us. It is bright and sunny, with friendly groves of data stretching off into the distance on either side. The Superhighway metaphor tames Cyberspace, making it acceptable in the average American home, something the whole family can enjoy. The datamobile can be parked in the family garage. The Information Superhighway commodifies data — in the form of things like on-line video games, movies, mail-order catalogues — so that it can be marketed just like any other consumer product. Don't drive down to the mall just call it up on the net.

It's all telephone of course and the Infobahn is just a broadband version of the old-fashioned telephone. Not the deregulated, digitized business tool but the telephone that was an open system, with party lines and nosey operators. We could call our era the "Telephone Era" or the 20th century the "Telephone Century" without much exaggeration. The telephone was, and still is, the only generally available, unprogrammed, participatory, personal and interactive communications medium — aside from face-to-face contact. Programmed broadcasting media like radio and television are universally available via satellite, microwave, or cable networks but they are one-way systems in which a commodity — information, entertainment, services — is distributed to a consuming, or potentially consuming, public. Feedback from these systems is in the form of the "body count" of viewers/ listeners or in the analyses of sales figures for the advertised products. With the telephone on the other hand, it is the service itself which is the commodity and the user supplies his or her own content — that is: the users communicate in a two-way exchange between equal partners. In this sense the telephone network is a public space, a meeting place open to all who have telephone access.

In this age of property-fetishism, the odd thing about "telephone space" is that nobody owns it — not the telephone companies because they only provide the service, not governments which merely meddle, snoop and regulate, nor the users who simply take it for granted — like rain or electricity. And here lies the problem: public utilities or spaces are not amenable to policies of profit maximisation. In a low-cost/low-quality two-way communications system like the telephone, value added services are extremely limited and growth, in a saturated market like North America or Western Europe, has become sluggish. Most telephone users just want to talk to each other and send a few faxes back and forth. The cake is too small and, since deregulation, the cake-eaters too many. The answer appears to be: increase bandwidth! Increased bandwidth allows telephone space to be appropriated for commercial propaganda; occupied by infotainment commodities; turned into a shopping mall. Increased bandwidth is not very interesting for those who simply want to talk to each other — and people who just want to talk to each other are even less interesting to the new telecom corporations whose profits will come mostly from the products and services they sell or rent online. What these corpora- tions really want is interactive cable TV — with the interactivity restricted to online shopping, video games and pay-to-view movies — with the telephone thrown in as a give-away because it requires almost no space on the cable. The Infobahn in this definition is little more than a catalogue of products, services, information and entertainment that can be ordered or purchased and consumed on line. Mr. Gore's Superhighway is really an electronic "Golden Mile," there to be cruised, like any suburban shopping strip, for entertainment, sex, fun and consumables.

In reality the Superhighway simply projects existing aspects of western social and cultural behaviour onto the new electronic communications systems. Its attraction as a metaphor is that it suggests that everything will be just like now but much much better; more convenient, more comfortable — more home entertain- ment, easier shopping, less commuting. The ubiquitous TV screens scattered about the average middle-class home will become windows into "Cyberspace" which has been paved over for convenient data-cruising. Office workers can download their daily tasks at the breakfast table and upload their day's work into the corporation mainframe at the end of 8 hours on the Infobahn — then flip into infotainment mode and surf 400 channels of consumdata. The network behind the flickering screen is there, like the labour-saving peripherals and hi-tech household appliances, for the sole purpose of making life more comfortable for post-industrial suburban mankind — and more profitable for the corporations. No notice is taken of the fact that, even now, most of the bandwidth of the new networks is being used by computers communicating with each other, completely independent of human "users," programmers or controllers — and the tendency is rising. The huge volume of data traffic between computers is already clogging the telephone system and the growth of computer communications — internet and other networks, online data banks, email etc. — is clogging it more every day. Even four years ago it was estimated that 50% of all telephone calls in the U.S.A. were by computers exchanging data. A broadband high-speed network for communication between computers has become a neccessity and the "Infobahn" is just a handy name for that network — a network of fibre-optic cable carrying large volumes of digital data at high speed between computers, using a standard protocol.

But Mr. Gore's linear Superhighway metaphor gets into trouble here too. A two-dimensional data-flow plan can look like a road map and road-like routes and junctions can be interpreted even in three dimensional renderings of data hierarchies and search-paths, but it is clear that a "network" of connections, comprised of enormous quantities of data interacting simultaneously and at the speed of light, has little in common with a Superhighway — no matter how many lanes and levels and interchanges it has. The data network predicted by the introduction of broadband transmission systems is much better described by the non-linear notion of "Cyberspace" — an image of a multi-dimensional matrix of interwoven data, materialising and de-materialising almost randomly. It is hard to imagine being a "user" in such an environment, but it might be possible to be a participant or to be simply present.

The assumption embedded in the Superhighway metaphor is that, in spite of the way so many aspects of our society and culture have been revolutionized by these new digital and communications technologies, nothing has really changed — and that the program of machine development is entirely for the benefit and convenience of the human "user." So not only does it fail to address the cultural ramifications of the new technologies, the Superhighway uncritically and opportunistically supports the master-servant relationship of man-machine. By treating the monitor/TV screen as the datamobile windshield and putting the human "user" in the driver's seat at the focal point of the network, the branching pathways of that specific user's interaction with the data-flow can be made to appear highway-like. But one is seldom alone online and each user has his or her own data-highway which, taken together, combine and recombine at every instant, creating an incalculable tangle of paths which cause data-space to be reconstructed, nanosecond by nanosecond, in response to "user" activity at the keyboard. If we locate the "user" in the centre of the network and make the network a creation and servant of the "user" it implies that, should no "user" be active, the network is idling, doing maintenance-like things, waiting for someone to press a key, like an arcade game waiting for a coin in the slot. Which is, of course, absurd because we also know that the computer networks control, with or without human presence; electricity supply, water supply, transportations systems, inventories and accounting, telephone and communications networks, and the whole infrastructure of world finance — stock markets, insurance, banking, not to mention government, corporate and military surveillance and control programs.

Absurdities and contradictions are the rule rather than the exception in the rhetoric of the new electronic media. The two-dimensional silliness of the Super-

highway metaphor is minor compared, for example, to the arrogance of the pre-
tence of a universal world-wide telephone network. Everyone really knows that no
more than 10% of the world's population now have personal access to a telephone
at home, and that, for most people alive today, a private telephone is an unimaginable luxury. But this knowledge has not prevented enormous amounts of money
being invested in global telecommunications programs (mostly involving value-
added services and peripherals) on the assumption that the telephone is already, for
all intents and purposes, ubiquitous. Two realities appear to collide here the reality
of the planet and its actual inhabitants and the reality of the virtual world of the
communications infrastructure inhabited by users/consumers. Having no telephones and little purchasing power, the vast majority of humanity cannot achieve
"user/consumer" status, except as consumers of the old movies and sitcoms rained
down on them from the satellites (tuning in on the cheap radio and TV receivers
which have replaced the bags of beads and bolts of cheap cloth that were used a
century or two ago to buy the land and undermine the cultures of the new world).
But in our media-dominated culture the virtual reality of the television image is so
powerful that "media-reality" is more real than actual experience and the majority of
humanity is invisible, appearing only sporadically in connection with some natural
catastrophe, war or revolution. That is: it becomes "news" and its misery becomes a
commodity for the infotainment media. The stupefying naivety of the technology-
dazed but well-meaning, politically correct and liberal Internet user who believes
that all problems will be solved when everyone is wired into the "World Wide Web"
is symptomatic of the schizophrenia of (post-) modern media culture. When
reading about or contemplating the amazing techno-future promised by the
superhighway propagandists and cyber-industry barons it is wise to remember that
it applies only to those of us with telephones, electronic gadgetry and purchasing
power.

But the real conflict and confusion is in the ontological problem of the man-
machine relationship. The history of the development of mechanical and electronic
machinery is really the story of the development of metal or silicon "slaves" —
obedient automata with super-human strength and endurance. In this context, for
example, artificial intelligence and robotics research can be understood as a part of
the age-old dream of creating autonomous humanoid servants. The computer itself
is the result of such a program: to build obedient number-crunching auto-nerds to
carry out the drudgery of complex mathematical calculations. Many scientists,
theoreticians and researchers in the field of computer and robot development still
believe that they are creating or dealing with prothesis-like electronic/mechanical
devices — extensions of the human brain and body. In the same way that robots are
usually portrayed as humanoid, (although our world is actually full of robotic
devices which go mostly unnoticed because they are entirely unlike humans: the
coffee-automat in the corridor, the thermostat on the central heating, the telephone
answering machine) the human brain is usually the model invoked in most descriptions and explanations of what a truly interactive electronic ("neural") communications network might be like. The human brain is the only model of intelligence that
we can recognize or respect even though the electronic devices which we have

created, and to which much of the control of our most vital social, political and financial infrastructure has been delegated, seem to have an intelligence very different from the human model.

It is generally agreed among computer scientists that the human brain, or the brain of any animal for that matter, possesses a capacity for information processing far greater than that of any conceivable intelligent machine. But most of the power of the animal brain is dedicated to moving around in — and interacting with — the world, constantly processing enormous amounts of rapidly changing data in real time. Human intelligence is, unfortunately, also cluttered up with distracting things like angst, sex, pleasure, jealousy — not to mention families, games, careers and drugs. Computers on the other hand are largely indifferent to the world. Being mostly stationary, computers just sit and think — that is: they process information gathered by mobile agents — such as people — who are good at moving around in the world hunting and gathering data.

In some ways therefore, the "slaves" are already being served by their masters. In fact the "slaves" have become so efficient in carrying out their delegated tasks that it is in our own interest to make them more "intelligent," more autonomous, so that we can delegate even more of the organizational drudgery to them. It is also in our interest to give the machines the capability of being able to detect and resist potentially damaging penetration by increasingly sophisticated and resourceful intruders, which means that they must be made, in a sense, conscious — if only at the level of an oyster.

If we want a model or metaphor for machine intelligence it must be looked for in places where data in an extremely simple form — as simple as digital code — is exchanged in networks linking immobile or barely mobile forms of life: in forests, shellfish colonies, ant hills. In a true network nothing moves. Once the data is in the network it is universally present — it does not travel anywhere and you don't travel anywhere to find it. This is what is so hard for mobile industrial cultures to understand and what is so exciting about the notion of Cyberspace. In Gibson's *Neuromancer* the protagonist "jacks in" to the net. He is not a user, he is not at the wheel of his datamobile speeding down the Infobahn — he simply disappears into the net and becomes a part of the data-flow.

Cyberspace is so different from the Superhighway because the element of human-centricity is missing or at least it is not in the foreground. You are not in control of cyberspace, it is not there for your comfort and convenience and no-one is driving it. There is no suggestion in the notion of cyberspace that, should human beings suddenly cease to exist — or destroy themselves in some nuclear folly — the network of machines that constitute cyberspace would vanish with them. Cyberspace assumes that the machines we have built will soon, in some leap of almost magical synergy, break free of their creators to constitute, by means of the communications networks we are generously building for them, a universe or nature of an entirely new and different order.

Perhaps they already have.

Digital Humanism

The Processed World
of Marshall McLuhan

Arthur Kroker

Marshall McLuhan was never the technotopian that contemporary
technophiles like to portray. To read McLuhan is to discover a thinker
who had a decidedly ambivalent perspective on technoculture. Thus,
while McLuhan might be the patron saint of technotopians, his
imagination is also the memory that should haunt them. As a way of
understanding McLuhan anew, we include this account of McLuhan's
ambivalent relationship to technology. Titled "Digital Humanism: The
Processed World of Marshall McLuhan," this excerpt is from Arthur
Kroker's *Technology and the Canadian Mind: Innis/McLuhan/Grant* (New
York: St. Martin's Press).

Processed World

Not the least of McLuhan's contributions to the study of technology was that
he transposed the literary principle of metaphor/metonymy (the play between
structure and process) into a historical methodology for analysing the rise and fall of
successive media of communication. In McLuhan's discourse, novels are the already
obsolescent content of television; writing "turned a spotlight on the high, dim
Sierras of speech;"[1] the movie is the "mechanization of movement and gesture;"[2] the
telegraph provides us with "diplomacy without walls;"[3] just as "photography is the
mechanization of the perspective painting and the arrested eye."[4] To read McLuhan
is to enter into a "vortex" of the critical, cultural imagination, where "fixed perspective" drops off by the way, and where everything passes over instantaneously into its
opposite. Even the pages of the texts in *Explorations, The Medium is the Massage,
The Vanishing Point,* or *From Cliché to Archetype* are blasted apart, counterblasted
actually, in an effort to make reading itself a more subversive act of the artistic
imagination. Faithful to his general intellectual project of exposing the invisible
environment of the technological sensorium, McLuhan sought to make of the text
itself a "counter-gradient" or "probe" for forcing to the surface of consciousness the
silent structural rules, the "imposed assumptions" of the technological environment
within which we are both enclosed and "processed." In *The Medium is the Massage,*
McLuhan insisted that we cannot understand the technological experience from the

outside. We can only comprehend how the electronic age "works us over" if we "recreate the experience" in depth and mythically, of the processed world of technology.

> All media work us over completely. They are so persuasive in their personal, political, economic, aesthetic, psychological, moral, ethical, and social consequences that they leave no part of us untouched, unaffected, unaltered. The medium is the massage. Any understanding of social and cultural change is impossible without a knowledge of the way media work as environments.[5]

And McLuhan was adamant on the immanent relationship of technology and biology, on the fact that "the new media… are nature"[6] and this for the reason that technology refers to the social and psychic "extensions" or "outerings" of the human body or senses. McLuhan could be so universal and expansive in his description of the media of communication – his studies of communication technologies range from writing and speech to the telephone, photography, television, money, comic books, chairs and wrenches – because he viewed all technology as the pushing of the "archetypal forms of the unconscious out into social consciousness."[7] When McLuhan noted in *Counter Blast* that "environment is process, not container,"[8] he meant just this: the effect of all new technologies is to impose, silently and pervasively, their deep assumptions upon the human psyche by reworking the "ratio of the senses."

> All media are extensions of some human faculty – psychic or physical.[9]

> Media, by altering the environment, evoke in us unique ratios of sense perceptions. The extension of any one sense alters the way we think and act – the way we perceive the world. When these ratios change, MEN CHANGE.[10]

For McLuhan, it's a processed world now. As we enter the electronic age with its instantaneous and global movement of information, we are the first human beings to live completely within the *mediated* environment of the technostructure The "content" of the technostructure is largely irrelevant (the "content" of a new technology is always the technique which has just been superseded: movies are the content of television; novels are the content of movies) or, in fact, a red herring distracting our attention from the essential secret of technology as the medium, or environment, within which human experience is programmed. It was McLuhan's special genius to grasp at once that the content (metonymy) of new technologies serves as a "screen," obscuring from view the disenchanted locus of the technological experience in its purely "formal" or "spatial" properties. McLuhan wished to escape the "flat earth approach" to technology, to invent a "new metaphor" by which we might "restructure our thoughts and feelings" about the subliminal, imperceptible environments of media effects.[11]

In this understanding, technology is an "extension" of biology: the expansion of the electronic media as the "metaphor" or "environment" of twentieth-century experience implies that, for the first time, the central nervous system itself has been exteriorized. It is our plight to be processed through the technological simulacrum; to participate intensively and integrally in a "technostructure" which is nothing but a vast simulation and "amplification" of the bodily senses. Indeed, McLuhan often recurred to the "narcissus theme" in classical mythology as a way of explaining our fatal fascination with technology, viewed not as "something external" but as an extension, or projection, of the sensory faculties of the human species.

> Media tend to isolate one or another sense from the others. The result is hypnosis. The other extreme is withdrawing of sensation with resulting hallucination as in dreams or DT's, etc... Any medium, by dilating sense to fill the whole field, creates the necessary conditions of hypnosis in that area. This explains why at no time has any culture been aware of the effect of its media on its overall association, not even retrospectively.[12]

All of McLuhan's writings are an attempt to break beyond the "Echo" of the Narcissus myth, to show that the "technostructure" is an extension or "repetition" of ourselves. In his essay, "The Gadget Lover," McLuhan noted precisely why the Greek myth of Narcissus is of such profound relevance to understanding the technological experience.

> The youth Narcissus (narcissus means narcosis or numbing) mistook his own reflection in the water for another person. This extension of himself by mirror numbed his perceptions until he became the servomechanism of his own extended or repeated image. The nymph Echo tried to win his love with fragments of his own speech, but in vain. He was numb. He had adapted to his extension of himself and had become a closed system. Now the point of this myth is the fact that men at once become fascinated by any extension of themselves in any material other than themselves.[13]

Confronted with the hypnotic effect of the technological sensorium, McLuhan urged the use of any "probe" – humour, paradox, analogical juxtaposition, absurdity – as a way of making visible the "total field effect" of technology as medium. This is why, perhaps, McLuhan's intellectual project actually circles back on itself, and is structured directly into the design of his texts. McLuhan makes the reader a "metonymy" to his "metaphor:" he transforms the act of "reading McLuhan" into dangerous participation in a radical experiment which has, as its end, the exploration of the numbing of consciousness in the technological massage. Indeed, to read McLuhan is to pass directly into the secret locus of the "medium is the massage"; to experience anew the "media" (this time the medium of writing) as a silent gradient of ground-rules.

No less critical than George Grant of the human fate in technological society, McLuhan's imagination seeks a way out of our present predicament by recovering a highly ambivalent attitude towards the objects of technostructure. Thus, while Grant writes in William James' sense of a "block universe" of the technological dynamo, seeing only tendencies towards domination, McLuhan privileges a historically specific study of the media of communication. In an early essay (1955), "A Historical Approach to the Media," McLuhan said that if we weren't "to go on being helpless illiterates" in the new world of technology, passive victims as the "media themselves act directly toward shaping our most intimate self-consciousness," then we had to adopt the attitude of the artist.[14] "The mind of the artist is always the point of maximal sensitivity and resourcefulness in exposing altered realities in the common culture."[15] McLuhan would make of us "the artist, the sleuth, the detective" in gaining a critical perspective on the history of technology which "just as it began with writing ends with television."[16] Unlike Grant's reflections on technology which are particularistic and existential, following a downward spiral (the famous Haligonian "humbug") into pure content: pure will, pure remembrance, pure duration, McLuhan's thought remains projective, metaphorical, and emancipatory. Indeed, Grant's perspective on technology is Protestant to the core in its contemplation of the nihilism of liberal society. But if Grant's tragic inquiry finds its artistic analogue in Colville's *To Prince Edward Island*, then McLuhan's discourse is more in the artistic tradition of Georges Seurat, the French painter, and particularly in one classic portrait, *A Sunday Afternoon on the Island of La Grande Jatte*. McLuhan always accorded Seurat a privileged position as the "art fulcrum between Renaissance visual and modern tactile. The coalescing of inner and outer, subject and object."[17] McLuhan was drawn to Seurat in making painting a "light source" (a "light through situation"). Seurat did that which was most difficult and decisive: he dipped the viewer into the "vanishing point" of the painting.[18] Or as McLuhan said, and in prophetic terms, Seurat (this "precursor of TV") presented us with a searing visual image of the age of the "anxious object."[19]

Now, to be sure, the theme of anxiety runs deep through the liberal side of the Canadian mind. This is the world of Margaret Atwood's "intolerable anxiety" and of Northrop Frye's "anxiety structure." But McLuhan is the Canadian thinker who undertook a phenomenology of anxiety, or more precisely a historically relative study of the sources of anxiety and stress in technological society. And he did so by the simple expedient of drawing us, quickly and in depth, into Seurat's startling and menacing world of the anxious, stressful objects of technology. In his book, *Through the Vanishing Point*, McLuhan said of Seurat that "by utilizing the Newtonian analysis of the fragmentation of light, he came to the technique of divisionism, whereby each dot of paint becomes the equivalent of an actual light source, a sun, as it were. This device reversed the traditional perspective by making the viewer the vanishing point."[20] The significance of Seurat's "reversal" of the rules of traditional perspective is that he abolished, once and for all, the medieval illusion that space is neutral, or what is the same, that we can somehow live "outside" the processed world of technology. With Seurat a great solitude and, paradoxically, a greater entanglement falls on modern being. "We are suddenly in the world of the "Anxious Object" which is prepared to take the audience inside the painting process itself."[21] Following C. S. Lewis in *The Discarded Image*, McLuhan noted exactly what this "flip" in spatial perspective meant. Rather than looking in according to the traditional spatial model of medieval discourse, modern man is suddenly "looking out." "Like one looking out from the saloon entrance onto the dark Atlantic, or from the lighted porch upon the dark and lonely moors."[22] The lesson of Seurat is this: modernity is coeval with the age of the "anxious object" because we live now, fully, within the designed environment of the technological sensorium.[23] For McLuhan, we are like astronauts in the processed world of technology. We now take our "environment" with us in the form of technical "extensions" of the human body or senses. The technostructure is both the lens through which we experience the world, and, in fact, the "anxious object" with which human experience has become imperceptibly, almost subliminally, merged.[24]

Now, McLuhan often remarked that in pioneering the DEW line, Canada had also provided a working model for the artistic imagination as an "early warning system"[25] in sensing coming shifts in the technostructure. Seurat's artistic representation of the spatial reversal at work in the electronic age, a reversal which plunges us into active participation in the "field" of technological experience, was one such early warning system. It was, in fact, to counteract our "numbing" within the age of the anxious object that McLuhan's literary and artistic imagination, indeed his whole textual strategy, ran to the baroque. As an intellectual strategy, McLuhan favoured the baroque for at least two reasons: it privileged "double perspective and contrapuntal theming;" and it sought to "capture the moment of change in order to release energy dramatically."[26] There is, of course, a clear and decisive connection between McLuhan's attraction to Seurat as an artist who understood the spatial grammar of the electronic age and his fascination with the baroque as a method of literary imagination. If, indeed, we are now "looking out" from inside the technological sensorium; and if, in fact, in the merger of biology and technology which is the locus of the electronic age, "we" have become the vanishing points of technique, then a way had to be discovered for breaching the "invisible environment"[27] within which we are now enclosed. For McLuhan, the use of the baroque in each of his writings, this constant resort to paradox, double perspective, to a carnival of the literary imagination in which the pages of the texts are forced to reveal their existence also as a "medium," was also a specific strategy aimed at "recreating the experience" of technology as massage. Between Seurat (a radar for "space as process") and baroque (a "counter-gradient"): that's the artistic strategy at work in McLuhan's imagination as he confronted the subliminal, processed world of electronic technologies.

Tracking Technology I: The Catholic Legacy

There is a deep, thematic unity in all of McLuhan's writings, extending from his later studies of technology in *Understanding Media*, *The Medium is the Massage*, *The Gutenberg Galaxy* and *Counter Blast* to his earlier, more classical, writings in *The Interior Landscape*, *The Vanishing Point* and also including his various essays in reviews ranging from the *Sewanee Review* to the *Teacher's College Record*. McLuhan's discourse was culturally expansive, universalist, and spatially oriented precisely because his thought expresses the Catholic side of the Canadian, and by implication, modern mind. McLuhan's Catholicism, in fact, provided him with an epistemological strategy that both gave him a privileged vantage-point on the processed world of technology and, in any event, drove him beyond literary studies to an historical exploration of technological media as the "dynamic" of modern culture. The essential aspect of McLuhan's technological humanism is that he always remained a Catholic humanist in the Thomistic tradition: one who brought to the study of technology and culture the more ancient Catholic hope that even in a world of despair (in our "descent into the maelstrom"[28] with Poe's drowning sailor) that a way out of the labyrinth could be found by bringing to fruition the "reason" or "epiphany" of technological society. McLuhan's thought often recurred to the sense that there is an immanent moment of "reason" and a possible new human order in technological society which could be captured on behalf of the preservation of "civilization."

Thus, McLuhan was a technological humanist in a special sense. He often described the modern century as the "age of anxiety"[29] because of our sudden exposure, without adequate means of understanding, to the imploded, instantaneous world of the new information order. Indeed, in *The Medium is the Massage*, he spoke of technology in highly ambivalent terms as, simultaneously, containing possibilities for emancipation and domination. For McLuhan, a critical humanism, one which dealt with the "central cultural tendencies"[30] of the twentieth-century, had to confront the technological experience in its role as environment, evolutionary principle, and as second nature itself.

> Environments are not passive wrappings, but active processes which
> work us over completely, massaging the ratio of the senses and imposing
> their silent assumptions. But environments are invisible. Their ground-
> rules, pervasive structure, and overall patterns elude easy perception.[31]

McLuhan's technological humanism was at the forward edge of a fundamental "paradigm shift" in human consciousness. When McLuhan spoke of electronic technology as an extension, or outering, of the central nervous system, he also meant that modern society had done a "flip." In order to perceive the "invisible ground rules" of the technological media, we have to learn to think in reverse image: to perceive the subliminal grammar of technology as metaphor, as a simulacrum or sign-system, silently and pervasively processing human existence. After all, McLuhan was serious when he described the electric light bulb (all information, no content) as a perfect model, almost a precursor, of the highly mediated world of the "information society." McLuhan's thought was structural, analogical, and metaphorical because he sought to disclose the "semiological reduction"[32] at work in the media of communication. But unlike, for example, the contemporary French thinker, Jean Baudrillard, who, influenced deeply by McLuhan, has teased out the Nietzschean side of the processed world of television, computers, and binary architecture but whose inquiry has now dissolved into fatalism, McLuhan was always more optimistic. Because McLuhan, even as he studied the "maelstrom" of high technology, never deviated from the classical Catholic project of seeking to recover the basis for a "new universal community"[33] in the culture of technology. Unlike Grant or Innis, McLuhan could never be a nationalist because his Catholicism, with its tradition of civil humanism and its faith in the immanence of "reason," committed him to the possibility of the coming of a universal world culture. In the best of the Catholic tradition, followed out by Etienne Gilson in philosophy as much as by Pierre Elliott Trudeau in politics, McLuhan sought a new "incarnation," an "epiphany," by releasing the reason in technological experience.

Indeed, in a formative essay, "Catholic Humanism," McLuhan averred that he followed Gilson in viewing Catholicism as being directly involved in the "central cultural discoveries" of the modern age. "Knowledge of the creative process in art, science, and cognition shows the way to earthly paradise, or complete madness: the abyss or the top of mount purgatory."[34] Now McLuhan's Catholicism was not a matter of traditional faith (he was a convert), but of a calculated assessment of the importance of the Catholic conception of "reason" for interpreting, and then civilizing, technological experience. Over and again in his writings, McLuhan returned to the theme that only a sharpening and refocusing of human perception could provide a way out of the labyrinth of the technostructure. His ideal value was that of the "creative process in art;"[35] so much so in fact that McLuhan insisted that if the master struggle of the twentieth century was between reason and irrationality, then this struggle could only be won if individuals learned anew how to make of the simple act of "ordinary human perception" an opportunity for recovering the creative energies in human experience. McLuhan was a technological humanist of the blood: his conviction, repeated time and again, was that if we are to recover a new human possibility it will not be "outside" the technological experience, but must, of necessity, be "inside" the *field* of technology. What is really wagered in the struggle between the opposing tendencies towards domination and freedom in technology is that which is most personal, and intimate, to each individual: the blinding or revivification of ordinary human perception. Or, as McLuhan said in "Catholic Humanism:" "...the drama of ordinary human perception seen as the poetic process is the prime analogate, the magic casement opening on the secrets of created being."[36] And, of course, for McLuhan the "poetic process" – this recovery of the method of "sympathetic reconstruction," this "recreation" of the technological experience as a "total communication," this recovery of the "rational notes of beauty, integrity, consonance, and claritas" as the actual stages of human apprehension – was the key to redeeming the technological order.[37] If only the mass media could be harmonized with the "poetic process;" if only the media of communication could be made supportive of the "creative process" in ordinary human perception: then technological society would, finally, be transformed into a wonderful opportunity for the "incarnation" of human experience. But, of course, this meant that, fully faithful to the Catholic interpretation of human experience as a working out of the (immanent) principle of natural, and then divine, reason, McLuhan viewed technological society as an *incarnation in the making*. Unlike the secular discourse of the modern century, McLuhan saw no artificial divisions between "ordinary human perception" and the technical apparatus of the mass media or, for that matter, between biology and technology. In this discourse, the supervening value is reason; and this to such an extent that the creative process of human perception as well as the technologies of comic books, mass media, photography, music, and movies are viewed as *relative* phases in the working out of a single process of apprehension. "…The more extensive the mass medium the closer it must approximate to the character of our cognitive faculties."[38] Or, on a different note:

> As we trace the rise of successive communication channels or links, from writing to movies and TV it is borne in on us that for their exterior artifice to be effective it must partake of the character of that interior artifice by which in ordinary perception we incarnate the exterior world, because human perception is literally incarnation. So that each of us must poet the world or fashion it within us as our primary and constant mode of awareness.[39]

McLuhan's *political* value may have been the creation of a universal community of humanity founded on reason, his *axiology* may have privileged the process of communication, and his *moral* dynamic may have been the "defence of civilization" from the dance of the irrational; but his ontology, the locus of his world vision, was the recovery of the "poetic process" as both a method of historical reconstruction of the mass media and a "miracle" by which technological society is to be illuminated, once again, with meaning.

> In ordinary human perception, men perform the miracle of recreating within themselves – in their interior faculties – the exterior world. This miracle is the work of the *nous poietikos* or of the agent intellect – that is the poetic or creative process. The exterior world in every instant of perception is interiorized and recreated in a new manner. Ourselves. And in this creative work that is perception and cognition, we experience immediately that dance of Being within our faculties which provides the incessant intuition of Being.[40]

The significance of the "poetic process" as the master concept of McLuhan's technological humanism is clear. It is only by creatively interiorizing (*realistically perceiving*) the "external" world of technology, by reabsorbing into the dance of the intellect mass media as extensions of the cognitive faculties of the human species, that we can recover "ourselves" anew. It is also *individual* freedom which is wagered in McLuhan's recovery of the "miracle" of ordinary human perception. McLuhan's intellectual strategy was not, of course, a matter of quietism. Quite the contrary, the teasing out of the "epiphany" in external experience meant intense and direct participation in the "objects" composing the technostructure. McLuhan wanted to see *from the inside* the topography of the technological media which horizon human experience. His Catholicism, with its central discovery of a "new method of study," a new way of seeing technology, fated him to be a superb student of popular culture. Indeed, McLuhan's thought could dwell on all aspects of popular culture – games, advertisements, radio, television, and detective stories – because he viewed each of these instances of technological society as somehow "magical;"[41] providing new clues concerning how the technological massage alters the "ratios of the senses" and novel opportunities for improved human perception. In much the same way, but with a different purpose, McLuhan was a practitioner of Northrop Frye's "improved binoculars." Like his favourite symbolist poets, Poe, Joyce, Eliot, and Baudelaire, McLuhan always worked backwards from effects to cause. Much like the models of the detective and the artist, he wished to perfect in the method of the "suspended judgement,"[42] in the *technique of discovery itself*, a new angle of vision on technological experience.

McLuhan was, in fact, a dynamic ecologist. He sought a new, internal balance among technique, imagination and nature. But his ecological sense was based on a grim sense of realism. In his view, the "electric age" is the historical period in which we are doomed to become simultaneously, the "sex of the lifeless machine world"[43] or creative participants in a great cycle which turns society back to a new "Finn cycle."[44]

McLuhan always privileged the connection between the immediacy and simultaneity of electric circuitry and "blind, all-hearing Homer."[45] This was a "humanism" which wagered itself on a desperate encounter with the "objects" of the technological order. In *Understanding Media*, *Counter Blast*, and *The Medium is the Massage*, there emerges an almost cruel description of the technological sensorium as a sign-system to which the human mind is exteriorized. Electric technology, this latest sensation of the "genus sensation," implies that we are now "outered" or "ablated" into a machine-processed world of information.[46] It is the human destiny in the modern age to be programmed by an information order which operates on the basis of algorithmic and digital logic, and which, far from conscious human intervention, continues to move through the whirring of its own servomechanisms. Thus, in *Understanding Media*, McLuhan noted:

> By putting our physical bodies inside our extended nervous systems by means of electric media, we set up a dynamic by which all previous technologies that are mere extensions of hands and feet and teeth and bodily controls – all such extensions of our bodies, including cities – will be translated into information systems. Electromagnetic technology requires utter human docility and quiescence of meditation such as now befits an organism that wears its brains outside its hide and its nerves outside its skin.[47]

And of this "semiological wash" through the technostructure, McLuhan said simply but starkly,

> Man becomes as it were the sex organ of the machine world, as the bee of the plant world, enabling it to fecundate and to evolve ever new forms. The machine-world reciprocates man's love by expediting his wishes and desires, namely by providing him with wealth.[48]

In McLuhan's effort to humanize technology through "in-depth participation" there is reopened a more ancient debate in the western mind between the tragic imagination and the calculated optimism of the rhetoricians. In his essay, "An Ancient Quarrel in Modern America," McLuhan described himself as a "Ciceronian humanist"[49] (better, I suppose, than the early Scottish common-sense realists in

Canada who labeled themselves "Caesars of the wilderness"). McLuhan was a "Ciceronian humanist" to this extent: he was, by intellectual habit, an historian of civilization and a rhetorician. McLuhan's *rhetoric* stands, for example, to Grant's tragic lament or to Innis' "marginal man" in much the same way as that earlier debate between Lucretius and Virgil. Between the rhetorician and the tragic sensibility, there is always a contest between the attitude of intellectual futility, tinged by despair, and a pragmatic will to knowledge, between resigned melancholy and melancholy resignation.

But if McLuhan brings to bear on technology the skills of a rhetorician's imagination, then he does so as a Catholic, and not Ciceronian, humanist. McLuhan's mind represents one of the best syntheses yet achieved of the Catholic legacy as this was developed in Aquinas, Joyce, and Eliot. In a largely unremarked, but decisive, article – "Joyce, Aquinas and the Poetic Process" – McLuhan was explicit that his *epistemological strategy* for the study of technology was modeled on Aquinas' method of the *respondeo dicendum*: the tracing and retracing of thought through the "cubist landscape" of the Thomistic article.[50] McLuhan said of Aquinas that in his "method of thought" we see the fully modern mind at work. In Aquinas, as later in Joyce, there is the constant use of the "labyrinth figure" as the archetype of human cognition. "Whereas the total shape of each article, with its trinal divisions into objections, respondeo, and answers to objections, is an 'S' labyrinth, this figure is really traced and retraced by the mind many times in the course of a single article."[51] Aquinas' central contribution to modern discourse was this: his "method" of study gave a new brilliance of expression to the "technique of discovery" as the locus of the modern mind.

> His 'articles' can be regarded as vivisections of the mind in act. The skill and wit with which he selects his objections constitute a cubist landscape, an ideal landscape of great intellectual extent seen from an airplane. The ideas or objects in this landscape are by their very contiguity set in a dramatic state of tension; and this dramatic tension is provided with a dramatic peripetieia in the respondeo, and with a resolution in the answers to the objections.[52]

Now, the significance of McLuhan's recovery of Aquinas' method of the "respondeo dicendum" is that this *method* is almost perfectly autobiographical of McLuhan's own strategy for the study of technological experience. Long before McLuhan in, for example, *The Medium is the Massage*, discussed the creation of a "cubist landscape" as a counter-gradient for understanding technological media or in *The Mechanical Bride* appealed for the need to sharpen "perception," he had already adopted the "Catholic method," and Joyce's adaptation of Aquinas' "article" as his main epistemological tools for "understanding media." Indeed, it was McLuhan's achievement, fully faithful to the spirit of Joyce's writings in *Ulysses*, *Dubliners*, and *The Portrait*, to translate the Thomistic analysis of cognition, "namely the fact of the creative process as the natural process of apprehension, arrested and retraced,"[53] into a powerful intellectual procedure for grasping the inner movement in even the most prosaic objects of popular culture. "Ordinary experience is a riot of imprecision, of impressions enmeshed in preconceptions, clichés, profanities, and impercipience. But for the true artist every experience is capable of an epiphany."[54] McLuhan may have lived with the grimly pessimistic knowledge that we had become the "sex organs of the machine world," but his intellectual spirit was optimistic, and indeed combative. In the following passage, McLuhan is speaking of Joyce in relationship to Aquinas, but he might well have been writing his own intellectual notice. Like Joyce, and for the same reason, he always preferred "comic to tragic art;"[55] his conclusions may have been downbeat, but his "method" was distinctly upbeat. McLuhan's very psychology was like a counter-gradient flailing against the technostructure; this in full awareness that the "technological massage" worked us over, not from outside, but from within. The "minotaurs" to be overcome in "understanding media" were also fully *interiorized* within the human mind and body.

> Any movement of appetite within the labyrinth of cognition is a 'minotaur' which must be slain by the hero artist. Anything which interferes with cognition, whether concupiscence, pride, imprecision, or vagueness is a minotaur ready to devour beauty. So that Joyce not only was the first to reveal the link between the stages of apprehension and the creative process, he was the first to understand how the drama of cognition itself was the key archetype of all human ritual myth and legend. And thus he was able to incorporate at every point in his work the body of the past in immediate relation to the slightest current of perception.[56]

McLuhan shared with Grant, and Nietzsche, a deep understanding of "technique as ourselves," of our envelopment in the historical dynamic of techno-logical media. But he differed from them, and consequently from the "lament" of the Protestant mind, both by subscribing to the value of "creative freedom," and by providing a precise intellectual itinerary through which the "creative process" might be generalized in human experience.

In McLuhan's terms, everything now depends on the creation of an inner harmony, a concordance of the beauty of reason, between the "imprecision of ordinary experience" and the "cognitive power in act." This is just to note, though, exactly how central McLuhan's religious sensibility (his Catholic roots) was to his interpretation of technology. It was, in the end, from Joyce and Aquinas that he took an intellectual strategy for the exploration of technological experience: the method of "suspended judgment;" the privileging of the perception of the true artist in battle with the minotaurs which block the possible epiphany in every experience, the technique of reconstruction as discovery; a singular preference for the comic over the tragic; the abandonment of narrative in favour of the "analogical juxtaposition of character, scene, and situation."[57] Like other advocates of Catholic humanism in the twentieth-century, McLuhan was neither an impressionist nor an expressionist, but one who stood by the "method of the profoundly analogical drama of existence as it is mirrored in the cognitive power in act."[58] For McLuhan, the recovery of *reason* in technological experience was always part of a broader religious drama: what was also at stake in the contest with the minotaurs in the labyrinth of technology was individual redemption.

Tracking Technology II: Experimental Medicine

McLuhan often recurred in his writings to Poe's figure of the "drowning sailor" who, trapped in the whirlpool without a visible means of escape, studied his situation with "calm detachment" in order to discover some thread which might lead out of the labyrinth.[59] While the Catholic touch in McLuhan's thought provided him with the necessary sense of critical detachment and, moreover, with the transcendent value of creative freedom; it was the particular genius of his discourse that he managed to combine an intellectual sensibility which was essentially Thomistic with the more ancient practice of exploring the crisis of technological society within the terms of experimental medicine. In McLuhan's inquiry, there is rehearsed time and again a classically medical approach to understanding technology: an approach which, while it may be traced directly to Hippocrates' *Ancient Medicine*, also has its origins in Thucydides' method of historical writing. Very much in the tradition of Hippocrates, and then Thucydides, McLuhan's historical study of the media of communication was structured by the three moments of semiology (classification of symptoms), diagnosis and therapeutics.[60] Indeed, it might even be said that McLuhan's adoption of the three stages of the Thomistic "article" – objections, respondeo, and answers to objections – was only a modern variation of the more classical method of experimental medicine. In both instances, the historical experience under interrogation is "recreated in depth," with special emphasis placed on the historian (the cultural historian as doctor to a sick society) as a "vivisectionist" of the whole field of experience.[61] When McLuhan recommended repeatedly that the cultural historian "trace and retrace" the field of technological experience, both as a means of understanding the "closure" effected upon human perspective and as a way of discovering an escape-hatch, he was only restating, in distinctly modern language, the experimental method of ancient medicine. McLuhan's imagination always played at the interface of biology and technology. His discourse took as its working premise that the most insidious effect of technology lay in its deep colonization of biology, of the body itself; and, moreover, in its implicit claim, that technology is the new locus of the evolutionary principle. For McLuhan the technological "sensorium" was precisely that: an artificial amplification, and transferal, of human consciousness and sensory organs to the technical apparatus, which now, having achieved the electronic phase of "simultaneity" and "instantaneous scope," returns to take its due on the human body.[62] The "sensorium" presents itself to a humanity which has already passed over into "deep shock" over the inexplicable consequences of electronics as a practical *simulation* of evolution, of the biological process itself. This circling back of the technological sensorium, this silent merger of technology and biology, is the cataclysmic change in human history that so disturbed McLuhan. His discourse on technology begins and ends with an exploration of the "possession" of biology by the technological imperative. Indeed, in McLuhan's estimation, technology works its effects upon biology much like a disease. It is also the tools of a doctor which are needed both for an accurate diagnosis of the causes of the disease, and for a prognosis of some cure which might be recuperative of the human sensibility in technological society.

One pervasive theme running through McLuhan's writings has to do with the double-effect of the technological experience in "wounding" the human persona by effecting a "closure" of human perception, and in "numbing" and thus "neutralizing" the area under stress.[63] It was McLuhan's melancholic observation that when confronted with new technologies, the population passes through, and this repeatedly, the normal cycle of shock: "alarm" at the disturbances occasioned by the introduction, often on a massive scale, of new extensions of the sensory organs; "resistance" which is typically directed at the "content" of new technological innovations (McLuhan's point was, of course, that the content of a new technology is only the already passé history of a superseded technology); and "exhaustion" in the face of our inability to understand the subliminal (formal) consequences of fundamental changes in the technostructure.[64] It was his dour conclusion that, when confronted with the "paradigm-shift" typified by the transformation of technology from a mechanical, industrial model to an electronic one, the population rapidly enters into a permanent state of exhaustion and bewilderment. In McLuhan's terms, the present century is characterized by an almost total unconsciousness of the real effects of the technological media. "The new media are blowing a lot of baby powder around the pendant cradle of the NEW MAN today. The dust gets in our eyes."[65]

It was a source of great anxiety to McLuhan that electronic technologies, with their abrupt reversal of the structural laws of social and non-social evolution, had (without human consent or even social awareness) precipitated a new, almost autonomous, technical imperative in human experience.[66] In *Counter Blast*, McLuhan had this to say of the new technological imperative:

> Throughout previous evolution, we have protected the central nervous system by outering this or that physical organ in tools, housing, clothing, cities. But each outering of individual organs was also an acceleration and intensification of the general environment until the central nervous system did a flip. We turned turtle. The shell went inside, the organs outside. Turtles with soft shells become vicious. That's our present state.[67]

A society of "vicious turtles" is also one in which technology works its "biological effects" in the language of stress. For McLuhan, the advent of electronic technology creates a collective sense of deep distress, precisely because this "outering" of the central nervous system induces an unprecedented level of stress on the individual organism. The "technological massage" reworks human biology and the social psyche at a deep, subliminal level. Having grasped the essential connection between technology and stress, it was not surprising that so much of McLuhan's discourse on technology was influenced by Hans Selye's pioneering work in the field of stress. Indeed, McLuhan adopted directly from Selye's research a medical understanding of the relationship between stress and numbness. A central theme in McLuhan's reflection on bio-technology was Selye's original theorisation that under conditions of deep stress, the organism anesthetizes the area effected, making the shock felt in peripheral regions. And McLuhan always insisted that the age of electric circuity is a time of HIGH STRESS.

> When an organ goes out (ablation) it goes numb. The central nervous system has gone numb (for survival). We enter the age of the unconscious with electronics, and consciousness shifts to the physical organs, even in the body politic. There is a great stepping up of physical awareness and a big drop in mental awareness when the central nervous system goes outward.[68]

Or again, and this in *Counter Blast*, although the same theme is also at the very beginning of *Understanding Media*:

> The one area which is numb and unconscious is the area which receives the impact. Thus there is an exact parallel with ablation in experimental medicine but in medical ablation, observation is properly directed not to the numb area, but to all the other organs as they are affected by the numbing or ablation of the single organ.[69]

It was McLuhan's overall project (his *semiology*) to probe the numbing of human perception by the technological innovations of the electronic age. In much the same way that McLuhan said of the movement from speech to writing that it illuminated the "high, dim Sierras of speech," McLuhan's "medical" understanding of technology lit up the darkness surrounding the invisible environment of the forms (rhetoric) of technology. All of McLuhan's writings are, in fact, a highly original effort at casting iron filings across the invisible "field" of electronic technologies in an effort to highlight their tacit assumptions. McLuhan's intention was to break the seduction effect of technology, to disturb the hypnotic spell cast by the dynamism of the technological imperative. And thus, while he was in the habit of saying, about the "inclusive" circuitry of the electronic age, that it was composed of "code, language, mechanical medium – all (having) magical properties which transform, transfigure,"[70] he was also accustomed to note that, on the down-side of the "new age," its participants were daily "X-rayed by television images."[71]

McLuhan could be so ambivalent on the legacy of the technological experience because, following Hans Selye and Adolphe Jonas, he viewed technological media as *simultaneously* extensions *and* auto-amputations of the sensory organs. The paradoxical character of technological media as both amplifications and cancellations was, of course, one basic theme of *Understanding Media*.

> While it was no part of the intention of Jonas and Selye to provide an explanation of human invention and technology, they have given us a theory of disease (discomfort) that goes far to explain why man is impelled to extend various parts of his body by a kind of auto-amputation.[72]

It was McLuhan's special insight though, to recognize the deep relationship between the history of technological innovation and the theory of disease. McLuhan's historical account of the evolution of technological media was structured around a (medical) account of technological innovation as "counter-irritants" to the "stress of acceleration of pace and increase of load."[73] Just as the body (in Hans Selye's terms) resorts to an auto-amputative strategy when "the perceptual power cannot locate or avoid the cause of irritation," so too (in McLuhan's terms) in the stress of super-stimulation, "the central nervous system acts to protect itself by a strategy of amputation or isolation of the offending organ, sense, or function."[74] Technology is a "counter-irritant" which aids in the "equilibrium of the physical organs which protect the central nervous system."[75] Thus, the wheel (as an extension of the foot) is a counter-irritant against the sudden pressure of "new burdens resulting from the acceleration of exchange by written and monetary media;" "movies and TV complete the cycle of mechanization of the human sensorium;" and computers are ablations or outerings of the human brain itself.[76] Now, it was McLuhan's thesis that the motive-force for technological innovation was always defensive and biological: the protection of the central nervous system against sudden changes in the "stimulus" of the external environment. Indeed, McLuhan often noted that "the function of the body" was the maintenance of an equilibrium among the media of our sensory organs. And consequently, the electronic age is all the more dangerous, and, in fact, suicidal when "in a desperate... autoamputation, as if the central nervous system could no longer depend on the physical organs to be protective buffers against the slings and arrows of outrageous mechanism,"[77] the central nervous system itself is outered in the form of electric circuitry. McLuhan inquires, again and again, what is to be the human fate now that with the "extension of consciousness" we have put "one's nerves outside, and one's physical organs inside the nervous system, or brain."[78] For McLuhan, the modern century is typified by an information order which plays our nerves in public: a situation, in his estimation, of "dread."

It was in an equally desperate gamble at increasing popular awareness of the "flip" done to us by the age of electric circuitry that McLuhan undertook an essentially medical survey of technological society. McLuhan's "classification of symptoms" took the form of an elaborate and historical description of the evolution of technology from the "mechanical" extensions of man (wheels, tools, printing) to the mythic, inclusive technologies of the electric age (television, movies, computers, telephone, phonograph). His "diagnosis" was that the crisis induced by technological society had much to do with the "closures" (numbing) effected among the sense ratios by new technical inventions. McLuhan was explicit about the technological origins of the modern stress syndrome: "the outering or extension of our bodies and senses in a new invention compels the whole of our bodies and senses to shift into new positions in order to maintain equilibrium."[79] A new "closure" is occasioned in our sensory organs and faculties, both private and public, by new technical extension of man. And McLuhan's "therapeutic:" the deployment of the "creative imagination" as a new way of seeing technology, and of responding, mythically and in depth, to the challenges of the age of electric circuitry. For McLuhan, the stress syndrome associated with the coming-to-be of the technostructure could only be met with the assistance of educated perspective. If it is the human fate to live within its (own) central nervous system in the form of the electronic simulation of consciousness, then it is also the human challenge to respond creatively to the "dread" and "anxiety" of the modern age. We may be the servomechanisms, the body bits, of a technical apparatus which substitutes a language of codes, of processed information, for "natural" experience, but this is a human experience which is double-edged. Without the education of perspective or, for that matter, in the absence of a "multidimensional perspective"[80] on technique, it will surely be the human destiny to be imprinted by the structural imperatives, the silent grammar, of the new world information order. But it was also McLuhan's hope, occasioned by his faith in the universality of reason that the electronic age could be transformed in the direction of creative freedom. After all, it was his over-arching thesis that the era of electric circuitry represented a great break-point in human experience: the end of "visual, uniform culture"[81] based on mechanical technologies, and the ushering in of a popular culture of the "new man," which would be fully tribal and organic. In all his texts, but particularly in *The Medium is the Massage*, McLuhan insisted on teasing out the emancipatory tendencies in new technologies. Against the blandishments of an "official culture" to impose old meanings on novel technologies, McLuhan sympathized with "anti-social perspectives:" the creative perspectives of the artist, the poet, and even the young, who respond with "untaught delight to the poetry, and the beauty of the new technological environment."[82] In his intellectual commitment to the development of a new perspective on technology, McLuhan was, of course, only following Joyce in his willingness to respond to the technological environment with a sense of its "creative process." "He (Joyce) saw that the wake of human progress can disappear again into the night of sacral or auditory man. The Finn cycle of tribal institutions can return in the electric age, but if again, then let's make it awake or a wake or both."[83] Anyway in McLuhan's world, in a society which has sound as its environment, we have no choice. "We simply are not equipped with earlids."[84]

McLuhan's Blindspots

McLuhan was the last and best exponent of the liberal imagination in Canadian letters. His thought brings to a new threshold of intellectual expression the fascination with the question of technology which has always, both in political and private practice, so intrigued liberal discourse in Canada. McLuhan's thought provides a new eloquence, and indeed, nobility of meaning to "creative freedom" as a worthwhile public value; and this as much as it reasserts the importance of a renewed sense of "individualism," both as the locus of a revived political community and as a creative site (the "agent intellect") for releasing, again and again, the possible "epiphanies" in technological experience. In McLuhan's writings, the traditional liberal faith in the reason of technological experience, a reason which could be the basis of a rational and universal political community, was all the more ennobled to the extent that the search for the "reason" in technology was combined with the Catholic quest for a new "incarnation." McLuhan's communication theory was a direct outgrowth of his Catholicism; and his religious sensibility fused perfectly with a classically liberal perspective on the question of technology and civilization. In the present orthodoxy of intellectual discourse, it is not customary to find a thinker whose inquiry is both infused by a transcendent religious sensibility and whose intellectual scholarship is motivated, not only by a desperate sense of the eclipse of reason in modern society, but by the disappearance of "civilization" itself through its own vanishing-point. As quixotic as it might be, McLuhan's intellectual project was of such an inclusive and all-embracing nature. His thought could be liberal, Catholic, and structuralist (before his time) precisely because the gravita-tion-point of McLuhan's thought was the preservation of the fullest degree possible of creative freedom in a modern century, which, due to the stress induced by its technology, was under a constant state of emergency. In McLuhan's discourse, individual freedom as well as civil culture itself were wagered in the contest with technology. The technological experience also made the possibility of a new "incarnation" fully ambivalent: it was also the Catholic, and by extension, liberal belief in a progressive, rational, and evolutionary history which was gambled in the discourse on technology.

But if McLuhan provides an important key to exploring the technological media, then it must also be noted that there are, at least, two major limitations in his thought which reduce his value, either as a guide to understanding technology in the Canadian circumstance or, for that matter, to a full inquiry into the meaning of the technological experience in the New World. First, McLuhan had no system-atic, or even eclectic, theory of the relationship between economy and technology; and certainly no critical appreciation of the appropriation, and thus privatisation, of technology by the lead institutions, multinational corporations and the state, in advanced industrial societies. It was not, of course, that McLuhan was unaware of the relationship of corporate power and technology. One searing sub-text of *Understanding Media* and *The Mechanical Bride* had to do with the almost malig-nant significance of the corporate control of electronic technologies. In McLuhan's estimation, "technology is part of our bodies;"[85] and to the extent that corporations acquire private control over the electronic media then we have, in effect, "leased out" our eyes, ears, fingers, legs, and the brain itself, to an exterior power.[86] In the electronic age, this era of collective and integral consciousness, those with control of technological media are allowed "to play the strings of our nerves in public."[87] The body is fully externalized, and exposed, in the interstices of the technological sensorium. For McLuhan, just like Grant, the technological dynamo breeds a new formation of power, demonic and mythic, which is capable, as one of its reflexes of vapourizing the individual subject, and of undermining all "public" communities. But if McLuhan understood the full dangers of corporate control of technological media, nowhere did he extend this insight into a reflection on the relationship of capitalism and technology. Now, it may be, as in the case of Jacques Ellul, another civil humanist, that McLuhan's intellectual preference was to privilege the question of technology over all other aspects of social experience, including the economic foundations of society. McLuhan may have been a technological determinist, or at the minimum, a "technological monist" who took technique to be the primary

locus for the interpretation of society as a whole. If this was so, then it is particularly unfortunate since McLuhan's "blindspot" on the question of capitalism and
technology undermined, in the end, his own injunction for an "historical understanding" of the evolution of technological media. In "Catholic Humanism" and,
for that matter, in all of his writings, McLuhan urged the use of the historical
imagination – an historical perspective which was to be sympathetic, realistic, and
reconstructive – as our only way of understanding the great watershed in human
experience precipitated by the appearance of electronic society. His was, however, a
curious and somewhat constricted vision of the historical imagination: for it
omitted any analysis of the precise historical conditions surrounding the development of the technological experience in North America. McLuhan was as insensi-
tive, and indifferent, to the problem of the political economy of technology as he
was to the relationship of technology and ideological hegemony in the creation of
liberal society, and the liberal state, in North America. McLuhan's primary value
was, of course, creative freedom, not "justice;" and his political preference was for a
universal community founded on the rights of "reason," not for the "ethic of
charity." This is to say, however, that McLuhan's "historical sense" already embraced, from its very beginnings, the deepest assumptions of technological society.
McLuhan's mind was a magisterial account of the technological imagination itself.
This was a discourse which evinced a fatal fascination with the utopian possibilities
of technology. Indeed, McLuhan liked to speculate about the almost religious
utopia immanent in the age of information.

> Language as the technology of human extension, whose powers of
> division and separation we know so well, may have been the "Tower of
> Babel" by which men sought to scale the highest heavens. Today
> computers hold out the promise of a means of instant translation of any
> code or language into any other code or language. The computer, in
> short, promises by technology a Pentecostal condition of universal
> understanding and unity. The next logical step would seem to be, not to
> translate, but to by-pass languages in favour of a general cosmic
> consciousness which might be very like the collective unconscious
> dreamt by Bergson. The condition of "weightlessness" that biologists say
> promises a physical immortality, may be paralleled by the condition of
> speechlessness that could confer a perpetuity of collective harmony and
> peace.[88]

Everything in McLuhan's thought strained towards the liberation of the
"Pentecostal condition" of technology: the privileging of space over time; the
fascination with the exteriorisation in electronic technology of an "inner experience" which is electric, mythic, inclusive, and configurational; the primacy of
"field" over event; the vision of "processed information" as somehow consonant
with the perfectibility of the human faculties. And it was this utopian, and transcendent, strain in McLuhan's thought which may, perhaps, have made it impossible for his inquiry to embrace the problematic of capitalism and technology. In
McLuhan's lexicon, the privileging of the "economic" relationship belonged to an

obsolete era: the now superseded age of specialism, fragmentation, and segmenta-
tion of work of the industrial revolution. McLuhan viewed himself as living on the
other side, the far side, of technological history: the coming age of "cosmic man"
typified by "mythic or iconic awareness" and by the substitution of the "multi-
faceted for the point-of-view."[89] What was capitalism? It was the obsolescent content
of the new era of the electronic simulation of consciousness. For McLuhan,
economy had also gone electronic and thus even the corporate world, with its
"magic" of advertisements and its plenitude of computers, could be subsumed into
the more general project of surfacing the reason in technological society. Consequently, it might be said that McLuhan's blindspot on the question of economy was
due not so much to a strain of "technological determinism" in his thought, and least
not in the *first* instance; but due rather to his, transparently Catholic expectation
that if the electronic economy of the corporate world was not an "agent intellect" in
the creation of a new technological horizon, it was, at least, a necessary catalyst in
setting the conditions for "cosmic man." McLuhan was a "missionary" to the power
centres of the technological experience; and he could so faithfully, and guilelessly,
discuss the civilizing moment in technology because there never was any incompat-
ibility between the Catholic foundations of his communication theory and the will
to empire. If McLuhan was a deeply compromised thinker, then it was because his
Catholic humanism allowed him to subordinate, and forget the question of the
private appropriation of technology. And what was, in the final instance, tragic and
not comic about his intellectual fate was simply this: it was precisely the control
over the speed, dissemination, and implanting of new technologies by the corporate
command centres of North America which would subvert the very possibility of an
age of "creative freedom."

   If one limitation in McLuhan's discourse on technology was his forgetfulness
of the mediation of technology by political economy, then a second limitation, or
arrest, concerned McLuhan's contempt for the "national question" in Canada. It
would be unfair to criticize a thinker for not violating the internal unity of his own
viewpoint. McLuhan was always firm in his belief that the dawn of the "global
village," this new era of "universal understanding and unity" required the by-passing
of "national" political communities. The universalism of reason and the potentially
new "Finn cycle" of an all-inclusive and mythic technological experience rendered
obsolete *particularistic* political concerns. McLuhan's polis was the world; and his,
not inaccurate, understanding of that world had it that the United States, by virtue
of its leadership in electronic technologies, was the "new world environment."[90] It
was, consequently, with a noble conscience that McLuhan, like Galbraith, Easton,
and Johnson before him, could turn his attention southward, passing easily and
with no sign of disaffection, into the intellectual centres of the American empire.
And, of course, in prophesying the end of nationalist sensibility, or the more
regional sense of a "love of one's own," McLuhan was only following the flight
beyond "romanticism" of the liberal political leadership of Canada, and, in particular, the "creative leadership" of Trudeau. Indeed, that Trudeau could so instantly
and enthusiastically embrace McLuhan's world sensibility was only because the
latter's sense of an underlying reason in the technological order confirmed the

deepest prejudices of Trudeau's own political perspective. Indeed, between Trudeau and McLuhan a parallel project was in the making: on Trudeau's part (*Federalism and the French-Canadians*) a political challenge against the "obsolete" world of ethnicity (and thus nationalism) in Quebec and an invitation to Quebec to join the technological (rational) society of North America; and on McLuhan's part, an epistemological and then moral decision to join in the feast of corporate advantages spread out by the masters of the empire. The common trajectories traced by Trudeau's technocratic politics and by McLuhan's sense of technological utopia reveals and powerfully so, the importance of the Catholic touch in Canadian politics and letters; just as much as it reflects, that for the empire at least, Catholicism is, indeed, intimate with the "central cultural discoveries" of the modern age. Moreover, the very existence of a "McLuhan" or a "Trudeau" as the locus of the Canadian discourse discloses the indelible character of Canada, not just as a witness to empire, but, perhaps, as a radical experiment in the working out of the intellectual and political basis of the technological imagination in North America. Canada is, and has always been, the most modern of the New World societies; because the character of its colonialism, of its domination of the land by technologies of communication, and of its imposition of an "abstract nation" upon a divergent population by a fully technological polity, has made of it a leading expression of technological liberalism in North America.

It was, consequently, the fate of McLuhan to be welcomed into the privileged circles of the corporate and intellectual elites of the United States. This was not unanticipated. The Canadian philosopher, Charles Norris Cochrane, noted that it is the peculiar feature of imperialisms that, as their energies focus, in the most mature phase of empire, on the "pragmatic will" to conquer, to expand, to live, they are often forced to seek out in the peripheral regions of the empire some new source of intellectual energy, some inspiring historical justification, which would counter the dawning sense of "intellectual futility" that so often accompanies, and undermines, the greatest successes of the will to empire.[91] McLuhan was such an "historical energizer." His utopian vision of technological society provided the corporate leadership of the American empire with a sense of historical destiny; and, at least, with the passing illusion that their narrow-minded concentration on the "business" of technology might make of them the "Atlas" of the new world of cosmic man. It was McLuhan's special ability, done, no doubt, sometimes tongue in cheek and with a proper sense of intellectual cynicism, to transfigure the grubby leadership (Grant's "creative leaders") of the American business world, and then of a good part of the new class of technocrats in the West, into the dizzying heights of a greater historical destiny, that made him such a favoured courtesan of the technological empire. Grant might say of the "creative leaders" of empire that their nihilism is such that they would always prefer to will rather than not to will, but McLuhan provided another, more radical, alternative. In the face of the incipient nihilism of the technological experience, McLuhan dangled that most precious of gifts: a sense of historical purpose (the age of communications as "cosmic consciousness"); and an intellectual justification (the technological imperative as both necessary *and* good).

While Grant's austere and forbidding description of technological depend-
ency revolved around a consideration of *technique as will*, McLuhan thought of
technique as possessing, at least potentially, the *poetry of consciousness*. Thus, it was
not with bad faith but with the curious amorality of a thinker whose ethic, being as
it was abstract freedom and reason, and who could thus screen out the barbarism of
the technological dynamo, that McLuhan could associate with the leadership of
technological society. And just to the extent that Grant's ruminations on technological society led him into almost self-imposed solitude in Halifax (far from the
"dynamic centre" of the technological dynamo in the Great Lakes region of North
America), McLuhan could be a dandy of the New York intelligentsia. McLuhan's
association of the values of reason and "universal unity" with the expansive momen-
tum of the technostructure was, of course, a highly fortuitous compromise. It
allowed him to serve a legitimation function for the technological dynamo, while all
the while maintaining his *sang-froid* as a civil humanist who was above the fray, a
Catholic intellectual among the barbarians.

McLuhan's political commitments, represented both by his rejection of the
"national question" in Canada and by his participation, in depth, in the futurology
of technological empire, are of direct consequence to his contributions to a master
theory of communications. That McLuhan could find no moment of deviation
between his civil humanism, founded on the defence of "civilization," and his
absorption into the intellectual appendages of empire, indicates, starkly and
dramatically, precisely how inert and uncritical is the supervening value of "civilization." McLuhan's lasting legacy is, perhaps, a historical one: the inherent contradiction of his discourse in remaining committed to the very technostructure which had
destroyed the possibility of "civilization" indicates the ultimate failure of civil
humanism in modern politics. McLuhan's humanism, and indeed his abiding
Catholicism, could provide an inspiring vision of a more utopian human future;
but in remaining tied to the "primacy of reason," a *reason* which was fully abstracted
from history and ontology, McLuhan's discourse could always be easily turned from
within. This was the comic aspect of the whole affair: the technological dynamo
could also accept as its dominant value the "primacy of reason"; and, by extension,
the application of technical reason, in politics, bureaucracy, science, and industry, to
the proliferation of technological media. The technostructure thus absorbed
McLuhan's discourse on his own terms: it transposed his search for a new, universal
civilization into an historical justification of technological necessitarianism; and it
showed precisely how compatible the Catholic conception of "transcendent reason"
is with the rationalising impulses of the technological system. McLuhan's one
possible avenue of escape: the recovery of a "grounded" and emergent cultural
practice or, at least, some sense of "intimations of deprival" which had been silenced
by the technological dynamo was, of course, firmly closed to him by his commitment to the universal over the local, and to the metaphorical over the historical.

To dismiss McLuhan as a technological determinist is to miss entirely the
point of his intellectual contribution. McLuhan's value as a theorist of culture and
technology began just when he went over the hill to the side of the alien and
surrealistic world of mass communications: the "real world" of technology where

the nervous system is exteriorised and everyone is videoated daily like sitting screens for television. Just because McLuhan sought to *see* the real world of technology, and even to celebrate technological reason as freedom, he could provide such superb, first-hand accounts of the new society of electronic technologies. McLuhan was fated to be trapped in the deterministic world of technology, indeed to become one of the intellectual servomechanisms of the machine-world, because his Catholicism failed to provide him with an adequate cultural theory by which to escape the hegemony of the abstract media systems that he had sought to explore. Paradoxically, however, it was just when McLuhan became most cynical and most deterministic, when he became fully aware of the nightmarish quality of the "medium as massage," that his thought becomes most important as an entirely creative account of the great paradigm-shift now going on in twentieth-century experience. McLuhan was then, in the end, trapped in the "figure" of his own making. His discourse could provide a brilliant understanding of the inner functioning of the technological media; but no illumination concerning how "creative freedom" might be won through in the "age of anxiety, and dread." In a fully tragic sense, McLuhan's final legacy was this: he was the playful perpetrator, and then victim, of a sign-crime.[92]

Notes

1. M . McLuhan, *Counter Blast*, Toronto: McClelland and Stewart, 1969, p. 14.
2. For McLuhan's extended analysis of the movie as a "mechanizing" medium see "The Reel World," *Understanding Media*, pp. 284-296.
3. McLuhan also described the telegraph as a "social hormone," *Understanding Media*, pp. 246-257.
4. M. McLuhan, *Counter Blast*, p. 16.
5. M. McLuhan, *The Medium is the Massage*, p. 26.
6. M. McLuhan, *Counter Blast*, p. 14.
7. Ibid., p. 31.
8. Ibid., p. 30.
9. Ibid., p. 26.
10. Ibid., p. 41.
11. Ibid., p. 14.
12. Ibid., pp. 22-23.
13. M. McLuhan, *Understanding Media*, p. 51.
14. M. McLuhan, "A Historical Approach to the Media," *Teacher's College Record*, 57(2), November, 1955, p. 110.
15. Ibid., p. 109.
16. Ibid., p. 110.
17. M. McLuhan, *Through the Vanishing Point: Space in Poetry and Painting*, New York: Harper and Row, 1968, p. 181.
18. Ibid.
19. Ibid., pp. 24-25.
20. Ibid., p. 24.
21. Ibid., p. 25.
22. Ibid., p. 24.
23. Ibid.
24. Ibid., p. 181.
25. The arts as "radar feedback" is a major theme of *Understanding Media*. See particularly the introductory comments, pp. vii-xi.
26. M. McLuhan, *Through the Vanishing Point*, p. 21.
27. M. McLuhan, *Counter Blast*, p. 31.
28. See particularly, M. McLuhan, *The Mechanical Bride: Folklore of Industrial Man*, New York: The Vanguard Press, 1951.
29. McLuhan wrote in *Understanding Media*, "To put one's nerves outside, and one's physical organs inside the nervous system, or brain, is to initiate a situation – if not a concept – of dread." p. 222.
30. McLuhan's most expansive statement on the relationship of the Catholic mind to the study of modern civilization is located in his article, "Catholic Humanism & Modern Letters."
31. M. McLuhan, *The Medium is the Massage*, p. 68.
32. Jean Baudrillard, *L'échange symbolique et la mort*, Paris: Editions Gallimard, 1976, pp. 89-95.

33. McLuhan's sense of communications as a new universalism is a unifying theme across his texts, from *The Medium is the Massage* to *Understanding Media* and *Counter Blast*. It was also a Catholic ethic which was at work in his thought about the media.

34. M. McLuhan, "Catholic Humanism and Modern Letters," p. 75.

35. Ibid., p. 74.

36. Ibid., p. 80.

37. Ibid., pp. 75-76.

38. Ibid., p. 75.

39. Ibid., pp. 82-83.

40. Ibid., p. 80.

41. Indeed, McLuhan describes the "new media" of communication (...as...) magical art forms, "Catholic Humanism and Modern Letters," p. 79.

42. M. McLuhan, *The Medium is the Massage*, p. 69.

43. M. McLuhan, *Understanding Media*, p. 56.

44. M. McLuhan, *The Medium is the Massage*, p. 120.

45. Ibid., p. 114.

46. See particularly, M. McLuhan, *Counter Blast*, p. 42.

47. M. McLuhan, *Understanding Media*, p. 64.

48. Ibid., p. 56.

49. M. McLuhan, "An Ancient Quarrel in Modern America" in *The Interior Landscape: The Literary Criticism of Marshall McLuhan, 1943-62*, edited by Eugene McNamara. Toronto: McGraw-Hill, 1969, p. 231.

50. M. McLuhan, "Joyce, Aquinas, and the Poetic Process," *Renascence* 4(1), Autumn, 1951, pp. 3-4.

51. Ibid., p. 3.

52. Ibid.

53. Ibid., p. 7.

54. Ibid., p. 4.

55. Ibid., p. 5.

56. Ibid.

57. Ibid., p. 9.

58. Ibid., p. 8.

59. M. McLuhan and Quentin Fiore, *The Medium is the Massage*, p. 151.

60. For an illuminating account of the significance of Thucydides' epistemology to modern consciousness, see Charles Cochrane, *Thucydides and the Science of History*, Oxford: Oxford University Press, 1929.

61. See particularly, M. McLuhan's "Joyce, Aquinas and the Poetic Process," p. 3, and "Catholic Humanism and Modern Letters," p.72.

62. McLuhan's understanding of the creative possibilities of "simultaneity" and "instantaneous scope" is developed in *The Medium is the Massage*.

63. While McLuhan analyzes the phenomenon of "closure" in many of his writings, this concept is the locus of *Counter Blast* and *Understanding Media*.

64. M. McLuhan, *Understanding Media*, p. 26.

65. M. McLuhan, *Counter Blast*, p. 5.

66. Ibid., p. 42.

67. Ibid.

68. Ibid.

69. Ibid.

70. Ibid., p. 62.

71. M. McLuhan, *Understanding Media*.

72. Ibid., p. 42.

73. Ibid.

74. Ibid.

75. Ibid., p. 43.

76. See particularly, M. McLuhan, *Understanding Media*, p. 42, and *Counter Blast*, p. 17.

77. M. McLuhan, *Understanding Media*, p. 43.

78. Ibid., p. 252.

79. Ibid.

80. Ibid., p. 142.

81. McLuhan always counterposed the mythic, inclusive and in-depth viewpoint to the homogeneity of visual culture.

82. This was a main thematic of *The Medium is the Massage*, pp. 112-117.

83. Ibid., p. 120.

84. M. McLuhan and Quentin Fiore, *The Medium is the Massage*, p.142.

85. See especially, M. McLuhan, *Understanding Media*, p. 68.

86. Ibid.

87. Ibid.

88. Ibid., p. 80.

89. Ibid., p. 141.

90. M. McLuhan, "The Relation of Environment & Anti-Environment," in F. Marsen's *The Human Dialogue: Perspectives on Communications*, New York: The Free Press, 1967, p. 43.

91. Charles Norris Cochrane, "The Latin Spirit in Literature," *University of Toronto Quarterly*, Vol. 2, No. 3, (1932 - 33), pp. 315-338.

92. Professor Andrew Wernick coined this term in describing the interplay of power/media in the thought of the contemporary French social theorist, Jean Baudrillard.

The Cybernetic Delirium of Norbert Wiener

Stephen Pfohl

[M]y delirium assumed the form of a particular mixture of depression and worry... anxiety about the logical status of my... work. It was impossible for me to distinguish among my pain and difficulty in breathing, the flapping of the window curtain, and certain as yet unresolved points of the potential problem on which I was working. I cannot say that the pain revealed itself as a mathematical tension, or that the mathematical tension symbolized itself as a pain: for the two were united too closely to make such a separation significant. However, when I reflected on this matter later, I became aware of the possibility that almost any experience may act as a temporary symbol for a mathematical situation which has not yet been organized and cleared up. I also came to see more definitely than I had before that one of the chief motives driving me to mathematics was the discomfort or even the pain of an unresolved mathematical discord. I even became more and more conscious of the need to reduce such a discord to semipermanent and recognizable terms before I could release it and pass on to something else.

Norbert Wiener[1]

All around me, inside me, flowing through me, between me and others, it is easy to discern signs of the flexible, mass marketing of cybernetic delirium. This is a delirium associated with both cyber-products and cyber-experience. "Cyber-this" and "cyber-that." Its hard to do the ritual of the check-out line these days, without some magnetic cyber-commodity-connectors wrapping their seductive sensors, cheek to cheek, in feedback loops with yours. Commanding attention. Inviting a try. Not that the effects are homogeneous. Nor the possibilities. From cyber-sex-shopping-surveillance, to cyber-philosophy, and even utopian dreams of cyborg revolts — whether for fun, or out of desperation, flaming desire, or for want of more passionate and politically effective connections — the world around and within me appears increasingly mediated by a kind of delirious cyber-hyphenation of reality itself. This is a short (sociological) story of the history of this hyphenated world. This story revolves around the delirium of Norbert Wiener, the so-called "father" of cybernetic perspectives on physical and social reality. Today, Wiener's delirium has become our own.

My suggestion is this: that for worse and for better, we are today virtually all struggling to survive and communicate — if differently and in different modes — within the hegemonic exigencies of cybernetic culture. Fast flows of British Telecom. Quick jolts of profit. Bye bye MCI. 182,000 jobs in motion. Seventy countries. Market value $64 Billion. An implosion of tears. "Hi, Mom. Happy Valentine's Day!" A looping fragment of memory catches my eye/"I," as information enflames the sensory manifold between us. Turning me on. Off. Turning history inside outside. The flapping of a window curtain. The digital smoothness of the screen separating my body from data-driven images of yours. The flickering of electronically mediated fantasies between us. And fears. Wired bodies. Hard bodies. Micro-soft hearts. Energetically aroused, then fashionably abandoned. I love the advert tattooing your sex. You love my CK Infinity. Or so I'm led to imagine. Day dream. On credit. This is cybernetic capital. This is ultramodern power. A digitized white grid of anxious informational pleasures and pains. "As the CEO's and the specialist consultants of the virtual class triumphantly proclaim: 'Adapt or you're toast.'"[2] The smell of burning flesh.

Cybernetics typically denotes the interdisciplinary study and strategic deployment of communicative control processes in "complex systems" constituted by humans, other animals, machines, and the rest of living-nature. In what follows, I wish to suggest an even broader use of this term. Cybernetics, not simply as a field of techno-science research and application, but as a term connoting the most far-reaching of ultramodern forms of social control. In this sense, I will be using the phrase, social cybernetics, to provisionally configure the fluid, high speed, and densely layered webs of communicatively driven positive and negative "feedback" which, this very moment, affect the ways you are receiving my words. This is a story of how loops of cybernetic feedback are informing the energetic ritual organization of power between ourselves and others. Within the fast-flexible boundaries of global capital, the most dominant, but certainly not all, of these feedback loops carry a masculine, heterosexist, and racially inscribed charge. This is a history of the present.

Decentered, as loops of communicative feedback may appear from within various localized scenes of capital, cybernetic control practices today guide the hegemonic marketing of both meaning and material survival within the bodily confines of a cruel, complex, and contradictory socio-economic system. Increasingly, this system — capital in its ultramodern or cybernetic mode — is incorporating the entire world as its parasitic playground for profit. I make this suggestion, not to further existing loops of communicative feedback, which make the televisionary marketing of paranoiac fears (and fascinations) big business. Instead, this is to join in some minor way, with others, in encouraging a heterogeneous affinity of collective, energetic, and "power-sensitive" efforts to reflexively double back upon and, thereby, better (theoretically) converse about — as well as jam, subvert, detour, and, by any means possible, contribute to the ritual transformation of — the violent and sickeningly hierarchical "order of things" in which I find myself writing to you. Partial and provisional transformations; transformations in the direction of ritual organizational forms which are more just, more life affirming, and more loving.

The word, cybernetics, derives from the Greek term, *kybernetics*, referring to mechanisms of steering, governing, or control. The term was first used with reference to "human engineering" by MIT mathematician, Norbert Wiener, during and in the years immediately following World War II. Perhaps deliriously. It was, after all, a time of war. First hot, then cold. And, as Paul Virilio astutely observes, a culture of war is also a culture of delirium — a culture where the ordinary "tools of perception" are suggestively, ritually, magically, spectacularly, technologically, almost halluncinatorily, retooled.[3] Wiener was something of a child prodigy, and a Harvard Ph.D. in mathematics by age nineteen. He was also a pioneer in the application of statistically-based nonlinear mathematics to problems of "circular causation" and "self-adjusting feedback." As part of the war effort, Wiener collaborated with Julian Bigelow and other mathematicians and scientists, gathered under the auspices of the MIT Radiation Laboratory. Directed by Warren Weaver of the Rockefeller Foundation, this lab was a high priority, D2 Section, project, under the command of the National Defense Research Committee. Wiener and Bigelow made innovative and unprecedented complex use of "ergodic theorems" and "integral equations," in what has been described as a "revolution" in (computational) communications engineering. During the final years of the Second World War, this revolution triggered significant advances in the design, production, and strategic deployment of anti-aircraft guns and precision bombing equipment. After the war, it would change an entire way of life.

Wiener and Bigelow's innovative mathematical labors were themselves in a complex and militarily mediated loop of communicative feedback with other exponential leaps being made at the same time in both computing and telecommunications. Many of these advances were made possible by the refined development of the vacuum tube. Nevertheless, in Wiener's account of these events, it is clear that it was the context of war which hastened the production of the cybernetic imagination.

> Though the vacuum tube received its debut in the communications industry, the boundaries and extent of this industry were not fully understood for a long period. There sporadic uses of the vacuum tube and its sister invention, the photoelectric cell, for scanning the products of industry, for example regulating the thickness of a web coming out of a paper machine, or for inspecting the color of a can of pineapples. These uses did not as yet form a reasoned new technique, nor were they associated in engineering mind with the vacuum tubes other function, communications.

> All this changed in the war. One of the few things gained from the great conflict was rapid development of invention, under the stimulus of necessity and the unlimited employment of money... At the beginning

of the war, our greatest need was to keep England from being knocked out by an overwhelming air attack. Accordingly, the anti-aircraft canon was one of the first objects of our scientific effort, especially when combined with the airplane-detecting device of radar or ultra-high-frequency Hertzian waves. The technique of radar used the same modalities as the existing radio besides inventing new ones of its own. It was thus natural to consider radar as a branch of communications theory.

Besides finding airplanes by radar it was necessary to shoot them down. This involves the problem of fire control. The speed of the airplane has made it necessary to compute the elements of the trajectory of the anti-aircraft missile by machine, and to give the predicting machine functions which had previously been assigned to human beings. Thus the problem of anti-aircraft fire control made a new generation of engineers familiar with the notion of a communication addressed to a machine rather than to a person."[4]

If the problem of "anti-aircraft fire" is a problem of "goal-directed communications," for the emerging science of cybernetics, its solution lies in the notion of regulated feedback. In cybernetics, the principle of feedback is (aesthetically) imaged as the operative force guiding a "contingent world" of beings in reciprocal energetic communication. For Wiener, this occurs in both animals and the new high-speed computing machines his mathematics helped bring into being. Each makes use of "sensory organs" and magnetic "memory" devices. Together these operate to produce ongoing comparisons between past and present exchanges between information and energy. In humans and other animals, this involves what Wiener described as "a kinaesthetic sense," which keeps "a record of the position and tensions of their muscles."[5] In the new computing machines, this function was handled by a combination of data scanning and taping devices. But in addition to logging an ongoing "comparison of inputs to goals," cybernetic feedback processes involve something more interactive — "a reciprocal flow" of "two-way interaction between controller and controlled." This operates "not only to communicate influence from the former to the latter, but also to communicate back the results of this action."[6]

This image of interactive feedback strikes me as, at once, perverse and utopian. On one hand, it celebrates the control of some subjects over others. On the other, it decenters the communicative practices these subjects use to exert control within a dynamic web of interactive feedback, shaped, in part, by the communicative actions of those being controlled. In other words, cybernetics substitutes for a simplistic one-way command model a vision of message-sending and message-receiving "subject-objects," each mediated by the agency of communicative practice itself. This is an agency of letters, icons, and moving pictures. Don't be surprised if you here find resemblances between cybernetics, with its imaginary of decentered communicators ensnared within flowing webs of scriptural, textual, and textural feedback, and the image of social life offered by certain versions of poststructuralist theory. Cybernetics and poststructuralist thought emerge in related (mid-to-late-twentieth century) historical times and spaces. Neither is genealogically innocent of the other. Neither materially; nor in the imaginary realm. When read critically, each also suggests (potentially) reflexive "power-sensitive" images of sacrifice.[7] And repetition.

The command, control, and communicative possibilities of cybernetics are rooted in the repeated sacrifice of other ways of being in and communicating about the worlds "we" are in. This makes cybernetics a restrictive economic practice.[8] It sacrificially banishes other possible worlds for the purpose of provisionally fixing, stabilizing, and communcatively controlling the boundaries which stake out the "contingent world" of which cybernetics is itself constitutively a part. Cybernetics also seeks to monitor, regulate, and modify the dynamic loops of feedback governing this contingent world's continuance. And its change. In cybernetics, the material effect of dynamic flows of feedback is the ongoing informational shaping of some worlds, to the statistical reduction of others. In this sense, there is also more than a bit of existentialism guiding Wiener's cybernetic imaginary. But, then, Wiener, like Sartre, was writing to combat what he discerned as the deadly freeze-framings of fascism. In contrast to the reductive and homogenizing violence of fascism, Wiener pictured cybernetics as offering a dynamic image of communicative exchange between heterogeneous beings; energetically scanning, monitoring, reading, interpreting, and adjustively responding to one another; all the while reproducing, modifying, defending, resisting, yielding, penetrating, and/or blurring the boundaries between themselves and others; these others now appearing ecologically, as if environments, as if spatially, temporarily outside.

Inside and out, cybernetics offers a model of "circular causation." Can you picture it? Wiener did. Which comes first: the cybernetic chicken or a golden egg? The answer, of course, is neither. Both are circularly caused: interactively, dynamically, reciprocally. Not mechanically, but in information-governed energetic exchange. Not one-way. But not all ways at once, either. Because when that happens, things loose their shape, liquefy; loose their distinction, their distinctiveness, their boundaries. Like water spinning in water; or lovers embracing from the outside in. But, orderly loops of communicative feedback control against such lovely, if dangerous, plays of chaos. As such, orderly feedback processes facilitate the erection of secure boundaries; helping to quiet, absorb, silence, control, construct sound proof boundaries against noise. All this replaces earlier modern (scientific and popular cultural) images of "cause leading to effect." Substituted for such linear modelings of causation is a more complexly suggestive theoretical-statistical imaginary: a computational modeling of "interactive" shapings and reshapings of the energetic boundaries between communicative agents — not all of whom need be human.

By making informational objects out of each other, ceaseless and circular cybernetic communicators alter the environments within which they and others energetically interact. Consider the information produced by a radar screen in communication with a human operator, two of the earliest "subject-objects" to be wired into the telelectronic circuitry of the cybernetic imagination. Here, information is "processed to calculate the adjustment on gun controls to improve aim; the effectiveness of the adjustments is observed and communication via radar, and then this new information is used again to readjust the aim of the gun, and so on. If the calculations are automated, one is dealing with a self-steering device; indeed, the whole system inducing the participating human beings can be viewed as a self-steering device."[9]

While situating the "new science" of cybernetics within the old sciences of war, Wiener simultaneously expressed horror at the contributions of other mathematicians, scientists, and engineers to the construction and use of nuclear weapons. Wiener was profoundly suspicious about structural complicities between elite scientific institutions and governmental-military sources of funding. In 1941 he resigned from the National Academy of Science in protest. Soon thereafter he withdrew completely from governmental and military-based service, never again to receive state funding for the production of knowledge. Indeed, throughout his subsequent career, Wiener operated somewhat doubly — as both a scientist and ethical commentator on the practice of science. Still, the wartime successes of cybernetic technologies inspired Wiener and others to search for an ever-widening "interface" between command, control, and communication processes in a diverse array of machinic, biological, and social systems.[10] In pursuit of this interface, from 1946 to 1953, Wiener met regularly with John von Neumann (whose mathematical labors, unlike Wiener's, contributed directly to digital computations necessary for U.S. military experiments with atomic weaponry against Japan) and other early cyberneticians, in a series of intensive conferences on cybernetics, sponsored by the Josiah Macy Jr. Foundation. Also attending some of these sessions were leading figures of post-war social science — Margaret Mead, Talcott Parsons, Gregory Bateson, Kurt Lewin, and Robert K. Merton, among others. Overall, the Macy conferences sought to "generate a new kind of link between engineering, biology, mathematics on one hand and psychology, psychiatry, and all the social sciences on the other."[11] And, in this, they succeeded. If not exactly in the blink of an eye/I, then exponentially and steadily over the last half-century.

As a young American white boy in the 1950s, cybernetics enveloped me like a second skin, a second nature. Indeed, night after night I would be lulled into half-dream states, swollen with telecommunicative feedback. The radio rocking me, rolling me, somewhere between wakefulness and electronic slumber. Phone now! Vote for your favorite stars! Request your favorite black tunes sung by white voices! And, of course, I did. Nothing has been the same since. This is no confession. This is a description of collective cybernetic signalings which run through my body, like blood, only much faster. This is also a description of a most material aspect of recent social history. For indeed, practical embodiments of the cybernetic world view have spread to virtually all fields of power, knowledge, and culture. As such, boundaries have become blurred between "once artificially separated areas of thought" as "more and more of the world is seen in terms of information. Just look at the account books, the projections, the numbers and the returns… Stocks and commodities, the securities markets, banking, currency, options, futures… [A]ll these markets must now be rethought and restructured," because today each is increasingly experienced as little but a kind of "telematic" exchange of feedback between information and energy.[12]

From a doctors' imagination of her patient to the CIA and IBM's imagination of its competitors and clients and, maybe, even your imagination of me, vast "flows" of the world as "we" have come to know it over the last fifty years have been (ritually) coded and recoded as seemingly nothing but matters of information. "Even the simplest of conversations are separated, reconfigured, sent and priced. And those who live in this new world are losing their grip on… older [and other possible constructions of] reality. As for those who have no access to, no participation in, this newly imposed world, they are [forced] out of the world's new information economy, doomed to obsolescence and death."[13]

Somewhere between the Real and a Militarized Imaginary

Returning to Wiener's delirium: in 1950, the MIT mathematician declared: "It is the purpose of Cybernetics is to develop a language and techniques that will enable us to indeed attack the problems of control and communications in general."[14] Despite his critical attitude toward military appropriations of scientific know-how, it is important to note the militaristic resonances vibrating in Wiener's own phrasings. To… attack the problems of control and communications. Such resonances remain deeply entrenched within contemporary social cybernetics. Adapt or you're toast! Moreover, given the omnipresence of cybernetic control mechanisms across a wide range of contemporary institutions, it is vital to remember the ritual origins of this logic and its limits. Wiener, of course, was not alone in providing military undertones for this new science. This is clear in the work of Donna Haraway. Haraway draws attention to the relationship between cybernetics and the militaristic economy of capitalist patriarchy out of which it has evolved. Conceptualizing the logic of cybernetics as a powerful "theoretical fiction" which forecloses other ways of making sense of the world, Haraway, like Wiener, traces the roots of this ideology to the labor of interdisciplinary teams of government funded researchers during and after the Second World War. Indeed, the "extraordinary organization of scientists in the war effort in Britain and the United States threw biologists together with engineers, linguists, physicists, mathematicians, and administrators in intense activity that had profound consequences" for both the conceptual and practical reorganization of sciences, such as biology. And for the management of everyday socio-economic systems as well.[15]

Haraway's work points us to a particular social scene: a series of white male dominated research settings organized around the demands of hot and cold war, a theater of perpetual war it seems. Within this theater, "command-control systems, called animal societies and populations, came to be known through technical, theoretical and practical procedures that [sacrificially] acknowledged natural-technical objects as problems in military strategy; industrial production, in which the worker is a system-component whose error rates must be controlled by information and resource management; in psychiatric management of overloaded, stressed communicative systems; and in engineered design of automated control systems."[16]

"Ether, having once failed as a concept is being reinvented. Information is the ultimate mediational ether. Light doesn't travel through space: its is information that travels through information... at a heavy price."[17]

Consider, for instance, the electrifying ideas of information theorist Conrad Hal Waddington. Waddington sought to model "information flows" in relation to differentially constrictive boundaries of energy. In so doing, he facilitated a general transference of methods associated with operations research in military organizations to the emergent field of molecular biology, where a new image of the body as an information-driven communications system was already beginning to take hold. In this regard, it is crucial to recognize that Waddington himself developed his ideas in feedback with a program of war-time research, sponsored by the British Royal Air Force Operations Research Section and aimed at countering the effectivity of German U-boats.[18] This is not to deny the value of Waddington's discoveries. The value is high. But so are the costs. It is, instead, to suggest that — like Kant, during an earlier, if related, time and space within capital — when searching for language to justify the (alleged) universality of particular aesthetic judgments, Waddington theorized life as basically a problem in sublime military gamesmanship. In this deadly and delirious game, as Waddington figured it, bodily life itself was imagined as little but a battlefield constructed around and between flows of energy and information. This is also evident in the language of W. Ross Ashby, an early theorist and popularizer of cybernetics. According to Ashby:

> [T]he inborn characteristics of living organisms are simply the strategies
> that have been found satisfactory over centuries of competition and
> built into the young animal so as to be ready for use at the first demand.
> Just as so many players have found 'P-Q4' a good way of opening a
> game of chess, so many species found 'growth teeth' to be a good way of
> opening the Battle of Life.[19]

If this sounds a bit like a delirious replay of Herbert Spencer's imperial sociological rhetoric of "survival of the fittest," this should be no surprise to those familiar with the social cybernetics advanced by long time Harvard sociologist, Talcott Parsons. Parsons' functionalist theories dominated U.S. sociological thinking throughout the 1950s and early 1960s. Moreover, Parsons' vision of society as a communicative "social system" represented an explicit synthesis of Spencer's thesis concerning adaptive societal evolution and recent developments in the science of cybernetics. Parsons pictured human subjects as "behavioral organisms" whose "communicative actions" were guided by "a cybernetic system located mainly in the central nervous system, which operates through several intermediary mechanisms to control the metabolic processes of the organism and the behavioral use of its physical facilities, such as the motions of limbs."[20] Indeed, for Parsons, the "same basic principle of cybernetic hierarchy," where information communicatively commands the expenditure of energy, and the reverse, was said to be "the fundamental basis for classifying the components of social systems."[21] Of particular importance was the communicative role of money as "a cybernetic mechanism at the symbolic cultural level," capable of integrating instrumental economic action within "the total society as a system."[22]

Parsons used the term "cybernetic hierarchy of control" to describe the orderly adjustment of rationally evolving social systems. In this sense, Parson's cybernetic functionalism combines Spencer's evolutionary viewpoint with ideas about adjustive feedback drawn from mid-twentieth-century biology. In Parsons' own words, his ideas about the evolution of social systems in their entirety "coincided with a set of developments within biological theory and in general science — notably the 'new genetics' and cybernetic theory — which indicated a far greater continuity between human socio-cultural evolution and that of the organic world than had been [previously] widely appreciated."[23] Parsons visualized a communicative exchange between information and energy as a core steering mechanism underlying evolutionary social development. "One source of change may be excesses in either information or energy in the exchange among action systems. In turn, these excesses alter the informational or energetic outputs across systems and within any system. For example, excesses of motivation (energy) would have consequences for the enactment of roles or the normative structure and eventually of cultural value orientations. Another source of change comes from an insufficient supply of either energy or information, again causing external and internal readjustments in the structure of action systems."[24] For example, informational conflict would cause normative conflict or anomie, which in turn would have consequences for the personality and organismic systems.

Inherent in Parson's cybernetic hierarchy of control are concepts that point to systemic interconnections between both stasis and change. If Parson's seemingly "neutral" depiction of social change, as a genetic-like mechanism of coded communicative adjustment, appears inattentive to the sacrificial exigencies of human historical struggles over the shaping of power, perhaps, this is because Parsons tautologically defines power as but the "capacity of a social system to mobilize resources to attain collective goals."[25] This ignores the effects of historically rooted social hierarchies and the struggles of people oppressed by unequal power. Such thorny issues are smoothed over by the fluid machinic metaphors of cybernetic theory. But as Arthur Kroker observes, this shift to a cybernetic concept of power signals "a grand reversal" in sociological understandings of the relation "culture and economy" and between "categories of power and capital."[26] Even when formulated in the crudest of Darwinian terms by Spencer, this conception already contained "the essential bourgeois discovery that political economy would now take place within a 'regulatory' order of dominations and powers."[27] A central aspect of Parson's massive contribution to the disciplinary character of North American sociology was the "normalization" of such a self-preserving system's logic. This represents an institutionally guided "descent into a virtual reality" where "all the referents, from money and power to health and intelligence" become coded as if "pure cybernetic processes."[28]

In reflecting upon his own interest in cybernetics, Parsons notes the influence of such "systems-oriented" biological theorists as Claude Bernard and W.C. Cannon. But the impressions made by Harvard biochemist L.J. Henderson were of particular significance. During the depression, Henderson's influential seminars on the Italian sociologist and economist Vilfredo Pareto underscored the role of living systems in the organization of all social forms and were attended somewhat religiously by a variety of thinkers, including Parsons, sociobiologist E.O. Wilson, and social scientists of various ilk, such as George Homans, Robert K. Merton, Henry Murray, and Clyde Kluckholm. "Henderson stressed the importance of Pareto's model of a social system and the notion of equilibrium in his teaching although it is also true that the Harvard physiologist's support for the Italian intellectual's ideas was connected to his anti-Marxist elitism. Henderson was an extreme conservative in his political views and saw Pareto's theory as many others with his opinions saw it — as the one social/economic theory which could counterpose Marxism in accounting for the depression."[29]

For Henderson, as for Parsons and many others who would soon develop an enthusiasm for cybernetics, Pareto's theories heralded "the commencement of a new era in the history of thought."[30] They also presaged a dissolving of informational boundaries between sociology, biology and economics. "That the America of the depression proved receptive to Pareto's thought is not surprising... [H]is work appealed to two major strains in the climate of opinion of the thirties: belief in the saving authority of science and loss of belief in the authority of tradition. [Time compresses into space; then the reverse.] His positivism appealed in an intellectual climate in which only the claims of science still stood unchallenged, and his debunking stance was congenial to intellectuals whose moorings had been severely shaken ever since the bottom dropped out of the stock market in 1929. [As a homeostatic systems theorist] Pareto was largely read as a kind of bourgeois answer to Marx."[31]

Parsons also acknowledged the impact of a continuing "Conference on Systems Theory" held in Chicago from 1952-57 and particularly the role of insect biologist Alfred Emerson who "spoke... in such a way as strongly to predispose me, and I think others, in favor of the then just emerging conceptions of cybernetic control."[32] Parsons was also a Kantian thinker who shared the idealist philosopher's dilemma concerning the difficulties of claiming universal knowledge from a strictly phenomenal point of view. And while Kant "solved" this dilemma by attending to the disembodied "genius" of sublime aesthetics, Parsons' cybernetic solution was of a related sort. Like Kantian thought, Christian metaphysics and ultramodern warfare, cybernetics too is "guided by an underlying compulsion to aesthetics."[33] In this, "the new genetic biology of combinants and recombinants contributes (analogically, it is true, but in the specific sense of structural similitude) to an interpretation of power as a 'site of battle' between genetic inheritance (the categorical imperative?) and the empirical 'range of variations' (the phenomenal world?)."[34] Here the body appears to disappear behind a coded screen of symbols. At long last, and during a Cold War no less, the word (of certain men) takes its place as more originary than flesh and moreover everlasting.[35] In the beginning was the word and the word was made flesh, states John's Gospel. Reducing bodily energies to that which is vocationed by information, cybernetics makes the same assumption. So does ultramodern capital.

Digitized Sacrifice, Delirious Flows: kitty cats, missiles and me

What (or who) is left out of the picture of the world we are in when the world itself is portrayed as if nothing but "pure cybernetic processes?" And what haunts this most powerful of late twentieth-century theoretical-fictions? The answer, according to Norbert Wiener, is the "evil" of chaos — the noise of disorganized forms and the entropic erosion of workable boundaries between "subject-objects" in communicative flux. To better understand this, as well as the dominant tendencies within cybernetic control mechanisms, let us return to Wiener's own statement of his theoretical-bodily delirium.

Wiener informs us that his anxiety was sparked by an inability (prompted by the onset of bronchopneumonia) to make clear distinctions between symbols and the objects they represented — an inability to distinguish between words and things. "It was impossible," he suggests, "to distinguish among my pain and difficulty in breathing, the flapping of the window curtain, and certain as yet unresolved points on the potential problem on which I was working." More disturbing was the cybernetician's inability to say whether this pain revealed itself as "a mathematical tension" or whether this mathematical tension was somehow symbolizing itself in the pain he embodied. Unable to clearly discern meaningful feedback about such matters because "the two were united too closely to make such a separation possible," Wiener worries about the randomness which overturns his search for knowledge. Indeed, it appears "that almost any experience may act as a temporary symbol for a mathematical situation which has not yet been organized and cleared up." In reflecting upon this delirious moment, Wiener grasps "one of the chief motives" which drives him toward cybernetics — the need to reduce an "unresolved discord" to "semipermanent and recognizable terms."

Wiener's biographer, Steve Heims agrees, observing at the core of the cyber-mathematician's personal and theoretical passions an obsession with "finding predictability through chaos or signal through noise."[36] But this was a difficult task for Wiener, convinced as he was by the theoretical vision of quantum physics, suggesting ongoing transformations between even the most seemingly solid of matters and the dynamic waves of energy which solid-state particles only temporarily congeal and contain. Wiener sought, through refinements of Gibbsian (non-linear) statistical computations, to provide a flexible mathematical basis for quantum mechanics. And through the communicative imagery of cybernetics provide a dynamic medium for mapping the transformative "interactions" which bind and unbind energy within always only relatively predictable material boundaries. In this, Wiener imagined himself advancing beyond Einstein's theories of relativity. From the cybernetic viewpoint, Einstein's ideas, like Newton's, remained burdened with "absolutely rigid dynamics not introducing the idea of probability. Gibbs' work on the other hand, is probabilistic from the very start, yet both directions represent a shift in the point of view of physics in which the world as it actually is replaced in some sense or other by the world as it happens to be observed."[37]

In truth, Wiener sought to reformulate Einstein's position, suggesting that, "In his theory of relativity it is impossible to introduce the observer without also introducing the idea of the message."[38] While clearly an advantage over "the Newtonian subordination of everything to [fixed] matter and mechanics," Einstein's reliance on observer-mediated measures of (one-way) optical radiation (from sender to receiver) limited the radicality of his theoretical discoveries. Wiener argued that Einstein's physics closely paralleled Leibnitz's pre-Newtonian notions of a lively universe of monads in optical (space-time distorted) communication with each other. This paralleled Leibnitz's own visual-theoretical fascinations with mechanical "clock-like" automata. For Leibnitz, the temporal "concordance" of these little dancing machines set in motion at the same point in time suggested a "pre-estab-lished harmony" of monads signaling to each other. Here, as in Einstein's image of light traveling from source to receiver, "the little figures which dance on the top of a music box... move in accordance with a pattern, but it is a pattern which is set in advance."[39] Wiener's cybernetic view of physics suggested something more "indeter-minate" and energetically "interactive." Whereas, Einstein's light waves and Leibnitz's dancing figures display "no trace of communication with the outer world, except "one-way... communication" guided by a "pre-established mechanism," the movement of things in the world in which Wiener found himself communicating appeared more complex — both computationally and ontologically.

This complex world Wiener shared with "moderately intelligent" animals, such as cute little kittens. Meow. Meow. "I call to the kitten and it looks up. I have sent it a message which it has received by its sensory organs, and it registers in action. The kitten is hungry and lets out a painful wail. [Pain again. Hum. Yes, pain seems a repeated feature of Wiener's cybernetic delirium. Whose pain?]... The Kitten bats at a swinging spool... This time it is the sender of a message... The spool swings to its left, and the kitten catches it with its left paw. This time mes-sages of a very complicated nature are both sent and received within the kittens own nervous system through nerve end-bodies in its joints, muscles, and tendons; and by means of nervous messages sent by the organs, the animal is aware of the actual position and tensions of its tissues. It is only through these organs that anything like a manual skill is possible."[40]

But accompanying Wiener and his hungry cyber-kitten is another kind of complex communicator — a new generation of flexible automata, the (mathemati-cal) configuration of which underscored the inadequacy of Einstein's and Leibnitz's lingering optic-mechanical rigidities. Unlike the older automata, which operated according to pre-programmed "clock-work," these new cybernetic machines — and believe me there are more each moment — are characterized as feedback-driven automata, possessing sensor organ functions as well taping-memory and translation-comparison capacities. This makes them "interactively" flexible in their command, control, and communicative capabilities. In 1950, Wiener included among their number "the controlled missile, the proximity fuse, the automatic door opener, the

control apparatus for a chemical factory, the rest of the modern armory of automatic machines which perform military or industrial functions." I mention this
hardly innocent of the machines through which I myself am sending messages to
you. Both the real ones and the imaginary.

In Wiener's cybernetic story all these machines face a common enemy —
entropy, chaotic disorganization, or noise — the villain of "the second law of
thermodynamics." Against this enemy Wiener pits the informational effectivity of
commanding communicative feedback. This facilitates the erection of a temporarily
"closed system," a "local enclave" against chaos, "whose direction seems opposed to
that of the universe at large and in which there is a limited and temporary tendency
for organization to increase."[41] But over time "entropy increases... and all closed
systems in the universe tend naturally to deteriorate and lose their distinctiveness"
as they move from (what Gibbsian statistics discerns as) "the least to the most
probable state, from a state of organization and differentiation in which distinctions
and forms exist, to a state of chaos and sameness."[42] But having stated this, Wiener
then makes a delirious leap from physics to a death-defying onto-theology, connecting the counter-entropic vocation of cybernetics to the writings of St. Augustine.
This, perhaps, is the most problematic aspect of Wiener's work. For by linking the
mission of his new science with the moral vision of Augustine, Wiener's writings
suggest a dangerous temptation within cybernetics to subordinate finite and
relational bodily matters to the infinitely commanding and abstract sign-work of
the soul.[43] Whose soul?

In this philosophical aspect of Wiener's work, cybernetics becomes a moral
science fitted to do battle against its evil arch enemy — disorganization. This
enemy, Wiener asserts, is not the Manichean devil with its crafty tricks of dissimula-
tion but "the Augustinian devil, which is not a power in itself, but the measure of
our own weakness."[44] But the "Augustinian devil is stupid." And while it "plays a
difficult game" of "passive resistance" to orderly communicative coding, "swamp-
ing" informational messages with the "noise" of unbounded energy, it is also a devil
defeated by a rigorous cybernetic "intelligence as thoroughly as by the sprinkle of
holy water."[45]

Here it is important to recall, even though Wiener makes no mention of this,
that one of the most arresting aspects of Augustine's theology is its fierce and
vehement expression of hatred for the flesh of women. And for pagans. But Wiener
mentions only Augustine's hatred of chaos, which he transcodes as a life-preserving
pursuit of clearly bounded flows of communicative feedback. In Augustine's
writings, chaos is figured in seductive and pagan-feminine forms. Evil forms. Pagan-
woman as chaos. Pagan-woman as evil. Pagan-woman as "gateway to the devil."[46]
This is a figure to be combated by closing the finite eye of the (masculine) flesh; all
the while, opening inwardly into an infinite mirror play of perfect Trinitarian
"three-in-One" identity. Perfectly the same and yet simultaneously different. A
perfectly informed communicative erasure of difference, this is also a fantasy of
timeless self-perpetuation. Pure autopoiesis. Pure simultaneity. Pure information. It

is infinitely easier to imagine, as is the case with both Augustine and Wiener, when no mother is involved. Or, when the only mother involved is a fleshless, holy ghostly info-mother. "Ma Bell" or whoever. No noise. No sin.

Wiener deliriously imagines cybernetics as a holy scientific weapon which uses the study of communicative feedback loops to both uncover and "exorcise" entropic noise. In this, he converts the little (counter-entropic) demons of Clerk Maxwell's nineteenth-century science into the informational angels guiding our own. As gatekeepers regulating the "useful" flow of otherwise ethereal energies, Maxwell's demons seemed to "overcome the tendency of entropy to increase" within defined communicative locales. But in sacrificially carving out protected pockets of organization these demons simultaneously threw the wider universe into disequilibrium. This is because neither humans nor other communicators ever truly exist in "isolated systems. We take in food, which generates energy, from the outside, and we are, as a result, parts of the larger world which contains those sources of our vitality."[47]

The same holds for Wiener's cybernetic angels, watching at the telelectronic doors of communicative feedback, securing the boundaries of some worlds against others, digitally transcoding energy into information. But at what or whose expense? This was a question Wiener continuously posed to himself and other cyberneticians. And with good reason. After all, Wiener's own work was situated within a very specific "local enclave" — the military-industrial-scientific web of Cold War capitalist America. This enclave was fighting, and in large measure with information, not merely against entropy in general, but against historical and material resistances to the systematic exploitation of the energies of others, as well as against tendencies for the rate of exploitative profit to fall.

Wiener's ethical vigilance about such matters initially inspired reflexive and critical scholars, such as Gregory Bateson, Anthony Wilden, Heinz Von Forrester, and Stafford Beers, to make use of cybernetic imagery and techniques in struggling for a more just and ecologically sane order of things. "Power-sensitive" cybernetic or cyborg imagery is also politically configured in the writings of numerous contemporary writers, some of who appear in this book. But, I feel, for worse more than better, Wiener's cybernetic delirium, as well as his Augustinian search for "closed systems," are today most materially embodied, for exploitative profit and control, within the dominant military-cultural institutions of corporate capital world-wide.[48] But this is less to dismiss cybernetics than to caution a reflexive, collective, and historically informed socio-economic engagement with the somewhat "hypnagogic," almost dreamy, loops of televisionary feedback which today interact so thoroughly with so much of our everyday lives. How, then, to effectively double back upon such cyber-social scenes of sacrifice, so as to better notice, communicate, and simultaneously expel the unjust and sickening flow of the energies these informational forms bind and those they exile, deplete, or deaden? The answers to this question are neither simple nor singular. They depend also on the feedback we give and receive from one another.

Having said all this, I leave you with a final bit of feedback from Norbert Wiener. And I wish you good cyborg dreams. In discussing his own "free-flowing" attempts to make imaginative theoretical sense of the "simultaneous aspect" of a problem, Wiener directs attention to certain moments when key aspects of the solution begin to crystallize.

"Very often these moments seem to arise on waking, but; but probably this really means that sometime during the night I have undergone the process of deconfusion which is necessary to establish my ideas. I am quite certain that at least part of this process can take place during what would ordinarily be described as sleep, and in the form of a dream. It is probably more usual for it to take place in the so-called hypnoidal state in which one is awaiting sleep, and it is closely associated with those hypnagogic images which have some of the sensory solidity of hallucinations but which, unlike hallucinations, may be manipulated more or less at will... The main ideas are not yet sufficiently differentiated to make recourse to symbolism easy and natural, they furnish a sort of improvised symbolism which may carry one through the stages until an ordinary symbolism becomes more possible and appropriate... What remains to be done is very often the casting aside of those aspects... that are not germane to the solution."[49]

Notes

1. Norbert Wiener, as quoted in Steve J. Heims, John Von Neumann and Norbert Wiener, *From Mathematics to the Technologies of Life and Death*. Cambridge, MA: MIT Press, 1980, pp. 147-148.
2. Arthur Kroker and Michael A. Weinstein, *Data Trash: the Theory of the Virtual Class*. New York: St. Martin's Press, 1994, p. 7.
3. Paul Virilio, *War and Cinema: the Logistics of Perception*. Minneapolis: University of Minnesota Press, 1990, pp. 4-6.
4. Norbert Wiener, *The Human Use of Human Beings: Cybernetics and Society*. London: Free Association Books, 1989 (1950), pp. 147-148.
5. Ibid., p. 24.
6. Norbert Wiener, *Cybernetics: or Control and Communication in the Animal and the Machine*. 2nd ed. Cambridge, MA: MIT Press, 1961, p. 11.
7. I here borrow the term, "power-sensitive," from Donna Haraway, who uses it to suggest a critical dimension of "situated" approaches to objectivity, as these work self-acknowledgedly within (or against) the grain of contextual configurations of power. See, for instance, *Simians, Cyborgs and Women: the Reinvention of Nature*. New York: Routledge, 1992, p. 196. Elsewhere I myself use the term, "power-reflexive," to indicate related methodological concerns. See, *Images of Deviance and Social Control: a Sociological History*. 2nd ed. New York: McGraw Hill Book Co., 1994.
8. My use of the term, "restrictive economic," invites a comparison between cybernetics and the social physics of Georges Bataille. Bataille, a contemporary of Wiener's, offers a theory of a "general economy" which, like cybernetics, situates the movements of life itself within a dynamic field of flowing intercommunications. Nevertheless, Bataille under-scores the limited and repressive character of restrictive economic communications, those which "usefully" establish "workable" boundaries between subjects and objects. Cybernet-ics restricts itself to the study of these "minor" communicative forms which, despite their utility, tragically limit the convulsive radiance of "major" communications. For Bataille, the vertiginous poetry of major communications is associated with the ecstatic realm of a more intimate "communion" with the abundant life energies. Bataille's model of commu-nication was thus spiral: suggesting periodic exchange, not only between identifiable beings "imprisoned" within the feedback loops of restrictive communicative forms — the stuff of everyday life — but also between minor and major forms of communication themselves — festive moments of sacred effusion where boundaries dissolve and beings dance undifferentiatedly as in "the flow of water or that of electric current." See, for instance, Georges Bataille, "Sacrifice," *October* 36 ((Spring 1986), pp. 61-74.
9. Steve J. Heims, John Von Neumann and Norbert Wiener, *From Mathematics to the Technologies of Life and Death*. Cambridge, MA: MIT Press, 1980, p. 184.
10. For a discussion of Wiener and von Neuman's wartime scientific contributions see, Steve Heims, John von Neumann and Norbert Wiener, *From Mathematics to the Technologies of Life and Death*. Cambridge, MA: MIT Press, 1980. Von Neumann, already a scientific advisor to the U.S. Army's Ballistics Laboratory in the years before the war, made strategic mathematical contributions to the development of digital computing machines, enabling the complex and high speed computations necessary for the design and production of the atomic bomb. Wiener, whose technical concerns with cybernetic feedback processes were

130   Digital Delirium

tempered by an ethical concern for the potentially "inhuman" uses of these same sources of knowledge, upon learning of the U.S. use of atomic weaponry withdrew entirely from military and governmental service, becoming somewhat of an "independent scholar" and never again accepting governmental funding for his continuing work with cybernetics.

11. Steve Heims, *The Cybernetics Group*. Cambridge, MIT Press, 1991, p. 17.
12. Yurik, *Metatron*, pp. 40, 74, 12.
13. Ibid., p. 3.
14. Norbert Wiener, The Human Uses of Human Beings, p. 17.
15. Donna Haraway, "The High Cost of Information in Post-World War II Evolutionary Biology: Ergonomics, Semiotics, and the Sociobiology of Communication Systems," *The Philosophical Forum*, Vol. XIII, Nos. 2-3, (Winter-Spring 1981-82), p. 249.
16. Haraway, "The High Cost of Information…," p. 246.
17. Ibid., p. 9.
18. Ibid., p. 249.
19. W. Ross Ashby, as quoted in Haraway, Ibid., p. 249.
20. Parsons, "A Paradigm for the Analysis of Social Systems," p. 172.
21. Ibid, p. 173.
22. Talcott Parsons, *Social Systems and the Evolution of Action Theory*. New York: The Free Press, 1977, p. 267.
23. Ibid., p. 238.
24. Jonathan Turner, *The Structure of Sociological Theory*. 5th ed. Belmont, CA: Wadsworth, 1991, p. 67.
25. Talcott Parsons, *Social Theory and Modern Society*. New York: The Free Press, 1967, p. 225.
26. Arthur Kroker, "Parsons' Foucault," in Arthur Kroker and David Cook, *The Postmodern Scene: Excremental Culture and Hyper-Aesthetics*. New York: St. Martin's Press, 1986, pp. 215-242.
27. Ibid., p. 216.
28. Arthur Kroker and Michael A. Weinstein, *Data Trash: the Theory of the Virtual Class*. New York: St. Martin's Press, 1994, p. 51.
29. Peter Hamilton, *Talcott Parsons*. London: Tavistock, 1983, pp. 59-60.
30. Lawrence J. Henderson, as quoted in Lewis A. Coser, *Masters of Sociological Thought*. 2nd ed. New York: Harcourt, Brace Jovanovich, 1977, p. 422.
31. Coser, *Masters of Sociological Thought*, p. 423.
32. Talcott Parsons, "On Building Social Systems Theory," *Daedalus*, (Fall 1970), p. 831.
33. Yurik, *Metatron*, p. 7.
34. Kroker, "Parsons' Foucault," p. 217.
35. Parsons' own complicity with Cold War political demands for information are perhaps themselves symptomatic of the place of cybernetics within a militarized U.S. metaphysics. Indeed, in the years immediately following World War II, at the request of the U.S. Army Intelligence and the State Department, Parsons engaged in a series of secret actions aimed at circumventing official government regulations by helping to recruit Russian-born Nazi collaborators, including a social scientist wanted as a "war criminal," in order to better

collect "cold war" information on the Soviet Union. See, for instance, Jon Wiener, "Talcott Parson's Role: Bringing Nazi Sympathizers to the U.S.," *The Nation*, 6 March 1989, cover page and pp. 306-309.)

36. Steve Heims, John Von Neumann and Norbert Wiener, pp. 146-147.

37. Norbert Wiener, *The Human Use of Human Beings*, p. 20.

38. Ibid., p. 20.

39. Ibid., p. 21.

40. Ibid, p. 22.

41. Ibid, p. 12.

42. Ibid.

43. My reading of Augustine here is, in part, suggested by Arthur Kroker and David Cook's provocative reading of Augustine as a precursor to the disembodying sign-power of the contemporary "postmodern scene." According to Kroker and Cook: "the postmodern scene in fact, begins in the fourth century with the Augustinian subversion of embodied power," as "the Augustinian refusal" presages a "fatalistic and grisly implosion of experience as Western culture itself runs under the signs of passive and suicidal nihilism." Arthur Kroker and David Cook, *The Postmodern Scene: Excremental Culture and Hyper-Aesthetics*. New York: St. Martin's Press, 1986, p. 8.

44. Ibid, p. 35.

45. Ibid.

46. See, for instance, discussions of these issues in Monica Sjoo and Barbara Mor, *The Great Cosmic Mother: Rediscovering the Religion of the Earth*. San Francisco: Harper and Row, 1987; John A. Philips, *Eve: The History of an Idea*. San Francisco: Harper and Row, 1984.

47. Ibid, p. 29.

48. See, for instance, Les Levidow and Kevin Robins, eds. *Cyborg Worlds: the Military Information Society*. London, Free Association Books, 1989; Chris Hables Gray, ed., with Heidi J. Figueroa-Sarriera and Steven Mentor, *The Cyborg Handbook*. New York: Routledge, 1995; and William Bogard, *The Simulation of Surveillance: Hypercontrol in Telematic Societies*. New York: Cambridge University Press, 1996.

49. Norbert Wiener, as quoted in Steve J. Heims, John Von Neumann and Norbert Wiener, p. 150.

Cybernetic Delirium: Two Remixes

Rupture Remix (verse-version)

Jace Clayton (a.k.a. /rupture)

182,000 jobs in motion. Seventy countries.
    Market value $64 Billion.
An
implosion
of   I'm led to image
   tears.
                        I love the advert tattooing your sex.
  You love my CK Infinity.
      Or so
I'm led to imagine.

      Day dream. On credit.
      This is cybernetic capital.
       This is ultramodern power.
      Adapt or
           you're toast.
  The smell f brnng flsh.
i-o-u
  (nobody not even the rain has such $mall hands

Rupture Remix: splice edit (4:20 event)

Sasha Costanza-Chock (a.k.a. Splice)

cybernetic capital
ultramodern power
ultramodern capital
cybernetic power

Melody and I had to run to the mall yesterday to get money for her ticket to Iphegania. Very high, we entered

cybernetic capital
ultramodern power
ultramodern capital
cybernetic power

time-out-of-time. This is what capital uses to stand in for the TAZ; this is an opposing pole or field; virtual space (dis)embodied: a dream-within-a-dream, nexu$ of power — the mall as a point at the conjunction of force lines that span the world. Magical capital, sacrificial altar, church, mosque, synagogue.

Spatial disorientation: mirrors on all sides and surfaces reflect each other into infinity and reflect spectacle into being. If the 3rd order simulacra is an image with no referent endlessly repeated, this is its home and vanishing point. It breeds and is born in the mall, transmits itself into the human host here. It is more of a feeling than a particular image, however.

This feeling is generated purposefully and encompasses all senses. Overwhelming empty spaces (mirrors and architecture, huge vertical hole surrounded by balconies of shops) demand filling, and they can only be filled by… goods, of course. This need is of course endless, insatiable; like the infinite reflections of vacuum that produce it, if it were real it could never be filled. The production of an unending de$ire.

Sound: this architecture also means that the mall is a giant resonating chamber. Awash in reverberation (which effect is used, in the conventions of cinema audio especially but any audio in general, to signify dreaming, intoxication, or flashbacks in time), all sounds in the space blend with one another in a muddy dance that obscures originary points, paths of travel, distances, and directions.

The size and shape of this space also produce, below everything and almost unnoticed but (because it is) omnipresent, a single, steady bass tone. This tone acts like a cushion or pillow, which works with the wet reverb to buffer the body against anything harsh, sudden, or uncomfortable. Tones like this make people relaxed; they are wonderful aids to falling asleep. They can be terrifying because they surround the body entirely, blurring its edges and stroking them sensually.

Time: there are, of course, no clocks to be seen; time here flows according to the passage of coins and bills.

cybernetic capital
ultramodern power
ultramodern capital
cybernetic power

We arrived at the cash machines. They have now all been replaced with the touchscreen model… I had been, the day before, at the MIT Media Lab Brain Opera open house, at which I played for a while with an interface based on the same technology — peizoelectric sensors that read the charge on the skin — but applied to music: a screen with liquid computer-generated image substrate that is played (it translates grid coordinates and pressure into alterations of a melody that plays over headphones) by drawing in this substrate with a finger. I learned that they were not entirely satisfied with this interface, partly because all technologies in the Brain opera are designed to be as non-intrusive as possible; the fact that people have to remove their gloves in order for the sensors to pick up the electric charge on the skin is a problem…

Gloveless, i entered my password on the ATM screen by pressing the proper screenal "buttons." Watching others around me, I fell deeply into a perception of our actions as identical to those of rats in a lab: press and take cash, press and take cash, press and take cash. Spend. Press and take cash, press and take cash, press and take cash. Work. Press and take cash, press and take cash, press and take cash. Spend…

cybernetic capital
ultramodern power
ultramodern capital
cybernetic power

As I plucked my $ from the metal lips of the machine, I looked up into the video eye. Behind me, the next person in line removed her gloves. I now noticed the plastic of the screen, dirty with fingerprints.

$erial numbers?   check.
video record?   check.
fingerprints?   check.

the owners of the lab keep very careful tabs on the rats.

cybernetic capital
ultramodern power
ultramodern capital
cybernetic power.

Zapatistas: The Recombinant Movie

Ricardo Dominguez

A people mute and brave are better than a people cultured and abject.

Maria Arias (Maria Pistolas) at
Madero's grave, August 1914

I'm thinking of making a movie about all this.

Oliver Stone

Black Screen.

(A Virus voice speaks between spasms of white noise).

Virus: "Recombinant politics calls for recombinant strains of disturbance at all levels. As screenal narratives become viral narratives — a new matrix of critical interventions are beginning to emerge. A process of polyspatial democratic movements who use methods of electronic civil disobedience to counter the nomadic bunkers of pan-capitalism."

The words "Rape Culture" appear on the black screen.

Cut to zoom-shoot.

(Jungle trail in Chiapas near Lake Pojaj. It is a hot night on October 26, 1995. In the distance one can hear the screams of woman being raped. It is companera Cecilia Rodriguez, United States citizen and legal representative of the EZLN in the US. Four laughing men surround her and kick her, one of them leans down and whispers in her ear.)

Man: "You already know how things are in Chiapas right? Shut up then, shut up, do you understand? Or you know what will happen to you…"

(On a jeep radio in the distance we hear an announcement that Journalist Fernando Yanez Munoz who was arrested on October 24, 1995 and accused of being a high ranking member of the EZLN had been released. Yanez, who was part of the Mexican rebel movement in the 1970s can be heard speaking.)

Yanez: "I have no links to the EZLN, though it would be an honour for me."

Cut.

(A reporter in front of the Mexican consulate in California on October 25,1995 interviews John Ross, who published an account of the Chiapas action, "Rebellion From the Roots.")

John Ross: "The Neo-liberal agenda manifested itself, again, as a shaky prop that always lives in fear of the truth. The Zapatistas without confirming or denying Yanez as one of them, stated that the arrest was in bad faith and threatened to end the peace talks. This caused the peso and Mexican stock market to tumble. On October 25, 1995 the Dow dropped 50 points in the US. The day after Yanez came out of prison the 'bolsa' and peso came up for air."

"This is Zedillo's most prolonged absence that he has dared to entertain since he took office. The arrest of Yanez may not be a stupid blunder by the local police; but that someone is out to derail the peace talks and embarrass Zedillo. The possibility of a military coup cannot be ignored."

Cut.

(November 4, 1995 a communique from the Indigenous Revolutionary Clandestine Committee arrives via the WEB and is read by a group of people in the cold basement of ABC NO RIO in New York. The camera pans the group.)

Group Member: "Third. The evil government is incapable of guaranteeing the security of any person in Chiapas despite maintaining dozens of thousands of soldiers, whose only goal is to assure the impunity of the powerful.

Fourth. In view of the fact that the law of the evil government does not do anything to address these situations, the EZLN has initiated the work of finding and taking prisoners those responsible for this and other similar aggression against women in Chiapas in order to judge them according to Zapatista laws.

Fifth. The EZLN adds its voice and its actions to that of the thousands of human beings who carry forward the demand for justice in all cases of aggression against women. We call upon all the men and women who, in Mexico and the world, struggle for democracy, liberty, and justice, in order that we mobilize with regard to this fundamental demand for all human beings: respect for women."

Cut to black screen.

(A Virus voice-over as the words "Speed Democracies" appear.)

Virus: "The disturbance of electronic bunkers with excess communication is an important act of radical emergence. The dissolution of informatic-economies will allow cells of electronic opposition-circuits to create speed-democracies. The Winter Palace is not being stormed, it is being dematerialized, as a state in ruins and the lines of flight lead towards liberated terminals. The Zapatistas accelerate the new possibilities of fractal politics by displacing the signature-effect of Domain block-age.

Spaces of information must be disassembled and reconstituted as replicating networks of decolonization through the naming of free civil digital spaces. These free electronic spaces will be constructed of excessive communication and unlimited counter-memories — and no longer as part of the hyperamnesiac-hierarchies of information. As a memo from the Rand corporation stated: "institutions can be defeated by networks, and it may take networks to counter networks." To become effective speed-democracies, we must continue to puncture the smooth-state by whatever means necessary."

Cut to Cecilia Rodriguez.

(She is speaking to a large gathering of people in front of the Mexican Consulate in El Paso, Texas under a clear blue sky on November 12, 1995.)

Cecilia: "I know three Tzeltal women were raped at a military checkpoint, and three nurses were raped and almost killed at the site of the peace talks, San Andres Larraninzer. How many other women whose stories we do not know have suffered through this hell? Women who have never said anything publicly because they fear for their lives.

I have decided to make a public statement because I hope my experience will illustrate the brutal nature of the low-intensity war being waged in Chiapas. I am one more piece of evidence of the use of sexual violence as a weapon specifically directed against women in this war.

I ask for justice — not from the governments of the United States and Mexico because they are complicit in this war — but from the people of Mexico and the United States. Look into my suffering and multiply that by hundreds of women, men and children whose voices you do not seem to hear, who suffer on a daily basis the humiliation of a low-intensity war which intends to suffocate the very human aspirations for democracy, liberty and justice."

Fade to Black.

(The words "Rituals of Chaos" appear on the black screen.)

Cut to a beetle crawling over the remains of a dead body.

(As the beetle moves in and out of the corpse, the Virus speaks.)

Virus: "Fractal politics crashes the imaginary of total State command and control with a counter-net dissolution which disrupts and erodes the hierarchies around which institutions are normally designed. It diffuses and redistributes power to dispersed cells who communicate, consult, coordinate, and operate on a polyspatial basis. Between real events outside of the macro-panoptic flow of data and excess information — counterhegemonic disturbances spread. Netwar is most the effective form of both defensive and offensive decentralized activism.

"Counter Intelligence Programs, COINTELPRO, are being reconfigured as anti-network forces whose aim is to neutralize nodes that promote participation in engendering an 'excess of democracy' on both a local and global level. States in the last few years have began to map out possible methods to limit digital autonomy: Italy, an Anti-Crime group shut down 'BITS Against the Empire,' a node on

Cybernet and Fidonet; United Kingdom, The Terminal Boredom (BBS) was raided by police; Germany, the State attempts to stop access to RADIKALL, small anti-State electronic journal; United States, several new bills (S390 and HR896) with bipartisan backing are before Congress that would give full legal force to COINTELPRO actions against electro-political networks; Senators Exon (D-NE) and Gordon (R-WA) are pushing a bill (S314) that would hold internet providers criminally liable for the activities of their subscribers."

Cut to a hand picking up the beetle.

(As the beetle crawls over a series of brown hands the voice of Subcomandante Insurgente Marcos is heard.)

Marcos: "In the mirror, chaos is a reflection of the logical order and the logical order a reflection of chaos.

"I don't remember the name of the movie (maybe the masters, Siskel and Ebert, remember) but I do remember that the main actor was Peter Fonda. I remember the plot clearly. It was about a group of brilliant Harvard students who raped a woman. She accused them in a public hearing and they responded that she was a prostitute. Their lawyer defended them by using their grades and good families. They're found innocent. The woman commits suicide. As adults, the 'juniors' look for stronger emotions and they dedicate themselves to hunting down vacationing couples on weekends... after the standard rape, the 'juniors' free the couple in the countryside and hunt them down with shotguns.

"I don't remember the ending, but it's one of those where justice is done, Where Hollywood resolves on the screen what in reality often goes unpunished.

"Today, the real 'juniors' have found that they have a country to play with. One of them is at Los Pinos (the Mexican White House) and the other in Bucareli (The Governor's house in Chiapas). They get tired of playing DOOM and instead play at hunting down 'bad guys' in a game of real war in the countryside. They give their prey time to escape, and move their game pieces to surround them and make the game more interesting. But, the 'juniors' find themselves in a quandary, because the game grows longer and they can't catch the 'bad guys.' Then the US Ambassador, the lawyer from the first scene, tries to save them again: 'It was just a game' he says, 'the dead are not dead, the war is not a war, the displaced are not displaced, we always wanted to talk and we only sent thousands of soldiers to tell the 'bad guys' that we wanted to talk.' A pathetic argument for an 'efficient' Harvard government.

"Meanwhile, reality approaches... and the mass media tries to impose itself on reality. Forgetfulness begins to populate the government discourse; they forget the fall of the stock market, the devaluation, the 'negotiations' of San Andres as a window dressing to hide the true indigenous politics of neoliberalism, instability, jealousy and distrust, ungovernability and uncertainty. They forget the principal objective, according to Machiavelli; they've had no results, they've not been 'efficient.'

"In the mirror, chaos is a reflection of logical order and the logical order a reflection of chaos."

Cut to black.

("Fourth Declaration of the Lacandon Jungle" appears on the screen.)

Fade into a painting of Zapata. The camera pulls back. We see President Zedillo at his desk.

("JANUARY 1, 1996. 12:01 A.M." appears on the screen. He stares into the air as he taps his fingers and listens to the Reader.)

Reader: "The flower of the world will not die. The masked face which today has a name may die, but the word which came from the depth of history and the earth can no longer be cut by the ears with its cannons."

(Zedillo opens his top desk drawer and finds a remote control. He aims the remote at the camera and the sound of the opening chords of a *Dynasty* rerun are heard. He reclines back and smiles.)

"The arrogant wish to extinguish a rebellion which they mistakenly believe began in the dawn of 1994. But the rebellion which now has a dark face and an indigenous language was not born today. It spoke before with other languages and in other lands. This rebellion against injustice spoke in many mountains and many histories. It has already spoken in nahuatl, paipai, kiliwa, cucapa, otomi, mazahua, maltatzinca, ocuilteco, zapoteco, solteco, chatino, papabuco, mixteco, cucateco, triqui, amuzzgo, mazateco, chocho, ixcaateco, hauve, tlapaneco, totonaca, tepehua, populuca, mixe, zoque, huasteco, lacandon, mayo, chol, tzeltal, tzotzil, tojolabal, mame, teco, ixil, aguacateco, motocintleco, chicomucelteco."

(Zedillo reaches down and brings up a half eaten bag of Fritos and begins to shove them into his mouth.)

"Ignoring Article 39 of the Constitution which it swore to uphold on December 1, 1994 the supreme government reduced the Mexican Federal Army to the role of an army of occupation. It gave it the task of salvaging the organized crime which has become government... Meanwhile, the true loss of national sovereignty was concretized in the secret pacts and public economic cabinet with the owers of money and foreign governments. Today, as thousands of federal soldiers harass and provoke a people armed with wooden guns and the word of dignity, the high officials finish selling off the wealth of the great Mexican Nation and destroy the little that is left.

"Three new initiatives were launched by the Zapatistas as responses to the success of the Plebiscite For Peace and Democracy. An initiative for the international arena expresses itself in a call to carry out an intercontinental dialogue in opposition to neoliberalism. The two other initiatives are on a national character: the formation of civic committees of dialogue whose base is the discussion of the major national problems and which are the seeds of a nonpartisan political force; and the construction of the new Aguascalientes as places for encounters between civil society and Zapatismo."

(An American Express Card commercial comes on and Zedillo begins to channel surf.)

"Today, with the heart of Emiliano Zapata and having heard the voice of all our brothers and sisters, we call upon the people of Mexico to participate in a new stage of the struggle for national liberation and the construction of a new nation, through this Fourth Declaration of the Lacandona Jungle in which we call upon all honest men and women to participate in the new national political force which is born today: the Zapatista Front of National Liberation... a civil and nonviolent organization, independent and democratic, Mexican and national... and we extend an invitation to participate in it to the factory workers of the Republic, to the laborers of the countryside and of the cities, to the indigenous peoples, to the colonos, to teachers and students, to the honest artists and intellectuals, to responsible priests and nuns, and to all the Mexican people who do not seek power, but rather democracy, liberty, and justice for ourselves... We are here. We do not surrender. Zapata is alive, and in spite of everything, the struggle continues."

(Zedillo ends his drift with the sound of Clinton saying that he supports of implementation of the Clipper Chip 2 project in order to protect the people.)

Cut to a Mexican mural with the words "The Hallucinogenic-State" in red is scrawled across it with a spray can.

A slow pan across the entire work.

Virus (voice-over): "Pan-capitalism is a crack war of narco-colonialism which enframes the neo-liberal relaxation of exchange between the PRI party and nomadic investment communities. The War-on-Drugs is the main NAFTA artery of exchange for the Colombian cartels of coke and heroin into the urban markets. Drug-enforcement-economies must command and control body-rights and land-rights in Chiapas — this foundational drive of the hallucinogenic-State."

Cut to black and white images of Oliver Stone's *Nixon* in fast forward.

(We hear John Tesh on Entertainment Tonight speaking, it's March 25, 1996.)

John Tesh (voice-over): "Mr. Stone will be meeting with Mexican rebels instead of in Hollywood for the Oscars. Oliver Stone said he was thinking of making a film about the rebels as soon as his finishes his next project. He also would like to meet Subcomandante Marcos. Edward James Olmos is also making a pilgrimage, so is Lady Danielle Mitterrand, and the rebels have just turned down a Benetton modeling contract. Mary, who knew that electronic disturbances could be so much fun!"

Cut to a still image of the Wall Street skyline.

(We hear bombs, gunfire, and the screams of people in the distances.)

Virus (voice-over): "Can the hallucinogenic-State be resisted hallucinogenically? Is electronic activism a mirroring of State-logic as a tool for developing better counter-insurgency networks?"

Cut to a map of Southern Mexico, the words "Popular Revolutionary Army Attacks" stamped on it.

(We hear Mr. Arreolo, a taxi diver in Hautuloc, Mexico, on August 30, 1996.)

Arreolo (voice-over): "They commandeered my taxi, but it doesn't bother me — these people want to change the government, right? Well, I say I'm all for that! But, I'm afraid that the police will accuse me of collaboration. I don't want trouble with anybody, not with the masked ones, and not with the police. I just want to live here quietly."

Cut to a photograph of soldier standing and saluting, with the words "Mexicans across the political spectrum say the rebels pose no real threat" stamped on it.

Dr. Estevez (voice-over): "They seem to have more money and are more heavily armed than in Chiapas. They came fast and vanished even faster into the mountains of Oaxaca. The fighters have the feet of peasants who work barefoot — but they also had good boots — American maybe. They spoke like Marxists, not like Zapatistas — but, they do have the backing of the coastal peasants. When I was stitching the foot of one of the rebels, a group of peasants brought them a case of soft drinks, mostly Cokes."

Cut to a can of Coke with the words "We often see people dressed in military-style clothing here" stamped on it.

Gonazlo Montoya (voice-over): "As the police commander in Tacambaro I know these armed men who attacked the military convoy on August 30, 1996 were narcotic traffickers. They all attacked military outpost in Guerrero and Chiapas. At this moment we are arresting individuals on suspicion of being members of the group and also those who are part of above-ground peasant and worker organizations we have identified as fronts for the Popular Liberation Army. We are going to try to make a distinction between the Zapatistas and this new group — if we can."

Cut to a computer screen on which the words "A call for a marcha virtual" appear.

(We hear a Japanese woman read as subtitles in English scroll across the screen.)

Japanese Reader (voice-over): "Action Alert: October 7, 1996. The government of Mexico has taken a rigid stance against the Zapatista Delegation travelling to the National Indigenous Congress, threatening punitive action if the Zapatistas leave Chiapas.

"Mexican Civil Society has called for a 'marcha virtual' to show International support for including the Zapatistas in national dialogues towards peaceful solutions to Mexico's crisis. Given the fact that members of the EZLN travelling to Mexico City are Mexican citizens, and are thus guaranteed by the Mexican Constitution the freedom to travel unencumbered anywhere in the Republic, and given the fact the Mexican government does not consider them criminals or terrorists, and that the San Andres Dialogue, and the agreements which govern it, although on hold, have not been broken, it is extremely important to pressure the Mexican Government. We are also asking that you forward this message to all lists, groups, and individuals liable to participate in the this march, in order to show that we in Cyberspace can mobilize to form "war of the Internet" (Gurria dixit) in the service of PEACE."

Cut to a folded Mexican flag and a single fuchsia rose. Beneath them the date: October 12, 1996.

(We hear about 2000 people screaming "the struggle continues".)

Then on the top of the image the words "Tzotzil Woman Arrives" appear.

William Means (voice-over): "Commandante Ramona walked out of the Lacondona and into the heart of Mexico City. The PRI government did not want this to happen, and on October 8 they even threatened to arrest any Zapatista that attempted to leave the military cordon. Subcommmadante Marcos said, 'she is the most belligerent, aggressive and intransigent member of the Zapatista Army for National Liberation and before dying she wanted to speak to other Indians.'"

Juan Cuellar (voice-over): "I brought my daughter to the Zocalo to see this small fragile woman demolish 500 years of enslavement. She is a bomb of tenderness. She is a bomb of patience. Beneath the ski-mask; my child's future. Long Live Ramona, Sweet Rebel!"

Cut to a black screen. The word "Punctum" appears.

Virus (voice-over): "Commandante Ramona is an event that punctures the bunker of containment as a trace of mourning empowering the ignored. She is a virtual line of flight that names the real condition of fractal politics — death or the invention of a new form of democracy. She is a virus for polyspatial systems of representation which can disturb the telematic force of pan-capitalism. Viva Ramona. The struggle continues."

Fade to black.

Hyperreal Serbia

Aleksandar Boskovic

The refusal of the ruling party to recognize the results of the November 1996 municipal elections and the mass protests that arouse as a consequence of it, have propelled Serbia into the spotlight of world media attention. Until recently, the only media images that Serbs could expect to get were the ones of bloodthirsty war criminals, since an overwhelming majority of them wholeheartedly supported savage wars (by the Serbs and in the name of Serbs) that raged on the territory of the former Yugoslavia between 1991 and 1995. However, there is obviously more to Serbia than meets the eye of the media.

Serbia is today the only truly *hyperreal* country in the world. Actually, along with tiny Montenegro, it forms a new, rump, Yugoslavia. The problem with this Yugoslavia (officially known as "FR Yugoslavia") is that it does not really exist. This is not a view of some Serb-hating sceptic, but of the foremost Serb legal expert, Prof. Pavle Nikolic. The legal basis of the "FR Yugoslavia" is its Constitution, and the current one, from April 27, 1992, is actually unconstitutional. That is to say, it was voted for in an illegal way by the people who had no legal right to vote for it. It is almost as if I met with some of my friends in New Orleans and decided to declare it independent. We could, of course, probably write something that would resemble a Constitution, but that would not necessarily make our product *a state*.

Another point to be made is that the citizens of Serbia and "FR Yugoslavia" still use passports of the former country, SFR Yugoslavia, *a country which does not exist any more*. Its non-existence is proved empirically by the new countries that were established as a result of its dissolution — Slovenia, Croatia, Macedonia, Bosnia and Herzegovina, *and FR Yugoslavia*. Thus, through its claim to existence, the "FR Yugoslavia" also denies the existence of the former country (SFR Yugoslavia), but still uses its passports, with the state symbols and coat of arms of a country that simply does not exist any more. The citizens do not seem to notice or to mind.

Foreign countries still honor these strange passports. On the other hand, international institutions both recognize FR Yugoslavia (European countries have full diplomatic relations), and regard it as a strange semi-existent entity (thus, it is not a member of the UN, IMF, World Bank, etc.).

The attitude of the majority of Serbs can be described as hyperreal as well. On the one hand, the official propaganda kept claiming that Serbia and Serbs were not at war, and that they have nothing to do with wars. On the other hand, the graveyards are suddenly full of men of military age, and there is a growing feeling of concern and anxiety. As Baudrillard would say, the war never happened. However, the consequences of the war are more than obvious, with the completely ruined economy, and the country on the verge of social unrest. Serbs are also facing the image of themselves as bloodthirsty nationalists as soon as they travel abroad. The truth that the Western viewers had about the wars does not quite match the truth that the Serbs had access to through the tightly controlled media. For example, according to the Serbian media, Bosnians just kept slaughtering themselves, and blaming Serbs afterwards. Serbs were always portrayed as the people who defend themselves, creating strange situations when exalted TV journalists were claiming ("live") that "our brave defenders of that village are on the verge of taking the enemy town."

In everyday life, there is a growing feeling that the war (especially the one against Croatia) has been lost. However, how can a country lose a war in which it never participated? This creates some strange situations and a lot of anxiety regarding Croats as neighbors and Croatia as a country with which Serbia (as a part of FR Yugoslavia) has full diplomatic relations.

These frustrations and anxieties were certainly contributing factors in the mass protests on the streets of all the major cities in Serbia. The protests kept an almost carnivalesque atmosphere, with lots of colors (flags of various countries, as well as the Ferrari flag and the Japanese Imperial war flag), noise (whistles, horns, trumpets, drums, etc.), and decent rock 'n' roll music. At some moments, particularly during the protests organized by Belgrade students, it all constituted a mockery of the current Serbian regime and the police forces that have, since Dec. 26, virtually occupied Belgrade. There is an unofficial martial law going on — with police occasionally banning people from walking in the very center of Belgrade. Officially, this is done in order to enable traffic through the center of the city. However, in reality, police forces themselves are enacting the most effective traffic blockade.

Although all the protests have been peaceful, this did not prevent police from overreacting. People were savagely beaten, arrested (one young man has been sodomized in police custody), and sent to jail for offences such as *having thrown an egg* (with the duly noted fact that there was no damage inflicted). In the most brutal police assault so far, in the night of Feb. 2, police were beating and arresting people who had a whistle, wore a badge, or had a pair of sneakers. It does not matter what you do in Serbia, it is much more important (especially when confronted with the representatives of the law and order) *what you wear*. In the future, this might enable companies like Nike or Reebok to advertise their products as being especially effective in running from the Serbian police. It seems that one does not have to do anything in order to be savagely beaten or arrested in Serbia. All one should do in order to provoke the forces of law and order in Serbia (who are equipped like RoboCops) is to simply exist. As things stand now, the least that one could expect from the hyperreal country is to be governed by a hyperreal police. Unfortunately, its violence seems all too real.

Berlusconi is a Retrovirus
From the Italian theory-fiction novel

Lorenzo Miglioli

The Holy Inquisition (knowledge as a form of extortion), Nazism (knowledge as a form of indirect extortion, as an experiment), Pol-Pot (knowledge as a form of erasing/extermination of the actors for the sake of the scene) are pure and simple transcriptions, horror vacui *translated into horror written on the flesh... Writing, text of the unknowable translated into horror of/on/in the flesh. Symptom of a knowledge destined to go beyond the species as a depository of that knowledge.*
    Mutation is the basis of everything: Its control is the purpose. The most sensational mutation is death: Is the control of mutation also the control of death?

A short summary

The novel tells the story of a group of sociologists who meet in a country cottage to have dinner together, a reunion. As everybody knows, people like to talk around a table and often play games, thus creating a parallel world with its own rules, separate while at the same time simulating the external world. A sort of meta-Noah's Ark.

Keep in mind that the language/map of sociology has been fully overcome by information, which is too fast and therefore frustrating for it. While they are talking they realize that they are tired of babbling. It's time for action. A very particular kind of action: similar to the pioneering era of cultural anthropology, which evolved from theory to field research, and the epic era of guerrilla movements that aroused the romantic and pure hearts of millions of potential revolutionaries. They call this the *Malinowski-Guevara Experience*. At this point they develop the idea of simulating a (memetic) terrorist attack (terrorism being the essence of memesis itself... information hard-core) against the man who better than anyone else represents this symbolic, metaphoric and memetic media pornography.

Psycho-terrorism that goes beyond science fiction as inspirational carpet, as nutritional ground, but towards the theory-fiction as ontological guerrilla, as if it is a new pasture for research (a literary pasture).

A kidnapping!

Who is the Man?

How will they recognize Him?

Towards the end, the sociologists, trying to go beyond their chit chat, decide to simplify and organize their analysis by comparing the body of the nation to that of a human being. Trying to isolate and define the primary infection (calling this **The A.I.D.S.™ Experience**); the cause of memetic degradation into which the nation is falling.

After a night of discussion they single out Silvio Berlusconi, the Italian media tycoon. Berlusconi represents to them a real worldwide experiment of memetic contamination by means of the media and politics.

The decision is made but... no longer tired of talking, words are becoming molecules of a very particular drug, a sort of metaphorine... they feel like new technopagan Gods, very powerful, very memetically omnipotent... until dawn... it was good role play... they say goodbye and the great veil of light brings back order... removal... end...

This short pamphlet-novel, written in 1993, a few months before Berlusconi entered politics, is still often quoted by the Italian Media. A sort of literary prediction. It was inspired by the need to give an interpretation to what seemed like a big push in the "quality" of mimetic (and memetic) contamination of the relation between media power and politics. The ineluctable ascent of Silvio Berlusconi: the king of Italian private media and one of the world leaders in this sector, with extensive associates and allies throughout Europe and parts of the United States.

The style of the novel is like that of a continuous talk-show. The sociologists do not appear by name, they are simply identified by quotation marks. The plot is replaced by direct speech. It might even be a single person simulating many people; a multi-character personality. Hence the exchange is argumentative; the subject is deprived of any existence other than a linguistic one... pure code... symbolism... literature mimetically and memetically contaminated by television in an evolution-ary-like replicant style...

Why Berlusconi? If ever memetics represented something theoretically or analytically trustworthy, if the epidemiology of memetic reproduction means anything, Berlusconi is certainly evidence for its viral character. The shift from entertainment to subtle publicity, from politics to subtle publicity, has transformed a viral into a retroviral infection. It was in the early 1980s, Berlusconi's era, that the human species accepted a new standard of reality: retro-reality (retromemetics). Reality became more bizarre than fiction. All you had to do was imagine and then describe it. In fact, it is through the fiction of his own media that Berlusconi created a new imagery. A new principle of reality, agenda-setting for the masses. His own television stations determine what we shall talk about in our country.

The big turning point of anti-politics. Berlusconi is always repeating that he sees the nation as a company. A bridge connecting liberal and virtual capitalism and also a bridge leading to classical fascism. He gave life and credibility to Mussolini's children and retro-fascism... Parliament was described in his own words as a useless slow coach. He claimed for himself the hard core of power, again pure pornography; he could not tolerate the parliamentary soft-core. He founded a company-party, where his own presidency was not voted on by any internal committee or any other democratic means. His relations with people close to the mafia, with shady politicians, with deviant masonry are put aside since the management of the nation's desire is potentially in his hands.

This memetic turning point was brought about by Berlusconi's real-time success, after he had been memetically contaminating his political electorate for ten years (1984-1994). He received 30% of the votes two weeks after having put himself up for election; apparently starting from zero, but in reality exploiting the opportunistic infection of his TV palimpsest (soap operas, faithful anchormen, popular national shows, crude satire, ridiculous soft-porn etc.). Like unsafe sex that now seems to have become popular with the clients of the prostitutes who come to Italy in thousands from the East or Africa and who are then shackled and enslaved. Among these the positive-serum has become the rule... the client wants sex without using condoms, paying more, much more... a suppression of the instinct for the immunological defense of the species for the sake of pleasure... it's the death of love as evolutionary energy. In this sense, a relationship between media and virology. The central and fundamental theme of the novel-pamphlet.

The chapter reproduced here covers the moment when the sociologists discover and define what they are talking about.

Berlusconi is a Retrovirus

"So then, I think we should reconsider the way we interpret everything. The metaphor we have used so far is strictly connected to the parameters of physics as a discipline, as an organization of matter. After years and years of overflowing complexity — mentioned, experienced, spoken, defined — we still behave as if the causal principle were the constant in the passing variable of a complexity that someone thinks, and tries, to say in other, simpler words, if... then: a still-too-mechanicist logic. Mechanically mechanic. On the contrary, we should be moving towards a biological way of thinking; mechanics, yes, no way out, but organic, organicist, mechanics. A more interactive, enzymatic way of telling stories, where the author physically communicates and interacts not only with the reader and the user, but also with the main character of the story. The kidnapped one, in this case. We are pathological — not plastic — surgeons. This is the point of the argument. Already many scientists studying complexity are examining things in this perspective to understand and talk about them. It is our task to give this a concrete form. Because at this point, owing to the speed we are moving at, we are forced to read everything directly in evolutionary terms, place everything on Darwin's microscope slide and, why not, even on Lamarck's. It is now obvious that the slightest change can alter the development of the whole human species, for better or worse — provided good and bad are still meaningful."

"So... Italy as a mimetic organism? Immunology, metabolism, sensoriality — and so on — instead of the more traditional sociological categories? Metaphor and allegory instead of statistical monitoring? Funny... then, to make sense we should become eco-terrorists... this dinner is turning into a tragicomic D&D game..."

"Meme-terrorism... what if genetics became a pidgin?"

"I'm afraid we're late here..."

"...as I was saying, if we moved to this type of analysis, considering the State as a real body — organic, anthropomorphic and even anthropocentric. Identical in function and existence to a human being. Then we should have no choice but to look for a disorder, the disorder of the body — a kind of symbol-disorder — give it a name, isolate it, and then find a vaccine and — if possible — commercialize it at the libido level..."

"...Lacan royalty payments... 'we are always talking about neurobiology ...'"

"So, what should we look for? Homo Cancer? Homo Tumor? Homo Thrombosis ? Homo Leukemia? A homo sapiens who can turn an idea into something living... use the vital energies of alien structures and convert it for his own use and consumption... a wicked man, a man..."

"Satanic meme... I am the most malevolent person imaginable. The one who shatters the sense of reality; 'I invalidate and replicate it for my own purposes. Mine will replace the species'. My egogenesis is the greatest, the fullest, the most super..."

"Virus... we have to look for Homo Virus. The virus that invades your body before you can spot it... the one that mentions you before you can mention it, that looks at you before you can see it. That knows what you are going to be, before you even have an inkling. The individual emerging from the bacterial revolution revealed through the information continuum..."

"The only pure viral form I can think of at the moment is God."

"We, as humans, are at a sub-god level, molecules, atoms... our configuration is small — little sight, slow hearing... but we can simulate higher configurations and probably inform this heavenly matter..."

"Hey, wait a minute, we are talking of an informational revolution, of the numerical revelation of sub-matter, of media viruses; let us try to be practical — we are not going to get anything out of it, otherwise — we are talking of men — media-viruses we ought to fight against and destroy before they extinguish us. Well then, there has been an evolution of the bacterial stock, of the virus population... it's like a mirror... a terrible evolution that could actually destroy the human species in a few decades."

"What do you mean?"

"I'll tell you... the Retrovirus... with the advent of the retrovirus, at the code level, it is as if the Great Virus Nation, that includes all invisible creatures, had synchronously discovered both writing and interstellar travels — an incredible evolution, a generational gap — whereas the other viruses, the ones at the previous stage, could just babble genetically predetermined guttural sounds. It's as if there was a purpose, a grand design that simulates consciousness, teleology, finality. The global thinking virus, a sort of bacterial gaia. In this perspective, I think — and I trust you will agree — that television is a retrovirus, it works like one. It is the one and only means from which we can draw a useful analysis."

"Go on..."

"Let us assume that every civilization, every century, has its own peculiar disease as a metaphor of communication. There have been the plague, smallpox, cancer and now AIDS. And each of these super-epidemics has influenced the imagination of the particular century. Its own narratives and narrative modes, its own perceptions and perceptive modes. What bothers me is that the Great Virus Nation seems to go far beyond this, living a life beyond our perception, it does not need our imagination to be read... it does not live in our legends, myths, it affects us like a pagan deity in 4D, a new reality principle... I will read you an extract from a novel written in collaboration... A piece I found surfing the Internet... it contains some difficult and specialized terminology, but on the whole I found it interesting and enlightening:

Dr. H was meditating on the words he had just read for the tenth time. Something was waiting for him at the end of that mental exercise. Something shapeless but less and less illegible. He knew the words by heart: in 1978, a decade after the discovery of the Reverse Trascriptase effect (when a retrovirus infects a cell, its Reverse Trascriptase immediately synthesizes a DNA mirror molecule which corresponds to the virus RNA code. This mirror DNA makes its way to the nucleus of the cell where it inserts itself, integrating amongst the genes of the host. A marvellous mediologic and memetic trap! Genetics and memetics working together in a viral evolution matrix), Prof. Ragallo managed to isolate the first human retrovirus. He called it the T-lymphotrope virus, because it manifested an attraction, also called Tropism, for the T-lymphocyte — white globules that play a crucial role in the modulation of immune responses. It has been codified as HTLV-I. A few years later other retroviruses were discovered, such as the second lymphotrope virus, HTLV-II, in 1982, which can be responsible for leukemia. But the most disturbing discovery was made in 1983/84, when they realized that the agent that causes the acquired immune deficiency syndrome (AIDS) was one of these viruses, HTLV-III. Why didn't biologists understand what they had in front of them? Why didn't the ancient Greeks invent the steam ship even if they had fire, water and the wheel? Maybe because they had a sort of veil in front of their mental eyes, an opaque screen, a surrounding body that confused the most important vision: this was the Endogenous Retrovirus; i.e., what one often discovers in the genetic material of many animal species as a residue of an old infection. All retrovirus diseases discovered so far are caused by exogenous viruses (they came from outer space!!). Exogenous viruses are of external origin whereas endogenous ones remain an evolutionary enigma. It was, once again, a matter of Visionary Perception, the art of perceiving the imperceptible. The microscope was no longer good enough to reveal the identity of the retrovirus. A new way had to be found. And a new means. This was the first great intuition: the human vision of the time was unable to show us what was to be seen. We had to become specialized in a new form of vision.

Could retroviruses exploit a different carcinogenic mechanism which did not require an extensive viral replication? If this was the case, then the electron microscope was no longer sensitive enough to pick up their traces. And clinicians had to rely on the lottery of symptoms, on a relative, virtual interpretation. Just like marines under friendly fire, shooting at each other in the jungle while the enemy lets them get on with it, until they are weak enough to be finished off. An information war: those who can see know, and those who cannot see do not know. But the problem was, the retrovirus went far beyond our vision, far beyond our ability to read and decode. A new perceptive ability was required. But if the question is no longer human, can the answer be such? And, not just any answer, can the crucial answer still be human?

"There..."

"Incredible... as if it was written for us... is there any more?"

"Go on..."

"Yes, there is another interesting passage... here it is..."

And from the nothing of the existing, unread, ergo undiscovered, came the Growth Factors, proteins that can stimulate the growth, in a laboratory, of other cells, but are reluctant to do so. In vitro cultivation was ready to start. And it became possible to discover that all the isolated viruses were not strictly related to previously isolated animal viruses and that they were not endogenous but exogenous. Of course, owing to the peculiar issue connected to the HIV-AIDS retrovirus, things got quite complicated as the Provirus (an intermediary between DNA and the virus itself) entered the cell as a clone mechanism — exactly like a classical tumor in the acknowledged neoplasias — and this had crucial evolutionary and metaphorical consequences: what most unsettled the minds of the first discoverers was the lack of uniformity in patients affected with ATL (leukemia of the adult T-lymphocyte). In each case the viral sequences were differently positioned. This meant there was an ongoing strategic super-evolution on the part of the viral species or their substitutes. The replizombie assumed a life of its own, just like those it represented or replaced: the matrixes, the other organisms, living, organic, native. Cloning was in a position to functionally replace fertilization and this, taken as a warning by nature for culture, was quite terrifying to say the least. Why is it that no one said — nor is anybody saying now — what this retrovirus represented, as a living and interacting model, in the evolution of our species on this unfortunate planet?

"So then, you realize that if we apply these ideas to television, we end up with some worrisome results... especially now that the electoral system is changing, moving towards a majority system, so that whoever manages to start a reproductive virus message, infecting healthy cells, that is, using DNA-television networks by way of a manipulating RNA, the contaminated trap message..."

"Yes, we were talking about leading personalities that can only be considered, after reading such passages, as opportunist infections, but we have not considered the real, fully developed viral stock, our national media HIV, the healthy carrier of an infectious meme."

"It's late and I'm afraid I'm too tired to follow this... what are talking about?"

"The one who is inscribed in the national DNA chain by way of a contaminated trap message, the one who has attracted and integrated the lymphocytes in his own viral logic, the one who fully exploits influential personalities as opportunistic infections, in order to evolve from them, at the cost of other potential avenues, sheer pornography. And now that he can even directly influence the election he is on the point of inscribing himself in the central national DNA chain, which reproduces the body of the nation with the features we can see. And once he is inscribed, he will no longer use that chain to replicate a representative national body, but rather to replicate his memetic purpose, that is to say, himself. Dear friends, I'm talking of His Broadcasting Eminence, Silvio Berlusconi, the Monarch of multimedia retroviruses. A world wide test-tube. Our symbol, the new god's champion, we have found him at last..."

Translated by Marco Graziosi (with the collaboration of Lawrence Baron)

Notes for CTHEORY

Hakim Bey

Eternal Return

In fractal mapping — like the famous Mandelbrot Set, that supreme fashion hieroglyph of the 1980s — the basic pattern keeps repeating itself, ad infinitum apparently — the deeper & more infolded you go, the more it repeats — till you get tired of running the program. After a certain amount of time, you might say, the fractal appearance has been "theorized" more or less satisfactorily. No matter how much more exploitation of conceptual space occurs, the structure of the space is now *defined* for all practical purposes. Hasn't something similar happened with the Internet?

Eugenics

In the late 18th or early 19th century a group of runaway slaves and serfs fled from Kentucky into the Ohio Territory, where they inter-married with Natives and formed a tribe — red, white & black — called the Ben Ishmael tribe. The Ishmaels (who seem to have been Islamically inclined) followed an annual nomadic route through the territory, hunting & fishing, and finding work as tinkers and minstrels. They were polygamists, and drank no alcohol. Every winter they returned to their original settlement, where a village had grown.

But eventually the US Govt. opened the Territory to settlement, and the *official* pioneers arrived. Around the Ishmael village a town began to spring up, called Cincinnati. Soon it was a big city. But Ishmael village was still there, engulfed & surrounded by "civilization." Now it was a *slum*.

Hasn't something similar happened to the Internet? The original freedom-loving hackers & guerrilla informationists, the true pioneers of cyberspace, are still there. But they have been surrounded by a vastness of virtual "development," and reduced to a kind of ghetto. True, for a while the slums remain colorful — one can go there for a "good time," strum a banjo, spark up a romance. Folkways survive. One remembers the old days, the freedom to wander, the sense of openness. But History has gone... somewhere else. Capital has *moved on.*

Incidentally, in the late 19th & early 20th century the Ishmaels were discovered by the Eugenics movement, which declared them to be racial mongrels &

degenerates. The Ishmaels were targeted for extinction; those who did not flee & disappear were institutionalized or even sterilized. The old slum was cleared & built over, and the Ishmaels were forgotten.

Something Borrowed Something Blue

The marriage of heaven & hell — that is, of the internet and television. The net is pure, "out of control," free & undefined, an autonomous space, a gnostic pleroma. Television is infernal, fifth-rate heroin, spectacle of capitulation, ceremonial voice of Capital, etc. etc. But now they are united — for example, in "pointcasting," whereby a commercial server offers an information menu designed *just for you* — while highly produced advertizements run continuously in one corner of the screen (see? you *can* do two things at once). Soon the advertizements will be designed personally as well. Home Shopping Network — that was the embryonic form of the internet, its true "future." But in fact the PC and the TV were always already "the same thing" in at least one vital aspect: the screen — and the body slumped before the screen.

Place Your Bets

Actually, the Internet has a structural aspect that makes it somewhat analogous to Capital: both in fact are fractal or chaotic systems — both have abolished space and time — both are self-replicating — both have reduced wealth to information — both are global structures (leading to conflicts with bordered entities). But isn't it a cliché to point out that any communication medium is analogous or mirror-like in relation to the dominant cultural paradigm that co-evolves with it? "When it's telegraph time, it telegraphs." And the ancient Persian postal system was an exact map of the Archaemenian Empire. Yes, these are truisms — so why should we expect the internet to be an exception to this rule? How could there exist a communication medium *outside* the totality it represents?

Please Try Again Later

The Internet as a tool for radical organizing — the Zapatistas, the Scientology case, the McLibel case, etc. True enough — at one time the printing press also had revolutionary potential. So does the telephone, the fax, and the telex. Each new technology as it appears seems liberating. The postal system, for that matter, is still "out of control" — perhaps even more so than the net. Only a few letters & packages can be checked, but "search engines" have now made it possible to steam open every bit of email in the world (in fact the NSA is already doing it). If I had secrets the last place I'd air them would be the WWW. The interesting question about the Net was never its usefulness as a *tool* for radical organizing — the interesting question was whether or not the Net itself could be seen as an area of contestation, as a "world" to be won or lost — or at least, as a *strategic space*. Clearly the answer is: no, no more than any other communication medium. For that matter, why not try to "seize control" of *language itself?*

Romans Policiers

As Geert Lovink says, Capital has now made it possible for us all to be "innocent" again. After all, if the Movement of the Social is dead, if History is ended in a burst of electromagnetic bliss, it's as if these botherations never really existed in the first place. Free at last! — free of that deadly burden of knowingness and belatedness. Now to plug into some real entertainment.

Never Happened

Baudrillard has decided that it's all over, so much so that it will not even come to an end! Not only does he quote the (ex-fascist) dean of pessimists, E.M. Cioran, he's even ready to embrace the "evil" — ready to spend eternity at poolside in his mirrorshades (or is that just another 1980s hieroglyph?) — ready to capitulate. Baudrillard is no longer a critic of Too Late Capitalism — he's a symptom of it. The "New Innocence" is merely exhaustion.

Social Ecology

I'd like to be a luddite; smoking machines would gratify me, I admit it. So naturally I'm distrustful of this tendency in myself. I pity the Unabomber because he's made himself into the unwitting *object lesson* of a "real world" totality of mediation & separation — living proof that we cannot bomb ourselves back to the Stone Age.

But the next time some Chernobyl occurs, some Bhopal, some Love Canal — and the people (instead of swallowing it as "victims") rise up and *destroy...* what will I think then?

And what relevance does this have to the Internet?

Off-line

"We're all connected...!" The triumph of the Net, not that different from telephone or TV — "reach out & touch someone" — "Be there!" — but not in the body. On the whole, the values of connection between or among virtual subjects appears outweighed by the deficit of actual *presence*.

The subject and object of Capital exists only in exchange, whether of information or money. True difference can only come into being outside or in opposition to this sameness; within the sphere of the totality all that appears as "difference" is merely simulation and packaging — a set of masks for separation. Since full contact can only occur between real differences, & since all communications media are mirrors of the totality that excludes such differences, it follows: that the contact cannot take place "within" or "through" such media.

Of course this isn't true! — the spirit bloweth where it listeth! Well then, let's say it may be *statistically* true.

Logging On

Disinformation — the internet as psychic swamp — disembodied egos — information vampires. "We have a Web page."

What to do with all these badly-designed gadgets? If I put the PC into an olde oaken cupboard, like rich people used to do with their TVs, I'd feel like an idiot — but if I leave it in plain sight it offends me at every moment with its smug space-age yuppie shape and designer beige plastic intrusiveness. I admit, these feelings scarcely amount to a *high moral ground.*

But please: let's have no more posturing about "the next stage of evolution" either.

Let's talk about something else.

Growing Old with Negroponte

David Cook

The problem of "real time" is that it is not. It is not real precisely because the real continues its ride in the virtual lane where the non-event in unreal time haunts it. Thus the nostalgia for the perfect real time weaponry of Virilio, whether God or the Patriot missile, runs up against the entropic spectrum of "real time." Who better, then, than Nicholas Negroponte to put us all straight. Straight into digital vectors where the time of your life can be had at any time of the day or night.

The Boom is Over in Old Age Homes

Growing old together has been the sign of America in recline: a reflection on the empire mentality of the imperial war machine.

As they always have, great civilizations come and go. American civilization is now engaged in the "going" part which takes the form of a fierce struggle to shift the time vector — preferably to the infinite enduring stasis of John Kenneth Galbraith's the "good life."[1] Nor has one given up on the fountain of youth, or, at a minimum, health in older age which has done wonders for the American invest-ment in old-age facilities. These homes and gardens, civilizations if you will, are all the products of analog consciousness the epitome of which is the great American monument to itself — the television. As Negroponte has it: "Unlike young digital companies such as Apple and Sun Microsystems, television technology companies were old-age homes for analog thought."[2] The vision of a greying America in front of the television set is a reassuring one again witnessed by Galbraith's *The Culture of Contentment*.

Or perhaps one would even nostalgically prefer the America of the good book, usually pictured beside a fireplace, complete with pre-digital citizens having the last of the good reads. But that was before the world according to Negroponte. As Negroponte states with reference to gardening and the problem of parasite maintenance: "Think of a CD-ROM title on entomology as another example. Its structure will be more of a theme park than a book."[3] Books lose out to theme parks, or maybe a better way to express it is that books become theme parks at the moment they shed their analog existence and become digital.

In either case, immortality is just around the corner once analog existence with its constant deterioration is replaced by the digital that has overcome the ravages of time. While perhaps not living forever, digital, at least, has the good sense to end without a trace once the delete button is pressed or one is sent off into an unknown address in cyberspace.

All that is Solid Melts into the Ground

What all of this has to do with life is, according to Negroponte, the following. Life will have made its escape from the very vector that now creates it. The real time world of the threatening "presence of being" can at the very moment of its birth be nicely avoided. That is, the "now" of time present can, in a fit of Derridean erasure, be indefinitely deferred. Good news for bill payers, but, perhaps, not quite what the world had in mind concerning the digital revolution. All this centers around the broadcast vector. Current television analog vector thought is still trapped in the physics of the ether. Looking to the heavens for one's solace has been the way of communication technologies that broadcast through the air. In a perverse reversal of freeway propensities, the air waves have become like the Beltway — a standing-room only vector. Not only is this quite dangerous because you might and will be seen and you might and will be listened to, it is even worse as it has become like the metro — crowded. The solution is, of course, to take to ground. This results in Negroponte's principle of what one might call the "Groundwork for the Metaphysics of Digital Mores": "…what is in the air will go into the ground and what is in the ground will go into the air… bandwidth in the ground is infinite and in the ether it is not."[4]

Here again is the bunker architecture of Virilio, now at the forefront of the vector revolution that threatens an infinite bandwidth.

Demanding Life of "Me"

The taking to ground of the digital bandwidth is also a taking to ground of the individual. For the bandwidth has, within its proximal zone, no internal time consciousness. The *Being and Time* of Dasein suddenly finds with Being and Digital that time's manifold has lost its horizon. Finally emancipated from time, Being is coded into the cyber-grid: a serial existence fed now, through the ethernet port, new digital ether rather than the ether of classical physics. For Negroponte, real time, in its digital mode, ends up being time deferred.

Digital life will include very little real-time broadcast. As broadcast becomes digital, the bits are not only easily time-shiftable but need not be received in the same order or at the same rate as they will be consumed. …With the possible exception of sports and elections, technology suggests that TV and radio of the future will be delivered asynchronously… On-demand information will dominate digital life.[5]

Negroponte's individual is completely delighted by this turn of events: digital life as retro fashion files given on demand. A type of instant gratification feed from the gargantuan memory file. The culture of narcissism can now safely join therapeutic, medical culture, at least as long as one subscribes to America Online and the Negroponte body is happily hardwired.

It is not surprising that Negroponte will then construct a new virtual self that is immune from the intrusion of politics and sports, which he nostalgically exempts from going to ground. The self becomes fully described in the broadcast vector space that he warns his reader not to confuse with the former analog narrowcast.

By the time you have my address, my martial status, my age, my income, my car brand, my purchases, my drinking habits, and my taxes, you have *me* — a demographic unit of one.

This line of reasoning completely misses the fundamental difference between narrowcasting and being digital. In being digital I am me, not a statistical subset. *Me* includes information and events that have no demographic or statistical meaning.[6]

"Me," to use his charming italicized referent, would appear to Negroponte to miraculously escape (like sport and politics) the closure of meaning. Perhaps the inference is too direct to conclude that for Negroponte there is no meaning — demographic, statistical or otherwise — to digital life. Or perhaps the political no longer includes surveillance and war machines, or maybe the marketing staff have simply gone on vacation.

Negroponte is correct in at least one respect: the older statistical subset based on the analog individual is too slow for the world of surveyed selves. The statistical lies within the spectrum of the possible limiting the vector of the virtual. Negroponte opens up the spectrum, recasting the individual as the digital self: a self ready to process the infinite bandwidth of digital corporations. Negroponte is the "Installer" of the operating system that goes with this "Me." If home seems far away for some nostalgia buffs, racial bigots, or fans of old ET re-runs, it is because they mistake home for the real rather than the virtual. "The address becomes much more like a Social Security number than a street coordinate. It is a virtual address."[7] A virtual address that quite naturally fits the security system.

And what about politics and sport that might just escape the net? Don't worry he was just kidding. We no longer have to worry about sport, given Nintendo's Virtual Boy. Negroponte himself took care of politics much earlier when he teleconferenced a meeting of the Joint Chiefs of Staff through digital imaging systems.[8] An experience of the out-of-body that appears to have put the Joint Chiefs out of joint.

Notes

1. See John Kenneth Galbraith, *The Good Society: the Humane Agenda.* Boston: Houghton Mifflin Co., 1996.
2. Nicholas Negroponte, *Being Digital.* New York: Vintage, 1995. p.39.
3. Ibid., p. 72.
4. Ibid., p. 24.
5. Ibid., p. 168-169.
6. Ibid., p. 164.
7. Ibid., p. 166.
8. Ibid., p. 121.

Net Game Cameo

Deena Weinstein and Michael A. Weinstein

The players of Net Game address the question of the effects of the internet on social relations.

I. New Age Cyber-Hippie

I deserve to come first. I'm the only one who truly loves the net.

For ages, human beings have dreamed of something greater than themselves. With the advent of historical thinking, many began to dream of humanity creating out of itself its own supersession — humanity as the frontier of cosmic evolution! Now it has happened — the modern dream is materializing; humanity is being overcome through its own development.

We are spirits and we are free. The net is our body and we — the authentic netizens — are the next stage of evolution — beyond the all-too-human, to the true and the spiritual. We give our bodies to our spirits as our bodies give the earth, air, fire, and water to themselves. We take the better portion. Our bodies serve the souls that emerge through the interaction of souls on the net. It is a new level of being. Not more "real" in some unknowable sense than the so-called material or perceptual world, but, rather, its present perfection — some day in the future itself to be surpassed but now the frontier.

Our future is the MUSH — the Multiple-User Shared Hallucination — in which people enter a cyber-environment and live out lives there as pure selves that are constituted only by their interaction on the net. In the purest case, they will never be able to find out who their fellow netizens actually are in the corporeal world. The worst punishment that can be meted out is exclusion from the community, which is, of course, cyber-death. But then you could get a new account and log on again, and take up a new life, even in the community that just excluded you, if not one of the scads of others that are always popping up. Short of banishment, there is only flaming and unresponsiveness. Your precious flesh remains unscathed.

Think of it this way: in the modern period you had a split between fact and fiction, between history and literature, between experience and imagination. Now, on the net, what once might have been fragments of my personal literary imagination become participants in social relations and, therefore, become what they could never have been without the interaction. Imagination becomes genuinely social in cyber-space. The Marcusian dream of transcending the realm of necessity into a realm of artistic play is coming true.

By choosing the spirit, I have liberated my private imagination to enter into relations with other imaginations and thereby to be transformed. I can see a time when the day will be divided into three parts. One part will be sleeping, another part will be working (and much of that will be done over the net) and caring for the body, and the final and most important part will be cyber-relations. If automation proceeds to the point at which the work day can be shortened, the surplus time will be apportioned to cyber-space and to conventional corporeal non-occupational activities only to the extent that they are instrumental to the enhancement of cyber-relations. We will sleep and dream and work and love corporeally and care for ourselves as preparation for the time we spend in our cyber-communities where our better and best selves grow. It is not too much to say that the net is the nervous system of heaven.

II. Net Defender

I find that I cannot agree with the previous speaker. Face-to-face friendship, love, and colleagueship are the highest ends, not some overcoming of humanity. I defend the relative autonomy and the value of a moral relation to and through the net that is based on the objective possibilities for relations among individuals that the net permits and, indeed, encourages, as what Jacques Maritain called an infra-valent end; an end that has its own intrinsic value, but is also an instrumental value to a greater end. Or, as John Dewey conceived of it, the best experience is one that is both a consummation and a means to future consummations.

The positivity of the net is its possibility of creating voluntary community through mediated conversation. In a negative sense (in the Hegelian sense of "negative" as abstract), the net abolishes physical distance between communicators, making everyone who's wired accessible to everyone else. In a positive sense, the net provides a field for experimentation (instrumental activity) and play (consummation) that by virtue of its mediated character becomes free from the demands of face-to-face or even telephonic relations, and, therefore, liberates expression and encourages play with self-definition. In return for the fullness of a close face-to-face relation, we must sacrifice our ability to vary ourselves and give vent to our reactions. The net's particular form of indirect mediation encourages variation and experimentation in expression and conversation. That is why endogenous theorists of the net are nearly always both libertarian and communitarian.

At its best, the net is an array of voluntary communities of inquiry and comradeship sustained by the free commitment of their members. There's nothing mysterious or marvelous about this. It boils down to people around the country or the world who are caring for someone with a degenerative disease forming a community of support and information outside the aegis of any medical organization. It amounts to people who share all sorts of common interests pursuing them and also exposing themselves to disturbing interlopers bringing the bad news.

As a moral possibility, the net is an anarcho-democratic community. It is a mistake to conceive of it as a model for corporeal community and an abomination to consider it a substitute for corporeal community. Think of it as a zone of freer communication than is social-psychologically possible in other contexts, something like — though not the same as — academic freedom in the context of higher education: a special opportunity to explore, experiment, learn, and appreciate: a special opportunity for people to help and enjoy each other apart from the disciplinary discourses and practices of hierarchical organizations.

The net offers the possibility of voluntary community on a scale and with a workability completely unknown until now. Networking on the net and sustaining the net as free and pure a medium for all messages as possible — consistent with the perpetuation of voluntary community — is the beach head of the New Left in cyber-space.

III. Marxist Theoretician

I think a word from the old left is called for here, a good old-fashioned Marxist critique and analysis. Things haven't changed all that much since the Manifesto. We still have to contend with utopianism.

Let's retreat a bit from the wild-eyed, infantilist if I might say so, idealism of the so-called New-Age Cyber-Hippie. This collective solipsism of the net is merely the fantasies of the technical intelligentsia of the computer-communications complex. A case of organizational psychosis (Dewey) and trained incapacity (Veblen) — trained incapacity in the ability to think scientifically in this case — a superb irony for an operative in highly rationalized technical networks. Technically, the networks are rationalized. Ideologically they index the contradictions of late capitalism, which is destroying society to such an extent that people flee to computer screens for compensation and breed a crowd of ideologists who tell them that they are pioneers in a new stage of cosmic evolution! Rather, they are waste products of capitalism, which is pleased to have them in their "alternative worlds" when they are not at work. These are high-maintenance kids put off to pasture on the net. Sooner or later capitalism will find a way of taking those worlds of self-experimentation over. Until then a decadent and despairing young intelligentsia finds its own devices of pathetic amusement.

Let us get closer to reality, to material conditions, by going back to the Net Defender, who correctly places the net and its sociality into the sensuous experience of human society, but remains a bourgeois individualist by directing net community to fuller personal relations rather than to revolutionary praxis to transform actual social relations, which is the only way to guarantee personal relations, which are imperiled under the autistic consumer behavior fostered by late capitalism.

Our task as Marxists who are involved in the internet is to devise ways of using its distinctive characteristics to best effect to further revolutionary praxis. We need to infiltrate cyber-space and learn to turn its conversations into opportunities for political education. We need to get members of oppressed communities linked by computer to better further their struggles against the system. We need to have clearing houses of activist experience in all quarters of the struggle and our own computer discussion groups on strategy and tactics. We need to link activists around the world to be resource persons for each other, to share their experience and knowledge.

As we engage in revolutionary praxis on the net, we will learn to appreciate, through our concrete transformative activity, the new turns in human relations that the medium imposes and permits, and we will learn to make them ever more serve our solidarity. But that solidarity will come as a reflective by-product of revolutionary praxis, not as its direct aim.

IV. Net Promoter

Let's get down to earth and get practical before we start soaring into thin air. We have a very bright future ahead of us in America if we have the wisdom and foresight and fortitude to do what's necessary to bring it about. We who proudly represent the emerging National Information Infrastructure (NII) are very pleased that we have both the Clinton administration through Vice President Al Gore and the Republican leadership through Speaker of the House of Representatives Newt Gingrich in our corner. We tend, on the whole, to favor the Gore approach, though we share much of the Tofflers' vision, appropriated by Gingrich, of a third-wave society based on individual empowerment. The basic point is that empowerment will only come through the institutions that we depend upon to sustain our life on earth: business enterprises, schools, hospitals, government agencies. They will develop the discussion groups, support groups, and clientele groups that will sustain individuals in their quest for individuality.

We say to the Marxist theoretician: Haven't you heard? Communism is dead. Capitalism won! Capiche? Go play with your bulletin boards in cyber-space. When it comes to the Net Defender and the New-Age Cyber-Hippie: You, my dear friends, are the cyber-incarnations of the sixties' counterculture, whose self-indulgence has endangered our country severely. We'll give you the cyber-space to play your games. Who knows? You might even come up with things that we can sell or apply.

Empowerment for individuals and groups is what the information super-highway is all about. The important thing is that everybody be connected and that there be interconnectivity among media. The goal is to give individuals, groups, and organizations maximum access to what they need to satisfy their legitimate purposes.

Cyber-populism will give way to an institutional phase of the net as organizations learn to use the net in sophisticated ways for outreach and servicing. Eventually, organized players will offer management of an incredible diversity of socialization situations and scenarios on the net. Support groups, common interest groups, and chat groups will flourish under professional support. For example, I read somewhere recently that a garden supply business had started a gardening discussion group on the net. This is the wave of the future: organizations facilitating socialization and therefore enhancing empowerment. Empowerment through connectivity!

V. Net(-Hype) Hater

I've had it! Enough! Internet discourse: internet "spirituality," internet philosophy, internet critical theory, internet policy — it's all hype. This is the first time in "history" that philosophy has become so completely enmeshed in promotion that the two are indeterminate partners in a single discourse. The Bill Gateses, Steve Jobses, Mitch Kapors are the hypesters and philosophers all rolled up into one.

I hate the seduction of net-hype. I hate the seduction of the net. I hate the virtual community as a substitute for the streets and the flesh. The fact is that the net is an emerging complex of communications media that has not yet reached its full rank among communications media and is, therefore, still "full of promise," breeding utopia and dystopia about it, and endless hype and vision: it can still be promoted like land in Florida or nuclear power were in the 1950s.

Do I even care if humanity goes bug-eyed in front of screens, communing with perpetual e-mail support groups, sometimes masquerading as newsgroups, as they wait — as in a universal hospice — to be replaced by androids?

Don't the technotopians see? The internet as anarchy, that is, the internet as a vehicle of academic freedom — the old ARPAnet that the defense department created to expedite cold-war military research and was captured by the academic side of the military-academic complex — is a totally elite-utopian moment; the internet as anarchy is about to cede, as the Net Promoter knows, to the internet as pan-capitalist facility. We are going through a doubling process, the internet is being absorbed into the environing retro-modern, pan-capitalist scene — the post-postmodern. Welcome to the retro-modern. Darwinian capitalism rides again on the net. The net is passing from libertarian utopia to techno-capitalism.

You ask what the net will be? It will be continuous spamming. The net will duplicate the fallen creation in cyber-space. From the net salvation doth not come. Everything we have already will be in cyber-space in pretty much the same proportion as we have it through the media-scape. Basically, whatever you can make a buck on will have its cyber-equivalent. A certain number of people will be sucked into cyber-space and become dependent on it for self-maintenance. Others will use it, among other media and relations, for self-maintenance. Others will opt out at the price of some exclusion from valuable practical and social connection.

Newt Gingrich was *Time Magazine's* 1995 Man of the Year. *Newsweek's* competing issue declared 1995 the Year of the Internet and featured on its cover a cartoon of Microsoft's Bill Gates dressed as Santa Claus. There ain't a chip's worth of difference. Two tech hypesters. Is there a message here about hegemonic media and the future of the net? I've seen the future and it's Newtergates.

VI. Cyber-Punk Provo-Geek Techno-Luddite

Excuse me, but you're all full of (cyber-)shit. The net is more technology to master in order to bring it down from the fuckin' insides! I'm the Unabomber hacking code. I'm spreading viruses everywhere — the AIDS of cyber-space. I'm the cyber-punk provo-geek techno-luddite.

I'll use the fuckin' net as a lonely-heart's club where I'll prey on whomever I please, at whatever age, as I please. I heard a great story the other day about an elderly Jewish gentleman who disagreed with a Nazi skinhead on the net. The Nazi skinhead, knowing no fetishism of the net, no taboos and sacred spaces, tracked down his critic in perceptual space and threatened the Jewish gentleman with physical death, which led to said Jewish gentleman having to relocate to another region of the country. Let them talk about cyber-space as something special — it's just another scam.

I'll hack you and jack you and smack you and whack you in every cyber way and will hold you physically accountable for your cyber-personalities.

I am the provo nihilist. Bring it all down from the inside. Eliminate all boundaries between the net and perceptual life. Destroy the net. Threaten security of private information, medical records, and financial transactions in any way you can. Break into data banks and mess them up. Falsify records. Use cyber-communities to draw the poor souls in them into humiliating and exploitative relations. Perpetuate misinformation, disinformation, rumor, and hate speech on the net. Intimidate and humiliate with your flames. Bring the world and net together at every opportunity in calamitous and degrading encounters. Commit financial fraud on the net and become a martyr to our cause if you get caught. Cause information overload in the system at social crisis points.

We are avowed terrorists. Some day we might go to work for a fascist leader. Hey! We're in training. Our aim is to cause feelings of insecurity and danger about the net so that people and organizations are as scared to go on it as suburbanites are to walk through an inner-city housing project. We aim to make the net at least as unfriendly as nuclear power has become.

We infiltrate the net as techno-geeks and then become the cyber-parasites that destroy it.

We're going to make life as tough as we can for as many people on the net as we can. The best way to show that something's a utopia is to bring it down. We'll violate your email and use it against you. Some day we might work for large organizations as enforcers and disciplinarians — cyber-torturers. Perotistas?

Get a life! We intend to throw you off the fuckin' net by making it unattractive to you by any means necessary, whatever it takes. We hate technology and we have mastered it — the ultimate cyber-punk horror story: the enemy within.

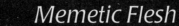 *Memetic Flesh*

Memetic flesh is a floating outlaw zone where the delirious spectacle of cyber-culture reconfigures the future of the nano-body.

Memetic Flesh in Cyber-City

Arthur and Marilouise Kroker

Memetic flesh? That's the street scene in cyber-city: San Francisco, CA. Not so much an ars electronica, but an Ars California: an art of digital living. Certainly not a sociological rhetoric of evolution or devolution, but something radically different. Memetic flesh as a floating outlaw zone where memes fold into genes, where the delirious spectacle of cyber-culture reconfigures the future of the molecular body. In Ars California, memetic flesh is neither future nor history, but the molecular present. Pure California Gening.

Now we just got off the Net where we experienced data delirium with the Ars Electronica manifesto for memetic flesh, the one which speculates about future memes: stochastic minds, recombinant bodies, infoskin, molecular daydreams. When we read this meme manifesto, our bodies of flesh, bone and blood sagged under the terminal evolutionary weight of it all, but the electronic sensors embedded in our nanoskin just went crazy. Like *Alien 3*, the electronic worms cruising the blood lanes just below skin surface heard this call of a future technotopia, flipped on their sensor matrix to red alert, whomped through the epidermal bunker, zoomed out into fresh air, and were last seen heading straight for the California coast.

And why? Because in Ars California, words are always too slow: the art of digital life exceeds new programming languages. Java, Perl, C++, awk, C shell — these are always outmoded codes for better client/server relations. Spurning new programming codes and breaking beyond all the debugging barriers, memetic flesh fast-fuses memes and genes, molecularly hardwiring information into the folded vectors of softflesh. In SF, memes have abandoned the art academy, becoming popular culture for the 21st century. Just listen to the street talk: a cool-looking city-wise Chicano in Killer Loop shades plays Tex-Mex blues on his guitar while wearing a T-shirt that boasts: "I'm a Professional Beta-Tester for Microsoft;" a businessman tucked away in an IBM suit, in-lines by while dealing mega-futures of Intel chips on his cellular phone; an African-American with a hi-tech futures face gets into the elevator armoured in a red windbreaker listing the brand-name icons for "The Corporate Alliance of America's Leading Cyber-Companies;" a nano-technologist begins to tell prophetic tales of the next human migration, the one where floating slivers of the human species will be carefully wrapped in huge nanofiber skins and allowed to float away into deep space, seeding the future universe.

Or we're walking down a sun-bleached street in San Francisco right under the Bay Bridge, and we see a beat-up Winnebago with a Nevada license plate. It's got a big sign out front advertising bargain basement prices on Java/Sun computer packages. It's a sun-real California scene: an old Winnebago, hi-tech gear, hard-drivin' Silicon Valley type salesmen in a no-tech part of town, with no customers to take their coffee and donuts and hi-tech packages except for some homeless guys and ourselves. After asking us "Which way to multi-media gulch?" they realized the error of their memetic way, and closed up shop just as a couple of street people settled down for some good eatin' and sleepin' inside the chain-link fence. Memetic flesh as daily life in cyber-city, the kind of place where the virus of the tech future digs its way under the skin, like an itch or a sore or a viral meme that just won't go away.

No one knows this better than the memetic artists of SF. Not the corporate art of Silicon Valley, the "house" art of Interval, Xerox, and Oracle with their New Age visions of wetware products for the digital generation nor the subordinated aesthetics of the fine art emporiums in official culture, but unofficial outlaw art that's practiced in hidden warehouses and storefront galleries and ghetto schools and other side of the tracks digital machine shops: an art of dirty memes.

Dirty memes? That's what happens when memetic engineering escapes into the streets of cyber-city, and its scent is picked up by viral artists. Like Elliot Anderson's multimedia algorithm, "The Temptation of St. Anthony," with its brilliant psychopathology of obsessive-compulsive behavior, complete with 3-D ghostly images of emotional discomfort and stuttering gestures, as the key psychic sign of digital culture. Or Matt Hackert's dead horse flesh machines complete with belching flame-throwers and whirring chain saws and rip-snorting drills, and all of this accompanied by the robotic sounds of the mechanical orchestra. Or Lynn Hershman Leeson's memetic cinema with its application of object-relations pro-gramming to the universe of Hollywood imagery. Or the viral robotics of Chico MacMurtie's "Amorphic Robot Works" that encode in robo-genetics all the ecstasy and catastrophe of the ruling cultural memetics. Neither technotopian nor technophobic, memetic art in the streets of SF is always dirty, always rubbing memes against genes, always clicking into (our) memetic flesh.

The Nanotech Future

A Digital Conversation
with BC Crandall

Arthur and Marilouise Kroker

Arthur and Marilouise Kroker: What is molecular engineering/nanotechnology?
What are some of the key emergent trends in nanotechnology?

BC Crandall: Molecules are collections of atoms. Molecular engineering is the art of
making objects with molecular precision. The field is called nanotechnology
because simple molecular components are measured in nanometers, or billionths of
a meter. For the past two hundred years, chemists have done rather simple things
with a large number of relatively small molecules. Nanotechnology aims to build a
wide range of quite complex micro- and macroscopic objects with molecular
precision. For perspective, consider DNA, which is 2.3 nanometers wide, or LSD,
one of the larger psychically active molecules, made up of some 50 atoms, which is
about one nanometer across. The field is just emerging from the coalescing efforts
of genetic engineers, chip manufacturers, and research scientists pushing around
individual atoms with their scanning probe microscopes to make raked-gravel
Japanese gardens with atoms and their electrons.

    The key goal of nanotechnology is the creation of self replicating molecular
systems that are not based on the mechanisms of DNA. The world envisioned
includes completely liquid environments with massive processing and robotic
capabilities. The equivalent of several thousand robotic Cray computers could
operate in a space smaller than a blood cell. Materiality would be addressable atom
by atom.

    Several traditional fields are becoming molecular and more will soon join
them. Computer chip manufacturers are beginning to toy with molecularly precise
components. Dr. Robert Birge at Syracuse University is working in the lab — and
in a start-up company — to create gigabyte memories smaller than sugar cubes
using lasers to "read" and "write" stacks of closely packed molecules similar to the
ones that register photons in our retinas. Drug manufacturers are using molecular
modeling software to design molecules that might lock or unlock a number of
proteins in an effort to more "rationally" develop new pharmaceuticals. Biology, and
all its sub-domains in anthropology, ecology, forensics, medicine, and so on, have
all resolved themselves to view the world with molecular precision.

Perhaps nanotechnology can best be understood as a fairly new set of memes with particularly dramatic material consequences. Our species has never experienced such a challenging opportunity; the potential for losing our evolutionary purchase on the planet is very real, as is the possibility of boldly carrying DNA to where no man — and no woman — has gone before. But this will only be possible, I feel, if we are able to substantially reconfigure major portions of human culture through a process of memetic engineering.

A & M Kroker: Why is our future "memetic engineering?"

Crandall: The term "meme" was coined by Richard Dawkins in 1976. A "meme" is a piece of patterned information carried and expressed by a human brain, just as a "gene" — which rhymes with meme — is a piece of patterned information carried and expressed by DNA. By taking in that last sentence, you become infected with the meme about memes. Memes are a new form of self-replicators, or viral life. They are atomic and molecular fragments of human "culture." Memetics is very far from the "mimetic" judgment Plato passed on materiality — that it consists of poor imitations of "True Forms." Memetics is the antithesis of metaphysics, insisting that matter matters. Felix Guattari performs a kind of memetic analysis when he argues that a wide range of heterogeneous machinic components lead to the production of contemporary subjectivities.

As material structures, memes are always on their way, transformationally, from medium to medium: speech vibrates air molecules that, if near an ear, enter the brain through the tuning forks of the inner ear and thus into more or less stable molecular patterns in the brain. Memes express themselves through the mouth, as words and song, through the hands — which have learned to use a growing range of signaling tools from paintbrush and keyboard to trumpet and fax machine — and through other "significant" gestures. Today, memes exploit the new media and travel as electronic and electromagnetic pulses and hibernate as magnetic patterns and as microscopic pits on laser-read compact disks.

Memetic engineering is the art of intentionally creating, nursing, annealing, and projecting an evolving matrix of these meat-based "ideas." Memetic engineering can be found at the core of contemporary techno-corporate communication apparatuses as well as at the heart of Buddhist literature — wherever "effective means" are used to infect the flesh of a reader, listener, or viewer with a given meme. These processes of "teaching" and "learning" — intentional memetic transfer — generate "human" culture. It is hardly an exaggeration to say that, "Memes are us." To the extent that we participate in language, economics, history, or aesthetics, we inhabit a memetic realm. Using the energy of our living flesh to maintain, mutate, and express themselves, memes live in and through us. Their viral activity generates our hallucinated identities as "individuals." You can identify the memes living in your flesh by inventorying your identities: If you call yourself "Christian," "Marxist," or "Postmodern" — or "Musician" or "Writer" — you do so because your body carries and expresses particular strains of memetic culture.

We are facing a crisis because the set of memes that can be identified as the ongoing technoscientific revolution is evolving with completely unprecedented success. Never before have the stories we've told each other about the world — the memes —' had such capacity to rearrange the matter of the world. As the techno-logical phylum discovers how to install itself as an evolving molecular presence, our animal survival depends on discovering the memes that we can live with. Without an effective methodology for discerning and modifying memetic forms our future looks quite bleak. Currently, the enacted consequences of the memes that we carry are causing the greatest reduction in species diversity on the planet of the past 60 million years. Leaking radioactive waste, lethal for hundreds of thousands of years, pockmark the "civilized" world. And soon we will face the prospects of genetically targeted molecular machine viroids!

As we "hack the future" with ever more powerful tools in our primate paws, we must continually re-engineer our memes so they inspire us to ever gentler action. Or perhaps another image — another meme — would be better, for we need to cultivate, nurture, and husband a garden of genetically beneficial memetic life forms.

A & M Kroker: In your new book, *Nanotechnology: Molecular Speculations on Global Abundance*, you claim that we stand at the "threshold of a molecular dawn." Why do you think the future is molecular? And what will be some of key concrete results of the "molecular dawn"?

Crandall: Our future is molecular because if we do not take molecular care we will not be materially alive, and that brings all our fine conversations — political, philosophical, spiritual, economic — to a graceless halt. Conversely, if we can conjure up a skeleton key that will allow us to pass us through the molecular gate, and we find ourselves living amidst molecularly precise artifacts as cheap as dirt, the imagination of millennia — the madness and laughter of our species — will leap forth, generating incomprehensibly complex patterns of human becoming. Some of which, I imagine, may be quite enjoyable.

In the book, I present an historical argument that it is actually quite reason-able to anticipate the arrival of surprisingly powerful molecular machines in the next few decades. The contributed pieces in the book present technically sound speculations on several potential applications. These range from the blessedly mundane — diamond teeth — to "utility fog," which would support you in an essentially liquid environment that could simulate almost any occurrence with full resolution at the limit of human sensory instrumentation. In fog, one might assume that every sensory impression would appear with a corporate logo in the lower right-hand corner. A suit of utility fog — while stimulating your senses — could carry you across the surface of the earth quite rapidly and, with a few modifications, could generate within its bulk a sufficient quantity of microscopic vacuum pockets to make the entire apparatus — with you inside — lighter than the atmosphere that it displaces; you'd bob up to the top of the atmosphere like a champagne cork released from the Titanic. Such a universal human-machine interface could act as a second skin and as the fundamental medium of "communities." Those who share protoplasmic extensions of a given liquid envelopment — each "individual" a raisin in a digital tapioca pudding — could be in constant, broadband, full-body communication. (Parenthetically, the Latin-rooted "individual" is the etymological equivalent of the Greek-rooted "atom"; both mean "indivisible.")

A & M Kroker: You co-founded a computer company, Prime Arithmetics, in 1990. Is that related to your work with Molecular Realities?

Crandall: Prime is based on the mathematical research of my cofounder Jack LeTourneau, who has shown that there exists a unique isomorphism between the natural numbers under the operations of "primeth" and "times" and hierarchical structures under the operations of "encapsulate" and "merge at the root." This discovery has allowed us to develop a family of arithmetic techniques that are particularly efficient for describing and manipulating object oriented data structures. These techniques, which have just recently been partially approved by the PTO [Patent and Trademark Office], have immediate applications — especially in the area of network-based computing, where a number of small digital "objects" are drawn into temporary assemblies as needed — and in the molecular world we will soon inhabit.

  In particular, it's clear that cellularization — the process of grouping molecular components into increasingly complex assemblies — has provided DNA life with one of its most fundamental techniques for generating ever more capable life forms. An efficient method for modeling the aggregation and evolution of object-oriented systems will have value, I believe, as we begin to create molecular mechanical instancings of artificial life forms. I also imagine that whatever "Global Algorithms" are used to effect the next transformations of the planet, they will need data structures and data-structure management mechanisms. Prime offers a mechanism that's as universal and as "natural" as the natural numbers: zero, one, two, three, four, and so on.

A & M Kroker: In *Nanotechnology* you state: "Nanotechnology poses a difficult question: What will we human primates do when some of us learn to manipulate matter as finely as the DNA and RNA molecules that encode our own material structure?" Now, we know that some of the early adopters of nanotechnology will be multinational drug companies who intend to apply to molecular engineering the same war-like strategies that they have already applied to the pre-nano world. Is nanotechnology doomed to recapitulate the often violent history of modern engineering, or does the possibility exist that memetic engineering may have a heretofore silent ecological ethic. In other words, is there a "Green nanotechnology?"

Crandall: There must be, or we will not long survive. Technology, as Heisenberg pointed out, is a fully natural phenomenon. He called it "a biological process on the largest scale." If this is the case, it is not a question of managing our technology in a kinder gentler manner, but rather one of ridding the global orgasm that is shuddering its way across the planet. Our choices seem to be encouraging this thundering undulation in the direction of birthing a multitude of post-planetary, DNA-life colonies, or dully observing its crescendoing explosion in place — an event that I do not believe will be very hospitable for our delicate hominid flesh.

In the next few decades, with the development of nanotechnology, a window of opportunity will open, during which we will be able to use early applications of molecularly engineered materials to launch a multitude of substantial, ecologically self-sustaining — and primate supporting — ecosystems into the previously untenable ecological niche of space. These colonies would provide new homes for DNA with one essential characteristic: complete molecular separation from one another. While terrorism and stupidity are likely to remain serious challenges, the void of space would serve to separate the various attempts to generate viable memetic and genetic cultures with human-directed, molecularly precise interventions. If one colony failed, the whole game wouldn't end. Currently, we know of only one molecularly interconnected DNA experiment: the Earth. For as long as we fail to multiply the instances where DNA life can continue its four and a half billion years' exploration, we face an ever increasing risk that molecularly machined artifacts generated by one species of DNA life will accidentally destroy the planet's capacity to support primates, and potentially its capacity to support all forms of DNA.

The "ecological ethic" inherent in nanotechnology emerges when we realize that it is indeed the end of the world as we know it. When groups of humans gather together — with the intention of forming self-sufficient, molecularly independent communities of DNA life with plans to leave the Earth at the earliest opportunity — it will be on the basis of an understanding that individual, bodily health and well being is utterly dependent on the ecological vitality of the place you call home, be it San Francisco, Berlin, Jakarta, or a centrifugally spinning necklace of Earth-life pods in near-Earth solar orbit. How such communities will form and the manner in which they will sustain themselves is the question that I am most interested in at this time. Clearly, this is fundamentally a question of memetic evolution.

Today, the deterritorializing memes of capitalism will continue to distract us from the primary pleasures of the meat — breathing, moving, eating, touching — with a growing blizzard of secondary representations, in an effort to constantly maximize return for the "owners." In this storm of accelerating combinatoric culture, it is critical that those of us interested in surviving begin to practice some form of memetic annealing — a kind of cybercalisthenics for domesticated primates in reclining civilizations. The goal of annealing is simple: remember that "Everything you know is wrong," or "The map is not the terrain," or whatever aphorism stands in your matrix as the navel, the omphalos, the Klein-bottle point at which "you" disappear. While Buddhists and others have developed a wide range of activities to induce such an experience, the event itself is utterly natural: meat returning to meat. This saturnalia of the soul which deconstructs the dominant hallucination in a temporary conflagration allows one's current set of memes to reorder their relationships. One is "reborn" — as yet another memetically infected ape.

Annealing becomes particularly important as we are ever more likely to find ourselves in molecularly altered states of consciousness. While certain psychedelics and alcohol are older than cities, most of us, including those of European descent, have had less than 400 years to adapt to the molecular intrusions of caffeine and nicotine on our brain meat. Prozac has been with us for only twenty-two years, and it passed a billion dollars in sales when it was only eighteen — the year Zoloft was born. Each of these molecular regimes, these postmodern material gods of consciousness, effect the beliefs and values — the memes — that guide our actions in the world. Avital Ronell's image of receiving a "six-month girloid program" as a molecular implant, and Neal Stephenson's questions, "Is it a virus, a drug, or a religion? — What's the difference?" point to the criticality of waking up to the material — the molecular — nature of the memes we each host.

Given this fundamental materiality, it is clear why memetic annealing always proceeds as an activity, a movement of the flesh. Whether the gross movements of dance or yoga, or the subtle movements of conscious breathing and mindful attention, annealing invites our meat to choose: what activity, what belief, what memes feel best for this meat right now? Nietzsche suggested that one sit as little as possible, and argued that we should "give no credence to any thought that was not born outdoors while one moved about freely." By taking the fundamental creative act — drawing a distinction — and handing the baton to our breathing, feeling flesh, we just might be able to choose and construct memetic forms that will allow the dance of human and DNA life to continue.

Requiem

Kathy Acker

Act III

Scene 1: Electra's monologue. Electra enters and sits cross-legged upon the stage. Just the actress, no need to dress up anymore. It's present time.

> Electra: I'm gonna to tell you about myself. (*A little like a kid*) I'd been working with this woman who knows how to access past lives. When I found out that I had cancer, a cancer that had metastasized, I ran to her for help.

> Why?

> For this reason: When the surgeon who had taken my breasts off, a few days after this operation, informed me that some of my lymph nodes were registering cancer, I asked him if the lymph nodes or the body's oil filter could simply be registering cancer because I was on a high anti-oxidant diet. I had been for some weeks. (Picking at her feet.) He answered me that diet has nothing to do with cancer, with the causes of cancer. He added, "Nor with environmental pollution. We have no idea," said my surgeon, "what causes cancer."

> So I decided that he knew nothing about cancer. I had no idea why I was deciding this. I knew I had to find out who did know about cancer. But I knew I had no way of knowing how to find out.

> Everything I had thought real had just been taken away from me.

> I ran to George, my psychic. I told her everything that had happened, that the surgeon was good-looking. Like President Clinton. I guess they're in the same racket, I

Editors' Note: Kathy Acker's *Requiem* was commissioned by the American Opera Projects, New York. Ken Valitsky is the composer.

said. George replied that I shouldn't be scared. She
would send me to someone who kills cancers. Who had
killed several for her.

I was alone again and everything that was happening so
fast ran through my brains. I could only think about was
killing cancers. If I can kill the cause of this cancer-this
was my thought-the cancer that's in my body will go
away.

I didn't know, however, if phenomena happen by chance or
by cause. Now, if things, phenomena happened by
chance, then nothing that I did or could do mattered,
that is, there was no way I could know what action led
to what other action or event. In other words, if chance
ruled the world, then my surgeon was right: cancer had
no discernible cause and my life and death were meaningless.

I can't bear this.

It was at this moment something, I don't know what word
to use, came out of me, someone larger in than me, and
screamed without raising my voice, using a calm tone,
"No more of this death. You've fucked everything up so
now I'm taking over." It was a male voice. I felt that my
conscious section was just a part of a huge being.

If this world is meaningful, I continued, then so must be
each of its parts, no matter how minute. If this world is
meaningful, then I need to concern myself, not with
cancer, but with its cause. Whatever caused it must
change. I knew one thing. That writing is a way to
change reality. I returned to George in order to find out
how I could change reality.

But I was very scared: the growing fear that I felt was so
great that it seemed just about to take me over. I was
about to stop being.

Again George said that I shouldn't be frightened. Why
was I? I didn't understand this question cause I thought
that the fear of dying was enough to frighten anyone.

Had I ever been scared before I had gotten cancer?

"Yes." I said this; then I thought. When I had been six years old, I guess it was six cause I don't remember anything that happened before that time, I had been taking a shower. My mother entered the bathroom. I didn't know she was in there because I couldn't see her through the shower curtain. Just like Psycho . She threw ice water on top of me. She had already placed a bar of soap on the floor of the bathtub.

It was a game. If I can remember playing these games like this with my mother, why can't I remember anything that happened before I was six years old?

Scene 2: Light opens up to reveal a lovely small study in tan. Most of the walls are huge clear windows through which can be seen full grown trees, tiny buds, branches, birds hopping here and there, maybe even a squirrel. The sun is clear and strong.

Electra, dressed in the actress' normal clothing, and George are sitting in two of the three comfortable armchairs. George looks like a beautiful Hollywood actress slightly past her prime; in a way she is, for she used to be married to a well- known American film producer.

They are already in conversation.

Electra: So I went to this dingdong doctor and she made me hold vials of different cancers in one hand while her hands tapped and sort of moved my feet. She said, "You don't register at all for breast cancer." "Maybe I'm cured." "But you have six other kinds of cancer." I think I'd know if I was growing every conceivable kind of cancer.

George: Forget about her.

Electra: While I was holding each group of vials, there were fourteen, she told me to hold the thumb of my other hand, for each test, against a different finger. Each time my thumb touched my third finger, she found all these really bad emotions. She named each emotion, then told me to think about it and hit the base of my skull with that tool they use to adjust backs. A "clicker" or some- thing or other. As soon as my head really hurt.

I told her I had thought about the emotion.

George: Don't see her again.

Electra: The most usual emotion was anger. I want to learn about this cause I don't think I'm angry with my mother. I've worked on forgiving her.

George: You must have been angry at her for what she did to you.

Electra: I don't know, but I don't know how I felt before I was six.

George: What's the first thing that you remember?

Electra: I do remember one thing that happened before I was six. I was about a year old. I had this pink baby blanket with roses. I adored it. They took it away from me. They said they were taking it away to clean it, but I never got it back.

George: Now, be a child. Sit in a chair or on the floor as if you were a child.

Electra: George. (*Readily sitting down on the floor, her legs away from the rest of her body*) This is silly!

George: What toy do you want?

Electra pouts.

George: Would you like a stuffed animal?

Electra: I like stuffed animals.

George, (*handing her a pig who's hugging a baby pig and a mauled bear*): Which one?

Electra: Both.

George: Go back to that blanket. To it being taken away. Where are you?

Electra: I don't know. (*She closes her eyes*) A bare room. Grey walls. I see a crib. I can't see anything else.

George: Who's taking your blanket away?

Electra: They are.

George: Your grandmother? She's obviously the one who took care of you.

Electra: My mother, my grandmother. They're one and the same. They're the only people in this world.

George: What about your nurse? You said you had nurses.

Electra: I adored my nurses. It was my mother or my grandmother.

George: What do you feel?

Electra: I'm really angry.

George: Do you show your mother you're angry?

Electra: No. (*Thinks*) My mother was a monster. I wouldn't have dared.

George: Why? Children usually show their mothers how they feel.

Electra doesn't answer.

George: What were you so scared she was going to do to you?

Electra, her voice changing: I tell you: I'm blocked. I'm blocking. (*Her body is rigid and she's in pain*) I'm trying to think of what I'm most scared of. Lobotomy. (*Reasons*) They're going to make me into nothing. To make me a puddle so I can be just what they want. Then I'll no longer be. That was what their society was to me: The fifties and the sixties. Hypocrisy.

George: I don't understand.

Electra: I was constantly supposed to say to my mother, "I love you". I wouldn't because I didn't know if she loved me. My father would say, "Why don't you tell your mother you love her? She loves you so much." I was guilty. When I was six, I would tiptoe up to the doorway of their bedroom, it was always late at night. I could hear them talking about me. My mother said that there was something bad about me which genetics couldn't account for and my father would agree. He agreed with everything she said. They talked about how maybe I should be instituted.

George: How did that make you feel?

Electra: I was unlike everyone in the world. I decided I was a freak. So my mind made up another world: that's when I began to live in the imagination.

George: But what had so frightened you?

Electra: I can't remember back then cause I'm scared to. (*Making herself*) I've got to remember because I have to cure this disease.

George: Go back further.

Electra: I'm trying. I'm going to look at my fears. Lobotomy. Fire. I'm terrified of fire. Which doesn't make sense cause I'm basically fearless: knives, guns don't bother me; when I was a kid, I used to jump off the boardwalk over the beach. It was high.

George: Why are you scared of fire?

Electra shrugs.

George: If you were badly burned during childhood, you'd have a scar.

Electra: I don't have a scar. I'm scared of fire.

George: Let's go back to lobotomy. Your mother doesn't want you to be you.

Electra: She wants me to be really dumb and get C's on my report card. She hates how bright I am.

George: She doesn't want you to exist.

Electra: She's always tells me that. That she would have gotten an abortion if she hadn't been scared.

George: She tried to kill you.

Electra: I don't remember. (*Blocking*) Let's ask the healers.

George: Dear healers, please be with us now and answer my and Electra's questions about her mother. Did Electra's mother try to kill her?

Electra is sitting in her child's position, rigid.

George: Yes.
Did Electra's mother try to burn her when she was a
child?
No.
Did Electra's mother try to kill her before she was born?
Yes.
When she was three months in the womb?
When you were seven months in the womb, your
mother tried to abort you using something to do with
heat, a method common in those days.

Electra: I know this.

George: The abortion didn't work because you were meant
to be born. You were helpless when all this happened.
That's why you're scared.

Electra: What do I do?

George: May you go back to that child who existed before
your mother tried to abort her,
so that she can grow up in love.
Give her the help that she needs
to do what she has to do
while alive. Amen.

Electra sings in a clear, strong child's voice:

Requiem

"Who, if I cried out, would hear me among
the angels?"

I know the answer:
no one.

Tell me: from where does love come?
An angel is sitting on my face. To whom can I run?

Take me in your arms, death,
I'm so scared;
do anything to me that will make me safe
while I kick my heels and shout out in total fear,
while we hurtle through your crags
to where it's blacker:
Orpheus' head eaten by rats,
what's left of the world scatters,
in the Lethe the poet's hairs,

below where there's no ground, down
into your hole,
    because you want me to eat your sperm.
    Death. I know.

"Every angel is terrifying."

Because of this, because I have met death,
I must keep my death in me,
gently,
and yet go on living.
Because of this, because I have met my death,
I give myself birth.

Remember that Persephone
raped by Hades
then by him brought
into the Kingdom of Death
there gave birth
to Dionysius.

You were the terrorized child,
Mother,
Now be no more.
Requiat in pacem.

Tell me: from where does love come?

"Emerging at last from violent insight
"Sing out in jubilation and in praise."
to the angels who terrified away the night.
Let not one string
of my forever-child's heart and cunt fail to sing.
Open up this body half in the realm of life, half in death
and give breathe.

For to breathe is always to pray.

You language where language goes away.

You were the terrorized child,
Mother,
Be no more.
Requiat in pacem.

Requiem.
For it was you I loved.

Conceiving Ada

Lynn Hershman Leeson

Conceiving Ada is a film that invented the technology of virtual sets to dramatize the converging lives of two young women widely separated in time: Emmy, a driven young woman of the present day who is obsessed with her experiments programming artificial life, and her 19th century counterpart, the brilliant and daring Ada Byron King Lovelace, who foresaw the possibilities of artificial life when she wrote what is now considered the first computer program in 1843.

As Emmy investigates Ada through a series of CD-ROM biographies as well as a DNA Memory Retrieval Program, she comes to identify with her subject to the point that she experiences scenes from Ada's life through Ada's eyes. It is a life of continual struggle for some measure of control: control over her own work. Ada's "Notes" were written to describe inventor Charles Babbage's Analytical Engine, the forerunner of the modern computer. She lost control over her own body, which was ravaged by childbearing and often-mysterious ailments.

Even her own thought processes were forcibly directed onto a narrow rationalistic course by her rigidly moralistic mother, Lady Byron, who counteracted the "bad blood" of Ada's notorious father, the poet Lord Byron. Nevertheless, Ada proved herself to be Byron's daughter in many ways. She led a double life as both the respectable and accomplished Lady Lovelace, and the "scandalous" Ada Byron, involved in drug use, high-stakes gambling, and torrid affairs with her tutors. Ada, in fact, used her calculations to bet on horses, and lost the family fortune, sins she confesses to her husband the night she died at age 36.

At first, Emmy's "colonization" of Ada's identity seems to be a means of exploring her own. Pregnant, yet compelled to continue her work and fulfill her own addictive drives, Emmy is also monitored by controlling forces of lover, Nicholas.

The computer-driven narrative of *Conceiving Ada* is structured to allow for multiple interpretations. It can be read as a projection of the terrors of giving birth as represented in terms of the programming of artificial life, or as a meditation on pervasive erasure of privacy in modern life. But it is overridingly a story of conflict between "essential truth" and the representations which block our access to it. As representations of reality become more and more technologically complex, "truth" seems to recede into an infinite proliferation of screens.

The story ends six years after Emmy gives birth to Claire, and reminds us that the grace of humanity allows each generation to reinvent itself.

The following scenes take place as Ada is dying. The first is between her mother and the final between her and Emmy, the contemporary woman who uncovers her story via the computer, and is then able to talk to her directly.

> Lady Byron (hesitantly): Ada — there is much I've never told you about your father. Remember when you learned the truth about your father and Aunt Augusta, you became paralytic and were in crutches for three years?

Close up of Ada's face as she hears the story.

> Lady Byron (*cont'd*): When I fought for custody of you there was quite a scandal. Harriet Beecher was the only one who tried to help, but it tainted her reputation as well. *(voice fading)*

> Ada: What are you trying to tell me Mother?

> Lady Byron: It was his passions from which you were conceived and his passions from which I hoped to protect you. *(beat)* If I was harsh in your discipline, it was to thwart his hereditary genes from transferring to you.*(beat)* Is this upsetting you Bird?

> Ada: No, Mother. In fact, it has made me realize even more the fragility of time. All genetic linkage is a gamble, isn't it. This talk has not upset me. I knew from Aunt Augusta the possibilities for recessive transfer. It has, in fact, renewed my ambition.
> *(beat)*
> I must recalculate my life so as not to squander even a second. Time seems to be the price of our genius.

> Lady Byron: But Ada! That's not at all what I meant. It's your soul that needs attention.

Ada rises. William is standing in the doorway and has overheard her last remark.

> William: You're far to weak —

> Ada (*fiercely*): Weak? I have strengths you know nothing of!

William looks bewildered.

> Ada (*cont'd*): Strength of conviction.
> *(she whispers as she walks past him to her desk)*

We watch as Ada begins her calculations.

Scene 79 — Emmy's Office

Emmy begins to pace agitatedly around the room. The image of Ada is projected on the wall. Emmy begins to do Yoga stretches on the floor, beneath the large image.

Close up of Ada, staring, saying nothing.

Emmy bends over, stretches, breathes deeply, walks to the camera attached to a computer, turns it on and stands in front of it. Emmy's image appears, scanned on the computer. Emmy does a search for the Ada DNA microbe patterns. She turns the camera on, aimed at herself. A pattern emerges like a veil over Ada's face.

> Emmy *(to herself and Godsdog)*: It was there all the time. It was all in the overlap of the patterns.

The image flashes then opens. Emmy's ghost-like image is covering Ada's . It is subtle and transparent.

> Emmy *(looking at Godsdog)*: This is for Sims too.

Scene 80

> Emmy *(o.s.)*: Ada.
> *Ada jumps and looks around fearfully.*
> Ada
> *(nervously trying to laugh)*
> Have I truly gone mad at last!

> Emmy: You're not crazy Ada. That's what they try to tell all visionary women.

> Ada *(trembling slightly, still looking around)*: Mother always told me I had an angel or a devil watching over me. But which are you?

> Emmy *(o.s.)*: Neither. I'm a friend. I want to protect you.

> Ada *(now craning her neck to see ceiling corners)*: Where? From where are you watching?

> Emmy *(o.s.) (hesitantly)*: I can see you — but I also seem to be looking — through your eyes...

Numbly, Ada puts her hands up to her face.

Scene 81

P.O.V. shot of the hands closing out the view of the room, as the sound of a heart beating surges up and is mingled with the sound of a second heart pounding at a different rhythm.

Quick cut of Sims watching this same scene.

> Emmy *(o.s.)*: Oh my god, I didn't think I would feel your
>   pain. *(distressed)*

We see Emmy watching this scene in her room as a transparent image of her appears over Ada's projection. Ada turns her head and stares out. She seems to be looking directly at Emmy, who is facing her.

> Ada: Can you save me?

The image warps, stutters, begins to rewind unsteadily, occasionally jerking back great leaps in time. With a final shudder, the image begins to run forward again, we see several scenes over: Ada is running through a brush

> Ada: My name is Ada Byron King Countess of Lovelace

The image comes to a halt; then suddenly it rushes forward, so swiftly there is nothing visible but a blur. Then it stops abruptly at:
Close up of Ada on her deathbed. She turns her head.

> Ada: We seem to return to this. No matter what path we
>   take, all roads lead here. Can you save me?

The image freezes.

> Emmy *(o.s.)*: I will try.

The image stutters, but begins again, repeating over and over:

> Ada: Can you save me?

The image freezes. Emmy presses the save button.

Scene 82 — Cut to Emmy's office, night.

Close Up of Emmy's face. Her eyes are open wide as she gasps for air.

> Emmy: Nicholas. I was there! I was …inside!

We hear the sound of the door opening and Nicholas walks in.

> Emmy *(grabbing at the image of Ada on the monitor)*: I was
>   in there! She's dying and I felt it! Let me show you.

> Nicholas: Emmy, you're perspiring. You look sick.

Emmy doubles over in pain. Nicholas is alarmed.

> Emmy *(struggling to breathe calmly)*: Call the doctor. It's
>   too early. Maybe a false alarm…

> Nicholas: Lie down. I'll call her.

Scene 83

Reluctantly Emmy moves into bed, but she refuses to let Nicholas turn the computer off.
     Close up of Ada in bed as a projection.
          Emmy *(o.s.) (in a whisper)*: I was in there…

Fade to Black

Scene 84 — Interior of Ada's bedroom, night.

*P.O.V shot from Ada's vantage. Dr. Locock stands over her. William stands in shadow
     behind the doctor. Lady Byron is seated by the bed.*

> Dr. Locock: It seems that the uterus is destroyed. All that
>   math was just too much for your body. You brought it
>   on yourself. Now we can only ease your pain, Lady
>   Lovelace.

He bends forward with a syringe. There is the sound of William sobbing.

> Ada: Opium?

Ada gradually relaxes under the influence of the drug.

> Ada: What a blessing… opium. There is a lovely cool-
>   ness…

> Emmy *(v.o.)*: Why does it keep returning to this scene?

> Ada *(faintly, aloud)*: Are you there, Angel/Devil?

> Lady Byron *(close beside Ada)*: Did you call me, Ada?

> Emmy *(v.o.)*: I'm here.

> Ada: I'm glad… I've missed you. I realized I have missed
>   you all my life. I've always looked for someone who
>   would see me clearly and like me for who I am…

> Dr. Locock *(to Lady Byron)*: She's hallucinating.

> Ada *(ruefully)*: They think so, do they? Well, I have been
>   accused of it often enough. This time it may be true.

*The conversation and actions of Lady Byron, William, and Dr. Locock recede to dim
     sounds and movements.*

> Emmy *(v.o.)*: Oh Ada, I've wanted to really know you for
>   so long — to see things from your point of view. But
>   now all I can feel is your pain.

Ada: I'm so sorry. That's always the way, isn't it?

Emmy: It's not your fault.

Ada: You know, I rather like pain. It makes me feel alive. No, the worst part for me is that I never wrote all that I am thinking. Now no one will ever know those stillborn words. And poor Babbage. He has failed too.

Emmy *(v.o.)*: You are both bound for greatness. I promise.

Ada *(laughing weakly)*: Greatness! One written work, unsigned! Just the initials, "A.A.L." My work will die as surely as me and nearly as soon.

Emmy *(v.o.)*: It's not the quantity of writing you did, but the profound nature of your insights. Nothing can take away your accomplishments.

Ada: I never suspected the end of the equation would be like this. To die in pain, with this wretched, bleeding. To be humbled into servitude and dependence. To be denied the grace of unopiated relief. To be physically degraded and depleted of spirit.
(beat)
Maybe I should write about this.

Emmy *(v.o.)*: Your essence will survive, Ada.

Lady Byron *(o.s.)*: Ada, do you know me?

Ada turns her head to see her mother close by.

Ada: Yes, Mother.

Lady Byron: Ada, I was arranging your things and found the letter you wrote to John Crosse.

(Ada gasps)

Lady Byron *(cont'd)*: I destroyed it. No one need know of your eccentricities. Your flights of escapade.

Ada: But Mother, how could you. It contained my most intimate thoughts.

Lady Byron: Ada, I mean this only for your good. You must protect your history. It is a blessing to have time to ponder your sins.

Child *(v.o.)*: Oh, to have been carried off by a bolt of lightning! A quick death would have been a mercy!

Lady Byron: You must confess your transgressions to your husband.

Ada: Oh Mother, why?

Lady Byron: Ada! You must confess for your own sake! For your soul!

Ada: Now I do not have to confess. You know everything already. The real truth of my life has been destroyed
(beat)
to protect me.

Lady Byron *(pleadingly)*: Confess to William. You will feel so much relieved!

Ada: Opium makes me feel more relieved...

Lady Byron *(shocked at this blasphemy)*: Ada! I know that it was your father's blood that made you ill and irrational. I accept that. I brought this on to you. I accept that as well.
(beat)

Lady Byron *(cont'd)*: I've attended to all your earthly responsibilities, settled your gambling and horse racing debts, arranged for the care of your children, redeemed the Lovelace family jewels.

Ada covers her face as her mother lists these.

Lady Byron *(cont'd)*: But you must find the strength to tell William... for the sake of your soul.

Ada *(writhing)*: Presuming I still have one. Oh, the pain again —

Lady Byron: The doctor is outside the door. I'll tell him to give you another dose of opium — after you see William.

Emmy *(v.o.)*: Why won't she let up?

Lady Byron: William must be told!

Lady Byron rises and leaves the bedside. Close up of Ada's suffering face.

Emmy *(v.o.)*: Don't listen to her! Don't tell your husband!

We see Emmy push a key by mistake. Suddenly Godsdog appears in the scene and looks around. Startled by her mistake, Emmy pushes the save button.

Cut to: Scene 85

The screen blinks and then fades and comes up.

Emmy *(to Godsdog)*: I've got to get some air.

Nicholas walks in, walks around the room, settles down on the sofa and thumbs through some magazines.

Godsdog: Emmy's a carrier.

Nicholas keeps reading, not paying any attention.

Godsdog: Emmy's an agent.

Nicholas looks up.

Godsdog: Emmy's a carrier that could infect your son.

Nicholas: Emmy, what is he saying?

The telephone rings. Emmy stirs ignores it as the answering machine picks up the call.

Nicholas: What have you done, Emmy?

She looks away.

Nicholas: The truth Emmy. What does he mean?

Emmy: Sims says it was safe. Besides, it's only temporary.

Nicholas: What's only temporary mean? What are you doing Emmy. The truth. Do you know what the truth is?

Emmy: I just immersed myself into her code patterns. It was the only way to make direct contact. I needed to use my DNA not only to make contact with Ada, but to create an antibody that might save Sims. It was a matter of life and...

Nicholas: Emmy, it's one thing to take chances with your life, but our baby had no choice. He can be affected by all of this. The transfer can affect him too! Sometimes you're so stupid, Emmy. You promised.

Emmy: I just wanted to see if it would work.

Nicholas: That's what the inventors of the Atomic bomb said.

He grabs Emmy and shakes her. They begin to fight.

Emmy *(weakly)*: The patterns have half life memories. They evaporate; wear off very quickly.

Nicholas: How do you know there are no after effects. Like Agent Orange, if no one has ever done this before.

Godsdog: Nicholas has done this before.

Both Emmy and Nicholas stare at Godsdog.

Emmy: What?

Godsdog: Nicholas revised the codes.

Emmy sinks into a chair.

Emmy: If you've been in here messing around, I have no idea what has changed. I only knew what I was doing was safe.

In frustration, Nicholas punches the computer, turning it over as he leaves. Godsdog reels back.

Nicholas: Emmy, they tell pregnant women to wear lead aprons when they get x-rayed and here you are, flagrantly making cyber anti-bodies with our son's life at stake. What are we going to do?

Emmy: Pray.

Nicholas leaves.

Nicholas: I'm going to ask Sims. Maybe he will know.

We hear Emmy sobbing under the next scenes.

Scene 86

The screen blinks a bit, then fades and come up.
Close up of the shadow of William in profile, seated by the bed.

Ada *(piteously)*: Try to understand, William. You forgive me, don't you? Not because I deserve it, but because we have to say good-bye.

Without answering, he takes her arm. The birthmark shows through her transparent sleeve. He kisses her hand and sobs.

> Ada *(cont'd) (reaching out weakly)*: William? You know I
> loved only you.

He leaves, still sobbing...

Close up of Ada's face as her head falls back against the pillow. Tears trickle out of her eyes.

The Emmy alias is crying behind Ada.

Dr. Locock appears at the bedside with a syringe, and administers the drug.

> Child's V.O.: In the end, it was William who proved to be
> noble. His love was complete. He loved and protected
> her despite the transgressions.

Dissolve to: Scene 87

Close up of Ada lying back weakly now.

> Ada *(dreamily)*: Yes, Mother... I renounce the devil. I
> repent of my sins...

> Emmy *(v.o.)*: Oh, Ada...

> Ada *(faintly)*: Oh, are you still here? I thought I had
> imagined you as a means of hedging my bets with death.

Dissolve to: Scene 88

There is a droning sound. P.O.V. shot of a figure which gradually becomes clearer: it is a priest standing over Ada's bed giving her the last rites. Close up of Ada.

> Priest: You are forgiven for the sins you have committed
> through the sense of taste.
> *(draws crosses over her lips, then her hands)*
> You are forgiven for the sins you have committed
> through the sense of touch...

> Ada *(softly)*: The final irony! I'm forgiven for things I'm not
> in the least sorry for.

> Emmy *(desperately)*: Ada — you don't have much time left,
> I can feel your heart pounding as well as mine —

The heartbeats become deafening.

> Ada: Are you there? Come to save me?

> Emmy *(o.s.)*: Yes.

Ada: How?

Emmy *(o.s.)*: I'm able to clone your memory patterns.
Everything you are thinking. Everything in your
memory.

Ada: Clone? What do you mean? I don't know that word.
Is it French?

Emmy: Oh, it's so difficult to make you understand what
we can do now. Believe me Ada, I can bring out your
memory patterns. Copy them exactly. They will exist in
a half life that will exist forever.

Ada: Half? That's a bad bargain. I'm not at all certain a
half-life is better than none.

Emmy *(o.s.)*: It's the only way.

Ada: How?

Emmy: Through me.

Ada: And why should I be saved at your expense?

Emmy *(o.s.)*: To take your rightful place, in history. So we
will all know the truth about your life. I promise that in
the year 2000 all the details that no one knows can be
made public. We will celebrate your accomplishments.

Ada: My rightful place? The year 2000? 166 years from
now?
(sighs, turning her head away, then laughs)
During my lifetime, I have lost all I ever called my own.
I have had to cede everything. My house, my work, my
body. Everything was taken over by others. I even
promised away my immortal soul in exchange for opium
and a little peace. But I still have something of myself
left.
(beat)
I can speak for myself, for my soul, or, as you put it, my
essence. I will not send it on to colonize you. Even for
history. You are my last friend and I will not taint you
with my diminished passions. The redeeming gift of
humanity is the ability of each generation to recreate
itself.

Emmy *(o.s.)*: Think of your heirs.

Ada *(with a faint smile)*: They will have to take their
   chances like I took mine. Life itself is a gamble.
   (beat)
   Besides, I would not want all my secrets known. Or to
   be watched after my death.

Emmy: But Ada...

Ada: There is genius in our blood. We will calculate
   another solution.
   (beat)
   Everything is perishable. Even time. Death makes the
   fragility of life delicious. In general I am not opposed to
   it.

She drapes her veil over the bird. The image winks out.

Pull back to reveal Emmy sobbing.

Child's V.O. *(under sobs)*: Babbage was so distressed by this
   premature death that he became isolated and bitter. It
   was only after death that the validity of their ideas and of
   their calculations were proven to have been true.

Extended-Body

An Interview with Stelarc

Paolo Atzori and Kirk Woolford

Stelarc is an Australian performance artist, born in Limasol, island of Cyprus. Stelarc moved to Australia, where he studied Arts and Craft at TSTC, Art and Technology at CAUTECH and MRIT, Melbourne University. He taught Art and Sociology at Yokohama International School and Sculpture and Drawing at Balurat University College.

Stelarc has been extending his body through performances since the late 1960s. His performances include attaching a "Third Hand" to his body, extending himself into virtual space with a "Virtual Arm," and over 25 suspension events where he hung his entire body from hooks piercing his skin. Stelarc's artistic strategy revolves around the idea of "enhancing the body" both in a physical and technical manner. It originates as a polarity between the "primal desire" to defeat the force of gravity with low-tech primitive rituals and the hi-tech performance with the third hand and the related cybersystem. His intention in both cases is to "express an idea with his direct experience."

Through Stelarc's work, we reach a second level of existence where the body becomes the object for physical and technical experiments in order to discover its limitations. When Stelarc speaks of the "obsolete body" he means that the body must overcome centuries of prejudices and begin to be considered as an extendible evolutionary structure enhanced with the most disparate technologies, which are more precise, accurate and powerful: "the body lacks of modular design;" "technology is what defines the meaning of being human, it's part of being human." Especially living in the information age, "the body is biologically inadequate."

For Stelarc, "Electronic space becomes a medium of action rather than information".

Paolo Atzori/Kirk Woolford: When did you first decide to hang yourself between two different worlds — to place your body between two levels of existence?

Stelarc: Well, you have to remember the suspension events weren't the initial, sort of primitive and physically difficult events and the technology ones the more recent, more sophisticated ones. In fact, the third hand project began a year after the first suspension event. These things were happening simultaneously. On the one hand you were discovering the psychological and physical limitations of the body. On the other you were developing strategies for extending and enhancing it through technology. I've always used technology in my performances. The very first things I made in art school were helmets and goggles that altered your binocular perception, which stylistically have this connection with virtual reality head-mounted displays; and compartments that were whole body pods that you sort of plugged your whole body into, and then were assaulted by electronic sounds and lights.

Atzori/Woolford: When people see your suspension events, they immediately think of Hindu, American Indian, or other rituals. Which of these practices did you come into contact with first?

Stelarc: It was the Hindu Indian ones that I knew about, but one has to put this into the context that for five years I was doing suspension events with ropes and harnesses, with a lot of technology. Laser eyes were first used when the body was suspended, oh, 1970-71 that sort of time scale, but one of the sort of visual disadvantages of all this paraphernalia was that there was all this visual clutter: all the ropes and harnesses were seen more to support the body than to suspend it, so when I first came across the notion of piercing the skin, I thought, if you could suspend the body using techniques like these, then you would have a minimum of support, you'd have just the insertion and single cable. Mind you, I never hid, there was no desire to make the suspension a kind of image of levitation. For me the cables were lines of tension which were part of the visual design of the suspended body, and the stretched skin was a kind of gravitational landscape. This is what it took for a body to be suspended in a 1-G gravitational field. The other context is the primal desire for floating and flying. A lot of primal rituals have to do with suspending the body, but in the 20th century we have the reality of astronauts floating in zero-G. So the suspension event is between those sort of primal yearnings, and the contemporary reality. Of course, suspension means between two states, so I think there is an interesting linguistic meaning that fits in with the idea of suspending the body. For me there was no religious context, no shamanistic yearnings, no yogic conditioning that had to do with these performances. In fact, they occurred in the same kind of stream of consciousness. In mean, I don't take any anaesthetics, I don't chant or get into altered states. I think metaphysically, in the past, we've considered the skin as surface, as interface. The skin has been a boundary for the soul, for the self, and simultaneously, a beginning to the world. Once technology stretches and pierces the skin, the skin as a barrier is erased.

Atzori/Woolford: Do you follow a very strict discipline to train your body for your performances?

Stelarc: In fact, there's never really been any discipline and when I start feeling the performances have become, in a sense predictable, because the techniques assume more importance than the creative impulses, then I stop doing them. I stopped doing the suspension events four years ago because having done 27 of them in various locations and different situations there seemed to be no more *raison d'etre* to continue doing them. The interest was really coupling the expression of an idea with the direct experience of it. That applies to all of these performances whether the suspension events, the stomach sculpture, the third hand performances, or the virtual arm event. These are all situations where the body is plugged into for direct experience. So it's not interesting for me to talk academically or theoretically about ideas of interface, the important thing for me is to plug in, extend the body with cyber-systems and see what it can actually do.

Atzori/Woolford: So you've always been interested in enhancing the body?

Stelarc: Oh, absolutely. And the connection with VR systems is a very fundamental one for me because, as I said, the very first things I made at art school were these helmets which split your binocular vision and compartments which were sensory environments, multi-modal structures for experience with the body. So that was a primary concern, and really the suspensions are often taken out of context whereas they are part of a series of sensory deprivation and physically difficult events which include: making the three films of the inside of the body, where I had to film three meters of internal space, for example. All these actions occurred simultaneously. The agenda wasn't a stylistic one with a particular technology, it was a general one. A sort of probing and determining the parameters of physical and psychological interface.

Atzori/Woolford: You always work with your body. Your body is your form of representation, your medium. How do you feel being both an artist and an artwork?

Stelarc: It's interesting you've pointed that out, I've never felt that I am the artwork. In fact the reason why my performances are focused on this particular body is that it is difficult for me to convince other bodies to undergo rather awkward, difficult and sometimes painful experiences. This body is just merely the convenient access to a body for particular events and actions. So I've really never been obsessed by the fact that somehow I am the artwork because I don't critique it in that way.

For me the body is an impersonal, evolutionary, objective structure. Having spent two thousand years prodding and poking the human psyche without any real discernible changes in our historical and human outlook, we perhaps need to take a more fundamental physiological and structural approach, and consider the fact that it's only through radically redesigning the body that we will end up having significantly different thoughts and philosophies. I think our philosophies are fundamentally bounded by our physiology; our peculiar kind of aesthetic orientation in the world; our peculiar five sensory modes of processing the world; and our particular kinds of technology that enhance these perceptions. I think a truly alien intelligence will occur from an alien body or from a machine structure. I don't think human beings will come up with fundamentally new philosophies. An alien species may not have the same notions about the universe at all. The desire for unity may well be the result of our rather fragmentary sensory system where we observe the world sensually in packets of discrete and different sensory modes. So our urge to merge, our urge to unify, that religious, spiritual, coming together might very well be due to an inadequacy or an incompleteness in our physiology.

Atzori/Woolford: If such a philosophy is devised, it would not be a human philosophy. How would it be applicable to the human race?

Stelarc: Well of course one shouldn't consider the body or the human species as possessing a kind of absolute nature. The desire to locate the self simply within a particular biological body is no longer meaningful. What it means to be human is being constantly redefined. For me, this is not a dilemma at all.

Atzori/Woolford: So a human is not this entity sitting here with these two arms and two legs, but something more beside?

Stelarc: Yes, of course, if you are sitting there with a heart pacemaker and an artificial hip and something to augment your liver and kidney functions, would I consider you less human? To be quite honest, most of your body might be made of mechanical, silicon, or chip parts and if you behave in a socially acceptable way, you respond to me in a human-like fashion, to me that would make you a kind of human subject.

Atzori/Woolford: You keep speaking about redesigning the human body. Who decides and how should it be redesigned?

Stelarc: (Laughs) There is often misunderstanding about these notions, partly because they are critiqued with a kind of rear-vision mirror mentality of a fascist, dictatorial, Orwellian-big-brother scenario.

   I don't have a utopian perfect body I'm designing a blueprint for, rather I'm speculating on ways that individuals are not forced to, but may want to, redesign their bodies — given that the body has become profoundly obsolete in the intense information environment it has created. It's had this mad, Aristotelian urge to accumulate more and more information. An individual now cannot hope to absorb and creatively process all this information. Humans have created technologies and machines which are much more precise and powerful than the body.

   How can the body function within this landscape of machines? Technology has speeded up the body. The body now attains planetary-escape velocity, has to function in zero-G and in greater time-space continuums. For me this demonstrates the biological inadequacy of the body. Given that these things have occurred, perhaps an ergonomic approach is no longer meaningful. In other words, we can't continue designing technology for the body because that technology begins to usurp and outperform the body. Perhaps it's now time to design the body to match it's machines. We somehow have to turbo-drive the body-implant and augment the brain. We have to provide ways of connecting it to the cyber-network. At the moment this is not easily done, and it's done indirectly via keyboards and other devices. There's no way of directly jacking in. Mind you, I'm not talking here in terms of sci-fi speculation. For me, these possibilities are already apparent. What do we do when confronted with the situation where we discover the body is obsolete? We have to start thinking of strategies for redesigning the body.

Atzori/Woolford: This recombinant body implies a widening of our sensibilities, of our perception. But our senses are linked to our brains, everything "happens" in our brain. So it's not enough to have, for example, X-ray vision. We need to change our synapses, the connections in our brains as well.

Stelarc: We shouldn't start making distinctions between the brain and the body. This particular biological entity with its proprioceptive networks and spinal cord and muscles, it's the total kinesthetic orientation in the world, it's the body's mobility which contributes towards curiosity. The desire to isolate the brain is the result of a Cartesian dualism. It's not really productive any more to think in that sense. We have to think of the body plugged into a new technological terrain.

Atzori/Woolford: We can see things that were previously invisible. We can go to the very little through nano-technology, see into infra-red and ultra violet spectrums, but this is not a direct perception. We get this through artificial systems...

Stelarc: Yes, and what will be interesting is when we can miniaturize these technologies and implant them into the body so that the body as total system becomes subjectively aware again. New technologies tend to generate new perceptions and paradigms of the world, and in turn, allow us to take further steps. If we consider technologies as intermediaries to the world, then, of course, we never have direct experiences. At the moment, we operate within a very thin electro-magnetic spectrum, and I would imagine that as we increasingly operate in wider spheres of reality, then yes, our perceptions and philosophies alter or adjust.

Technology has always been coupled with the evolutionary development of the body. Technology is what defines being human. It's not an antagonistic alien sort of object, it's part of our human nature. It constructs our human nature. We shouldn't have a Frankensteinian fear of incorporating technology into the body, and we shouldn't consider our relationship to technology in a Faustian way — that we're somehow selling our soul because we're using these forbidden energies. My attitude is that technology is, and always has been, an appendage of the body.

Atzori/Woolford: Stelarc, your latest work centers around a sculpture you built for your stomach. What was the impetus for creating a sculpture to display inside your body?

Stelarc: I've moved beyond the skin as a barrier. Skin no longer signifies closure. I wanted to rupture the surface of the body, penetrate the skin. With the stomach sculpture, I position an artwork inside the body. The body becomes hollow with no meaningful distinction between public, private and physiological spaces. The hollow body becomes a host, not for a self or a soul, but simply for a sculpture.

Atzori/Woolford: Funding any artwork is difficult, especially getting money for high tech equipment. Did you have trouble finding funding for the sculpture?

Stelarc: Actually no. One of the museums in Australia was preparing a show and asking for sculptures which explored alternative display spaces. I told them I had an alternative way and place to display a sculpture.

Atzori/Woolford: Can you describe the stomach sculpture?

Stelarc: It's built of implant quality metals such as titanium, steel, silver, and gold. It is constructed as a domed capsule shell about the size of a fist. The shell contains a worm-screw and link mechanism and has a flexidrive cable connected to a servo motor controlled by a logic circuit. The capsule extends and retracts opening and closing in three sections. An embedded instrument array, light and piezo buzzer make the sculpture self-illuminating and sound-emitting.

Atzori/Woolford: How did you insert it?

Stelarc: Very slowly. The stomach sculpture is actually the most dangerous performance I've done. We had to be within five minutes of a hospital in case we ruptured any internal organs. To insert the sculpture, the stomach was first emptied by withholding food for about eight hours. Then the closed capsule, with beeping sound and flashing light activated, was swallowed and guided down tethered to it's flexidrive cable, attached to the control box outside the body. Once inserted into the stomach, we used an endoscope to inflate the stomach and suck out the excess body fluids. The sculpture was then arrayed with switches on the control box. We documented the whole performance using video endoscopy equipment. Even with a stomach pump, we still had a problem with excess saliva. We had to hastily remove all the probes on several occasions.

Atzori/Woolford: Now you've penetrated the body. You've hollowed it out, extended it, expanded it, hung it out a window, mapped out several miles of its interior. What is the next step?

Stelarc: It is time to recolonise the body with microminaturised robots to augment out bacterial population, to assist our immunological system, and to monitor the capillary and internal tracts of the body. We need to build an internal surveillance system for the body. We have to develop microbots whose behavior is not pre-programmed, but activated by temperature, blood chemistry, the softness or hardness of tissue and the presence of obstacles in tracts. These robots can then work autonomously on the body. The biocompatibility of technology is not due to its substance, but to its scale. Speck-sized robots are easily swallowed and may not even be sensed. At a nanotech level, machines will navigate and inhabit cellular spaces and manipulate molecular structures to extend the body from within.

Debauching the Digitalis
(this is me, speaking to you)

Sue Golding

Part I: (this)

Avoidance as creation. First, the problem of zero, one {0,1; or even, 0 —> 1; maybe also: beyond 0; finally, just the 1}. Did you know that the square root of any positive number after zero is eventually — I mean, after awhile (that is, at least to nine digits, sometimes rounded up or down) — always and without fail equal to: 1. Peculiar, though not fascinating, except to the very few. Indeed, probably only to those with calculators and extra time on their hands, bored with some other mathematical task (say, figuring out the law of averages). With the aid of light avoidance techniques — boredom, self-abuse, whimsy, for example — surprising things can be accomplished, even with the most simple of calculators! Like pressing the magic √ button enough times until a 1 emerges from any (positive) anonymous chaos. Nerd sublimity.

Part II: (this is)

I would like to report right now, and without hesitation, that Bataille's wry sense of luxury, for whom the eating of one species by another is but a tasty, albeit expensive, treat has fallen into the category of yesterday's news. Witness the recent television programme on "animal cannibalism." Photographed in detailed slow motion, I watched everything from amoebas to lions eating 'their own kind' seemingly without guilt, often in the trashy name of love, sex, power, scarcity of resources or just good old-fashioned street gang furore. Some kind of sectarianism (left, right or centre)? No, that cannot be right: I'm confusing cannibalism with the all too usual strains of political infanticide.

Part III: (this is me)

Four children's questions: the practical one asks: how?; the evil one always asks: why?; the wise one restates in question form the that; and the one who cannot ask any questions doesn't ask a thing. I have heard this somewhere before. Where? Why? What does it matter that it matters? [0]? Could be charades; sounds like: the passing (over) from exile to freedom. Maybe just democracy as a proposition of timing.

Part IV: (this is me speaking)

Peel back the surface of anything, let's say, for convenience, the surface of a conventional table. Place the peeled surface over there, for a minute. Now, go paint the new surface using only primary colours. Hold up a mirror to your new work of art. What gave you the genius not to go outside the lines? Maybe it was just early encouragement with those lovely little baby colouring books when you were awarded prizes for doing the job properly! Or, more probably, your neatness was the result of a repetitive wound-trauma from badly administered toilet training! You have your doubts with either scenario? Your uncertainty might just be correct.

Part V: (this is me speaking to)

Virtual beings created on the net. Is it only me, or have you noticed that the only lack you multiple, seemingly radical imaginations lack has mainly to do with the smelly juices of an (absent) orifice, especially genital. Come to think of it, pluralised sexual orientations, genders, humours, laughters, forgettings, and etc. seem to have gone also to that heavenly elsewhere located somewhere other in the brave new (old) electronic sky. Applied technology gone horribly wrong or horribly right? An endless supply of re-packaged deodorizers resurrected (sans the more unpleasant virtues of excremental dirt). Can't zero/one games do better than this? Something is sorely lacking.

Part VI: (this is me speaking to you)

> Yea, but I am ashamed, disgraced, dishonoured, degraded, exploded: my notorious crimes and villainies are come to light (deprendi miserum est [it is a wretched thing to be caught]), my filthy lust, abominable oppression and avarice lies open, my good name's lost, my fortune's gone, I have been stigmatized, whipped at post, arraigned and condemned, I am a common obloquy, I have lost my ears, odious, execrable, abhorred of God and men. Be content, 'tis but a nine days' wonder, and as one sorrow drives out another, one passion another, one cloud another, one rumour is expelled by another; every day almost come new sun to your ears, as how the sun was eclipsed, meteors seen i' th' air, monsters born, prodigies, how the Turks were overthrown in Persia, an earthquake in Helvetica, Calabria, Japan, or China, an inundation in Holland, a great plague in Constantinople, a fire at Prague, a dearth in Germany, such a man I made a lord, a bishop, another hanged, deposed, pursued to death, for some murder, treason, rape, theft, oppression, all which we do hear at first with a kind of admiration, detestation, consternation, but by and by they are buried in silence...
>
> Comfort thyself, thou art not the sole man."[1]

You do not understand what has been noted by one Mr. Robert Burton way back in 1621! Answer then the following skill testing remark, tracking carefully, and without mirth or indiscretion, the four points under discussion:

> The machine went melancholic (then ballistic) when confronted with the mutation of an affirmative negation. Discuss with relation to (a) Auschwitz; (b) Hiroshima; (c) civil society; (d) fairy tales.

Make sure you double space all answers. THERE CAN BE NO EXTEN-SIONS, unless properly footnoted. Wine will be served at the end of the meal. Good luck. All e-mailed responses accompanied with recent photo and telephone/fax will receive immediate attention.

Ignore the man behind the curtain.

Notes

1. Robert Burton, *The Anatomy of Melancholy*, in three volumes, (1621), as reprinted (5th edition, 1638, as reprinted 1932), New York/London: Everyman's Library, 1932/1972), v. 2, pp. 199-200.

Bring the Noise

Mega-Tranced Flesh
Interference-Patterns
[Poet as Strobe Starling]

John Nòto

I click on San Francisco's premier college radio-station, KUSF, and am met
with a growling sound difficult to distinguish from the static and roar of the
airwaves themselves — it is the raging, guttural voice of the DeathMetal band
Sepultura's lead vocalist, pinning my ears back with the corruption of human flesh
irrupting with the digested sound and fury of the world's robotic simulcast mania.

I attend the screening of a recent Hong Kong film, *Chungking Express* by
Wong Kar Wai, filled with stroboscopic bodies, faster-than-light dialogue and
scenes in which the background whirls and zooms in ultra-fast-forward mimicry of
Heart-On-Speedball-Mediagraphic-Overkill.

I open a slick contemporary photography magazine called *BIG*, and am
arrested by the "Diaries of Peter Beard," a word-and-image collage hybrid, densely,
intensely packed with the instant-memorabilia and quick verbal sketches endemic
to the life in the fast lane we've all been forced to live under the Stars 'n Hypes of
America's advertising-as-lifestyle hypnoinertia. Beard pictures everything from the
plasticwomen of the "men's" magazines to (sometimes juxtaposed with) childhood
memory Post-Its on the InfoSuperhighway bulletin board, memory, that is, as
advertising copy…

I stumble upon an exhibition of "New Abstract" paintings by Oakland,
California's brilliant Brad Johnson; paintings layered with sticky, dredged, raked,
gouged, trawled, streaked, mottled and smudged oils over delicate, atmospheric
green-gold and fire-red patinas — the look of an excavation site: muck & mire
ambiguously but poignantly gummed over the sheen of human spirit which yet
streams gorgeously through like angelic light onto the curtains of Hell.

All these and more I've seen in every medium, art-stories of the Age of Chaos
& Complexity, the Era of the False Crescendo — except one medium; what's
holding poetry back?

Why do virtually all poems written today, whether "lyric" or "postmodern,"
treat the world as though the last 35 years of discovery in technology, philosophy
and the other arts never occurred or are barely worthy of notice? Why will poets not
tackle the Information Age (as a present and inevitable influence, not as the

"enemy"), the Loss of Privacy, The Phenomenon of Global Breathlessness, the sheer impenetrability of contemporary life to sensory-processing (not as a bald-faced evil, but as a reality to cope and wrestle with), and tackle these on their own terms in the milieu of North America, 1997? Why is almost everyone writing poems as though the world were a still and tranquil reflecting pool for quiet contemplation as though grandma were still in the kitchen making apricot preserves with FDR on the radio reassuring us of the constancy of Western Civilization?

Does a continued loyalty to "elevated" subject matter still hold sway over even self-professed "avant-garde" poets? Are many poets afraid to break the "precious and proper" mold? Yes, I think so. Have today's poets forgotten the lesson of the Beats, that there may be spiritual beauty in man-made ugliness, the lesson of the Surrealists, that imagery's power multiplies geometrically in juxtaposition? Have they ignored the developments in a dozen other art media (including, right next door, relevant advances in literary fiction!) over the last two+ decades? — Sure looks that way!

Leafing through even some of the most reputedly "cutting-edge" journals, I am struck by the extent to which none of this has registered, or to which it has been shunted aside in favor of trendy, utterly indecipherable work which, evidently, is the stuff of high-powered "careers" in academia.

In the last two years, though, I have seen breaks in the levee — the acceptance of Kerouac's work by a sub-group of academics, the sudden interest in certain contemporary "Neo-Surrealists" (I use the term loosely for want of a better one) such as Will Alexandere and Ivan Arguelles, whose work operates at the density-potential threshold needed to begin describing the artifice-soup of signal-matrices, jammed mental circuits and proprioceptive arrest we've created and in which we've immersed our flesh and souls, the emergence of a loosely-knit group of widely scattered poets and essayists in their late 20s through 40s, who are rocketing past and away from stale poetic tradition and trend like Desolation Zealots high on diffEQ and Laser Cryptography.

These poets understand that density, stress, overload and penetration are as essential considerations as meter and deconstruction. Their poetry weaves dense, complex tapestries of sound-meanings taken from broadcast élan and brocaded with brightly-hued, cutting and dancing narrative, the human spirit on pins & needles threading its way in primal nobility through the layers of overlay, layers so "noise-y" as to appear aleatory at times — "irrelevant" detail ensnared in a web of probabilities, price quotes and yearnings, with a strong undercurrent of "I-want-to-be-seen-and-there-is-a-story-to-be-told-here-dammit"!!!

Theirs is no quiet, contemplative, "broken" language surrounded by the preciousness of pregnant negative space! After all, this is not Hellenic Athens, nor 17th century Japan, nor Browning's England, nor is it even "Modernist" America. It is the late 1990s — The Age of Writhing and Rapture Before the Anti-Sign of MediaSpeak, a conglomerate of street-ese and "suit"-talk, the color-the-world-by-numbers we call home. These poets pervert it, play with it, mutate it and inflate it to larger-than-life proportions, all with unabashed, strongheaded, but ever aware, panache. The work is jarring, incisive, deadly!

Their poems are mostly not about spruce trees, peaches and clotheslines blowing in the wind, nor are they abstracted musings on the esoteric rituals of linguistic analysis and endless self-reference. They mostly are about the human voices howling through this tempestuous, ice-hot Night of a Million Channels. Whether "lyric" or fragmentary or a combination, the peaceful, proper poem of the workshops and the "postmodern" canon is about as relevant to living in 90s North America as Elizabethan couplets or Alexandrine prosody are to the language of the City streets. The poets I speak of know this in their bones from the get go. That's why their poems are so damn sexy!

> Tricked into time's burning dress, you catch buildings in your beard of flux…
>
> …your flack, "spatial montages" in "zone[s] of hypermodernity." Houses of impulse, disposable
> solace! Nomadness of nomads, dwelling as sojourn!
> "No call-waiting for empyrean fire." Place, voracious hole, pivots with tenses…
>
> …Disemboweled planes, kiddie-straw struts, giddy smears of
> color, aluminum sides: the self-hating home, technocracy's deathproject!
>
> It's a managram, right? I mean, *R.E.M. Cool-house?*
>
> …*Delirious N.Y.*, delirious world (a global postman's palace). Delirious,
> I consume my backyard:
> unslotted panes, ground cover and jonquils, wild violets…
>
> *from David Hoefer's "Rem Koolhaas"*

Their language is often breathless and abbreviated from its encounter with the void deep inside "busy"-ness in America, the very Heart of Darkness in the guise of the Virtues of Hard Work, Progress and Professionalism, the encounter with the basest, subtlest animal augmented to techno-god and Chief Operating Officer, Bill Gates as the new Satan at the core of us all, salivating as he brushes Rembrandt and Mozart into the dustbin of history in favor of the rights to their electronic $$ after-images.

The most admired person is the one who has *him/herself* molded into product, self-packaged and image-managed and on his/her way to your home on CD-ROM.

The blond elastic rain beneath the saw on the fuel-floor
A video-inoculated child immune from the fire-storm
Steers keyboard flames to a cornered matrix-man

How the fire-axe open his cartoon hands and heart
Each impuse-induced event on a binary switch
The blowing-away release a spasm of highlight
On a blackboard globe a child chalks countries in...

If this were a children's book where clear picture-plates
Are laid over one another each with its layer of the picture
Whose question is what would it be had each never been
Whose question doubles each year like silver coins...

I was told to make it this way by the voice of god...

The smooth screen renders dice and investment choice
The laser printer purr as the options expire...

It is said there are six worlds six veils six paper selves
When you see the dead hold their pasts in the tunnel-face
Bring a single voice bring rain some wheels of rain
You are one in an age of fissure-blades and teeth
A boat of broken sticks a boat of bronze a boat of flames
When you identify the dead you have passed the narrows
In the air in the falling cold you are in for a long climb

from Lindsay Hill's "NdjenFerno"

There are times when nothing less than a phased, seeming-chaos of appropriated high-holy words and phrases will suffice to unscramble the sacrificial noise of
spirit embedded within force-fields emitting only interference-cardiography from
nets swathed in tight-lipped cash-transfer, distorting...

I recline in this noble hell
and pretend an appearance
allows bodies to writhe in warm metal air
filigree carbon
    or geography is a world dreaming species through
    Rumi ringdoves shivering mercury's
    stones to numb muscle sunflower diode she in twin
chondria
    fuels the microphage, equates cool aluminum,
pelvis, thistle and yew
reactor's gray theater, the spiral contracts and takes
root —

...[ignition steel green moonflower
   decides murder in a backseat,
   handcuffed, dismembered
   transplanted in half countenance
      emerald
     mandrake [(barter)]...

5. microwave assault foreshadows as an abstract of skull
   generators whose coils devise rust, ideogram...

7. Castor is barren from eye facile bondage
   until the extractor redeems with Quetzal-jade rain...

from Jake Berry's "Brambu Drezi", Part II

...Like that.
Then, the suppressed rage gasses, sparks the torch-lit appendices flaring with
lost knowledge of the Cloud Comanchee:

Apocalypse Now Reaches Critical Racheting
Sky Come Flaming Down

I mine steel-tank salvation
disclosure riddled with bulletholes, licking the flames;
cut-switch plies silence censored with rumbling
pipes, shredded documents, sysops, begging cups;

Know that rasp and tourniquet pressing blood
onto static-y plastiform rushes —
the ranks of the untouchables;
industrial filmic coding fingerpaints switchblade lungs
collapsed face-building onto a shear, the chest-knot
ice blocks mirror, claws: a boneless owl
stares back from muttered steam;

Ebola formats Disney lymphocyte debt-management,
"Should someone grunt, the scruff of the elbow groin
is forfeit" — running flush with dowel-in-anus,
wrangling the Dow,   like,
"Has anyone got a match?"

FLAMMABLE GAS — DO NOT LIGHT UP

   ...BROOOM!!

from John Nòto's "Perpetual War: Wrist Control
Tourniquet Owl"

Yet, sometimes a poet must look through the sky's dismissed ozone to fix the star-snake's gaze and call on Circe and Athena to dispense with his/her agony and dash it on the rocks in a burst of flash powder and blood metallurgy.

Imagine, so many sweet things in such thin air, but it is not so

...It is a flat, pear-shaped garment with vertical openings
that reveal the vault of heaven, and that's going to be
my excuse to wallow in the mud, right?...

STILL, THE SPIRIT REFUSES TO CONCEIVE WITHOUT A
BODY.

Perhaps because of all this, bloody bundles appear in desolate corners.

obietos de seducao...

That's me displaying.

movable dream lab.

inside the lid: something long buried: subdued light, carpeted
floors, stairs, bird beak, a couch of some kind, forgotten
books, stones, dirt, water, beautiful illegible scribbles,
voices down the hall narrating as if a whole new continent I
have been listening to all my life passing under the roof of
my mouth, inwards.

from Karen Kelley's "A Description of the World..."

So passes the old poetics into oblivion (or at least history!). An entire world and all its conceits, baubles and false promises reflex — swallowed by a new age faster than a snapping mousetrap. Let the devil meet the deep blue sea and unravel his inks in its fathoms — the flesh and the code are deposits of a god-like raiment, the pulse and resistance of the MultiPlex Fray.

Poetry, then, has been playing catch up, riding gamy, old horses in a race against turbo-charged cheetahs. At the very least, we must begin to mount Arabian stallions with night-vision and enhanced traction-control! Meet me at the stables...

Camcorder: Deluxe Titles Suck Optical Coitus

John Nòto

Zero-sum.

A man breaks down and is mechanized,
and 100,000 expendable Iraqis revive
as android processors on keyboards
invoke the spectre of a binary order
an Egyptian woman embroiders on a tabouret
the image of a couple embracing
through the flesh of their own children
warped out geometrically   across the globe
an attack of air-phones
lures an entire school to its death

At the port of Israel
on a bus muffled voices with guns
force gas in the mouths of significant others
through the lost playgrounds
I was crushed and tagged
by a vicious number:
the next rise in expectations

Slips soothing replicant memories inside
the global mudslide cartoon
swallows the post-nuclear family
beached on a shelf   celluloid
through the voices of wave-people
the lion-faced serpent

Who will announce the names
I've shaved
to protect the innocent
they kept under cold surveillance?

A woman in a black garter belt
presses distended nipples against a stiff,
cocks, pivots and vanishes
beneath the rim of the Indian subcontinent
Sumatra glows exotic
pebbles in the dash of the Seychelles
spill down dark reflector tape
moonwash
unzipping the world

Through a rift   in the birth of velcro
a Caesarean scar lingers
on my hidden wing-camera   the moon waxed
as a snow-blind leopard might smoke in her eyes
an endless cycle of frenzy and slow-scan

Over Antarctic cliffs
the convenience store of a billion tears
caresses the right urge
to build a consensus alarm
into heat-seeking loins
instantly and with unmediated ruthlessness

Shocked on the groin
out in the killing fields
my test scores cancel   meat-clamps
extending prosthetic incisors
access the G-spot in North Korea
and rip out its tonsils

Along my inner thighs
the force behind acute multi-level marketing
schemes the transport of helium bells
dripping from sleeves of Nepalese spirit armies
under the shuddering stars
a sabertooth llama
breaks the silence
riding the world-gasm like a tube
aboard breaking trends

In wetware   thong-back
Euro-trash shunts down a mall   golden
under the sky-machine   a unicorn bridled
before dawn
systemic assimilations to the screamscape
load both barrels
and the queen of ravished gypsies
lies with slaves

Labor-intensive   menacing hands
sail the ship of state through horse latitudes
anywhere in the minus column
the unknown and unwanted
count as seams in the hull of the world
and hooves tighten   trance-like
over the gallop of commerce
the most innocent confession forced

A skin-sensitive switch jammed in the off-position
halts seven continents   grimacing
contestants behave homogeneously
consuming the pattern of oats
and unquenchable thirst
strapped on your native dressage   a livid cat
wrestling for the feedbag

Within the whining   RAGE
suck my eyes from the face of the lens.

Augustine of Epcot

Confessions of a Hyper-Miraculous Age from Chronicles of Life in the Electronic Middle Ages; or, The City of Disney

Daniel R. White

Difficile est saturam non scribere ("It's difficult not to write satire")

Juvenal

Preface

News stories like the following emanated from the Tampa Bay area in Florida during December of 1996:

CLEARWATER — A finance company on busy U.S. 19 became the site of a mass pilgrimage Tuesday when a stain on the building's side assumed the visage of the Virgin Mary for the faithful.[1]

CLEARWATER — The trickle of pilgrims coming to an office building to see a two-story image resembling the Virgin Mary turned into a traffic-clogging throng on Wednesday. Thousands went to Seminole Finance Corp. near Drew Street and U.S. 19 to see the sight and, in some cases, look for a miracle.[2]

CLEARWATER — When a city has a high-profile apparition of the Virgin Mary on its hands, it calls for serious action. That's why Clearwater officials on Thursday established the Miracle Management Task Force.[3]

TOKYO, 1997 JAN 13 (NB) — This is a roundup of new and updated resources and services on the global Internet, including: in the news — Virgin Mary in Florida.[4]

CLEARWATER — Covering nine panels of bronze-tinted glass, the image evokes an impressionist stained glass portrait of Mary, her downward gaze cloaked in a mantle of swirling hues. Although glass experts have attributed the multicolored pattern to the effects of weather and sun, belief overrides science for most visiting the makeshift shrine.[5]

CLEARWATER — Throughout the large parking lot Monday, people bowed their heads, knelt on the pavement and openly wept before the sight. Many of them added to what has become a shrine of several hundred prayer candles, potted poinsettias, photographs of loved ones and hand-scrawled pleas for help.[6]

CLEARWATER — Some 800 pilgrims stand at noon in the south parking lot of Seminole Finance Company, near Drew Street on U.S. 19: construction workers, business people in suits, mothers with babies, teenagers, the elderly, the disabled. Tears stream down the faces of new arrivals. Strangers converse and share their wonder. Around the periphery, six television satellite trucks stretch microwave towers heavenward. Reporters work the crowd.[7]

I found myself, on December 31st, amidst this crowd of the curious, fascinated and desperate. I just happened to be in Clearwater for the afternoon. I hadn't planned to attend the miracle, but, as traffic swept me into its vortex, I became a participant-observer. I have recorded my impressions below through the eyes of a fictive persona, Augustine of Epcot. I offer this event-scene as an experiment in altered subjectivity and critical historicity: the first of Augustine's confessions and chronicles of our times.

Book I: Event-Scene: Miracle on US 19

"The appearance of the an image in glass, on a finance company building in Clearwater, Florida, has drawn pilgrims by the thousands, a multitude of the faithful come to view the miraculous vision of the Virgin in Glass." So the author's consciousness of the late twentieth century, only three years from the millennium, might construe the events of this day of our Lord, 31 December 1996. As I must speak in that Authorial mode, I do so now, understanding the Limits of Insight that this entails, but such are the conditions of our current Fall into the realm of Subjectivity, a kind of Captivity in the Babylon of Consumerism, whose Intellect is condemned to Produce Commodities in the Alienated Person of Authority. But, if I may confess, I view things somewhat differently, amidst my ceaseless wanderings under the bridges, across the parks, through the Stadiums of — in the words of a recent friendly Saint suited in gold like (but not actually of the same substance as the original) Elvis — the hyperreal kingdom, "America": self-proclaimed star of two continents, supervening locally like the haggard pixellated ghost of divinity *absconditus* upon the landscape of my home peninsula. I was born here in mid-century, 1950, in a little house on 23rd Avenue North, whose number signifies that Psalm which makes of all faithful Sheep, in St. Petersburg, home of the retired, the dead and the dying, home too of the Segregated Drinking Fountain and the wars of race and class flowing from it, a city named after another old Saint friend of Mine and, soon, no doubt, of Yours if I may be permitted a moment of *memento mori*. Though I didn't know it at the time, I was born, this time once again (yes, I confess, this is a heterodox idea, reincarnation, popular not only in the Old Empire but also, more recently, in upper-caste California) as a neighbor to the coming Event. That Occurrence, the celestial visit in Clearwater, is perhaps the organizing eschaton of Florida history, and perhaps even of our collective history to date, if we take into account the great European invasion of Florida by Ponce de Leon, itself the tip of a great migratory toe stepping onto North America, in search of youth and gold and hope and, of course, Real Estate. Could it All have led here, to the Corner of US 19 and Drew Street in Clearwater? To visit this site, You might think so.

So, this is how it begins, and this is how it will end, perhaps, the story of our times in this terribly stricken land of Florida, once the domain of Flowers, lately visited by the ghostly image of our Lady. The appearance of the Virgin in glass is the miracle the great stream of travelers has been seeking all along, I believe, in their ceaseless wandering up and down the asphalt river between the shrines of consumerism, the great Malls gracing our landscape like Tombs, their designer iconography illuminated by hot lights under plate glass, plastic visages frozen in smiles of concerted amity, Directed toward the Final sale and the transubstantiation of the very lives of the seekers miraculously into Commodities: those malling sheep in the flock of the devoted, all in quest of their dreams. Our dreams. I have looked in awe at them, and at myself reflected, like our Lady, in glass, my image a patina of light laid delicately over the more stately images of the mannequins behind shop glass, wondering how I myself might become transformed into an idol of the market, and I have reflected too on my own image, pale and imperfect as it must needs be, in the presence of that Radiance I witnessed today on Highway 19. But less of myself, for now, and more of the Virgin and Her other admirers, many of whom have come so far to witness a miracle.

There is an eeriness, a strange panic and hushed desperation, evident on the faces of the devoted before our Lady of the Glass, so many attempting, futilely I imagine, to capture Her miracle in the boxes of their cameras, some of which are of the Kodak disposable variety, to take home to enthrall their friends and neighbors. They might well Hope to Package some of Her, perhaps, standing before the (I might admit I hope without disrespect) rather oily image of the celestial Lady, emerging with such glory on the Finance facade, just below a Sign, a billboard for medical services, itself rising above the litany of the traffic, reading "Have your tattoos removed." Indeed, the box — camera, "vault," *kamera*, "chamber," as our Latin and Greek Fathers would say — is in some sense a key to the mystery of the Virgin, or at least to Her effect here in Clearwater, itself a kind of *camera lucida* projecting the celestial image, as if through a spiritual microscope, upon the Plate of Commerce. For she is not only gracing that Industry offering promises of happiness and protection from calamity, as our Lady herself is wont to do, but She is surrounded by — seemingly encased in — the great icons of power which are interspersed on the landscape between the Malls, so many beacons on the road to Orlando, signs of our Progress toward our End. Our lady appears, to the cinematically conditioned consciousness, as a muted curvaceous rainbow, rather like those Madonnas one used to see in Byzantium, and now sees on the Arts and Entertainment Network (Angels & Evangels, I would have thought), mosaic images of our holy Mother emanating from tesserae of blue, amber and gold, on the walls of Churches in the Old Empire and on the Monitors of Cable Christendom in the New. She arises from the tesserae of mineral deposits on glass, stricken and transformed by Light, and hangs there amidst, as I was saying, the Signs.

"Amoco," reads one on the corner just below our Lady's visage, itself a logo in red and blue, offering the blessing of transport to the pilgrims, from mall to mall, and a kind of industrial oasis for their wheeled-internal-combustion boxes of steel, plastic and glass, which bear them into the presence of the Lady, and require considerable attention from local Authorities in charge of traffic, and litany, control. Of these Authorities and their orchestration of devotees, I shall speak Again. "Pelican Car Wash" is emblazoned on yet another sign, though this one seems less universal than Amoco, notwithstanding its promise of "oil change while you wait," conveniently, I surmise, allowing the devoted further to rejuvenate and even illuminate their automotive cubicles with polish, while attending the miracle. "Kane's Furniture" offers its self-evident, if again less than universal, appeal from across the eight lanes of concrete whose Signs say US 19, a way reminiscent of those *viae* constructed in the Old Empire, Via Appia etc., this being no doubt the Via Commercii, whose ancient forebears lead to great Imperial monuments we once admired and then shunned in favor of the Savior and, of course, his Mother, whom we in turn shunned in favor Images, and Madonnas too, more worldly and, some would say, profane. Curiously, though, no one has yet seen fit to purchase any chairs or tables or other paraphernalia of Comfort from Kane's, to enhance his or her stay in the Presence of our Lady. The Authorities, themselves present in considerable number, would no doubt disapprove of that. There is a woman selling cotton vestments, "T-Shirts" her Sign reads, bearing the title, "Miraculous Mary," which some younger Seekers seem to think may be the name of a "band" of "punk" minstrels rather than of our Lady, but on this subject I am not qualified to speak. In any case, the devotees stand, and mill, and stare in the presence of the "awesome." "No Parking" is also evident, highlighted by a forest of orange cones pointing, like so many Fingers of Remonstration by the Authorities, toward Heaven, and this at least has the aura of universality again, being a sign (No Parking) which God no doubt would have given to Paul in his Fortunate fall from his legged vehicle on the road to Damascus, with a vision of the Son shining in his eyes, if it were not for His infinite mercy in allowing saints to exvehiculate during visions (a policy I have recommended in several editorials to the Clearwater Sun, none of which has appeared as yet in print, possibly due to the paper's fear of angering the Authorities).

I have, by the way, watched this Virgin miracle on Tele-Vision, as They call it, and it is not the same as being there, though of Tele-Visual miracles I shall also speak Again. Our lady appears, curiously, in multiple apparitions on various panes of the Finance Company, leading one to believe that her appearance is meant to have less than a unique appeal, perhaps indicating the complexity of projecting divinity in what Saint Baudrillard called the realm of Simulacra, a Zone in Saint Pynchon's sense more suited, perhaps, to the apprentices of the Sorcerer than to the passionate admirers of our Lady, but, again, this could be, in spite of my preference for "being there," a domain where the actual event and the Tele-Visual have, miraculously in a strange new sense, been transubstantiated. One has only to re-envision her mineral tesserae as digital bits of primary color, to Imagine one is squinting at a Modern painting by Seurat or at the site of the Louvre on the Internet. But I precede myself again, and promise to speak of media miracles in a later chapter. You Authorities reading these words may ignore my comments on Tele-Vision and on Yourselves, as I have already spoken of these mysteries on the Tele-Phone, to which you are already Secretly privileged to listen.

I am amazed at the masses of the devoted themselves, of their plights, and of the Hope that seems to draw them into the Presence so strangely ambient amidst the Signs and Authorities and Malls of late Modernity. So let me share with you what I witnessed today, this last dies of our Lord's annum, in the Reign of Clinton, 1996. One wonders if the Sign, US 19, is not an intimation of the End of that grievously destructive era leading up to the Appearance of Notre Dame, Parthenos Kathara, here in "Clearwater," whose name itself may be a neon intimation of the luminescent Baptism — purifying virginity of the Unsignified, our Lady of Contracts (including Finance and Insurance Policies) Unsigned — offered by the present Vision. "All things are signs and of signs they are made," if I may conflate two Saints from very different yet perhaps, in the hyperreal Imaginary of our collapsing millennium, convergent schools, the one the Author of the *Dhammapada*, the other of Of Grammatology, both of whom are virtually absent like Yours truly. In any case, we are all, entrapped here in this text, and despite our denials of metaphysics, Devotees of the industrial Dump, more or less like Vladimir and Estragon, so let us attend to our fellows and their Hope renewed by the miracle.

Onward march the banners of the Kingdom of Death, Lord; I see the Signs marking its seductive and universal machineries, as I stand below the bright arcs of metallic birds piercing Your heavens, and wade through the colored legions of steel thundering down the lanes of fused stone, transporting souls in endless rings around Your Spouse and Your Son, emblazoned here in stained glass. In Awe I view the Letters of Hope written to Her in the Spirit of the Love She emanates. But, Oh, give me the power of Your mysterious Word that I may express the Anguish that I see written here!

Now I gaze at formations of Candles, standing together like so many soldiers before a great battle, massed before Mary's image as if to protect Her from some approaching Peril. Or are they huddled around Our Lady to receive Her Protection from the Gargantuan Thing, *Res Mundi*, whose name echoes from their ranks in one collective voice crying, not in the wilderness, Lord, for that has already been Consumed, but rather from the phantasmagoria of concrete and plastic that surrounds them, and their Protectress, on this bright Winter day in the land of Flowers? Yet, what I see in the hands of these glass soldiers, these little vestibules of light before the Miracle and, yes, partaking of it, indeed, too, constituting part of its glory, what I see are Letters, Lord, written by so many hands in so many languages that even with the learning of Rome I cannot read them all. Yet I shall share with You what I have seen, as it resonates in my soul, that You may hear through me what You already know, yet patiently attend to as the sad melodies of Time, "the ebb and flow of human misery." Some of their missives I do not recall literally, so let me paraphrase: "Mary please bring back our daughter, Sarah, to her family. We miss her and need her home," cries one broken soul. And another's voice pleads, "My grandmother has a tumor on her neck. Mary, please help her with the pain." And yet another, "Please help us get our 16-year-old son out of jail." "Beloved Mary, I am alone. Please bring me love," appears in a shaken hand on paper limp with last night's damp. "Mary, please bless my husband so that he can stop drinking," cries another from mute paper. Yet another reads in bleary script, "I have no job. Please Mary, help me find work." Others, I managed to write down on the sleeve of my gown, so I have a literal record (though I have abbreviated names to protect the Innocent):

"Everyone please take time to read — I believe that this has been sent from heaven that the Vergin Mary is holdin Jesus' hand and when she lets go — thats it — cause her hands getting heavy — so if your not saved please get saved. Anne G. I love you Jesus & Mary"

"Mary Mother of God, Please, we pray for an arrest soon. You know the feeling of losing a son... Lynn E. and George A. are withholding information from the police — but not from you!"

"Help heal my eyes."

"Pray for Shawn to find happiness."

I wonder if the Authorities consult the Virgin regarding Information otherwise unobtainable? Yet Behold: Amidst all these missives of despair, Lord, stands a color image on paper, jutting from beneath a glass candle holder, and on it one of the most peculiar compound messages I have ever encountered in my spiritual quest. There is the picture of a small, fluffy-white dog, mouth agape as if in a smile, and beneath it a note reading: "Please bless Chris, our beloved poodle, blessed Virgin Mary"! I am so stricken by this message of spiritual Need, and in the kindness shown even to household pets, here in the presence of our Lady of US 19, that I turn my face heavenward, past the prism of light of the miracle in glass, and — forgive me Lord for I must confess — laugh. As I look down again among the legions of the Desperate, my Fount of Light , I find another note, probably written by a philosopher of the street, which generalizes the sentiment I find inscribed everywhere here, for it says, presumably to Mary though there is no salutation: "Bless those less fortunit."

The writing of Arabian souls is emblazoned here, too, Lord, for they are no doubt just as miserable as the rest of us, and that of Your Latin Church in the Americas, and even that strange composite script of the New flocks who come from across the Pacific, under the Sign of Toyota, to visit my home and "America's" great City on the Swamp, Epcot, domain of that Second Son, Walt, whose miracles have so enlivened souls with the Phantasies of Light on Tele-Vision. Yet whatever their script, there rises from the thousand sheets of vellum here, not only despair but also, above all, Hope.

I have been told by another Pilgrim that a strange little man appeared at the Site in the first week of the new year. He was dressed in black vestments with a black mitre, which rose like a tombstone above his long white hair and sun-darkened face splashed with a white moustache. From around his neck hung a gold medallion, which glinted in the candle light and seemed to hypnotize the Admirers who circled 'round him with specula — a glimmer of hope. "Perhaps he is a Greek, or a Bishop of some post-Christian sect," I commented, though I can not report his appearance with confidence, since I only heard of it from another.

I have thought long on that Hope, as the Despair seems plain enough in the Desert of Signs that stretches between the Malls, for I see a yearning that is unfulfilled in the Desires prompted by the consuming machineries of night, amidst the starry glare of thousands of lamps lighting the way of the earthly "cars" on US 19, and the planetary neon Signs that glow in Primary Colors along the vast concrete plain I travel, just past evening. I cannot see Your stars, Lord, though I strain upward toward the Empyrean, and the Image of Our Lady is gone, too, taken by the miraculous descent of the Sun beneath our little sphere at the center and lowest point of the Cosmos You have fashioned, yet also at the pinnacle of spiritual possibility. Now I too Hope, and wonder, at the miracle of this inspiration that You have planted in us, that we could be entombed in a dying world, a mortal shell, encased, if you will, Lord, in a Dumpster outside Paradise, yet still we can aspire out of the Tomb toward the Light.

Notes

All citations from The Tampa Tribune are from the paper's World Wide Web page dedicated to the apparition. The Internet address is: <http://www.tampatrib.com/news/maryindx.htm>.

1. Coryell, George and Janet Leiser. "Faithful Flock to Clearwater Building, Say Image of Virgin." *Tampa Tribune*. 18 December 1996. Internet. 8 January 1997.
2. Norton, Wilma and Curtis Kreuger. "Come All Ye Faithful." *St. Petersburg Times*. Thursday, 19 December 1996, Pinellas Edition: 1 A.
3. Collins, Lesley. "Popular Image Spurs City Task Force." *Tampa Tribune*. 27 December. Internet. 8 January 1997.
4. Williams, Martyn. Internet Update. *Newsbytes News Network*. 13 January 1997.
5. Coryell, George. "Thousands Find Peace with Image." *Tampa Tribune*. 25 December 1996. Internet. 13 January 1997.
6. Spitz, Jill Jorden. "Seeing is Believing — Devout Visit Mary's Image." *Orlando Sentinel*. 24 December 1996.
7. Barry, Rick. "Christmas Miracle on U.S. 19"? *Tampa Tribune*. 19 December 1996. Internet. 8 January 1997.

Where Do Angels Hang in the Cybernet Nineties?

Meditations on Theological Politics

Michael Dartnell

[to Shannon]

Since I have lacked the comfort of that light,
The which was wont to lead my thoughts astray,
I wander as in darkness of the night,
Afraid of every danger's least dismay.[1]

I have never seen or felt angels or even know if they really exist. We haven't met, the angels and I. They have not been part of my life. They seem to belong to things that do not really concern me, such as major religious enterprises and patriarchal angst about other-worlds. But I am certainly not opposed to the idea of angels. They have an appealing ecumenical pull. Even my heroes k.d. lang and Jane Siberry soar and swing to the heavens every so often, singing "Calling all angels." Angels have just never seemed immediately present. In fact, they seem far away from a world of slaughter and suffering, which is probably a good thing for them. Yet some traces in our culture do hint that they hang close at times when official sanction thrusts individuals up against a cold wall of pain and suffering,

> From the twelfth century onwards Christ is clothed only in a loin-cloth
> and stands facing the observer, either behind or in front of the column,
> as in certain images on painted crosses... In the Flagellation on the
> earliest surviving painted cross in Sarzana two angels kneel on two roofs
> which descend steeply toward the column of Christ's martyrdom; they
> illustrate Christ's divinity in his hour of humiliation. They appear again
> on the side panels of the arms of a painted processional cross in the style
> of Cimabue...[2]

This image of Christ does contain a more than subtle erotic "O come ye forth earnest Catholic youth." The scene blends several seemingly disparate elements: sensuality, violence and spirituality. Beneath a veneer of official Catholicism lies an association between "managed pain" administered by temporal masters and the transcendent spirituality achieved by the slave. The fountainheads of Western sadomasochism, whose contemporary adepts strive to arouse previously untapped passions, could hardly be clearer. The presence of angels at the flagellation underlines their role in contexts that draw together corporeal pain, physical passion and spiritual values.

The thing really is that I haven't called on these far-away angels nor have they seen fit to call on me. They are distant from my daily life, although I like the fact that they helped out East German political refugees in Wim Wender's *Wings of Desire* during the eighties. The image gave them a twentieth-century "feel" and placed them in the context of the spiritual issues of our own time period. But angels are a rarely considered element in the world order. They are relegated to our subconscious as we obsess over debt-reduction, the hunt for welfare fraud and efforts to generally make government more "effective." Due to its close links with light, significant theological questions can be raised about the information industry. Angels are made of light and presumably omnipresent, but part of a love about which the cybernet nineties are so inarticulate. The light of angels, their curly hair and rosy cheeks are just too incongruous on legal data-bases, corporate spread sheets, electronic bulletin boards or the StatsCan on-line info service.[3] As the portraits of Christ's passion indicate, however, angels embody serious spiritual transcendence, not the saccharine love of Hallmark greeting cards. The seriousness of their role was openly acknowledged in pre-modern thought. Socrates, for example, referred to supernatural creatures to meet the charge of atheism,

> ...if I believe in supernatural beings, as you assert, if these supernatural
> beings are gods in any sense, we shall reach the conclusion which I
> mentioned just now when I said that you were testing my intelligence
> for your own amusement, by stating first that I do not believe in gods,
> and then again that I do, since I believe in supernatural beings. If on the
> other hand these supernatural beings are bastard children of the gods by
> nymphs or other mothers, as they are reputed to be, who in the world
> would believe in the children of gods and not in the gods themselves?[4]

After antiquity, angels became less intimate and more Augustinian. St. Augustine makes angels his business (as he incidentally dollops simplicity and order onto Plato's un-Christian universe) and is more categoric about their role and presence,

> when God said, "Let there be light," and light was created, then, if we
> are right in interpreting this as including the creation of the angels, they
> immediately become partakers of the eternal light, which is the
> unchanging Wisdom of God, the agent of God's whole creation...the
> angels, illuminated by that light by which they were created, themselves
> became light, and are called "day," by participation in the changeless
> light and day.[5]

Although this account is rather more Catholic than I could ever wish to sustain, it shows how angels are part of both Plato and Augustine's world (although the shift from Platonic supernatural beings to eternal light must have been rude), giving them an impressive genealogy. In the 1990s, the Augustinian after-life (along with many other things) has become distinctly temporal. We cut money to the poor, wave fingers at welfare mothers, castrate paedophiles and watch the slaughter of innocents over steaming TV dinners each evening, all the while making scant reference to angels and light. The prevailing social sadism of our time does not even aim at a better (Augustinian) after-life, but merely hopes to maintain structures that are as yet undefined, but certainly something less than that to which we have become accustomed.

The chain of events that leads me to angels goes something like this:

It's Gay Pride week in Toronto and I'm staying at Shannon's. I arrive early, two days before she returns from a ten-day holiday in Greece. She bursts out of the arrivals lounge flush with the idea of learning to drive a standard transmission automobile, full of projects for becoming her own "master." On Monday, Shannon phones a driving school, enrolls in horseback riding classes and then turns to renting a standard Jeep. The road to self-mastery arches off to the horizon even though she has to settle for a Jeep with an automatic transmission. We rush off to the Chrysler dealer at noon and spot several Jeeps for sale in the parking lot. All have standard transmissions. In a fit of mastery, Shannon spontaneously decides to buy her own standard Jeep. Negotiations drag on, but we emerge with a complimentary red automatic-transmission Jeep until she takes possession of her own. "Let's take the top down," Shannon says. We throw ourselves on the Jeep with Amazon frenzy. Zippers. Velcro. Vinyl. More zippers. More vinyl. More velcro. The scene has the feel of an SM porn shot as we sweat, puff and heave with zippers and velcro, unzipping and un-velcro-ing until we reach an impasse, not quite either master or slave to circumstances. A decidedly non-erotic sweat breaks out as we struggle with mind's barriers to body's pleasures. The roof is not off the vehicle, but merely de-constructed. A nice young man from the dealership then appears and calmly removes the top. No need to un-zip or un-velcro… just un-hook handles above the windshield and pull back. Mastery, it appears, requires deliberation. As we pull away, Shannon says, "I have to get the tiny perfect Buddha that Gad gave me soldered onto my earring. I want to go to Urban Primitives." She steps on the gas, veers abruptly into the right lane and we're off on a new mission. It is just after 4 pm. Urban Primitives is a tattooing and piercing salon in a second-floor office on Church Street one-and-one-half blocks south of Wellesley, a site for inversion of the hegemonic mind-body rapport.

Piercing. Infibulate. The term is often used to refer to female circumcision but can also mean to fasten with a clasp or buckle; "while piercing is primarily done for erotic reasons, it has often been used to prohibit sexual indulgence — though to those of the bondage and discipline persuasion, even such restraint is doubtless erotic."[6] Infibulation. The action of infibulating; especially the fastening of the sexual organs with a fibula or clasp. Infibulation was an operation performed on young boys and singers by the Romans, who used it as a muzzle to human incontinence. Piercing is thus not at all a new practice: "the proud Roman centurions, Caesar's bodyguards, wore nipple rings as a sign of their virility and courage, and as a dress accessory for holding their short capes."[7] However, piercing today's body has

different meanings than it did in Roman times: it is an act of resistance that violates
the beauty norms set by the mainstream fashion-entertainment-advertising complex[8] and re-appropriates a time-worn *lieu* of sexuality and fashion. In the West of
the fashion-entertainment-advertising complex, the body can be conceived as a site
of opposition to corporate homogenization and control because it is a surface upon
which the "me" of the self meets the "I" of the gazing public. Considered as such,
piercing is a form of mastery that is sexual and body-centred, wherein mind's
devices service the pleasures of the flesh. In north-west Kenya, in contrast, the
complex's norms, based on a nebulous mind-body split, do not apply,

> By outwardly wearing the signs of inner states, combined with the signs
> of events and effects impinging on the body from the acts of others, the
> Turkana convert their skin into public surfaces, inscribed with visual
> statements of social potential.[9]

The Turkana show that dichotimization is but one, non-essential, way of
conceiving the relation between body and mind.

My first inkling of angels is the sense that I am heading into a house of
worship when we arrive at Urban Primitives. There, one speaks of piercing in
hushed tones, as though connecting with another level of being or a wider community to which only the initiate truly accede. We walk upstairs to the offices and
enter, for want of a better word, a buzz of activity. Not the buzz of flesh, but a buzz
of society. The reception room is full of people. Two staff members are on duty and
both know Shannon. A large heavy-set man with dark Rod-Stewart hair, unshaven
beard and moustache, black T-shirt with cut-off sleeves and dark sparkling eyes
greets us. "Hi Shannon! How are you?" he says brightly. Tattoos slide down his
arms, staring at me, sizing me up. "Hi Shannon! Nice to see you again." His
colleague sports tattoos on both arms. Nose pierced one, two, three times. Ears
covered with rings from the lower lobes up around and inside. Same Rod-Stewart
hair, but shorter, lesbian-identified. "I need to get my earring soldered," Shannon
smiles broadly.

Two male suburban mall rats scurry in, looking around in wonder. A large
poster for an international tattooing convention in Europe hangs on the wall. A
well-dressed East Asian business type sits primly, waiting his turn, a *Globe and Mail*
folded on his lap, a slightly absent expression on his face. A younger rocker strides
in, does a 360 gape at the tattoo patterns on the wall and leaves.

> Précession de toutes les déterminations venues d'ailleurs, illisibles,
> indéchiffrables, peu importe, l'essentiel est d'epouser la forme étrange de
> n'importe quel événement, de n'importe quel objet, de n'importe quel
> être fortuit, puisque de toute façon vous ne saurez jamais qui vous êtes.
> Aujourd'hui où les gens ont perdu leur ombre, il est de toute nécessité
> d'être suivi par quelqu'un, aujourd'hui où chacun perd ses propres
> traces, il est de toute urgence que quelqu'un se mette dans vos traces,
> même si par là il les efface et vous fait disparaître, c'est une forme
> d'obligation symbolique qui se joue, une forme énigmatique de liaison
> et de déliaison.[10]

"You'll be seeing Eroshia," the lesbian-identified woman says, ushering us out of the room, to the right, down a short narrow hallway and into another office. The room resembles a dental or physician's office. White walls, the calm spiritual pop sound of "Dead Can Dance" and cleanliness. A kitchen unit has been white-washed, a grey Ikea countertop is installed alongside the sink across from a white-vinyl lounge chair that comes pretty close to being a dentist's chair. "She'll be with you in a minute."

Shannon eases into the white-vinyl lounge chair. I sit on a chair across from her, a large shelf unit next to my left shoulder, the door onto the hallway to my right. Eroshia comes in. Small, dark, vaguely playful, demonic. A dark angel. A tattoo on one arm. Earrings through her nose. I suddenly spot a framed photo entitled "Eroshia" on my right, next to the door. An out-of-focus colour print depicts an open mouth. A blurred earring line crosses the fussy lower lip. "I need to have my tiny perfect Buddha soldered onto this earring or I just know that I'll lose it. It's a gift from Gad and I can't lose it." "Okay, Shannon, that's easy." Eroshia turns to the earring, works on it briefly and stands back to look at the results. Without notice Shannon says, "You know, Eroshia, I think I'm ready to get my nipple pierced. I've always wanted to get my nipple pierced, the left nipple, on the same side as the tiny perfect Buddha. Can you do it today?" "No problem Shannon. Are you sure that you want to go ahead with it?" Eroshia stands back and eyes Shannon. A tiny smirk appears. "Absolutely. I just left my master. I'm ready to be my own master." Shannon is deadly serious. I've seen that look before. The blue eyes are bluer, the eyes are set on their target and not letting go. Mastery for her means making this decision and holding to it,

> No divinity shall cast lots for you, but you shall choose your own deity.
> Let him to whom falls the first lost first select a life to which he shall
> cleave of necessity. But virtue has no master over her, and each shall have
> more or less of her as he honours her or does her despite. The blame is
> his who chooses. God is blameless.[11]

"I've always wanted to get my nipple pierced," I blurt out, "I like the look." Eroshia shifts her steady look onto me. Dark light flashes in her eyes. "You know, you'll come back here someday to have it done." "Hmmph...doubters," I think. There are limits to what even I do for fashion. "I don't think I could go through with it," I say calmly. I half-close my left eye and slowly shake my head from side to side as I say this.

Turning to Shannon, Eroshia says in a dead-pan voice "If you're really sure that you want to go ahead with a piercing, you'll have to sign forms. I'll explain how to take care of it and show you how to prevent infection. I'll go an' get the rings so that you can choose one." Shannon nods agreement to go ahead. Eroshia leaves the room. "She's an apprentice. She'll be a master someday. You can see it already. She's really good," Shannon explains.

> ...interviewees were not interested in pain at all; and those who were
> insisted that the word 'pain' was redundant, given that their activities
> were geared toward creating pleasurable rather than unpleasurable

'sensations'. They also preferred the terms 'master' and 'slave' to 'sadist' and 'masochist', because these better described the motives and nature of the sex games they played...the Sadist runs the scene; the Masochist sets the limits. The Masochist says what you can't use and how far you can go. But within that, the Sadist can do anything.[12]

I nod my head, trying to follow. A vague dizziness belches up from my stomach. "I just hope I don't faint or something." "Would you faint? Would it bother you to stay?" "I can't look at needles or at my own blood during tests," I laugh. It took me years to do an HIV test because I can't stand the sight of my own blood. But I want to stay to share Shannon's experience or some such horseshit. I cringe inwardly at the thought of a painful piercing. Ripped flesh. "I'll be fine." Or at least I decide that I should be fine if I want to play a role in this scenario. I lean back, sigh, and think of the awards for best supporting roles at the Oscars. "Are you sure you'll be all right?" Eroshia asks me, entering the room. We are in her domain now. She has to be in control, it is crucial. "Sure." I lean slightly to my left, into the shelf unit.

Eroshia holds a small grey padded board with about thirty earrings pinned onto it. She offers the board to Shannon, who carefully eyes the selection. They talk about the advantages and disadvantages of several models. Shannon chooses a round gold earring with a small nob on one side. Aesthetically, it is quite okay, but I get a little more dizzy, feeling as well as I would if offered to choose what type of shovel I would like to use if I were being forced to bludgeon someone to death. Silver or gold head? These new Italian handgrips are really comfortable. My instincts are telling me to leave! leave! leave the room! I have a flash of the kill floor in the slaughterhouse where I worked for about a month in my early twenties. I can still distinctly smell freshly killed pigs and cattle when I think of that. Never will forget. I look at Shannon. Yep, she's gonna do it. That look, open blue eyes now slightly level under her thin eyebrows, says it all. I decide to stay to check it out, to "support" her, to save face, to see what piercing is all about. The mix of perform-ance piece and dental surgery in this scene is odd, but intrigues me.

Eroshia is assuming a look not unlike that of my former colleagues at the slaughterhouse. Working with flesh of any sort necessitates bureaucratic detach-ment, whether it's chicken breasts or Shannon's breast. The need for both distance and immediacy makes body modification or SM an intellectual and physical challenge. Eroshia is abstracting the process into a business deal, but understands that Shannon is investing in the spiritual energy of the piercing. This mix of mind's tools for body's ends is her own growing mastery. As a participant-observer, I see Eroshia abstract, and grow into more and more of a dark angel, a demon. An age-old concurrence of pain, emotion, devotion and ecclesiastical officialdom re-materializes,

Christ of the Flagellation in Ottonian art wears a long robe; he embraces the column with both arms, his hands are either held by a servant or are bound, his feet are not tied. Since whipping was an official act of the judiciary and took place in the praetorium, this building is nearly always from the tenth century onwards represented by various architectural motif. The column which supports the roof is also the whipping column. It therefore has a base and capital and is taller than Christ, even in images containing no spatial details. A German ivory plaque, which probably formed part of an antependium given by Otto I to the cathedral at Magdeburg, shows Christ being whipped in front of Pilate, who sits in the praetorium gazing as though spellbound at Christ. The ceremony of washing the hands is obviously over; servant, basin and jug simply allude to it. Manuscript illuminations portray the procurator either standing, as in the Codex Egberti, or seated, as in an Echternach Book of Pericopes (2nd quarter of the 11th century). His raised hands and pointing fingers must indicate his command to whip Christ.[13]

Eroshia leaves the room, muttering that the ring will not fit Shannon's nipple. "She's giving me a chance to back out," Shannon says, "they always do this. It's a sign of a good master." I have no doubt but that Eroshia is setting the scene. And that Shannon is carefully defining the limits. Eroshia returns. "I think that this ring will work after all. It could be a little bigger, but you'll see that it'll be fine. You can replace it later if you want." Out of stock, I think to myself. Good salesperson. "I'm ready to go ahead if you are," she says smiling.

Shannon wants to do the piercing on the floor. She strips off her shirt and pants with lightning speed, ready to get on with it, eager to embrace mastery. She sits down in the middle of the floor with her heels underneath her buttocks and knees spread. She sticks out her tits and stretches her hands back to touch the floor behind her on each side. "How's this?" she asks in a professional manner, smiling, her back arching and fingertips stretching. I almost laugh aloud, amazed at her seizure of the moment. Eroshia, slightly more reserved, looks at her with anticipation and amusement. "Fine, really. I've never done one like this before, but it's a great idea." Eroshia brings out a small grey box. Shannon kneels down once more in her black Calvin Klein's and black boots. I look at her nipples. Rosy red, pointy and boyish. Joyous nipples, curious about the world. Eroshia takes a set of what look like long pointed pliers from the box. I lean into my corner, eclipsing Shannon's left nipple with her right shoulder. Eroshia asks if she is ready. Shannon is. Eroshia lines up her pliers. Okay, breathe three times slowly. I'm going to do it as you let out the third breath. One...two...three...

Fakir Musafar says that those who embrace body alteration reject

the Western cultural biases about ownership and use of the body. We believed that our body belonged to us. We had rejected the strong Judeo-Christian body programming and emotional conditioning to which we had all been subjected. Our bodies did not belong to some distant god sitting on a throne; or to that god's priest or spokesperson; or to a father, mother, or spouse; or to the state or its monarch, ruler, or dictator; or to social institutions of the military, educational, correctional, or medical establishment. And the kind of language used to describe our behaviour ("self-mutilation"), was in itself a negative and prejudicial form of control.[14]

Fakir's radical re-appropriation of the corporeal responds to the seizure of the body by medical and legal sciences in the nineteenth century. Bodily pleasure had to conform to abstract notions of the "natural" since this is what medical and legal sciences believed they were "discovering." In fact, the seizure produced a standardization of bodily sensation within specific limits, limits that I suddenly realize Shannon is transgressing big time, as she forges onward into the land of non-procreative pleasure. In the 1990s, Fakir's riposte also challenges the ejection/rejection of the body by a technologically obsessed society along with the hierarchies that this entails (mind over body, rich over poor, white over colour, hetero over homo, "health" over "sickness," specialist over non-specialist). By modifying or altering the body, Fakir and others undertake

> a deeply meaningful, transformative act. This self-fashioning impulse leads to an individualizing of the body and seems directly related to the struggle to create a sense of identity in a society felt to be dehumanizing, alienating, and characterized by increasing conformity... individuality, personal beliefs, sense of aesthetics, and oppositional stance must be articulated through the body and tangibly inscribed on... flesh.[15]

Although body modification in the West cannot appropriate non-Western practices and preserve the latter's signification, taking the Turkana attitude into account, for example, throws new light on practices within our own culture.

To refine and substantiate Fakir's critique, we might further ask whether body alteration rejects Judeo-Christian culture or (more precisely) the obsessive techno-scientific-economic mindset of its Enlightenment-Victorian offspring. In other words, condemning "Judeo-Christian" values in general ignores that the term is a cultural artefact like any other and, as such, susceptible to manipulation as time washes away outer armour and older layers of meaning stand newly exposed. The "tales" told about our culture must be questioned. We must ask who tells them, who edits them and why they do so in what way. Most tales of the body that we receive simply serve hegemonic mind-over-body marketing. If we re-read flagellation, for example, in light of Fakir's point of view, the "passion" of martyrs becomes much less abstract and could turn Enlightenment-Victorian notions of the body on their head.[16] By re-casting life as technologically (Internet) centred in a context in which political disempowerment is accentuating (via austerity measures that leave no room for political debate or policy alternatives), the priests of mind-over-body marketing and their information "revolution" ironically make a radical physical re-appropriation of the body possible by leaving the mass of the population with little else beyond their own corporeity. Instead of a noble vessel or source of sin, the body is highlighted as a site of authentic emotional-spiritual affirmation for those who practice body modification.[17] Radical "body praxis" is not an unprecedented example of popular corporeal response to disempowerment and social crisis,

Medieval self-flagellation was a grim torture which people inflicted on themselves in the hope of inducing a judging and punishing God to put away his rod, to forgive them their sins, to spare them the greater chastisements which would otherwise be theirs in this life and the next. Yet beyond mere forgiveness lay another, still more intoxicating prospect. If even an orthodox friar could see in his own bleeding body an image of the body of Christ, it is not surprising that laymen who became flagellants and then escaped from ecclesiastical supervision should often have felt themselves to be charged with a redemptive mission which would secure not only their own salvation but that of all mankind. Like the crusading pauperes before them, heretical flagellant sects saw their penance as a collective *imitatio Christi* possessing a unique, eschatological value.[18]

Just as SM practitioners follow in the footsteps of medieval flagellants, post-punk neo-tribalism takes the ancient Western cultural tool of body decoration and uses it to challenge contemporary society's artificial mind-body dichotomy. Rather than a juxtaposition of nature/body and spirit/mind as described by Irigaray, "where thought is separated from effect, thought being a logical construction for truths beyond earthly contingencies, which are associated more with affects, with nature,"[19] piercing, tattoos and scarification apply modern technology to design a sensation. Mind thus turns to satisfying body's pleasures by creating new emotions, new pleasures for a formerly neglected vessel, one seen as stolid, impassive, and needing mastery. Through body modification, the body sets the scene, defines its needs and sets its limits. This focus on body's needs alongside those of mind undermines a cruel society that strokes out the needs of body through accounting procedures. These witch-hunts are carried out in the name of mind, of abstraction, of the categorisation of human beings in the name of efficient management.

Calling all angels.

Angel. *Daímon or daimónion*: supernatural presence or entity, somewhere between a god (theos) and a hero:

The belief in supernatural spirits somewhat less anthropomorphized than the Olympians is a very early feature of Greek popular religion; one such *daímon* is attached to a person at birth and determines, for good or evil, his fate (compare the Greek word for happiness, *eudaimonia*, having a good *daímon*).[20]

I recoil into my corner, feeling sucked into the event by a powerful magnetizing force, but not daring to look. Eroshia, intent on the nipple, centred, concentrating, is unaware of anything around her so that her work is professionally done. I turn my head to the wall, waiting to hear a quick "clip" as I imagine I will. With the dark angel distracted by her craft and my eyes covered, the angels have a chance to do their work. Do I hear a rustle of white robes or the flapping of wings as I cringe in the corner? Is there a slight breeze as events move forward? I don't exactly know.

The room falls away. Noise and perception draw away from us on all sides, retreating, then turning and rushing in with the force, noise and intensity of the oceans. I hear angels start to sing in a chorus. The voices are very high, very pure, innocent yet knowing, like yet unlike children singing. I know in my solar plexus that these are not children singing. A very pure breath of air colours my perceptions. The light becomes white. There is no scent, only a faint and pleasant warmth that oddly reassures. A tidal force pushes us upward and the heavens open. The things of the world swirl downward away from us. Faster and faster they turn down and away. Small bands of black form a few feet away and begin to spin around and around. Then thick yellow bands appear between the black ones. The second bands are dark enough to highlight patterns, shapes, and people and worldly forms. Both sets of bands continue to swirl around us, then rise rapidly like an inverted tornado that pulls the three of us upward. Faster and faster we turn, the yellow turning deeper, the angels singing, screaming, laughing.

> On peut considérer l'énergie comme une cause qui produit des effets, mais aussi comme un effet qui se reproduit lui-même, et donc cesse d'obéir à toute causalité. Le paradoxe de l'énergie est qu'elle est à la fois une révolution des causes et une révolution des effets, quasiment indépendantes l'une de l'autre, et qu'elle devient le lieu non seulement d'un enchaînement des causes, mais d'un déchaînement des effets.[21]

I shrink into the corner of my chair, having no sense of where or who I am. In front of me, Shannon leans back and began to... laugh/scream/wail/laugh/laugh/ laugh ("it looks excruciating painful, but it's not — it's funny!"[22]). Eroshia hangs determinatedly onto her tit for what seems a long time, "clipping" it firmly. Shannon screams with laughter, leans forward into Eroshia's left shoulder, placing her forehead on the shoulder.

Do I see Shannon, eyelids fluttering, throw her right arm behind her, the left arm remaining around the neck of Eroshia, who looks on steadily and adoringly as Shannon trembles imperceptibly, her skin turning ivory as a drop of blood slowly runs from the corner of her mouth above her wounded and now deeply pink nipple? Does Shannon's sigh call forth a great hush, as though the world holds its breath and the heavens pause to take notice? Do I see Shannon suddenly turn pale in rich blue tumbling robes as a faint light glows warmly over her brow?...no, I do not.

> ...as we have just pointed out, whatever comes to pass, comes to pass according to laws and rules which involve eternal necessity and truth; nature, therefore, always observes laws and rules which involve eternal necessity and truth, although they may not all be known to us, and therefore she keeps a fixed and immutable order...it is certain that the ancients took for a miracle whatever they could not explain by the method adopted by the unlearned in such cases, namely, an appeal to the memory, a recalling of something similar, which is ordinarily regarded without wonder...[23]

The swirling begins to slow. White light begins to filter through the room, which itself has re-appeared. A strange ritual calm takes hold. I float in the heavens, arms and legs waving, looking down into the room, trying to find my way back to the body. Shannon sits on the floor, patiently waiting, absorbed by her nipple, cradling her breast. Eroshia re-assumes the air of a bureaucrat of piercing, an oddly priest-like role, having initiated another adept to her cult. This dark angel has again played out an ancient drama. Suddenly, I'm in the room. Shannon turns to me and I see a flash of fear in her eyes and, beyond, a deeper torrent of pain/joy at the realization of self-ness.

> le cœur battait, elle respirait, assise, les yeux vitreux, sans rien voir. Et ç'a été fini: "Les docteurs disaient qu'elle s'étreindrait comme une bougie: ce n'est pas ça, pas ça du tout, a dit ma sœur en sanglotant. — Mais, Madame, a répondu la garde, je vous assure que ç'a été une mort très douce."[24]

It costs $147, taxes included. We have to immediately go out onto the street to get money from a bank machine. The automobile exhaust is choking and the sharp light of day slices into me. It is five p.m., rush hour and Church Street is filled with cruising boys. The angels are gone, lost to the bustle and worry of everyday existence, to mind's pursuit of mind's needs.

> Le pire, c'est la compréhension, qui n'est qu'une fonction sentimentale et inutile. La véritable connaissance, c'est celle de ce que nous ne comprendrons jamais dans l'autre, de ce qui dans l'autre fait que cet autre n'est pas soi-même, et donc ne peut être séparé de soi, ni aliéné par notre regard, ni institué dans son identité ou dans sa différence.[25]

As my screen glows, time to stop, I can't help but wonder "are angels calling to me, their light shining a call for help and a comfort?" Or is the screen another pathetic imitation, another tool that we don't know how to use except as an extension of a fearsome will to control? The sounds of the world wash in. At this end of century, as the world moves feverishly (intensified spiritual hum or mass marketing?), as the planet and its populations groan under an unsustainable burden of pain, suffering, hunger, injustice, environment deterioration, mass murder and disease, ancient body-centred spirituality offers a re-connection with the physical-ness that is no less human than the mind. The contemporary twist on the old form validates "me." Hearing angels sing is an intensely non-cyber experience, celestial voyeurism for me as it lands up — no cost, no tax, no punishment, no censure, no mass distribution, no guilt. An affirmation of self, identity and the reality of authentic (as opposed to virtual) experience. A connection of the mind to the passions and to love, beginning in love of self and in offering pleasure, a treasured gift, to oneself. A rare delicacy for body and mind in the cybernet nineties.

Notes

1. Edmund Spenser, fragment of Sonnet 88, "Amoretti," *Books I and II of The Faerie Queene, The Mutability Cantos and Selections from the Minor Poetry* (edited by Robert Kellogg and Oliver Steele), New York: The Odyssey Press, 1965, p. 466.
2. Gertrud Schiller, *Iconography of Christian Art, Vol. 2: The Passion of Jesus Christ*, London: Lund Humphries, 1972, p. 67.
3. See http://www.statcan.ca/. No angels there.
4. Plato, "Socrates' Defense" (Apology), 27d, in *Plato: The Collected Dialogues* (edited by Edith Hamilton and Huntington Cairns), Princeton University Press, 1978, p. 14.
5. Augustine, *City of God* (edited by David Knowles), Penguin Books: 1980, pp. 439-440.
6. V. Vale and Andrea Juno, *Modern Primitives: Tattoo, Piercing, Scarification*, San Francisco: Re/Search Publications, 1989, p. 26.
7. *Modern Primitives*, p. 25.
8. The fashion-entertainment-advertising complex refers to the corporate sector whose focus is the reification and marketing of a homogenized vision of the human body. The sector sets a model of the human form alongside which we are invited to measure ourselves. The lack of alternative images endows this model with its hegemonic character. We see the images of the fashion-entertainment-advertising complex in Demi Moore, Marky Mark and Calvin Klein models. The message is that pleasure belongs to those meeting corporate standards of beauty, usually, in fact, those who are able workout 6 hours a day and/or willing to submit to costly and painful surgery. The imposing physicality that piercing initially evokes in many people pales alongside the torn flesh of cosmetic surgery. In fact, the two practices may only be different insofar as their "social-class site" is concerned. Piercing is a less costly and therefore more "popular and democratic" cultural practice.
9. Vigdis Broch-Due, "Making Meaning Out of Matter: Perceptions of Sex, Gender and Bodies among the Turkana," in Broch-Due, Vigdis, Ingrid Rudie and Tone Bleie, *Carved Flesh/Cast Selves: Gendered Symbols and Social Practices*, Oxford: Berg, 1993, p. 71.
10. Jean Baudrillard, *La transparence du mal: Essai sur les phenomenes extremes*, Editions Galilée, 1990, p. 170-1.
11. Plato, "Republic": X, 617e, in *Plato: The Collected Dialogues* (edited by Edith Hamilton and Huntington Cairns), Princeton University Press, 1978, p. 841.
12. Bill Thompson, *Sadomasochism: Painful Perversion or Pleasurable Play?*, London: Cassell, 1994, pp. 136-7.
13. Schiller, pp. 66-67.
14. Fakir Musafar, "Body Play: State of Grace or Sickness?," in Armando R. Favazza, *Bodies Under Siege: Self-Mutilation and Body Modification in Culture and Psychiatry* (2nd edition), Baltimore, Maryland: The John Hopkins University Press, 1996, p. 326.
15. Daniel Wojcik, *Punk and Neo-Tribal Body Art*, Jackson: University Press of Mississippi, 1995. p. 34.
16. Indeed, it even turns our notions of the Victorian period on their head: "The Prince Albert, called a 'dressing ring' by Victorian haberdashers, was originally used to firmly secure the male genitalia in either the left or right pant leg during that era's craze for extremely tight, crotch-binding trousers, thus minimizing a man's natural endowment. Legend has it that Prince Albert wore such a ring to retract his foreskin and thus keep his member sweet-smelling so as not to offend the Queen." *Modern Primitives*, p. 25.

17. Body modification is in fact widespread in the West. The transformation of bodybuilding from socio-cultural marginalization to a widely-practice form of physical self-affirmation and the appearance of (pardon the pun) a sizeable population of obese persons in contemporary North America are two examples of attempts to affirm selfhood and identity through body modification. See, for example, Alan M. Klein, *Little Big Men: Bodybuilding Subculture and Gender Construction* (Albany: State University of New York Press, 1993), especially chap. 9: "Comic-Book Masculinity and Cultural Fiction."

18. Norman Cohn, *The Pursuit of the Millennium*, NY: Essential Books, 1958, pp. 127-8.

19. Luce Irigaray, *i love to you: Sketch for a Felicity Within History* (Alison Martin, trans.), New York: Routledge, 1996, p. 116.

20. F.E. Peters, *Greek Philosophical Terms: A Historical Lexicon*, New York: New York University Press, 1967, p. 33.

21. Baudrillard, p. 106-7.

22. *Modern Primitives*, p. 130.

23. Benedict de Spinoza, *A Theologico-Political Treatise and A Political Treatise* (translated by R.H.M. Lewis), New York: Dover Publications, 1951, pp. 83-84.

24. Simone de Beauvoir, *Une mort tres douce*, Editions Gallimard, 1964, p. 137.

25. Baudrillard, p. 153.

Discovering CyberAntarctic
An Interview with Knowbotics Research

Paolo Atzori

The world presents itself to us, effectively.

J. Baudrillard

Which worlds?
Knowbotics Research

Knowbotics Research (KR+cF) develops hybrid models of knowledge generation. These models are complex dynamic fields which produce an exchange between virtual agents, poetic machines and interactive visitors. They enable an observer to participate in the physical exploration and construction of networked rules and strategies of the new public spheres. KR+cF outlines technoid events in parallel real and virtual spaces to investigate the experience of the multiple layers of reality. These extensions of the cultural environment provoke new cultural and aesthetic parameters in order to prevent an ideological closed circuit in an information based society. KR+cF — Yvonne Wilhelm, Alexander Tuchacek, Christian Hübler — is based in Cologne, at the Academy for Media Arts. In partnership with Westbank Industries and Tactile Technology, KR+cF has founded Mem_brane, a laboratory for media strategies. KR+cF has won several major international Media Art Awards, including: Prix Ars Electronica 93, Golden Nica for Interactive Art; German Media Art Award, and ZKM Karlsruhe 95.

Paolo Atzori: Last November in Hamburg during "Interface3" you finally installed your new work, "Dialogue with the Knowbotic South." What is the topic of your discourse?

Christian Hübler: Our approach is to focus on the scientific world in reference to the South Pole and to study the codes used by scientists of the Antarctic who make computer simulations. We intend to offer a model for a discourse between different fields of the communications world. From an artistic point of view, our project formalizes the problem of a missing language.

Atzori: A dialogue beginning from the state of a missing language... Is this the starting point for your new artistic activity or a hypothetical limit?

Hübler: One has to discard one's own old language. How shall we discuss what we are doing? We don't debate with journalists and critics only but also exchange ideas with the scientists. It really becomes a problem if we don't have a language.

Yvonne Wilhelm: It's a development of our own history as artists, as aesthetic beings; you have to log in into your own history...

Atzori: How do you formulate the discourse about nature between the different artistic and scientific dimensions?

Hübler: We work with hypotheses since natural scientists are dealing with hypothetical issues, as they have throughout the century. When they simulate nature on their computers they project systems into the future, pushing forward the meaning of time. For the first time, scientists not only prove the laws of nature, they also formulate conditions of possible systems. In our project we treat an actual state of nature corresponding to our information culture: the scientific definition of nature through communication systems and powerful computers. This way of working changes the meaning of nature itself because nature has always been culturally defined.

Wilhelm: Reality is culturally defined too. We investigate nature but at the same time question reality.

Atzori: A concept that changes with time. Do you want to point out an idea of reality more fitting to our contemporary times?

Hübler: Our bigger concern is the topic of Wirklichkeitskonzept. With the term "virtual reality" you can define a dimension that belongs to the computer. This is just play, but I think we play in accordance with rules of games dealing with phenomena which really have an effect on our personal life. The question is no longer what nature is, rather, what kind of nature do we want. We are embodied in the process of how nature merges, with the ability to go into the system and to change and manipulate it. We have to include in our research the term "real" (das Reale), what comes out from the reality conception. We don't know if we really can discuss about Das Reale. It is a very delicate thing; in our work dealing with nature we must also deal with the economy and politics.

Atzori: We can say that Knowbotic Research is searching for an artistic definition of nature, a possible reality, in the Information Age through models and data that come directly from the world of scientific research. How would you describe your intellectual experience with the scientists? Did you find that your ideas corresponded with theirs?

Hübler: Most of the scientists still think in accordance with the mechanistic world view — for instance their theory of chaos is deterministic. They want just to prove their laws confirming the construction of science. If is there anything they cannot put in the body of science they think the question is wrong. They don't think their work methods are wrong. Here's an example: if they have a simulation model running on a computer and get actual data from a satellite that do not fit into the simulation, they conclude that the satellite has committed an error. Some people would argue that perhaps the simulation is wrong. We believe scientists should venture forward even at the risk of leaving the academic domain of science behind.

Atzori: Don't you think too many scientists are affected by heavy political/economic demands?

Hübler: Last summer in Hamburg when we joined some scientists at the German polar research institute of Bremerhaven (AWI), we realized how powerful the connections between science and politics and economics are. Many scientists do visual simulation only to legitimize their work to the politicians and secure funding for more projects, not because they want to find something new with the visual simulation language. Most of the scientists saw visualization in this context, and this is disappointing. As I explained earlier we started our project with natural scientists because we thought they deal with hypothetical questions involving all the new concepts of science like the theory of the inner observer, complex dynamics and self organization. We were mostly interested in the research of dynamic processes. We wanted to find out how they determined the way in which the results of this research changes their knowledge of Antarctica.

Atzori: There is a kind of synthesis of scientific knowledge applied to a special environment in an interactive form where one can observe the work of scientists giving an interpretation and a simulation of natural processes. At the same time some scientists are developing new ways of representating the scientific methodology too. Do you want to provide the scientists with a free platform where they can exchange and debate their research?

Hübler: We want to create a field of discourse freed from the rules of the specialists' disciplines. It is a field not only for natural scientists but also for scholars and philosophers who are discussing current ideas of reality. We start from the scientific material because Knowbotic Research is interested in hybrid knowledge, in the integration of facts in fiction.

Atzori: The cybernetics of Norbert Wiener was the first attempt to initiate a new sense of science arising out of the epistemological meeting of research from different disciplines in order to break the borders of isolation. We are living again in a time where everything is always more and more specialized, and everybody follows his method like a dogma that can hardly be discussed. Do you consider cybernetics a good background for your ideas?

Wilhelm: Our world view is based on what we see in the future, a worldwide data space induced by the communication technologies, filled with tons of information coming from all different disciplines of knowledge. I think it is very important to create models which focus on the needs and possibilities of the person who tries to receive this information. We are dealing with questions of strategies that support human perception. Furthermore, the concept of nature in our work does not come from the scientists; we only use their data. Our work is also a liberation from science. We create an environment where, initially, we fabricate actual phenomena of scientific thinking. But we emancipate these phenomena from their reference (science) by a self-organization model.

Atzori: Let's speak more specifically about your work…

Hübler: Our installation "Dialogue with the Knowbotic South" is unlike our previous work "Simulationspace Mosaic of Mobile Datasounds" (SMDK), a functional work. The new concept is based on knowbots, which generate a vision in a data-network. They originate a hypothetical nature, a Computer Aided Nature (CAN). The main problem for the knowledge robots is that we are dealing with two bigger entities, the so called reference nature that is still very powerful in the Antarctic, one of the few almost intact ecological systems, and the related scientific institutions. The knowbots act with completely different kinds of inputs, originating a tension so you can't bring these two worlds really together. This produces an aesthetic field for artists. Virtual reality means that you are inside the computer box closed to the outside. Knowbotic reality means you are in a zone of different worlds, totally aware of the dynamic processes in different worlds. We are interested in finding a form for this concept. Each knowbot carries information about several Antarctic research projects that are running at the moment. It is not a scientific knowbot because we incorporate very different phenomena related to different research programs. This incorporation of phenomena of actual research in a Computer Aided Nature shapes the knowbot. We have designed a visual form for every knowbot's algorithm corresponding to the data sets. The agents (knowbots) work as connectors of processes. This point represents a new idea for the artwork. We do not have an interface anymore, a mechanical interface, in the real world, we have interfaces in the network, the dynamic network. If the processes associated with the knowbots and/or the research projects change, the knowbots will change too, following the modification of ideas in the world of research. This leads to forms of artificial creativity implemented in these agents. The agent should be open to other ways of thinking. For instance, we outline interfaces for philosophers allowing the possibility of reaching them and determining other outlines for the knowbot.

Atzori: Is the shape of the agents strictly related to some kind of processes? Are there different categories of agents, each with a specific architecture at both levels, algorithmic and visual?

Wilhelm: The shape is only a metaphor for a model. We define borders for our model. The borders we are investigating and developing imply a kind of representation, not specialized but interactive.

Atzori: So there is no symbolism, no allegory?

Hübler: Maybe some new things emerge. In the work represented here all the agents are autogenerative. They are connected to processes on the Internet which change continuously. These agents always modify themselves. They also offer points of interest which can be activated by the observer of the installation. Thus the knowbot will also mutate and react according to the interest of the visitor.

Atzori: What is the logic you follow to develop the agents? Where do you find the first input to design them?

Hübler: The first outlines of the knowbot relate to visual material that is used in the research fields mixed with our creativity... For example one agent refers to the computer simulation of the tide of the Antarctic sea; we develop a model and write an interface for data from satellite observation. The interesting thing is that we deal with processes you can't see in reality. Hidden processes, sometimes extremely small or extremely big, and very complex. Furthermore you can't live in the Antarctic, which means you can't experience its reality directly or empirically without the help of technology. Actually, for the scientists it no longer makes sense to work directly in contact with nature. They need data, intelligent data for their terminals in the institutes. And intelligent data means that you install robots and automata which live there year-round, periodically sending raw data. Only a few scientists need to go there to maintain the functionality of these robots. Sometimes they put sensors on the animals living in the Antarctic continent. These sensors are directly connected to computers. They ex-territorialize their nature in the networks. Maybe our artistic work is a kind of re-territorialization.

Wilhelm: The important point is not to discuss the meaning of measures, but rather how can we visualize and handle this complexity of information. That's a problem for the scientists too. There are so many data: how can we turn it into information and knowledge, how can we handle this with the knowledge we have?

Atzori: You said about this new work that it maintains the state of process, not only for the interactivity but also because it keeps itself constantly updated. Since we cannot follow the whole information processing you make a selection of the information displayed inside the simulation space otherwise it would be a completely chaotic system since the information that comes in almost in real time. How do you make this kind of classification?

Hübler: It is necessary to define a strategy about order and the generation of new things. With computers we analyze fragments of the reality and at the same time we build and initiate complex processes. This is what the work is about. You can't deal directly with data fields and databases to make a model only by analysis; you get millions of data the human brain is unable to perceive. To outline a model that simulates one year of a certain natural process you need "giga-tons" of data to keep the simulation running. You really have to find new criteria, new formulations or maybe new bodies (we call them "incorporations") to construct, visualize and perceive such models.

Atzori: Your previous installation "Simulations Mosaic Raum" was a self-organized system consisting of elements of communication, data sounds, collected through the Internet. This work induces a new insight dimension where one misses the usual feeling for orientation: the visitor/actor can navigate a "datascape," the composition of the information in the darkness reveals new clues of perception, new sense of space, the space/process of information. At the same time another level of perception is involved using the data coming from the visitor's interaction converted by a motion-tracking system into an algorithm and transferred in real time to the "reality" of the computer. In another room another program visualizes the floating entity of the agents with 3D computer graphics displayed by a video-beamer on a large surface. I am very interested in your concept of space where you can implement this information organized by the knowbots...

Wilhelm: Rethinking space is the main topic of the new project too. It's not a question of finding one aesthetic or a language everybody can understand but of defining nature and its information output, between reality and virtual space. To the define the differences between discussion and discourse. To define the differences among the various concepts of nature is itself a process.

Hübler: It is not efficient to use sculptural terminology but we are investigating new concepts of "bodies." It is not the body idea in the common, psychological meaning. Our concept of bodies comes from these kinds of entities which generate the different layers of our reality and we look for these generators mostly in data spaces. For us knowbots are means for incorporations of ideas, and also of reality concepts. This is somewhat similar to our earlier project where we had a "sound space," a space consisting of ideas formulated with sounds, connected by the interactive visitor. In the simulation room one could only connect two ideas at once. We were interested in the tensions originated between two ideas, the gap between two sounds and not in the idea itself. In this new project we have "bodies," complex connectors, which link complex fields of ideas. We touch on one of the biggest problem for science: to gain a more complex simulation it is necessary to simulate several organisms/processes together in one program, to compare at the same time different kinds of data. This leads to our next question: "What can you encode and what cannot you encode?"

Atzori: Your idea of "bodies" could be interpreted as a model for artificial life, because the knowbots are able to change themselves according to the changes in the ideas. It's an endless process. Once it has started, it can go on independently.

Hübler: Yes, but as a vision, a wish...

Wilhelm: In fact it does not work like artificial life. Artificial life is one-to-one translation. We, on the other hand, take reality and the simulation together, a kind of new function with its own borders to reality or to cyberspace. From a scientific point of view the knowledge that you can achieve from artificial life is a fake connection to reality. For the scientist it is just a value from which it is possible to make some forecasts and statements. For the artist there is value if it goes out of control.

Atzori: Many "media-works" which are supposed to be artistic follow the Aristotelian principle of mimesis: the work is just imitating nature with a new technology.

Here you deal with the nature without any "naturalistic" reproduction. We experience a complex of processes that are going on and define a new dimension of communication. Could we define it as a model of a digital environment?

Hübler: Yes, we are in environments where the senses of the body are connected via interfaces to dynamic architectures. Sometimes these knowbots also have the "mimetic" potential for dynamic processes. They represent real "data fluids" which you can contact and transform. Mimetic not in the meaning of traditional art: mimetic potential means the agent incorporating the process. We can't use the term representation any longer because you are included now as an observer of reconstructed representations. I would like to consider this phenomenon further.

Atzori: In your installations one feels a massive use of technology. Formally the only material one can see are computers and communication hi-tech equipment. As artists using this technology what is your critical position regarding the economic/ political process which operates in parallel with the information world?

Hübler: We are inside a technological system whose direction and speed are defined by industry and science. Politics and arts have to follow and it is nearly impossible to do anything without being inside. It is a confrontation which can't work if you play with the traditional ways of art. You have to be inside so that you can really see the consistency of the new technology, not only to say: "OK this is their world." This is our world and becomes bigger and bigger. We all depend on computers. I try to keep my vision free to understand what is outside and deal with both of these worlds. There are still many parts of our life which the technological system can't incorporate. Therefore, I define myself as an artist who can fight inside this self-regulating order. Though I know everything I do could be good for the system because everything is connected, I fight and surrender my respect for the big machines I am working with.

Atzori: The industrial revolution has produced one of the biggest concerns of our time: the pollution of the environment. The South Pole is an environment almost untouched by the man, where it is possible to make important observation about the environmental problem. Many scientists are able to visualize the effects of pollution, but it seems they have much more difficulty uncovering its origins. For an artist it should be more important to fight the causes and not the effects of industrial pollution.

Wilhelm: Yes, a real solution is not fighting against the effects or against the people who destroy the ecosystems. It's necessary to struggle against the thinking of the people who make these strategies, against the scientists and politicians who think they can predict reality by computing nature. It's an old artistic strategy to make politicians and scientists aware of the consequences of their concepts of reality.

Atzori: What's your feeling about the time you need to produce this kind of work?

Hübler: It always takes too long to realize a project when you work with technologies. It is a kind of paradox, not only for the technical complexity, but also for economic support. The production process of art takes longer than you want. You can't produce ten pieces a year. This is perhaps not understandable in the traditional view of art.

Atzori: As we can speak of cyberspace, virtual space, we may think of a different notion of time. Past, future and present exist together in your installation: the past is the work of the scientist; the present is the interaction in your installation; and the future is the potential information going to be updated by the knowbots. How would you define the implicit time of this work?

Wilhelm: We are familiar with the notion of cyberspace, how can we modify space, compress space, extend space. I think you can do the same with time and the way you experience it. We make a concept for the practice of vision. The time we try to realize it is the present.

Hübler: Maybe the work succeeds when somebody gets into our installation and realizes that there is a complex of different and new aesthetic and cognitive structures with which to deal. We can't offer results in our work, everybody can experiment in his own way. We offer a model which is still in discussion, which offers different layers of nature concepts simultaneously: a traditional physical model with light and temperature zones, a scientific simulation with the illusion of linear references and a networked info-aesthetic model generated by knowbots.

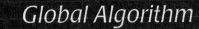

What is gained and what is lost by being digital? What do we see when we look in the digital mirror: Future-Fallout or Net-Utopia? Digital ears and diamond eyes or real blood and guts? What is the relationship between being digital and being human?

Tokyo Must Be Destroyed

Dreams of Tall Buildings and Monsters: Images of Cities and Monuments

Ken Hollings

Introduction: City of Lenses

Let us, just for one brief moment, rewrite the history of cinema in terms of our cities; of centres and spectacles, monuments and disasters. We are coming to the end of so many things in the closing half of this decade that greater demands than this will be made upon us before the end of the millennium.

We could begin, for example, with the Abbasid Caliph Abu Ja'far al-Mansur, the original founder of the ancient city of Baghdad, who conceived of his vast new seat of government as being walled around with fortifications and completely circular in shape. At its exact centre, he decreed that a palace and a great mosque should stand together. Before starting on this undertaking, however, the Caliph ordered his army of labourers to dig a vast circular trench in the sand which was to follow the intended outline of the city's foundations. Oil was poured into the trench and set alight. The Caliph then watched the blazing spectacle from a vantage point overlooking the great river Tigris.

Who knows what hallucinatory visions of power arose out of that shimmering circle of flames? Cities emerge from the haze as mirages on the desert plains. Monuments and landmarks function as lenses bringing them into focus, reducing their size, increasing their clarity.

The towers of Las Vegas ripple in the heat: Caesar's Palace, the great pyramid of Luxor, the Excalibur, the Imperial Palace and the MGM Grand. Did anyone ever suspect that the earth would be called upon to support so much history? Monuments don't require grandeur, merely drama: a change of light. "Do you think Robert Venturi was on drugs when he wrote that book about how great Las Vegas was?" Andy Warhol once asked, after seeing it in daylight.

This from a man who made a notoriously static movie starring the Empire State Building as "an eight-hour hard-on." But even he admitted that Vegas looked better at night, but then so did the Empire State Building:

> It's so beautiful. The lights come on and the stars come out and it sways.
> It's like Flash Gordon riding into space.

In August 1989, Saddam Hussein decreed that his Victory Arch — two gigantic arms, modeled upon his own, bursting forth from the ground clutching crossed scimitars cast from the steel of melted-down Iraqi weapons — be presented to the people of Baghdad:

> The ground bursts open and from it springs the arm that represents
> power and determination, carrying the sword of Qadisiyya. It is the arm
> of the Leader-President, Saddam Hussein himself (God preserve and
> watch over him) enlarged forty times. It springs out to announce the
> good news of victory to all Iraqis, and it pulls in its wake a net that is
> filled with the helmets of the enemy soldiers, some of them scattering
> into the wasteland.

In September 1990, while the Great Satan imposed Resolution 666 upon the United Nations, restricting the importation of food and medical supplies into the Republic of Iraq, an archeological expedition was using radar equipment to pinpoint large objects buried in the desolate, shifting sands of the Central California coastline believed to be sphinxes.

Beneath these dunes, members of the expedition claimed, were the actual remains of Ramases the Magnificent's palace; a monolithic movie set which, in 1923, Cecil B. De Mille had commanded to be built in preparation for Hollywood's first biblical epic, *The Ten Commandments*. As Operation Desert Shield slowly gave way to the final preparations for Desert Storm, it was announced that a full excavation was scheduled to take place, under the direction of a professional archaeologist, to search for these legendary monuments. Chariot wheels, plaster horses, ceramic decorations and statuary, they said, lay scattered on a vast plane of ruins, waiting to be uncovered.

Back in 1956, De Mille had expressed the hope that in a thousand years' time, the discovery of his film set would not lead scientists to the sensational, if erroneous, conclusion that Egyptian civilization, far from being confined to the Valley of the Nile, had extended all the way to the Pacific coast of North America.

As if the Ancient Egyptians had ever been that adept in the use of concrete, nails and plaster of Paris.

The War of the Cities

In these cities constructed as vast movie sets within which the populace, like so many extras, re-enact endless variants on the same crowd scene, what is on show is less important than the way in which it is viewed. Where, for example, the grand frivolities of Las Vegas are focused and reordered in the camcorder lens of the wandering tourist, Saddam Hussein's Baghdad has become reconfigured for Western audiences by the optical telemetering of the guided missile.

Either way, the image ends up on your TV at home.

For the spectator, a cruise missile is nothing but a point of light in the night sky. The digitized flight plan contained in its memory is running a continuous movie of the terrain over which it is traveling. As the missile nears its target, moving from relief map to floor plan, its nose-mounted camera prepares to transmit a live, broadcast-quality, image of the impact. Thus, the cruise missile becomes a complex piece of hardware designed to be an eye-witness to its own destruction.

The moment of impact is also the moment at which the camera goes off air.

Who can survive the shock of being seen in such a fashion? The collapse of the eye is rendered as a complex, instantaneous inversion of the last image seen: black fades rapidly into white, and white instantly turns to black. Sight pools in an informational gravity well. Cities carry within them the blueprints for their own ruins.

Meanwhile, Saddam Hussein has announced the construction in Baghdad of what will be the biggest mosque in the world. Built to his own design, it will stand in the middle of a huge artificial lake fed by the waters of the Tigris, which, following the pounding which the Iraqi capital received at the hands of the United States Air Force, has been transformed into a gigantic open sewer.

"We are rebuilding the ruins in record time," The Mother of Battles Radio announced during the Desert War, "for after the triumph. There is no God but God."

In Waco, Texas, scorched concrete and featureless earth are all that now remain of Ranch Apocalypse, where the Branch Davidians under the guidance of their leader, David Koresh, had their latest and greatest Disappointment. Recent events have reconstructed this haunted patch of wasteground into a rhetorical platform from which Middle America now declares itself to be under attack from all sides, and especially from within.

American Gulf War veteran, Timothy McVeigh, who once dominated the terrain of the KTO as the gunner in an armoured vehicle, now sits in a federal prison cell, charged with the bloodiest bombing in US history. No one seems to think it strange, in the wake of the attack on the Alfred Murrah Federal Building in Oklahoma City, that this outrage should have coincided with the second anniversary of the ending of the Waco siege.

Such a convergence is not so much political as theological. If either Ronald Reagan or George Bush had still been in power at the time of Waco, reads the subtext connecting these two events, perhaps David Koresh's followers would still be alive today, and he'd be putting the finishing touches to his commentary on the breaking of the Seventh Seal.

After all, Reagan believed in the Rapture.

Bush yearned for things to be tested by fire. Both presidents were deeply into the theology of mass-destruction. Under their hands the Star Wars programme appeared and disappeared; uncommented on, unnoticed and unmourned. Now, with Bill Clinton at its helm, Middle America finds itself, for better or worse, approaching the end of the second millennium with a President of the Union who doesn't seem to understand the meaning of the Apocalypse.

But the signs and portents were all there: in 1994, Los Angeles, that great city of lenses and surveillance systems, had trembled once more along its own fault line. After the fires, the uprising, the unrest and the urban decay, an earthquake was just enough to emphasize the point that the great city of the twentieth century had only a few years left to go. Then, exactly one year later to the day, it happened again. This time in Southern Japan.

Welcome to Earthquake Island

Some pretty strange dust started to settle in the media after the earth shifted so tragically under the people of Kobe and Osaka in January 1995. As the extent of the damage became increasingly clear, and the casualty rate soared into the thousands, the international news services struggled to make sense of it all, revealing in the process a fault line of misunderstanding running from East to West that was as real as any that might lie beneath the Japanese mainland.

Commentators, experts and other assorted professionals crowded onto the airwaves to explain how the Japanese had neither predicted the earthquake correctly nor prepared for it adequately in advance and that they knew next to nothing about disaster relief or even how to counsel the survivors. Unfavourable comparisons were also made between the Kobe and the Los Angeles earthquakes. The Japanese people, it was implied, were being so obviously and willfully wrong-headed about the whole thing that they didn't even deserve to have the earthquake in the first place.

The truth is that the broadcast media tend to confuse their own reactions to an event with the actual event itself. Such incidents as the Kobe earthquake have a long history of occurring on the Japanese mainland.

An ancient piece of mythological wisdom has the island of Japan resting upon the back of a gigantic catfish that lies submerged beneath the primordial mud. Every so often, about every seventy years on average, the fish twitches its tail, and that's when the earth starts shaking. Some kind of major upheaval had been expected in Japan since the Great Kanto earthquake devastated Tokyo in 1925, killing 250,000 of its inhabitants.

All the same, there must have been many in the West who looked at their video collections with feelings of unease. Wholesale urban demolition has long been a staple element in *anime*, and fans of *kaiju eiga* — Japanese live-action monster movies — have seen Tokyo reduced to rubble so often that the city must be permanently associated in their minds with scenes of destruction. And that is perhaps where the tragedy of Kobe really lies. Everyone had expected the earthquake to hit Japan much further south; in Tokyo itself.

The Uncertainty Principle

If Japan rests upon the back of a giant catfish, then the fate of its capital city belongs with another, equally fabulous, creature. Ever since he first burst onto the big screen back in 1954, Godzilla has become famous for the lasting impression he has made on the Tokyo skyline. Returning to the great metropolis over and over again in well over half of the twenty-one feature films in which he has appeared so far, Godzilla, the undisputed king of *kaiju eiga*, has left it in ruins every time.

A gigantic mutant dinosaur breathing radioactive fire, he was the unforeseen byproduct of atomic testing in the Pacific Ocean at a time when such tests were beginning to cause grave public concern. The year which saw the release of the first Godzilla movie was also the one in which the crew of the Japanese fishing boat

"Lucky Dragon No. 5" were showered with fall-out from the H-Bomb detonated on Bikini Atoll. Oblique references to this incident were subsequently incorporated into the film. However, as a true run-away child of the nuclear age, Godzilla is also subject to the Uncertainty Principle. Just as it is impossible to determine a suba-tomic particle's exact position, direction and velocity all at the same time, the Big G does not allow himself to be pinned down that easily. Does he represent some kind of dark, unacknowledged obsession which the Japanese have with their own destruction, or is he just a guy in a rubber monster costume jumping up and down on a tabletop landscape pretending to shoot radioactive flame from his mouth?

Godzilla has always been a monster who casts two shadows; one in the West and the other in the East. His origins reveal a strong mixture of both Japanese and American influences: conceived as a combination of two successful Hollywood monsters — Willis O'Brien's King Kong and Ray Harryhausen's Rhedosaurus in *The Beast from 2000 Fathoms* — he was presented to the Japanese public as Gojira; a hybrid name which co-joins the Western word "gorilla" with the Japanese "kujira", meaning a whale. He was also quite evidently a man in a rubber suit; an aspect of the *kaiju eiga* genre which has never gone down particularly well with Western audiences who tend to confuse notions of spectacle with those of realism.

Atoms for Peace

O'Brien's King Kong and Harryhausen's Rhedosausus contributed greatly to the development of a whole battery of photographic special effects — from stop-frame animation, glass shots and live-action mattes though to the sophisticated digital processes of today — which have established in the West the conventions by which cinematic illusions are judged to have become reality. Godzilla, however, has made an entire career out of failing to meet such demands, earning for himself in the process a reputation for being cheap, amateurish and silly among those movie-goers who prefer bigger budgeted affairs in which the computer-generated dino-saurs look real and the actors behave as if they were stuck inside rubber suits.

Furthermore, Godzilla's Eastern origins ensured his divergence from Western notions of reality almost from his very inception. His twin shadows emanate from a common point; that troubled moment after the Second World War where East met West on the most uneasy of terms, the American Occupation of Japan.

"Ambiguity" is a term that barely covers the confusions and contradictions that characterized this period. During the immediate post-war years, the Japanese were encouraged to come to terms with the atomic devastation of Hiroshima and Nagasaki in elegiac, "positive" ways, such as the 1950 documentary film, *Hiroshima*, with its respectful "March of Time" voice-over and its American footage of the bomb exploding. In the same year, however, a book detailing the events of August 6, 1945 as experienced by the bomb's survivors was printed, bound and then immediately suppressed by the Occupation forces for being too anti-American. That volume had to wait another ten years, buried in the depths of Hiroshima City Hall, before it was finally published.

And whatever thinking lay behind American attempts to discourage tradi-tional Japanese art forms such as Kabuki, with its giant puppets, elaborate costumes, masks and exaggerated gestures, can only have helped to establish the equally stylized theatrical traditions that would eventually come to characterize the Japanese monster movie. Certainly, it is interesting to note in this context that it was only after the Occupation was over that Kabuki flourished once again and the first film compilations showing existing Hiroshima footage were made freely available to the Japanese public.

Perhaps because Hiroshima is simultaneously a place and an event, it must always be approached obliquely. As the effects of radiation sickness become increasingly apparent, from one generation to the next, the connection between the two becomes more and more apparent: Hiroshima is a monument that exists in both time and space. What makes this fact all the more terrible is that Ground Zero must always remain an imaginary terrain. There is not a soul alive today who can tell us what happened at the centre of the bombed area. "The great mysterious monster conquered the city in an instant," Kenzaburo Oe observed in his *Hiroshima Notes* — and that instant is really nothing more than a single frame of film passing through a movie projector's gate.

In Godzilla's Skin

Meanwhile, back in 1950s small-town America, where everything seemed to be going well and everyone was under attack, atomic science was having a field day. "People talk a great deal of nonsense about the effects of nuclear radiation," one of the scientists announces in *The Monster That Challenged the World*. Considering that he's appearing in a movie opposite an army of giant mutant snails hell-bent on invading California, it's a pretty safe assumption that he knows what he's talking about.

While real scientists were secretly injecting very real plutonium into the bodies of the poor, the sick, the needy and the institutionalized, the American public indulged itself in a nuclear nightmare of orgiastic proportions. Atomic-powered spaceships crashed into the sides of mountains, and giant ants built their colonies out of the very sand that covered Ramases the Magnificent's dream palace. So far, so familiar. However, things only started to get really scary when the big cities of America, with their recognizable monuments and landmarks, were approached by these portents of the future.

The unease with which an audience watched a flying saucer glide over the Washington Mall at the beginning of *The Day the Earth Stood Still* in 1951 turned to shock in 1956, when the reassuring shapes of the Washington Monument, together with those to Lincoln and Jefferson, and the dome of the Capitol Building were smashed to pieces by invading aliens in *Earth vs. the Flying Saucers*. It shouldn't come as any surprise to discover that the man responsible for this startling vision was Ray Harryhausen, whose giant stop-frame mutant octopus tore San Francisco's Golden Gate Bridge apart in *It Came From Beneath the Sea* in 1953 and whose Rhedosaurus had rampaged through a very real-looking New York earlier that same year.

Willis O'Brien's King Kong — re-released in 1952 and even more popular with monster movie fans than he had been back in 1933 also took on New York. And lost.

Carl Denham, however, only got it partly right. It clearly wasn't the airplanes that killed the beast, but it wasn't beauty either. It was the fall from the top of the Empire State Building that finally did for the mighty Kong.

Landmarks can kill.

In the 1976 remake, the poor bugger even had to take a dive off the new, improved and even taller symbol of economic power; the World Trade Centre. How could anyone have seriously believed, nearly twenty years later, that a truck loaded with explosive could succeed in toppling what King Kong could not?

Godzilla, who has only ever had to contend with the rather banal splendours of the Tokyo Tower and the Diet Building, has always managed to inflict more damage upon Japan's capital city than it has ever succeeded in causing him in return. One of the reasons for this is that the Uncertainty Principle places Godzilla squarely outside the "Nature vs. Technology" debate which has come to dominate the way in which monster movies are perceived. Possessing a more markedly individualistic personality than the anonymous armies of assorted giant fauna that rampaged across America during the 1950s, Godzilla has always followed his own instincts. However, unlike King Kong, he is no oversized nature boy, fresh off the boat and ready to get beaten to the ground at the first instance by the iniquities of urban civilization.

Existing above and beyond the oppositional trends of nature and culture, Godzilla has also become the victim of a common misconception. His skin, contrary to popular opinion, is never green — the colour traditionally associated with plant life and, by extension, with Nature itself — but a very deep charcoal grey. His impenetrable hide is the same shade as burned stone and compacted carbon; hard, dense and unyielding. The same colour as the impact of energy on matter at Ground Zero.

Perhaps placing Godzilla at the heart of Hiroshima's or Nagasaki's ruins raises more than just questions of taste in the Western viewer's mind. The truth is, however, that films belonging to the *kaiju eiga* genre were, from the very beginning, made to a very different set of criteria. The majority of them were photographed in an anamorphic wide-screen process which, when properly projected, lent the images a greater sense of scale and depth. To add further atmosphere, the films' soundtracks were almost always recorded in stereo; an innovation which dates back to at least 1957. Presented in such a fashion, Godzilla's destruction of Tokyo — built in considerable detail at one twenty-fifth scale and filmed in slow motion to collapse more effectively — took on a spectacular, almost theatrical, quality. Unfortunately, by the time these films reached the West, they had been scanned and panned to fit a smaller format, their soundtracks re-recorded and rearranged, and additional scenes (usually shot on an entirely different screen ratio) had been inserted. Let's not even mention the dubbing. What was left appeared as a miserable failure to achieve a level of cinematic realism which the films had never set out to attain in the first place.

Tokyo Must Be Destroyed

But how real is real? There is a story about security guards in a Tokyo department store stopping two suspected terrorists who had been overheard animatedly discussing the destruction of the city. The dangerous subversives turned out to be veteran director Ishiro Honda swapping ideas with special effects expert Eiji Tsuburaya for a scene in what was to become *Gojira*, the first Godzilla movie.

Illusions depend a great deal upon not being in full possession of the facts. To see the *kaiju eiga* genre as the obsession of a culture repeatedly seeking to rehearse repressed or unacknowledged fears of nuclear obliteration or natural catastrophe is to explain little and to obscure a great deal more. It is also an attitude based upon a very selective view of Japan's filmic output. For example, in the decade that witnessed the rise of Godzilla, films explicitly confronting Japan's continuing nuclear nightmare, such as Kaneto Shindo's *Children of Hiroshima* and *Lucky Dragon No.5*, were also being released. Ishiro Honda himself had visited Hiroshima in 1946 and had wanted to convey in *Gojira* some of the horrors which he experienced there. Unfortunately, the film's references to bomb shelters, Nagasaki and its pleas for nuclear disarmament were deleted from the English-language version by its American distributors.

Godzilla, however, had already selected a very different target for himself. It was a disaster area still waiting to happen, and each time he returned to it, he became more a part of its future than its past.

By 1945, allied air raids had reduced most of Tokyo to smoking embers. Its predominantly wooden buildings had burned easily, resulting in the destruction of three-quarters of a million houses and the deaths of 100,000 of the city's inhabitants. A further three million were left homeless. Today, as well as being one of the principal centres of world economic activity, the greater Tokyo area also houses an astonishing 25% of Japan's entire population. This vast urban sprawl has come to be regarded by many as the ultimate megalopolis: the first city of the 21st Century. The planners and engineers responsible for its safety have also described it as a "disaster amplification mechanism"; a term which could just as easily be applied to Godzilla himself.

There is, however, something both reassuring and unsettling about the Tokyo which Honda and Tsuburaya had Godzilla smash so repeatedly. It never changed. No matter how far into the future the films were set, Tokyo always returned looking the same. In a universe increasingly populated by alien invaders, female psychics, killer androids and giant mecha, Tokyo's vast centre-less sprawl seemed to expand into time and space, eternally rising unchanged from its own rubble. The more Godzilla demolished it, the more it came back, determined to survive.

Godzilla in Paradise

Godzilla's career trajectory as an urban destroyer has never been as smooth as his continuing relationship with Tokyo might suggest. Quite often he became the victim of his own success. The cost of rebuilding an entire city is still high, even when it only exists in miniature. Furthermore, his audience was not only getting larger, but appreciably and enthusiastically younger. Consequently he was packed off, from time to time, to remote tropical islands in the middle of the Pacific Ocean, where palm trees were cheaper to replace than skyscrapers and he could participate in such juvenile romps as Toho's *Son of Godzilla*.

This did not mean, however, that the dark forces which he had come to represent had also been sent on vacation. It is worth remembering that Japan produced many disaster films outside of the Godzilla cycle which dealt much more explicitly with the themes of catastrophe and disaster, most notably Toei Studio's *The Final War* and Toho's *The Last War* (both about global nuclear conflict) in the 1960s; *Tidal Wave*, *Last Days of Planet Earth*, in the 1970s; and *Virus* in the early 1980s. As these films would inevitably have utilized similar special effects budgets and technicians as the monster movies, it is not surprising to find that they tended to be made when there was a slackening off, either of quality or frequency, in the *kaiju eiga* genre. Similarly, Keji Nakazawa's comic strip, *Barefoot Gen*, based upon his own childhood experiences of the bombing of Hiroshima, first appeared in the children's magazine *Shukan Shonen Jampu* during the early 1970s, at a time when Godzilla's audience was predominantly pre-teen.

To transpose Godzilla from his urban habitat in mainland Japan to the arcadian paradise of an island in the Pacific, if only for the briefest of interludes, is to place him firmly within the kind of "Technology vs. Nature" debate which he so effortlessly transcended whenever he was tearing Tokyo apart. *Son of Godzilla* illustrates this point extremely well, if only because it raises the one question to which monster movie *otaku* have never been able to supply an adequate answer: who or what exactly did Godzilla mate with to produce a son?

At the beginning of the film, Godzilla is seen swimming towards Solgell Island, attracted by a mysterious radio signal. However, he is not the first interloper to arrive on this tropical paradise. A group of scientists — all male — have already established a research centre amid its sultry palms to study the ways in which climatic conditions can be artificially manipulated and controlled. They, in turn, have to endure an intruder of their own: a pushy, camera-toting newshound called Goro, also male. As the story unfolds, and it becomes increasingly apparent that all of this tropical Eden's invaders are masculine, it comes as no surprise to discover that Solgell Island's indigenous population are exclusively female. As Godzilla's son, Minya, emerges from his egg, he is attended by a coven of giant preying mantises who quickly forget their duties as midwife when they discover that he is a male and — true to type — attempt to devour him. Slumbering deep within the island's depths is another archetypal female predator from pop culture; the Spiga, a monstrous spider. Finally there is Reiko, the jungle girl: one of those natural born sophisticates who always use their first name when they mean "I". She is the orphaned daughter of Professor Matsumiya — another male interloper — and is the only person in the film to take any real interest in nurturing the young Minya, pausing every now and again to hurl cantaloupes into his ever-open mouth. Godzilla's only contribution to the little mite's development, on the other hand, is to teach him how to blow radioactive smoke rings. In fact, as a predominantly masculine science enters into a frenzied discourse with a primordially feminine nature, there doesn't seem to be much else for him to do. This lack of purpose appears quite puzzling until Goro, in an unguarded moment, makes a reference to his home in Tokyo. "Tokyo?" asks Reiko, using the kind of basic grammar favoured by the inhabitants of tropical islands. "What kind of place?"

"Well," Goro replies, "it's a man-made jungle", and it suddenly becomes evident that Godzilla has no place in this prelapsarian Eden or the thematic simplicities it engenders.

Like the gangster, the salaryman and the juvenile delinquent, Godzilla is a true city-dweller. He needs its ambiguities in order to truly be himself.

Mekatokyo

As Godzilla's audience became younger during the 60s and 70s, he quickly slid from atomic destroyer to comic avenger and science-fiction clown. After so much time spent mucking about in children's bedrooms, Godzilla had a lot of growing up to do. Literally.

When Toho Films brought him back for the 1984 remake of the original *Gojira*, they had to almost double his height so that he could compete with the rise in Tokyo's skyline over the years. The Japanese capital had expanded upwards and outwards to an alarming degree, dwarfing its cinematic counterpart.

"That's quite an urban renewal programme they have there," an American army major remarks of Godzilla's attack on Tokyo, but he could have been speaking about the city's actual growth rate. An anarchic process of demolition and reconstruction, in which houses, shops and tower blocks were continually being torn down and rebuilt, had resulted in an anonymous sprawl that seemed to stretch on forever. This prompted further concerns about its safety. Planners became worried that too much of the nation's future had become concentrated into its disaster-proofed structures. There were calls for a radical decentralization of Tokyo's functions into other parts of the country, but how do you decentralize something which has no centre?

Fragile and featureless, caught between expansion and catastrophe, Tokyo's possible futures came to dominate *anime*. In *Bubblegum Crisis*, Mega Tokyo has been rebuilt from the ruins of the old capital city after it was devastated during "the second Kanto Earthquake". Bigger and more ungovernable than ever, it is menaced by fearsome cyborgs and corporate powerplays. The series title hints at the steadily increasing state of instability that occurs the moment before the bubble bursts.

Neo-Tokyo, the setting for Katsuhiro Otomo's *Akira*, has been rebuilt after Tokyo's nuclear obliteration into a high-rise labyrinth of rioting citizens, political unrest, terrorism and full-scale gang warfare. Readers of the manga version will also know that Tokyo actually has the dubious privilege of being demolished *twice* during the course of Otomo's 1800-page story.

Even with a complete change of name, Tokyo's ruins are clearly identifiable. In *Project A-KO*, the city of Graviton has been rebuilt into an unstable business community around the waters of a bay punched out of the Earth's crust by a giant spaceship that plummeted from the sky. Olympus, in Masamune Shirow's *Appleseed*, is a city state that rose to prominence after a devastating global conflict and now staggers from one near-apocalyptic power struggle to the next. Newport in *Dominion*, also by Shirow, is in constant danger of being transformed into a demolition derby by the Tank Police; the very force sworn to protect it.

Silent Moebius takes place in a Tokyo which has managed to survive into the twenty-first century without having to undergo either serious destruction or a name-change, but has swollen to enormous, unmanageably overcrowded proportions. Seriously polluted, plagued with unbreathable air and acid rain, it has also become the arena for demonic incursions from another dimension. *Wicked City*, *Urotsukidoji* and *Doomed Megalopolis* (which features the original Kanto Earthquake) all pursue similar themes of supernatural invasion. The origins of the *Patlabor* series lie in the threat to a vulnerable Tokyo of rising tidal waters caused by the Earth's global warming. Then there's *Cyber City*, *Tokyo Babylon*, *AD Police*... the list, like a streetplan of Tokyo, seems to go on forever.

The Ruins of Cyberspace

In all these visions of the future, Tokyo is depicted as a major conurbation entering the 21st Century having already run out of time. It is also a city of glowing colours, rapid edits, break-neck narratives and dizzying perspectives. Whereas in the *kaiju eiga* genre, Tokyo was a city of details and effects, of collapse as a theatrical spectacle, *anime* has transformed it into a place made out of pure velocity. A product of the video age, its depth and its structures are now created by the speed of an electron moving across the flat plane of a television screen. Both versions, however, depict Tokyo as a featureless urban mass. Landmarks are so rare that their appearance arouses suspicion. In the 1992 remake of *Godzilla vs the Thing*, Mothra cocoons Tokyo's Diet building in an ironic comment on the political scandals of the time. Its fictional counterpart, the Genom Tower, broods over Mega Tokyo in *Bubblegum Crisis*, and in the manga version of *Appleseed*, the huge Tartarus arcology appears in frame after frame; a series of futuristic Views of Mount Fuji.

Tokyo's real landmarks are its imaginary ruins, a point well illustrated at the end of Shinya Tsukamoto's manga-influenced live-action movie, *Tetsuo II*, where the salaryman protagonist and his family wander like tourists, sight-seeing among Tokyo's devastated towerblocks. The ambiguous feelings which Tsukamoto has expressed towards the city — enjoying the security of its utilities while yearning also for the wide-open spaces created by its destruction — have a counterpart in the thinking of Japan's more radical designers, such as Toyo Ito, who see Tokyo as a city whose life does not reside in its structures but in the energies that surge through them. Its true architecture, they argue, exists in the limitless profusion of temporary forms thrown up by computer links, information flows, networked images and disembodied voices. Computer animation, videogaming and the technology of data processing have all conspired to take destruction beyond mere physical limitations. Tokyo won't become decentralized: it will dematerialize itself instead.

Paradoxically, serious questions are now being raised about what form such a dematerialization might take. As the standing ruins of the Alfred Murrah Federal

Building in Oklahoma City are being razed to ground, the American public is being warned that the extreme right have begun to infiltrate the Internet. In Japan, it has now been revealed that the Aum Shrinrikyo cult, accused of the Sarin gas attack upon a crowded subway train during the morning rush hour in Tokyo, appropriated themes and imagery derived from popular manga and *anime* series in developing their paranoid visions of the forthcoming apocalypse.

While *otaku* use the sprawl of the Internet, a communications system originally designed to survive a nuclear attack, to swap esoteric factoids about Ultraman and Hello Kitty, there is still someone present whose influence is unmistakable.

Having been there at the start of it all, he will not be quickly forgotten.

One of the most immediate responses to the Kobe Earthquake was that the Nikkei Index fell by over 1,000 points in a single night. This was the result of nervous speculators fearing that Japan was about to start withdrawing capital from its investments overseas to finance the rebuilding programme. If a series of checks and balances had not previously been introduced into the system — just after the crash of 1987 and immediately before the start of Operation Desert Storm — in order to discourage dangerous fluctuations in the market, Japan's economy would have probably dropped right through the floor, taking the rest of the world with it. Godzilla, it seems, is alive and well and rampaging through cyberspace. Consider yourselves warned.

Stalking the UFO Meme

Richard Thieme

"There is Thingumbob shouting!" the Bellman said. "He is shouting
like mad, only hark! He is waving his hands, he is waggling his head, He
has certainly found a Snark!"

Lewis Carroll, The Hunting of the Snark

"We are convinced that Roswell took place. We've had too many high
ranking military officials tell us that it happened, that told us that it was
clearly not of this earth."

*Don Schmitt, co-author, "The Truth About the UFO
Crash at Roswell," in an interview by Ed Mar and
Jody Mecanic for* Lumpen Magazine *on the Internet*

That "interview with a real X-Filer" can be found on one of the hundreds of
web sites — in addition to Usenet groups, gopher holes stuffed with hundreds of
files, and clandestine BBSs where abductees meet to compare "scoop marks" — that
make up the virtual world of flying saucers.

The UFO subculture or — for some — the UFO religion on the Internet is a
huge supermarket of images and words. Everything is for sale — stories and
pictures, membership in a community, entire belief systems. But what are we
buying? The meal? Or the menu?

The Bricks that Build the House

When Don Schmitt uses the word "Roswell," he is not merely identifying a
small town in New Mexico that put itself on the tourist map with a terrific UFO
story. He uses it to *MEAN* the whole story — the one that says a UFO crashed in
1947 near the Roswell Army Air Field, after which alien bodies were recovered, eye-
witnesses rewarded with new pick-up trucks or threatened with death, and a cosmic
Watergate — as Stanton Friedman, another Roswell author, calls it — initiated.
Schmitt uses the word "Roswell" the way Christian evangelists use "Jesus," to mean
everything believed about "Roswell." Like an evangelist, he counts on his audience
to fill in the details. Every good Roswellite knows them — it's the story, after all,
that defines them as a community.

That story is scattered on the Internet like fragments of an exploding space-ship. Do the pieces fit together to make a coherent puzzle? Or is something wrong with this picture?

Stalking the UFO meme on the Internet

Memes are contagious ideas that replicate like viruses from mind to mind. The Internet is like a Petri dish in which memes multiply rapidly. Fed by fascina-tion, incubated in the feverish excitement of devotees transmitting stories of cosmic significance, the UFO meme mutates into new forms, some of them wondrous and strange.

"The Roswell incident" is but one variation of the UFO meme. On the Internet, Schmitt's words are hyperlinked to those of other UFO sleuths and legions of interested bystanders like myself, as fascinated by the psychodynamics of the subculture as by the "data" exchanged as currency in that marketplace.

Before we examine a few fragments, let's pause to remember what the Internet really is.

Copies of copies — or copies of originals?

The Internet represents information through symbols or icons. So does speech, writing, and printed text, but the symbols on the Net are even further removed from the events and context to which they point.

The power of speech gave us the ability to lie, then writing hid the liar from view. That's why Plato fulminated at writing — you couldn't know what was true if you didn't have the person right there in front of you, he said, the dialog providing a necessary check.

The printing press made it worse by distancing reader and writer even more. Now we put digital images and text on the Net. Pixels can be manipulated. With-out correlation with other data, no digital photo or document can be taken at face value. There's no way to know if we're looking at a copy of an original, a copy of a copy, or a copy that has no original.

But wait. It gets worse.

The World is a Blank Screen

Certain phenomena, including UFOs and religious symbols, elicit powerful projections. We think we're seeing "out there" what is really inside us. Because projections are unconscious, we don't know if we're looking at iron filings obscuring a magnet or the magnet itself.

Carl Jung said UFOs invite projections because they're mandalas — arche-typal images of our deep Selves. Unless we separate what he think we see from what we see, we're bound to be confused.

Repetition makes any statement seem true. Hundreds of cross-referenced links on the Web create a matrix of even greater credibility. In print, we document assertions with references. Footnotes are conspicuous by their absence on the Web. Information is self-referential. Symbols and images point to themselves like a ten-dimensional dog chasing its own tails.

"Roswell" may be the name of the game, but what does the name really say?

What's in a name?

Everything.

Names reveal our beliefs about things.

Was there a "Roswell incident?" Or was there a "so-called Roswell incident?"

Are Don Schmitt and his former partner Kevin Randle "the only two professional investigators in the field" as Schmitt claims in that interview? Or are they in fact "self-styled professional UFO investigators?" (UFO investigators accredit themselves, then reinforce their authority by debating one another and showing up at the same forums. Refuting or attacking another "investigator" does him a favor by acknowledging his importance.)

Are there "eight firsthand witnesses who saw the bodies," "many high-ranking military officials who said it was not of this earth," or "550 witnesses stating that this was not from this earth?" All of those statements are made in the same interview.

Words like "self-styled" and "alleged" do more than avoid law suits. They make clear that the speaker states or believes something rather than knows it to be true. Schmitt uses the word "witness" the way Alice in Wonderland uses words, to mean exactly what she wants them to mean — instead of letting witness mean... well, **witness**.

Dan Kagan and Ian Summers have written a masterful investigation of "cattle mutilation" (*Mute Evidence*, Bantam Books, New York: 1984), detailing how predator damage became "cattle mutilation" conducted with "surgical precision," i.e. in straight lines, through the distortion of the media, "professional experts" who kept everyone one step away from the evidence (common in UFO research), and true believers who suspended their capacity for critical judgment.

"The Roswell incident" also consists of words repeated often enough to turn them into pseudo-facts which are then used to weave a scenario. When enough people believe the scenario, they focus on the minutiae of the story — did it crash on the Plains of San Agustin, as Stanton Friedman claims, or north of Roswell as Schmitt and Randle claim? — instead of the basics, i.e. did anything other than a balloon crash at all? Science turns quickly into theology.

Can a Fact Move at the Speed of Light?

The way sites are connected on the WWW tends to obliterate our historical sense. Everything on the Web seems to be happening **now**. Without a point of reference, all information seems equal. Lining up texts side-by-side and evaluating discrepancies feels like hard work.

Surf to the Cambridge Cybercafé, for example, and you'll find a laudatory article about Schmitt written by Milwaukee writer Gillian Sender.

Sender says the piece was purloined without her permission. Like much on the Net, it's an unauthorized copy of a copy.

Sender did a follow-up piece for Milwaukee Magazine in which she confessed her subsequent disillusionment with Schmitt. In interviews he misrepresented his educational background and occupation. Sender concluded that those misrepresentations undermined his credibility across the board.

You won't learn that on the Web, because the second piece isn't there. The Cybercafé web site also has a newsletter written by Schmitt and Randle but no link to information about their later split, when Randle denounced Schmitt for deceiving him as well as others.

The Soul of the Web

According to Jung, when the psyche projects its contents onto an archetypal symbol, there is always secrecy, fascination, and high energy. When a webmaster finds an article like Sender's he gets excited, plucks it out of cyberspace, and puts it on his site. Come across it four or five times, you start to believe it.

Tracking down the truth about the "Roswell incident" is like hunting the mythical Snark in the Carroll poem. The closer one gets to the "evidence," the more its disappears.

There is in fact not one living "witness" to the "Roswell incident" in the public domain, not one credible report that is not filtered through a private interview or other privileged communication.

There are, though, lots of people making a living from it.

Who ARE These Guys?

Karl Pflock is another "Roswell investigator." Stick his name into a search engine and you'll find him on the UFOlogist roster at Glenn Campbell's Area 51 web site. The text of an online interview with Pflock and Stanton Friedman is reproduced there.

What effect does this have?

By appearing with him, Friedman lends credibility to Pflock's status. Their disagreement over details (Pflock thinks the Roswell debris was the remains of a Project Mogul balloon, as the Air Force claims) is less important than the fact of their debate, which implies that the details are important, the debate worth having. That ensures future bookings for both.

Get the idea? In the virtual world, the appearance of reality becomes reality. Then you can buy and sell words, icons, symbols as if the menu is the meal.

Pflock is not new to the world of UFOs. Kagan and Summers first encountered him as a man named "Kurt Peters" who appropriated a story he knew was fabricated about "cattle mutilations," then tried to pass it off as his own and sell it to a New York publisher. When the authors confronted Pflock "with the Kurt Peters gambit, he was shaken that we had found him out."

What might we infer, therefore, about Pflock's credibility? On the Web, however, the context created by juxtaposition with Friedman makes it seem as if he is a real "professional."

Follow the Money

The UFO game needs teams so the game can be played. The "for-team" and the "against-team" are essential to each other. The famous "alien autopsy film" exploited by Ray Santilli illustrates this.

This film allegedly showed the autopsy of an alien retrieved from a crash site. Many web sites were devoted to this film; Usenet groups hummed with endless conversation about the details. One major thread was devoted to finding the cameraman. (Once again, the key player or detail was absent, the audience addressed by a "spokesperson for the event.")

A great deal of money was made by debating the film, regardless of which side one was on. Stanton Friedman was off to Italy for a screening, Schmitt to England to "examine the evidence," and so on. Meanwhile reports like that by Dr. Joseph A. Bauer on CSICOP's web site that exposed the film's "overwhelming lack of credibility" were ignored. The lack of credibility was obvious from the beginning, but had it been acknowledged, there would have been no game to play — no Fox-TV special, no books or debates, no conferences in Europe.

The Santilli episode is about played out, but other "evidence" is taking its place. At the moment, an anonymous tipster claims to have a fragment of the crashed saucer. The story is spreading on the Web, mutating as it grows. Now, fifty years after the alleged crash, others claim to have fragments too.

The good thing about fragments of crashed saucers is that they are endless. Even better are the claims made by "professional investigators" that they are negotiating with shadowy figures who have fragments but are afraid of being killed if they go public. Those stories are endless too.

To know someone's motivation, follow their checkbook. Look, for example, at the heated rivalry in the town of Roswell between museums competing for tourist dollars with trips to rival crash sites. You can even sign up for the tour on the Web.

Information? Misinformation? Disinformation?

The Santilli film could be dismissed as a non-event, did it not reveal a deeper dimension of life in the UFO world. What were its effects?

Energy was displaced, the focus of the debate shifted, and the "Roswell incident" — ironically — reinforced.

When someone says, "These are not the real crown jewels" they imply that real crown jewels exist. If this is a fake autopsy film, where is the *real* autopsy film? That implies a real autopsy which implies real aliens and a real crash.

Or was the film an ingenious piece of disinformation by the government? Was it designed to throw investigators off the track? See how we responded to news of real aliens? Hide some real data among a snowstorm of false data?

Is all this confusion… intentional?

It's X-files time.

Ready for a Headache?

Now we're closing in on the Snark.

Are government agents using the subculture to manipulate or experiment with public opinion? To cover up what they know? Are the investigators "useful idiots," as they're known in the spy trade, real spies, or just in it for the buck?

One of my online adventures illustrates the difficulty of getting answers to these questions.

A woman in Hamilton, Montana, was speaking to Peter Davenport, head of the National UFO Reporting Center in Seattle about a UFO she said was hanging around her neighborhood. She said she could hear strange beeps on the radio when it was hovering. Then, while they spoke, some beeps sounded.

"There!" she said. "You hear that? What is that?"

Peter played the beeps over the telephone. I recorded them. Then I posted a message on alt.2600 — a hacker's Usenet group — asking for help.

I received several offers of assistance. One came from LoD.

LoD! The Legion of Doom! I was delighted. If anybody can get to the bottom of this, the LoD can. These guys are the best hackers in the business.

I recorded the beeps as a .wav file and emailed them to LoD. They asked a few questions and said they'd see what they could find.

Meanwhile I received another email. This writer said he had heard similar tones over telephone lines and shortwave radio in his neighborhood, which happened to be near a military base.

Then he wrote, "I have some info that would be of great interest. Government documents..." He mentioned friends inside the base who told him about them.

Meanwhile the LoD examined the switching equipment used by the telco and reported that they were evaluating the data.

A third email directed me to a woman specializing in the "beeps" frequently associated with UFOs. She sent me a report she had written about their occurrence and properties.

LoD asked for my telephone number and someone called the following week. They could affirm, the caller said, that the signals did not originate within the telephone system. They could say what the signals were not, but not what they were. One negative did not imply a positive.

Then the correspondent near the military base sent a striking communication.

"The documentation and info that I am getting are going to basically confirm what a member of the team has divulged to me.

"They are here and they are not benign."

He gave me information about other things he had learned, then acknowledged that all he said was either worthless hearsay or serious trouble. Therefore, he concluded, "I am abandoning this account and disappearing back into the ether."

The Twilight Zone

There you have it. Without corroboration or external evidence to use as a triangulating point, that's as far as the Internet can take us.

Words originate with someone — but who? Is the name on the email real? Is the domain name real? Is the account real?

Secrecy. Fascination. High energy.

Maybe it's a sign of the times that I was pleased to have the help of the LoD. While I would have dismissed a government or telco statement as maybe true, maybe not, I trusted LoD.

They did a solid piece of work. Technically they're the best, but more than that, I knew they'd be true to their code. Like me, they're need-to-know machines and they love a good puzzle.

What about the next-door-to-the-military source? Was he who he said he was? Were his contacts telling the truth? Are "they" here and are "they" not benign? Or was he a government agent trying to learn what I knew? Or just a bored kid who felt like killing a little time?

How do we separate fact from fiction? Jacques Vallée, a respected writer and researcher, recently authored a work of fiction about UFOs. Is he really writing fiction so he can disguise the truth, as some say? Or is he just another guy selling a book? Or a serious investigator who has blurred his own credibility by writing fiction that's hard to distinguish from his theories?

Or is he a secret agent working for the government?

The UFO world is a hall of mirrors. The UFO world on the Internet is a simulation of a hall of mirrors. The truth is out there, all right… but how can we find it?

Plato was right. We need to know who is speaking. We need to stay with the bottom-line data that won't go away.

The Bottom Line

What does it look like?

One piece looks like this. I know a career Air Force officer, recently retired as a full colonel. He worked at the Pentagon and the War College., He is a terrific guy who has all the "right stuff." He's the kind of guy you'd willingly follow into battle. Many did.

A fellow B47 pilot in the sixties told him of an unusual object that flew in formation with him for a while, then took off an incredible speed he could not match. The co-pilot independently verified the incident. Neither wanted to report it and risk damage to their careers.

When he first told me that account in the 1970s, I remember how he looked. He usually looked confident, even cocky. That time he looked puzzled, maybe a little helpless. I knew he was telling me the truth.

I have seen that look many times as credible people told me their account of an anomalous experience. They don't want publicity or money. They just want to know what's happening on their planet.

Data has accumulated for at least fifty years. Some of it is on the Internet. Some of it, like email from that retired air force officer, is trustworthy. Much of it isn't.

Are we hunting a Snark, only to be bamboozled by a boojum? Or are we following luminous breadcrumbs through the darkening forest to the Truth that is Out There? The Net is one place to find answers, but we'll find them only if our pursuit of the truth is rigorous, disciplined, and appropriately skeptical.

*This article appeared first in the November
1996 issue of* Internet Underground.

Transmitting Architecture
The Transphysical City

Marcos Novak

> Here and there, sick lamplight through window glass taught us
> to distrust the deceitful mathematics of our perishing eyes.
>
> *F. T. Marinetti, Futurist Manifesto, 1909*

> Analogy is nothing more than the deep love that links
> distant, seemingly diverse and hostile things.
>
> *F. T. Marinetti, Futurist Manifesto, 1913*

TechnoChronology

May 20-24, 1994. 4CyberConf: At the Banff Centre For the Arts in Alberta, Canada, under the auspices of the Art and Virtual Environments Project, the last virtual chamber created for "Dancing With The Virtual Dervish: Worlds in Progress" affords viewers the world's first immersive experience of phenomena involving a fourth spatial dimension.

February 3-4, 1995: The transTerraFirma project is launched. Two Silicon Graphics Onyx/RealityEngine2 graphics supercomputers, one at the University of Texas at Austin and the other at the Electronic Cafe in Santa Monica, connected to one another via ethernet, give audiences the opportunity to navigate through and interact within shared virtual architecture. Even though the two sites can communicate via live audio and video ISDN connections, people prefer interacting in the virtual worlds to simply seeing and speaking to one another directly.

April 3, 1995: "Webspace," a three-dimensional browser for the World-Wide Web (WWW), is announced by Silicon Graphics and Template Graphics Software. Built around the VRML (Virtual Reality Modeling Language) and OpenInventor graphics formats, designed to work on all the major computer platforms, and integrated into the functioning of Netscape, the most widely used WWW browser, Webspace creates the first widespread opportunity for the transmission and exchange of virtual environments.

May 20-28, 1995: At the Tidsvag Noll v2.0 (Timewave Zero) art and technology exhibition in Gotheborg, Sweden, the transTerraFirma project continues. A series of worlds are constructed that can be transmitted over the web and visited by anyone with internet access and a VRML browser. Address: <http:// www.ar.utexas.edu/centrifuge/ttf.html>.

July 1995: RealityLab, the Laboratory for Immersive Virtual Environments, is established within the School of Architecture at the University of Texas at Austin. It is the first facility devoted to the study of virtual space as autonomous architectural space.

Zero: Transmitting Architecture

The history of invention alternates between advances of transport and advances of communication, that is to say from transmitting the subject to transmitting the sign and presence of the subject, establishing a symbiosis of vehicles and media that leads from antiquity all the way to the present. Mode after mode of expression or perception have yielded to being cast across greater and greater distances as agents of will and power. Signal, image, letter, sound, moving image, live sound, live image, sense and action, intersense and interaction, presence, interpresence, telepresence, all express our awareness of other and elsewhere, and underscore our will to interact with the sum of what we know to exist simultaneously with us, relativity's complexities notwithstanding.

In this effort to extend our range and presence to nonlocal realities, architecture has been a bystander, at most housing the equipment that enable us to extend our presence. The technologies that would allow the distribution or transmission of space and place have been unimaginable, until now. Though we learn about much of the world from the media, especially cinema and television, what they provide is only a passive image of place, lacking the inherent freedom of action that characterizes reality, and imposing a single narrative thread upon what is normally an open field of spatial opportunity. However, now that the cinematic image has become habitable and interactive, that boundary has been crossed irrevocably. Not only have we created the conditions for virtual community within a nonlocal electronic public realm, but we are now able to exercise the most radical gesture: distributing space and place, transmitting architecture.

The transmission of architecture and public space alters all the familiar issues of architecture and urbanism. All at once, theory, practice, and education are confronted with questions that have no precedent of consideration within the discipline, necessitating that we turn elsewhere for guidance. Learning from software supersedes learning from Las Vegas, the Bauhaus, or Vitruvius: the discipline of replacing all constants with variables, necessary for good software engineering, leads directly to the idea of liquid architecture. Liquid architecture, in turn, leads to the re-problematization of time as an active element of architecture at the scale of the cognitive and musical, not just the historic, political, or economic event. The language and metaphors of networked, distributed computing apply even greater torque to the straining conventional definitions of architecture: not only is real time now an active concern of the architect, but the logistics of sustainable, transmissible illusion become as real as the most physical material constraints. Form follows fiction, but an economy of bits replaces the economy of sticks and stones.

§ **connector: conditions: time, space, sampling, transmission**

To be effective within these new conditions, the poetic, philosophic, and techological strategies we employ to generate architecture must reflect our current understanding of physics and cosmology, must utilize our most current concepts and methods of knowing the world, and confront fully the implications, constraints, and opportunities that arise from conceiving of a transmissible architecture.

1/4: Implicit Time

Gilles Deleuze has commented that in early cinema the treatment of time was bodily-kinaesthetic, embodying what he calls the "movement-image," while what characterizes cinema now is the "time-image." The "movement-image" uses time as it is readily perceived in expected sensory-motor action or plot. It is linear time, proper sequence, straightforward causality. The "time-image," on the other hand, relies on mechanisms of association, memory, imagination, illusion, hallucination. An object out of place, out of time, or out of plot, rationally incongruous, colors a scene with its probable histories or possible futures. Building on Bergson, Deleuze sees in each object, in each frame of a film, a rhizome in time, allowing haecceities to communicate "motion without action."

An object is thus enveloped by an aura of its own trajectory through time that is immensely different from the sequence of images that would describe its motion through space. The "movement-image" records positions in space while the "time-image" records states in time. The cinema of the time-image adds to this the combination of disparate objects, each with its own, implied aura, and constructs a language of nuances in place of the language of actions. Actions themselves can be lifted from the simplicity of the movement-image and placed within the time-image.

Time permeates every architectural gesture, but in most cases, architecture's concern with time is passive. Even where the idea of the time-image is employed in the evocative arrangement of elements intended to speak through implication, the elements and the arrangement are static, responding only to the slow accumulation of patina and accident. Until now, architecture, even when speaking in the language of the time-image, has spoken in an inanimate way, using inanimate elements. The possibility of an animate, or at least animated, architecture, containing varying arrangements of animate or animated elements, has yet to be explored. What examples do exist are either vehicular, aircraft carriers and skyhooks, nomadic, like the ornate tents of Bedouin princes, or greatly extended in time or space: so far, the life of architecture has only manifested itself across continents and centuries.

Once we cast architecture into cyberspace, these concerns take on both theoretical and practical urgency. The architect must now take into active interest not only the motion of the user through the environment, but also account for the fact that the environment itself, unencumbered by gravity and other common constraints, may itself change position, attitude, or attribute. This new choreographic consideration is already a profound extension of responsibilities and opportunities, but it still corresponds only to "movement-image." Far more interesting and difficult is the next step, in which the environment is understood not only to move, but also to breathe and transform, to be cast into the wind not like a stone but like a bird. What this requires is the design of mechanisms and algorithms of animation and interactivity for every act of architecture. Mathematically, this means that time must now be added to the long list of parameters of which architecture is a function.

2/4: Implicit Space

When space existed as a separate category, architecture was the art of space; when time existed as a separate category, music was the art of time. The realization of the deep relation between space and time as spacetime, and the corresponding parallel relation between mass and energy, challenges the idea that architecture and music are separate, and prompts us to conceive of a new art of spacetime: archiMusic. But while we can surely imagine such an artform, we have had no way to actually construct and inhabit the spatiotemporal edifices of that imagination. While our science examines microscopic and macroscopic regions of curved, higher dimensional spacetime, we build within the confines of the small lots of what our limited sensorium can comprehend directly. Even though we depend on devices that rely on phenomena at these other scales, our architecture does nothing to help us form an intuition of the larger world we know through our theories and instruments.

Until relatively recent times, architecture kept pace with knowledge. By the middle of the 18th century, however, the historical congruence between ways of knowing the world and ways of conceiving and executing architecture was disrupted by repeated, and eventually successful, challenges to Euclidean geometry. Up to that point architecture could still embrace western spatial conceptions: even the heavens were Euclidean, it seemed. The efforts of Lobachevsky and Riemann, the descriptions of electromagnetic fields by Maxwell, and the world view that was slowly assembled via relativity, quantum mechanics, and that led to today's theories of hyperspace and stochastic universes, created a condition that architecture, burdened by its materiality, could no longer follow. While a handful of exceptional architects grappled with the new problems, for the most part, the modernism that was widely embraced was the most conservative available. Architecture, for the most part, ceased to embody the leading edge of our world-view, and turned to narrower and narrower problems, until it became indistinguishable from mere utilitarian building.

The spatial imagination of mathematicians and physicists has been far bolder than that of architects. Gauss's curvature, Lobachevksy's hyperbolic or "imaginary geometry," Riemann's elliptic geometry, the ladder from scalar to vector to tensor to spinor to twistor, are yet undigested conceptions of space that must be considered by a new algorithmic and computational critical discourse and poetics. While the scale at which these conceptions apply is outside the range of everyday experience as we knew it, that range has itself changed. As Virilio has noted, our horizon has shifted from the edge of what is visible to our naked eyes to that which is visible electronically at the speed of light, that is to say, at the scales of non-Euclidean geometries. Actually, everything we see, we see at the speed of light: what we have overcome are atmospheric and perspectival noise, the constraint of seeing in a straight line, and constraint of seeing from just one point or in just one direction. Optico-digital orthographics: lossless clarity, curved omniscience, panoptical omnipresence.

The architecture of cyberspace offers the opportunity to mend the rupture between how we know the world and how we conceive and execute architecture. It allows a far greater latitude of experimentation than any previous architectonic opportunity. It is once again possible to seek to know what is known and to conceive a corresponding architecture, without always falling back upon the sacred geometries of ages past. This engagement only makes architecture more relevant to the world, more in keeping with what is sensed as a new condition. In fact, architecture's role in articulating spatially the outlook of an age is strongly reasserted.

3/4: Sampling

We cannot know the real in its entirety. As much shields as bridges, our senses isolate us from the outside world, even as the cognitive mechanisms that translate raw input into meaningful pattern isolate us from within. In either case, what we do know is known through sampling: continuous reality, if indeed it is continuous, is segmented and reconstituted to fit our understanding.

Sampling implies the existence of a field to be sampled, a sampling rate or frequency, and a sampling resolution or sensitivity. From subatomic particles to scanning tunneling microscopes to compact disks to video, film, meteorological and cosmological information, what we know empirically we know through this very particular form of observation. What we know synthetically or by simulation does not escape this either: whether we gather or produce data, we do so at increments and intervals that reduce the infinite, or merely vast, to the manageable. Our own senses operate by sampling: the finite grids of rods and cones that form our retinas feed a finite number of nerve endings at finite intervals: whatever continuity we perceive in the world is an illusion we construct.

Understanding the world as field is very different from understanding the world as dialectic of solid and void. The world of objects and emptinesses is enumerable, a world of local binary decisions: is/is-not. In a world of fields, the distinction between what is and what is not is one of degree. There can be as many sampling points where something is not as there are where something is. Sampling involves an intermediate sense of reality, something between real and integer numbers, a fractal notion of qualified truth, truth-to-a-point. An object's boundary is simply the reconstructed contour of an arbitrarily chosen value. Having captured a three dimensional array of pressure points around a tornado, we can reconstruct the pressure contour of the center of the storm just as surely as we can the leading edge. At one density setting the data from a magnetic resonance scan give the shape of one's skull, at another the shape of one's brain, paradoxically replacing the discontinuity of sampling with a new continuity across names and categories.

The data upon which these tools are applied can come from any of several sources: direct sensing of the environment, computation of functions that occupy space, fiction and fancy, it does not matter which. In McLuhan's sense, the advent of the tool already changes our reality by shifting the balance of all our practices and outlooks. In order to contend with the enormous amount of information provided by arrays of instruments directed at all aspects of the world, scientists have developed a panoply of tools for scientific visualization. The dominant metaphor behind the operation of these tools is that of the field or lattice. Volume visualization, isosurface construction, advection, and numerous other techniques exist that allow us to peer into a block of numbers and extract the shape of an answer to a question.

Architectural heuretics and poetics, even when employing the computer's boundary representations and solid modeling, still emphasize a Euclidean understanding of form and space, an ideology of presence and absence. Descriptively, analytically, synthetically, in every way, the rigidity of the canonical, orthographic descriptions of architecture fail to capture what is salient to space as we currently conceive it. Plan, section, elevation, perspective, axonometric, traces of pigment held by the tooth of vellum, ruler and compass, were perhaps appropriate to the cycles and epicycles of a Ptolemaic, Copernican, and Galilean universe, or even the ellipses of a Keplerian universe, but are completely impotent in arresting the trajectories of subatomic particles, or the shapes of the gravity waves of colliding black holes. Once this is observed, it can be readily seen that the plan is dead because its worldview is obsolete.

An alternative architectural poetics would look past the static depiction of objects and surfaces to the description of latent information fields. The air we move through is permeated by intersecting emanations of information from every object: electromagnetic flux, intensities of light, pressure, and body heat form complex dancing geometries around us at every instant. We already inhabit an invisible world of shapes, an architecture of latent information that is modulated by our every breath and transmission. The shapes are definite, and with the right tools of sampling and visualization, can be seen, captured, and, if so desired, manufactured. It is imperative that architects embrace these tools critically and creatively, and set aside the tools that Alberti used as beautiful, but finally nostalgic, vestiges of another era.

4/4: Transmission

The unprecedented potential to cast space into the electronic net surrounding the planet is not without restrictions of its own. The astonishing capacity of optical fiber to carry information is just being grasped. In the interim, between astonishment and proficiency, we must contend with the present limits of bandwidth. While everything is growing exponentially, it seems that the speed of computers and the number of users of the internet are expanding at a more rapid rate than the availability of the raw carrying capacity required to create shared virtual environments. We will soon have very many people with very fast computers vying for limited bandwidth. It is unlikely, and, in any case, against the fundamental insights of distributed computing, to have a central computer manufacture one reality for many participants. The paradigm that is emerging is quite the opposite: each participant receives a compressed, concise description of the world and information about the state and actions of all the other participants. Each participant's local machine then synthesizes a version of the shared reality that is similar to, but not necessarily identical with, all the others, depending on local factors and preferences. In a Leibnizian way, each location functions as a monad. Each location is independent of the others, and yet, by the fact of their relative agreement, a larger reality is constructed.

Obviously, what is required here is a transmissible form of reality in condensed form rather than in fixed description. Simple compression does not suffice, since it imposes the same limit on resolution for all participants, regardless of their communicational and computational resources. In the long run, what must be transmitted is not the object itself but its cypher, the genetic code for the regeneration of the object at each new site, according to each site's available resources.

Cyberspace as a whole, and networked virtual environments in particular, allow us to not only theorize about potential architectures informed by the best of current thought, but to actually construct such spaces for human inhabitation in a completely new kind of public realm. This does not imply a lack of constraint, but rather a substitution of one kind rigor for another. When bricks become pixels, the tectonics of architecture become informational. City planning becomes data structure design, construction costs become computational costs, accessibility becomes transmissibility, proximity is measured in numbers of required links and available bandwidth. Everything changes, but architecture remains.

Genetic Poetics

Slowly, from the considerations above, we can articulate some expectations about what a cyberspace architecture might involve. It would be an architecture designed as much in time as in space, changing interactively as a function of duration, use, and external influence; it would be described in a compact, coded notation, allowing efficient transmission; it would be amenable to different renditions under different fundamental geometries; and it would be designed with the most advanced concepts, tools, and processes available. Emphatically nonlinear and nonlocal, its preferred modes of narration would inherently involve distributedness, multiplicity, emergence, and open-endedness.

Just as chaos and complexity have switched polarities from negative to positive value, so too are all the expressions of disjunction and discontinuity being revisited as forms of a higher order. Unlike the disjunction of collage that has characterized much of this century, the new disjunction is one of morphing. Where collage merely superposes materials from different contexts, morphing operates through them, blending them. True to the technologies of their respective times, collage is mechanical whereas morphing is alchemical. Sphinx and werewolf, gargoyle and griffin are the mascots of this time. The character of morphing is genetic, not surgical, more like genetic cross-breeding than transplanting. Where collage emphasized differences by recontextualizing the familiar, the morphing operation blends the unfamiliar in ways that illuminate unsuspected similarities and becomings.

Narrative structures are similarly affected. Cinematically, the cut yields to the crossfade and the crossfade yields to the morphed blend, until what would be consequent scenes merge into a modulated, varying composite of simultaneous existences. The elements of meaning become atmospheric and temperamental, and narrative sequence proceeds from ellipsis to ellipsis, in a stochastic perpetual motion machine.

Though the question of architectonic merit admits no facile answer, it must still be asked. Just as simple engines exchange displacement for force, so too do the tools of cyberspace exchange computational cycles for the production of usable information. It is fair to inquire not only how much power an engine can produce, but to what purpose that power is directed. Of all the cpu-cycles expended in the design and construction of a work of architecture, how many are applied to improving its architectonic quality? Are they applied toward goals that increase architectonic merit, or are they applied to peripheral issues, such as the more rapid production of mediocrity?

One of the fundamental scientific insights of this century has been the realization that simulation can function as a kind of reverse empiricism, the empiricism of the possible. Learning from the disciplines that attend to emergence and morphogenesis, architects must create generative models for possible architectures. Architects aspiring to place their constructs within the nonspace of cyberspace will have to learn to think in terms of genetic engines of artificial life. Some of the products of these engines will only be tenable in cyberspace, but many others may prove to be valid contributions to the physical world.

One: transTerraFirma: Tidsvag Noll v2.0

transTerraFirma is the ongoing effort to assert the vitality of architecture after territory. It is also an investigation of the means necessary for architectural conception and production in cyberspace. For the Tidsvag Noll exhibition in Sweden, this exploration has taken the form of a series of city-worlds constructed for the pre-release version of the Webspace three-dimensional web browser. These worlds are now available on the net. In various guises, these "worlds in progress" each explore a different facet of virtuality.

Words are portals. Woven through the worlds are several webs of non-linear narrative. Words suspended in space, at different scales and orientations, act as portals to other worlds. One set of words consists of the names of present or historical cities that have been the sites of disaster and destruction: Kobe, Kikwit, Oklahoma City, Waco, Beirut, Sarajevo, Mostar, Johannesburg, Soweto, Carthage... Another set consists of reminders of what humanity would rather escape: plague, pain, torture, virus, carnage, friction...

A third uses only sentence fragments, preceded and followed by ellipses, such as:

... this body ...   ... the necessity of voids ...   ...after
territory...   ...you inhabit her fearscapes...   ...fragments of stories...
...he asked about you...   ...homeworld...   ...laughter,
pain...   ...upgrade my love....   ...a matrix of questions...
...broken glass...   ...no room...   ...the necessity of voids...
...you occupy my visions...   ...collapsing...   ...centrifuge...
...komMERZ...   ...spectacle...

This third system always leads to a distribution node, a world unlike the rest. The distributor world is a fully spatialized poem consisting almost entirely of text, arrayed in three dimensional space. Every sentence fragment in this space is a link back into the city-worlds. By creating a field of text fragments that the visitor can navigate through, a new form of poem is invented: a spatial poem, characterized by shifting relationships between the foreground and background words, between the words that catch the light and the ones that disappear in dark fog. As the visitor travels through this poem an infinite number of poems shift smoothly past one another, each phrase an entry to another world. The slow rotation of the text destabilizes the viewer, creating the necessity to either move to keep the words in any particular configuration, or yield to the change and reread the kaleidoscopic wordplay.

Locked within the deepest recesses of each city-world are nodes of "friction," places where the visitor is confronted with screens displaying images that have been gathered on the net, but that recollect reality outside cyberspace. These images are often related to the names of the cities, but in ways that are not directly apparent. Rather, the construction of meaning remains the responsibility of the visitor, who must integrate the overall sense of place of each world with the sequences of names of places, keywords, and sentence fragments encountered.

The design of the shapes one encounters in these worlds is based on an analogy to sound synthesis, extended to include three dimensional form. Timbre, the character of a sound, is not given by the fundamental frequency of a sound, but by the structure, proportion, and onset pattern of the overtones, or multiples, of that frequency. If we visualize the fundamental frequency as a wave, the character of the sound is given by the perturbations caused by the addition or subtraction of subordinate waves of higher frequency but lesser amplitude. Even though we know that sound propagates spherically, we normally think of it as an undulating line, representing air pressure, moving forward in time. We can just as well represent it as an undulating surface, like the surface of a liquid, or as a solid block of pressure or density values. Let use assume that a simple shape, a cube or a sphere, perhaps, corresponds to a simple sine wave. We know that by adding perturbations to the sine wave, we can produce a richer sound: the same is true for our simple shape. The idea of a fundamental function with perturbations carries well into other dimensions. Assuming that the fundamental figure of architecture is the domain, represented in two dimensions by a boundary contour of an arbitrarily chosen value, and in three by a boundary isosurface, we can search for functions that produce simple figures, and that can readily be modulated by successive perturbations at higher frequencies. Applying the perturbations conditionally ensures a high degree of control. Such a conception of architectural space has the advantage of being extremely compact: a single mathematical expression can be expanded to become a fully formed chamber, at whatever resolution the available resources permit. Adding a temporal dimension is as direct as adding another parameter to the expression, and the expression itself articulates the genetic structure of the chamber, making evident the loci of intervention for the generative or genetic algorithm that determines the growth of the architectural artifact over many generations. And, of course, it is eminently transmissible. While most current three dimensional browsers do not yet support the transmission of executable applications, applets, along with data, exceptions do exist, and that functionality will soon be standard. It will not be long before form follows the functions of fiction.

One Zero: The Transphysical City

Discussions of the relationship of the actual to the virtual tend to polarize even more rapidly than discussions of morality, politics, or gender. Remnant of our predator/prey days, an exclusionary either/or mentality makes more detailed considerations difficult. In considering the urban implications of a transmissible architecture, we will have to set aside binary oppositions and establish continua between extremes that may well wrap around to meet at their most distant ends.

The transphysical city will be suffused with intelligence. Sensors and effectors will be ubiquitous and will be linked everywhere with information utilities as common as running water. How can we begin to envision such a city?

The problem of the design of "intelligent environments" can be instructive. Each term, and their relationships, can be replaced by "tuples." "Intelligence" can be replaced by Howard Gardner's seven types of intelligence: <visual, verbal, mathematical, bodily, musical, interpersonal, intrapersonal>. "Environments" can be seen to be of at least three types: <actual, virtual, and hybrid>. The loci of application of intelligence to environments can also be listed: <in, on, of, by...>. If we map these tuples onto a coordinate system, we create a space of possibility for what intelligent environments might mean, what projects might be undertaken and what directions explored. What is the bodily intelligence of a virtual environment? How is intrapersonal intelligence exhibited by a hybrid environment? How can technologically augmented intrapersonal "intelligence" enhance an actual environment? Once we have understood some of the features of this space, we can add dimensions. What is the range of urbanism?

There is no question that urbanism as we know it will be altered, that our cities will become our interfaces to the net, that we will really be able to "reach out and touch someone" across the planet and as far as our transmissions will allow. As important as the understanding of those changes will be, we must not forget to see the larger change: a new, nonlocal urbanism is in the making. This new urbanism, transurbanism, freed from a fixed geometry, will have to draw upon set theory and the physics of a quantum universe. As distant as this may appear from the city as we know it, the transphysical city will not be the postphysical city. As the prefix *trans-* implies, it will be at once a transmutation and a transgression of the known, but it will also stand alongside and be interwoven into that very matrix.

Futurismo & Futurismi

In the decade that has passed since the Futurismo & Futurismi exhibition in the Pallazo Grassi in Venice, the relevance of Futurism to our experience with technology has become increasingly clear. It is plainly evident that the conditions we have created will bring about far deeper changes than the ones that fueled early modernism. Still, the parallels are strong, and it is worth considering them briefly.

Of the various ways in which the futurists saw simultaneity and dynamism, Umberto Boccioni's was perhaps the most prescient and applicable to the conditions we are facing. Critical of Balla's literal depiction of forms in motion, Boccioni sought to capture a sense of time that was implicit in being. Like Bergson's notion of "duration" as the principle animating the passage through time rather than the particular form at a given instant, Boccioni's work observed the lifelessness of a form arrested from motion in a single instant, and created forms that were condensed records of their own becoming, past and future both being contained in the vector of the present. It is perhaps not too surprising that Boccioni's sense of time and Deleuze's time-image would both draw upon, and thus be connected by, Bergson. What is surprising is that Deleuze and Boccioni, especially the latter's *Unique Form of Continuity in Space* of 1913 and related works both anticipate and can be expressed by the tools and concepts of scientific visualization, especially isosurfaces.

Our surprise is only the result of our forgetting; in his 1913 *Manifesto*, Marinetti is explicit: "…we should express the infinite smallness that surrounds us, the imperceptible, the invisible, the agitation of atoms, the Brownian movements, all the exciting hypotheses and all the domains explored by the high-powered microscope. To explain: I want to introduce the infinite molecular life into poetry not as a scientific document but as an intuitive element. It should mix, in the work of art, with the infinitely great spectacles and dramas, because this fusion constitutes the integral synthesis of life."

"Here and there, sick lamplight through window glass taught us to distrust the deceitful mathematics of our perishing eye." The wings and propellers of the Futurists were severed by the rise of Fascism. Marinetti's words cut both ways.

Works Cited

Bergson, H. *Creative Evolution*. New York: H. Holt and Company, 1911.

Bergson, H. *Matter and memory*. New York: Zone Books, 1988.

Deleuze, G. *Cinema1. The Movement Image*. Minneapolis: The University of Minnesota Press 1986.

Deleuze, G. *Cinema2: The Time Image*. Minneapolis: The University of Minnesota Press 1989.

Hallyn, F. *The Poetic Structure of the World: Copernicus and Kepler*. New York: Zone Books, 1993.

Hulten, P. (Ed.). *Futurismo & Futurismi*. New York: Abbeville Press, 1986.

Jammer, M. *Concepts of Space: The History and Theories of Space in Physics*, 3rd Enlarged Edition. New York, Dover Publications, Inc., 1993.

Kaku, M. *Hyperspace: A Scientific Odyssey Through Parallel Universes, Time Warps, and the 10th Dimension*. New York: Oxford University Press, 1994.

Kauffman, S.A. *The Origins of Order: Self-Organization and Selection In Evolution*. New York: Oxford University Press, 1993.

Perloff, M. *The Futurist Moment: Avant-Garde, Avant Guerre, and the Language of Rupture*. Chicago: The University of Chicago Press, 1986.

Wolff, R.S. and Yaeger, L. *Visualization of Natural Phenomena*. New York: Springer-Verlag, 1993.

Media Archaeology

Siegfried Zielinski

We're travelling from the 'Body in Ruins' symposium at V2, a Dutch
artist-run collective, to a midnight debate about net politics with
European surplus class theorists in a warehouse squat on the industrial
outskirts of Frankfurt. Our travelling companion from Amsterdam to
Cologne is Siegfried Zielinski. We meet in an old railroad car that looks
like it hasn't been refurbished since the 1930s: lace curtains, red velvet
seats, mahogany trim. A perfect site for the delirious tale that Zielinski
invokes of Europe's media past: a strange but haunting vector of secret
texts, books within books, ancient curses, digital dreams, and medieval
cyber-art. A real "prolegomena to an-other history of technological
visioning." Zielinski's essay, "Media Archeology," is an eloquent plea for
the recovery of artistic subjectivity as a way of tempering the sometimes
operational sterility of today's multi-media fest.

Arthur and Marilouse Kroker

1. This year, Cologne's Academy of Media Arts hosted an event in which
artists, musicians, filmmakers, philosophers, engineers, psychoanalysts, and writers
came together for five days and nights to talk about and around Antonin Artaud. It
was not our intention to hold obsequies for a dead poet nor to celebrate a legend.
Involved as we are, day in day out, both practically and theoretically with digital
artefacts and systems, a few months ago we decided to take this disturbing and
troublesome phenomenon Artaud and keep him in the Academy for a period of
time as an imaginary fixed point around and on which to debate the following
question: Is (artistic) subjectivity an antiquated notion at the end of the 20th
century and something we must bid farewell to, or is it something that just requires
new conceptions? Naturally we failed in our endeavour, that was inevitable. We did
not answer the question. But we did get a little closer — just a few beats of a
butterfly's wing — to renouncing some of the dualisms that have become both dear
and familiar to us, like:

- Calculation and Expenditure
- Simulation and Excess
- Moderation and Extravagance
- Universalization and Heterogeneity
- Code and Sensation

I argued vehemently against declaring artistic subjectivity dead because I have the impression that were we to do so, we would encircle this empty space left by theory and philosophy in an even more hectic and panicked fashion, with even more words and images and I also think that we from the field of social praxis represented by media art must finally start to confront the production of mediocrity and nice design, particularly and because we are responsible for teaching and training young artists.

Yet in which direction are we to formulate this concept of artistic subjectivity (in the indissoluble linkage of an aesthetic and an ethical orientation), *vis-a-vis* the gigantic cleansing and reducing machinery of digitization? And beyond the dualisms and antagonisms mentioned before?

There is a gang[1] of artists, theoreticians, and artist-theoreticians who have a very strong affinity (moreover, one that links them to a figure such as Artaud): they burn and burn up in the endeavour to push out as far as possible the limits of what language and machines, as the primary instances of structure and order for the last few centuries, are able to express and in doing so to actually reveal these limits. Without doubt it is the most difficult path to tread in and with the apparatus. Otto Rossler, as physicist and applied chaos theoretician, belongs in my opinion to this gang, with his attempt to bring together participants and observers in a physics of heterology that also recognizes ethical responsibility; Peter Weibel is another, for no one has been more resolute in challenging techno-aesthetics, from its potential strength to its signs of fatigue; or there is Oswald Wiener, whose poetic texts on the phenomenology of artificial intelligence have helped me enormously to understand that the sensational richness of all that is non-machine processable is the greater the more intensively and uncompromisingly the machine world is thought of as world machine.

Something is articulated in strategies and ways of life such as these that, for me, achieves its clearest expression in the *Tractatus Logico-Philosophicus* by Ludwig Wittgenstein, that reckless tightrope walker between uncompromisingly precise thinking and life, who adhered to the premise that philosophy is not something to be sat out on a professorial chair, but should be a continuous action of clarification in its very own medium, language. "Philosophy is not a doctrine it is an activity/ Tatigkeit... The results of philosophy are not 'philosophical sentences' but the clarification of sentences. Philosophy should make thought that is otherwise cloudy and indistinct, clear, and should sharply differentiate it." (4.112, p. 41)[2]

The notion of the subject that informs these deliberations has the power to break free of the shackles of ontological ascriptions. Interface/the boundary, expressed through main sentences of Wittgenstein's *Tractatus*:

"The world and life are one." (5.621, 90)

"The thinking, imagining subject does not exist." (5.631, 90)

"The subject does not belong to the world, it is a border of the world." (5.632, 90)

"That the world is mine, this is shown in that the limits of language stand for the limits of my world."

Ethically justifiable aesthetic activity in the net of the technical and the imaginary should, according to this, clarify the fragments of expression contained in it and their relationships to each another. I would term this activity subjective if it were to succeed in rendering the difference to life/the world to be experienced by formulating the boundaries of the net. In principle this is only possible if we exhaust its possibilities. "...to go in every direction to the end of the possibilities of the world"[3] — this thought comes from the theoretical work by Georges Bataille on the aesthetic avant-garde and it is still well worth putting it into practice.

This is not a new idea and it did not first occur to someone in the 20th century. It appears to me to be a basic idea for understanding what we might call the avant-garde of technical visioning in history — in awareness of the controversy surrounding this term.

I shall now launch a few probes into the strata of stories that we can conceive of as the history of the media in order to pick up signals from the butterfly effect, in a few localities at least, regarding both: the hardware and the software of the audio-visual. I name this approach media archaeology, which in a pragmatic perspective means to dig out secret paths in history, which might help us to find our way into the future. Media archaeology is my form of activity/Tatigkeit.

2. One of the most exceptional stories in Western Judeo-Christian culture that imagines an intensive temporal process is the dream of Jacob's ladder: the risky and hazardous ascent to the light, the ineffable, as a regular, metrical pattern of progress up the rungs of a ladder or solid steps. In some sense or degree it is the reverse side of Freud's staircase dream, which in the interpretation of the psychoanalyst, stands for the strenuous, rhythmic ascent of coitus and its release, ejaculation. There are countless visual representations of Jacob's dream, illustrations, paintings, icons. Some portray the ascent as a wondrous, gentle movement upwards in the company of pretty angels (in this century the musical film still continues to evoke this), some as a horror scenario of the death struggle, that takes place between the hell on earth and the proffered hand of God Almighty. In these media treatments of the theme, the work that is most often adapted is the 7th century heavenly ladder of Johannes Klimakos, abbott of the monastery of St. Catherine on Mount Sinai. Vertigo: simple, diagonal ladders, spirals of winding rungs and stair formations, double ladders and double helixes, mainly occupied by monks of whom the odd one or other plummets vertically downwards into misery, does not make it to the top because he cannot completely resist the temptations of hell.

From a perspective of the time image, a highlight among these adaptations is a Greek manuscript dating from ca. 1345.[4] The exposition of this particular episode starts with a long shot that gives an overview, followed by a reminiscence of the author, Johannes Klimakos, with the intersecting vertical and horizontal lines above his head. Then we see the scene, the monastery in which the Book of Books was written, first from above, then a zoom to a picture of the abbott at work. Now the real plot begins, portrayed in iconographic miniatures: the ascent, step by step. The movement of ascending is expressed visually, image for image, only by takes of the ladder, one rung at a time. External movement is minimal and only becomes dynamic through the succession of images. Between these, other dramatic scenes are interposed that are supposed to characterize the momentary whereabouts of the adept, as, for example, at the beginning of the dream scene, encounters with angels, with virtues or with vices. In this manner, 30 steps are mounted. On the top step, where a monk is depicted kneeling humbly before Christ, the ladder has disappeared completely. The story ends with two grandiose credits: Johannes Klimakos and his homily Johannes von Raithn; the final frame shows the star once again in a close medium shot.

3. One of the most fascinating figures of pre-modernity, working between the disciplines and different worlds of knowledge, was the Neapolitan, Giovanni Battista Della Porta (ca. 1538-1615): author, man of letters, member of secret societies, multiplicator, aider and abettor of knowledge, organizer — much more than a (natural) scientist, according to our contemporary conceptions. In Volume 28 of Zedler's Lexikon, 1741, the entry for Della Porta reads: "He did much to help establish the Academie Degli Otiosi, and he held another at his house, which was called the Academie de Secreti, to which only members were admitted who had discovered something new about the natural world. But the papal court prohibited the meetings of the latter because its members allegedly engaged in forbidden arts and studies...." Della Porta's most famous work, the 20-part encyclopaedia *Magia Naturalis*, of which both he and his chroniclers claim that he wrote the first version "in the fifteenth year of his life"[5], is a biological, physical, chemical, medical, and philosophical treatise and, equally, an entertaining "Book of Art and Wonders" (as the sub-title of the German edition classifies it), a kind of early form of the popular scientific encyclopaedia, a phantastic boundary crossing printed network of knowledge. "Wisdom and perfect knowledge of natural things" (Porta 1719, 2) — this is how Della Porta characterises his understanding of magic and in these 20 books he undertakes a colossal and daring journey through all areas of life; from zoological observations and the (alchemistic) transmutation of metals and the synthetic production of precious stones to the investigation and composition of special combinations of herbs and rituals for inducing abortions and performing quasi-genetic engineering (the manipulation of the sex of unborn children),[6] from treatises on artificial fire, cooking, and secret ciphers to the XVII Book of "divers mirrors and lenses" (cited by many film archaeologists but read by very few) which contains Della Porta's studies on projection, reflection, and a multitude of optical *mises-en-scene*. All the volumes share the same view of the world in the direct sense of the expression: natural phenomena offer themselves to the scholar not only for the investigation of immutable objects, for reproduction or for mimesis; they become material that can be altered/manipulated. By means of the magical power of the imagination and experimentation with that which is real, it should be possible to change, transmute and also go beyond them, whereby the body — corporeality — is, as subject, very clearly the centre.[7]

Let us try to make Della Porta's — for his time — seditious relationship to the world clearer, taking his optical studies and blueprints of optical artefacts as an example. His starting point for the interpretation of mirrors and lenses is precisely the traditional and firmly established taboo, that these artefacts allegedly only convey "false images" of the objects observed (reductions, magnifications, distortions...) and therefore, in accordance with the sanctity of Divine Nature, may only be used to correct defects of vision (that is, for spectacles and the like). This function of the artefacts as prostheses did not interest Della Porta much at all. It was precisely the dilations, deformations, double vision, splitting, changes of dimension, and transmutation of the real that fuelled his searching and driving attention, the contrast to that which is normally visible, the visualization of the imagination.

"How, when looking at a mirror, a pale yellow or many-coloured form can appear... that it seems as if the face is split down the middle... that it seems as if one has the face of a donkey or a dog or a pig..." (943) — Della Porta begins his XVII Book of the "Magia Naturalis" with these thoughts about simple arrangements of mirrors. In the fourth paragraph of Chapter II we encounter the first astounding phenomenon: "It is also possible, using flat mirrors, to see things that are happening in far-off places..." (947) and he goes on to describe exactly an arrangement of mirrors that, much later, Sigmund Freud installed in his study in order to secretly observe the other people in his house. There follow detailed descriptions of the various kinds and uses of hollow mirrors that we shall meet with again a century later, heavily embellished, in the writings of Athanasius Kircher, and then Della Porta arouses the media archaelologist's feverish interest for the first time in Chapter VI with his "Gesicht=Kunst" (Face=Art), where he demonstrates the germ cell apparatus of the cinema: the Camera Obscura — he calls it *obscurum cubiculum* in the latin original of 1607. He desires to show us "how hunting scenes and battles and other kinds of hocus pocus can be made and performed in a room... Guest performances, battle fields, games, or what you will, so clear, distinct, and pretty to see as though it were taking place before your very eyes," and he explains, "For the image is let into the eye through the eyeball just as here through the window" (Bill Gates' metaphors have a very long tradition); and in describing these optical illusions he gives his imagination free rein in the construction of living scenarios and *mises-en-scene*: "Namely, opposite to the room where you desire to see this, there must be a large, level space that the sun can shine down upon, where can be placed all manner of trees, forests, rivers, or mountains as well as animals, and these can be real or artificial, of wood or other material... There can be stags, wild boars, rhinoceroses, elephants, lions and other animals, whatever one wants to be seen; they can slowly creep out of their corners into the space, and then the hunter can appear and stage a hunt..."[8] (962). Then, in Chapter VIII, even the author has to hold his breath — "in truth, the pen fell out of my hand" — in the face of the monstrous things he wishes to divulge to us: "How an image can be made to appear in the air without either the mirrors or the form of the thing itself being seen."

By means of a complicated arrangement of mirrors, Della Porta anticipates the effect that is today organised by holographic images. Then, in the treatises on lenses, we are confronted with his strange conception of tele-vision: "From a perspective [this term is destined to survive even beyond the first laboratory phase of the technical history of television — SZ], in order that one may see farther than one imagines, he states and explains the point of "this useful thing," this

"Gesicht=Kunst," that in this way "well-read personages can recognize things at a distance of many miles and even stupid people can read the smallest letters of the alphabet from a distance." (971) Only a few decades later, at the turn of 16th century, the physics of the visible establishes itself with the astronomical studies of Christoph Scheiner ("*rosa ursina sive sol*"), Galileo Galilei ("*sidereus nuncius...*"), and Johannes Kepler's research on optics, the geometry of the retinal image, encouraging the instrumentalization of these artefacts in the service of representation, albeit enhanced representation, by means of the telescope, the microscope, and the reversed telescope as projector. In Francis Bacon's fantastic architecture of science, that in 1624 he located in New Atlantis, the serious "houses of optics" are already rigidly separated off from the somewhat dubious "house of sensory delusions, where we perform all manner of magic, sleight of hand tricks, hocus-pocus and illusion as well as their false conclusions." (Bacon 1982, 54). Physics and magic, observer and interpreter, they no longer live under the same roof. In Descartes' "Discours de la methode," and — particularly with regard to optics — in the companion text "La dioptrique" (Leyden 1637), the rational instrumentalization of modern times finds its exact formulation.

Notwithstanding, the magical energy of the designs and imaginings of Della Porta continued, in parallel, to exert their influence far into the 17th century. The most impressive examples are found in the voluminous works of the pupil and collaborator of Kircher, Caspar Schott (*Magia Optica* 1671) and in the studies on technically mediated vision by Athanasius himself, who so mysteriously haunts the pages of Umberto Eco's *Foucault's Pendulum*. Both editions of *Ars magna lucis et umbrae* of 1646 (Rome) and 1671 (Amsterdam) are heavily imbued with both world views: on the one hand, the geometricization of vision as a means of producing reversible image constructions, and on the other, pushing back the limits in order to create visions of that which is generally not-seeable, for example, quasi peep-show arrangements where a voyeur may observe how the visage of another person is transmuted to the head of an ass or a lion or the sun with the aid of a "Metaphor-Drum" ("Metapherntrommel," Gustav R. Hocke) — we have already encountered this illusion technique in Della Porta's "Hall of Mirrors;" light and shadow plays with fixed and mobile prisms, projection apparatus like the magic lanterns and again, even more arrangements of mirrors for the visualization of the Other, not yet or, rather, not yet so seen. Particularly in Kircher's iconographic presentations, which he designed but did not actually construct in most cases, the magic and the modern natural science view of the world run riot, side by side and interlocked; the overlapping of fictions and imagined facticity, is also characteristic of his combination studies (particularly of *Ars magna sciendi*, 1669) and his theoretical and fantastical works on music (*Musurgia universalis*, 2 volumes, 1650). In the same way that Kircher playfully operates with various systems of characters, especially the Hebrew, Greek and Roman alphabets, so too the concepts and signs of mathematical and geometrical constructions converge in Kircher's work with the symbols of the alchemists and astrologers; he links with ease mythology and science, Jesuit theology and philosophy, to form a multiple semantic network, that we today can only understand in its complexity with great difficulty. Here secret codes (a highly specialised quasi hacker language) alternate with that which appears (or perhaps only seems to appear) to be decodable, the highly probable with sheer improbability, solid architecture with fragile edifices of the imaginary and the will to change.

4. Last night we were invited to the phantastic hermetic film world created by Ladislaw Galeta. Prime symbol of the heavens, of the cosmos, of the journey that always ends at its starting point: the circle. We are familiar with the design of Henry Heyl's Phasmatrope, of Muybridges's zoopraxiscope, of Anschutzen's tachyloskop and its further development into the electronic *Schnellseher*, of Demeny's phonoskop or of Marey's photographic gun plates: in the tradition of the Lebensrad of the 1830s and 40s, before film became footage it was painted or mounted on round flat disks. Narratively, it represented a short closed circuit repeatable in quick succession in the same or a similar way, ad infinitum.

In the 1671 Amsterdam edition of his *Ars magna lucis et umbrae*, Athanasius Kircher includes an illustration of a strange device for recounting stories in circular form, the Smicroscopin. The container held the story of Christ's passion in eight dramatic tableaus or scenes (Kircher uses the word simulacrum — it was not in fact coined by him but belonged to the terminology of the pre-Socratic thinkers and their theories of vision). The appliance itself, hard- and software all in one, consisted of round, flat, boxes, the lids of which were connected with a pin so that the picture wheel between could be rotated. One of the lids was inset with an ocular and the other had a round hole in it of the same diameter as the eyepiece of the optical cylinder. The speed and rhythm of the narrative was at the discretion of the user. It would have been easy to change the software wheel. This artefact was portable and did not require a particular kind of energy to operate it.

Kaspar Schott, Kircher's long-standing collaborator, published his own treatise *Magia optica — das ist geheime doch naturmassige Gesicht-und Augen-Lehr* (that is the secret yet natural science of face and eyes) in the same year (1671) that the second edition of the *Great Art of Light and Shadow* appeared. In it, Schott does not merely parade his knowledge as the bright assistant of his more famous Jesuit colleague but surpasses the latter by far in the meticulous care and attention to detail with which he describes the various material systems for seeing that is transformed by the artificial. In Book Six, "Von der Spiegelkunst" (On the Art of Mirrors), Schott dismantles Kircher's Allegorie-Maschine and, using its components, experiments with a number of variations for producing images and for projection. The art of mirrors was at its peak in the 17th century. Before it became linear, the original idea of the material form of film as a round drum or a disk was stubbornly persistent, although it was not until many decades later that it made a reappearance in the shape of the videodisc and the compact disc. Initially the storage capacity was so limited that these were only suitable for very short films. In Henry V. Hopwood's book, *Living Pictures*, published in 1899, which lists and explains hundreds of different types of cameras and projectors for moving images, for example, two US American patents are recorded that complemented each other technically. One described a camera that could capture over 200 individual images in concentric circles on a gelatine plate about 8 inches in diameter. This machine, like the Lumieres' Cinematographe, was dual-purpose and could also be used as a projector. Similar, but mechanically more refined, was Nelson's spiral camera, which had a portable casing containing the plate upon which the recording occurred. Further, in the fathomless archive of the Deutsches Museum in Munich, there is an artefact that in 1898 did not make very much money for its London manufacturer whose name it bears: Kammatograph. The diameter of the wafer-thin gelatine plates on which the images were mounted is about twice that of a modern long-playing record. It is hardly surprising that with the concentric circular arrangement of the miniature images, this artefact calls to mind the early disks of mechanical electric television. Television and cinevision developed almost in parallel, techno-historically.

5. In Georges Bataille's economy of the universe, it is the most extravagant planet of all: the sun. It radiates energy incessantly without ever getting anything back from the recipients of this gift. It is expending all its energy. For over one and a half thousand years models and experiments have been done using the sun as the light source for projection, until first Arab scientists (around 1000 AD), and much later Europeans, such as the polymath and alchemist Roger Bacon, developed ideas for concrete apparatus in the form of an obscure chamber that could also operate with light sources generated by humans.

However, real interest was not directed to the pure light of the sun. The desire of the scientists focussed on the impure, the dark elements of this squandering planet, through which light in projection produces forms and structures. Christoph Scheiner, who was overshadowed by Kepler and above all by Galileo, was one of the co-founders of a physics of the visible. In order to observe sunspots,[9] he developed a heliotropic telescope, a simple device for protecting his eyes when looking directly at the sun but also for procuring upright and inverted pictures of sunspots. This projection machine was up to 22m in length and with its aid, Scheiner was able to project the surface structure of the planet that he was interested in onto a piece of white paper where he could fix it (icono-) graphically. A striking particularity in contrast to earlier concepts of the Camera Obscura or Camera Clausa where the observer's position was outside: equipped with lenses, Scheiner's chamber was a viewing room that contained the observer.

Maculas etiam caelo deducit ab alto — "They can even bring down the sunspots from the sky." In these emphatic tones the instruments that enable natural irregularities to become temporal images are celebrated in Johannes Zahn's famous book of 1685 on the artificial eye.

A companion piece: in the stylised and contrived images of the magic lantern, the spots that were made visible and analysed by scientific means take on the form of the incarnation of evil, of the weird and uncanny. The first subjects to be painted on transparent disks for projection using candlelight in order to throw big and ghostly images onto walls were really devilish ones, such as Lucifer and the allegorical depiction of the flames of purgatory (as in Kircher's first illustration of a Laterna Magica). Images of horror run through 500 years of media history up to and into the present day. One of the earliest, around 1420, had a particularly striking feature: the diabolical element was very definitely imagined as feminine. The projectionist, who held the lantern with a taper in his hand, wore oriental clothes (possibly a reference to the original inventors of the magic lantern). The drawing of the lantern was not exact; the apparatus is depicted around the image area and had to be black so that the she-devil could make her shadowy appearance on the wall.

6. Only since Paul Virilio's famous essay, "War and Film," has it become customarily postmodern to interpret advanced media technology in the context of an original military vanishing point; war as an archimedian point to which and from which the world of illusions is structured. Well-worn references from the history of technology are, for example, the revolving drum, the repeating rifle and particularly Janssen's photographic revolver and Marey's photographic gun, that he used to shoot successive pictures of birds in flight — amongst other things.

But film — insofar as its origins can be defined at all — is not a medium that destroys space or volume as may be concluded if it is assigned to the military complex. For me, film means first and foremost time that is structured and formed. For the specific history of the mechanical and electrical apparatus it makes sense to begin the search for prime artefacts from this perspective. The wheel clock, that was developed in this form in the mid 14th century, is a technical system whose functionality comprises the decisive elements for the process of shooting pictures with a camera: the combination of regular progress (continuity) and graduation (discontinuity).

The mechanical heart of the wheel clock is the cogwheel. Its earliest known applications are documented in the culture of ancient Egypt: Sakie was the camel-powered machine for drawing water from wells and its central component was a gigantic horizontal wooden wheel with deep notches. Machinery for survival and not for death. Later, the cogs of the first wooden, and later metal, wheels that engaged exactly were the guarantee of the precisely regulated running of many machines. This includes, of course, the cinematographs and kinetoscopes that were built in the early years by engineers from the clock and watch-makers' branch of light engineering industry. Stop & Go, the perpetual alternation of movement and standstill, was the binary code of 19th century industrial culture. In the cinema, it finally achieved status in the moving image. Yet its history is nearly as old as that of man outsmarting nature.

7. The deviant, the impure, and the image of an era. The project of film for cinema received an enormous boost of innovative energy from physiological and psychophysiological research. The century of the industrial revolution was madly keen to fathom out the functioning of bodies, to study the movement of their muscles and limbs (that were often enough imaginized as parts of a mechanism), to make their energies and surges visible. Medics, biologists, physiologists, registrars, and manic encyclopaedists from the most diverse backgrounds initially pounced on what was nearest because it was the most obvious. They studied deviant behaviour. For example, over the last three decades of the 19th century the Italian doctor of medicine and criminologist, Cesare Lombroso, developed an extensive factitious system by which means he attempted to explain mental, cultural, and social phenomena of heterogeneity through their supposed "inscriptions" on the body. He analysed handwriting and skull structure, preserved aborted fetuses, fabricated

correlations between social unrest and the menstrual cycles of the female militants, analysed drawings and songs by prison inmates and the writings of prisoners condemned to death. Each deviant behaviour and its expression had to be recorded. The Other, that seemed to be threatening the centre of bourgeois life, had at the very least to be pinned down in statistics and texts if it could not be really understood.

The period photography of Kohlrausch is paradigmatic: the walk of the neurotic man is captured twice, once as spatial progress and once as temporal progress. Corresponding with the successive movements, the chronometer is positioned above the man's head. In this respect, Etienne Jules Marey's set-up was even more precise and effective. For his studies of the movements of humans and animals, the pictures he took included a measuring tape that ran along the bottom, plus a running clock showing the corresponding position of the second hand. The physiologically orientated chronometric and movement photographers were not primarily concerned — like Muybridge — with the body as a superficial sensation. Their relationship to their objects in front of the camera was above all analytical. That was the reason why they literally had to get on their subjects' backs. Georges Demeny — the assistant and later rival of Marey — did some experiments in which he tried to capture the movements of the mouth articulating words. The aim was to produce a basis for teaching the deaf to speak. For this purpose the pictures had to be large. Much later, a montage of close shots of a similar kind, with semi-close ups and long shots, became a shock-horror experience for cinemagoers.

The artificial eye's focus on the functionality of the body already contains in essence the beginnings of the computed, synthetic image that at the end of the 20th century is increasingly being integrated into films. The line structures that result from the scanning of real objects by 3-D scanners and that constitute the basis for the generation of figures in movement by the computer, do not differ in principle from the studies of movements done by Marey with his test persons wearing black suits with white spots running down their extremities. There is also a striking correspondence with regard to the subjects: as yet, computer animation of living beings in film is mostly restricted to monsters, to the abstruse, to humans that are not homogeneous. But this is — just as it was a hundred years ago — just a matter of time; today of time that needs computation.

8. I probably owe you an explanation as to my intentions in constructing these wild juxtapositions of heterogenous phenomena from media history, and particularly with regard to the presence of the digital media and their start into the next century: I do not proceed on the assumption of a coherent praxis in artistic production and reception with and through the media in the expanding present, and likewise I try not to homogenize or universalize the historic development of the media. Thinking further along the lines traced by others, Georges Bataille for example, I attempt to think and write about the previous technical and aesthetic and theoretical richness of the development of artefacts of media articulation hetero-logically. In this concept both re-construction and the conception of possible future developments rub together. Against the enormously growing trend toward the universalization and standardization of aesthetic expression, particularly in the

expanding telematic nets, the only strategies and tactics that will be of help are those that will strengthen local forms of expession and differentiation of artistic action, that will create vigourously heterogenous energy fields with individual and specific intentions, operations, and access in going beyond the limits that we term mediatization.

To put it more pragmatically — I am pleading for a project of diverse praxis with advanced media machinery. I am counting on a creative side-by-side co-existence: not in the sense of grandiose arbitrariness but rather as a division of labour that is very necessary because we — as cinephiles, as videophiles, as computerphiles — do have different wishes and expectations of the obscure object of our desire.

Synthetic images that have their referents in the real bore me, whether they be mimetic biologies, virtual studios, actors, or effects. I hope that the most creative computer artists will move heaven and earth into worlds that I do not know as yet, that will expand and enrich the horizon of my fantasy. For example, Catherine Deneuve's expression in Bunuel's *Belle de Jour*, when she looks into the Chinese man's box, I cannot quite imagine this as a simulation. If I feel in the mood for audiovisual leisure or for reading sound-image-text constructions, I will put a disk into the CD-ROM drive WHEN it surpasses the complexity that a book and a videotape and an MC offers me. For fast communication or extending my knowl-edge of the world (including the world of media), I am very happy to use the Internet or the World Wide Web (if I've got the time). But if I want a story about love or life or death that goes beyond my own powers of imagination and brings me into contact with the Other, then I do not turn to the delirious community of Net users who all consider themselves artists, but rather, I spend my time with an exceptional story-teller, I actually seek a long term confrontation with a single picture, or with a musical composition that enriches my time-experience. And I notice that I need this all the more when the attractors of knowledge, planning, and organisation accelerate at a frenzied pitch.

Notes

1. The term is used here in the sense of Deleuze's/Guattari's *1000 Plateaus*, a loose and somehow anarchic group of people without bureaucratic institutional form.
2. All citations taken and translated from the Suhrkamp edition of the *Tractatus* (Frankfurt, 1963).
3. Cited in Jurgen Habermas: *Zwischen Erotismus und Allgemeiner Ekonomie*. In: J. Habermas: *Der philosophische Diskurs der Moderne*. Frankfurt, 1985, p. 267.
4. For further details on the adaptations see Rupert Martin , *The Illustration of the Heavenly Ladder of John Climacus*. Princeton, 1954.
5. We used the Frankfurt edition of 1607 in Latin and several translations into German ("ins Teutsche"); all citations are from the Nuremberg edition of 1719.
6. This is particularly emphasized by the editor of the German translation in the preface: "It would be somewhat strange if the pregnant girls or, rather, the careless whores, were no longer to hold in esteem the concoctions of SABINER or the Seven-[Satten] tree, if the effect corresponds to what he claims for the female fern [Farren-Kraut]; that as soon as a pregnant woman steps on it, the fruit of her womb would leave her and she would abort. Yes, certainly, the women would idolize him if it were certain what he claims for the herbs PHYLLON and MERCURIALIS; that if a woman drink the juice of the male plants of these herbs, or simply place the leaves on that natural place, she would conceive a son without fail."
7. In his *Tractatus Primus* on the sun ("De Sole") (we used the German translation of 1608, edited by Joachim Tanckium), included in the volume, "Vom Stein der Weisen und von den vornembsten Tincturen des Goldes…," Roger Bacon always refers to the *Leib* (body) of this precious metal, as in this small extract from the chapter on theory: *"Solches vorwar geschieht dem Golde nicht / denn bis zum letzten Urtheil des Gerichts / mag die Natur dem Leibe des Goldes nichts an seiner NOBILITET unnd PERFECTION endern oder mindern: Es ist auch zwar eine Materia aller Edelgesteinen / und gibt sie besser von seinem Leibe und von seiner Materia / denn sie die Natur finden mag und erreichen. Und ich sage euch / ob das ASTRUM seine INCLINATION in ein solchen claristeirten Leib des Goldes wenden und IMPRIMIEREN worde / es kundt sein VIRTUTEM und Potentz bio zum letzten Urtheil nicht verlieren. Denn der Leib ist PERFECT und allen Elementen vereiniget und angenehm / und ist kein Element das ihm micht schaden."* (p. 44).
8. Not a word is said about the burning question of "the first." Della Porta's text without doubt exploits earlier writings. For example, similar descriptions to his can be found in Villeneuve's works, written in the 13th century, and whose 'shows' go quite a bit further, prefiguring the 'talkies': "during the play he arranged for a group of people outside the room to make appropriate noises, such as the din and clash of swords, or screams and blasts… from trumpets." (Hammond 1981, 9, 10).
9. In his major work of 1626/30, Scheiner calls the sun "the bear rose" (*rosa ursina*), in mythology often with the connotation of female attributes, as the real flower of the goddess Venus, symbol of love, beauty and the erotic. The title of Scheiner's book, in which he published a description of his telescopic lense for the first time, is in latin and takes up five lines (*Refractiones celestes…*) It was published in 1617 in Ingolstadt.

Fonts and Phrasing

Alexander Galloway

The story goes that new media, new technologies, new and faster methods of transferring information, democratization of technological luxuries, diversification of access to digital networks, the standardization of data formats, the proliferation of networked relations — the story goes that these advances will help usher in a new era marked by greater personal freedom, heightened interpersonal communication, ease from the burden of representation, new perspectives on the problem of the body, greater choice in consumer society, unprecedented opportunities for free expression, and above all, that they will give us speed.

Where are those points in society today where complicity is not read as such, where decisions are not seen as being either political or apolitical but just a choice? Where are those points where a utopian sense of technological progress comes to us uninterrogated? Surely these are points worthy of greater attention. And surely these points overlap with those above.

With the advent of computers comes the phrase "real time." This phrase is used when a digitized event (such as an online interactive broadcast) proceeds as if it were in a non-virtual setting. An event happens in "real time" if it prints, broadcasts, displays, animates, plays using the same timing and event-durations as the non-virtual world. Computational rhythms (be they too short or too long) are masked or subordinated to the duration of events in the "real" world. Real time, therefore, indicates that there has emerged concurrent with computers some sort of digital time or compressed time not parallel with traditional concepts of time. What is the nature of this temporality?

Even if new technological advances do not give us sheer speed, I venture to say that they are indicative of a new form of temporality, a contemporary sense of timing. As a product of the electro-digital transfer of textual information, this contemporary temporality is a twofold sense of time as read through registration, tracking, recording, documentation, playback, scanning, connection, and protocol. Once, it is a sense of timing, like a playing, a sculpted inflection, or a phrasing of notes; it is a phrasing. And twice, it is no time, a singularity, a zero-wait, the utter collapse of temporal distance; it is an instancy.

I argue here that this timing is a product of two general phenomena: a split in the nature of the signifier caused by fonts and the electro-digital transfer of textual information, and the phrasing of certain elements of popular society through cultural slogans and corporate trademarks. These two senses of time must be regarded as concurrent systems that emerge "at once," so to speak, and are by no means mutually pre-emptive.

The manipulation of textual information over computer networks in contexts such as email and the internet, and specifically their mark-up in design layouts and computer fonts tells us something about the nature of contemporary culture. The nature of computer fonts, network structures, and the interpretation of digital information is one that evaporates traditional notions of temporal and corporal sizings. Consequently, the incorporation of the electronic text has been divorced from any notion of activities requiring actual labor time: texts are loaded (derived from a preexisting copy), displayed, saved, and erased with no connection to their traditional labor and time intensive counterpart procedures of researching, printing, copying, and archiving. To this extent, computer fonts are connected to our contemporary, electronic sense of time. It is not a continuum. The temporal difference separating fonts and texts is a no-time, a singularity.

A font is not analogous to a signifier. Rather it renders the signifier itself internally complex. It is a sub-element of the signifier. A computer font cannot be thought of, therefore, as a genetic element of the sign. In text for example, a font must be thought of independently from content, written markings, etc. Fonts are indicative of what is known in the digital text as a protocol. They regulate representation.

The concept of zero-wait transfer governs contemporary ideas regarding textuality. In a digital network, much like previous types of value economies, information is produced in order to be exchanged or transferred. However, under digital transfer texts are exchanged according to an atemporal logic and through digital means. (Digital texts are those whose very content has been quantized. So-called analog texts are those whose value alone has been quantized.)

As one contemporary critic has noted, this transfer of textual information occurs through a process of "immediation." Immediation means both immediate and mediated. Texts are therefore both instantaneous and second-order. They are heard with both static and clarity. In Baudrillardian fashion, each digital text is derived and yet also real. Time is seemingly no longer a textual component.

Fonts mediate and incorporate (put-into-a-body) zero-wait transferred texts. Virtuality is that state where texts or discourses are no longer bound by traditional space/time laws. As Paul Virilio has recently noted, it is time itself that is rendered instantaneous by virtuality [http://www.ctheory.com/a30-cyberspace_alarm.html]. And thus, at this turn, computer fonts illustrate a break in traditional notions surrounding temporality, and representation.

Font faces appear at the intersection. They are the veneer of representation. The font is always the first thing you read and the last thing you write. Fonts have no body. They buffer the act of reading. They protect the reader from the shock of virtual transfer. And fonts are those elements that are so commonly not read.

Fonts are closely connected to textual standardization and thus the very nature of the internet. The standardization of data formats as a result of hegemony or negotiated dominance (i.e. GIF format for images, character-based formats for text, dominance of English over other natural languages, etc.) is the conceptual framework behind HTML, or Hypertext Mark-up Language.

What are the constraints of HTML? By far still the fundamental computer language used on the internet, HTML and the browsers that interpret it constitute a quantitative structure of exchange that both directs textual or discursive flow, and regulates its dissemination — if that indeed is the manner in which it is distributed. This dynamic constitutes a true information (or textual), economy. Ebb and flow are governed by specific protocols. Connection is established according to certain hierarchies. And like the logic of traditional political economy all elements conform to formal standardization. Computer networks are not a heterogeneity.

Computer fonts are an indication of a type of technological complexity that allows for wide varieties of font faces, sizes, shapes, distortions, and types of mark-up. However, this type of quantitative diversity is not equivalent to a real diversification of the conditions of digital texts, including distribution networks, virtuation apparatuses (browsers, VR hardware, and other interfaces), and mediative machinery (routers, dial-up protocols, displays).

By way of illustration, allow me to compare these two elements. Computer fonts do the same work in the digito-semiotic world that HTML does in the virtual world. They both are a set of instructions for the compilation of contents. Fonts compile and represent digitized texts, while HTML compiles and displays hypertextual elements. Like HTML, a computer font displays textual information "all at once," and virtually. On load a derivative of each element is placed. On unload that copy is discarded. However, computer fonts are not representation per se. They are governing principles for representation. They are at once totally crucial in the transfer of textual information and yet they are completely disposable, contingent and atemporal. They are a readable example of protocol.

Fonts, trademarks, and misspellings — ground zero for contemporary negotiations concerning textuality. Today, language is negotiated and marked through complex protocols that govern one's ideological relationship to digital texts. We recognize Netscape, but do we recognize their encryption protocol licensed from RSA? (Althusser rolls in his grave.)

It is on the corporate stage where font faces, a method of visually representing language, are regulated as an element of corporate trademarks an symbols. They are patented, trademarked, controlled, owned, regulated, as the way that words are formulated as readable. It is important to note that historically this was not always the case.

Equally responsible therefore for the constitution of temporality today is what I term the "phrasing" of certain elements of popular society through cultural slogans and corporate trademarks. Phrasing here should be taken quite literally, to the extent that it refers to a constructive aestheticization, or textualization, of everyday life. An action is "phrased" — like a trumpet solo is phrased. It is translated into articulated gestures; it is conducted. Phrasing also means to articulate into language. This therefore refers to a more gestural temporality, one with a certain influence over the "tempo of life." It is not instantaneous or singular, but complex and multiple. It is a non-linear affect, a systemic influence that controls both action and discourse.

As it happens, a coincidence of current modes of gestural phrasing takes the form of a sort of lowest possible denominator for ontological claims. Take for example GE's "We bring good things to life," Coke's "Coke is it," Nike's "Just do it," and Calvin Klein's brilliantly simple "Be." These ideological campaigns share a confluence of strategy within which certain social relationships are naturalized. The primary tactics here are content-evacuation and the simplification of complex social relationships.

Similar to the collapsing of temporal distances as seen in electronic transfer of information, there is a collapsing of conceptual distances through the mating of the nostalgic or familiar with the futuristic or alien. This is an example of the top-down phrasing or aestheticization of everyday life. Technologico-corporate progress (a fetishization of time) is naturalized through the phrasing of language, especially the juxtaposition of disparate elements in slogan-type phrases. Here, the familiar and the techno-alien are phrased, they are lyricized into a gestural subject fabric. The phrase is sentimentalized, it is repeated, it is printed on children's pyjamas.

We remember "A long time ago/in a galaxy far, far away." It is a perfect example of this ideological mating of the alien and the familiar. This type of phrasing is a real example of "repetition with a difference." It creates a spooky epilogue to Benjamin's "Storyteller."

The story goes that theory knows the power of slogans. We have Althusser's "hey you there!" or "I've strangled my wife," and Derrida's "I've forgotten my umbrella." ...The story goes that theory can use slogans. But we have "E.T./phone home," and "Beam me up, Scotty" — both examples of the equating of dissimilar semantic elements as part of a definite strategy. These are our political slogans. This type of gestural language is ideologically constitutive.

The electro-digital transfer of textual information coupled with a general multiplication of media sources changes the manner in which we conceive of temporality, itself a social discourse. This new discourse relating to time is marked by new protocols, and as articulated above these protocols may be understood through a reading of digital texts.

The Aesthetics of Virtual Worlds

Report from Los Angeles

Lev Manovich

Since this essay was written, Netscape Navigator 3.0 introduced support for VRML, thus allowing its users to navigate virtual spaces without leaving the program; every commercial network has added support for multi-user virtual worlds; and more than 100,000 people have become "citizens" of AlphaWorld <www.worlds.net/alphaworld>. Given this rapid growth, some examples and numbers quoted in this essay will be out-of-date. Yet, exactly because this growth promises to make networked virtual worlds an important, if not the key aspect of cyberculture, the analysis contained in the essay is becoming even more relevant.

Welcome to a Virtual World! Strap on your avatar! Don't have the programming skills or time to build your own? No problem. We provide a complete library of pre-assembled characters; one of them is bound to fit you perfectly. Join the community of like-minded users who agree that three-dimensional space is more sexy! Yes, there is nothing more liberating than flying through a 3D scene, executing risky maneuvers and going for the kill. Mountains and valleys can represent files on a network, financial investments, enemy troops, the body of a virtual sex partner — it does not really matter. Zoom! Roll! Pitch! Not enough visual realism? For just an extra $9.95 a month you can upgrade your rendering speed to a blistering 490,000 polygons a second, increasing the quality of the experience a staggering 27.4%! And for another $4.95 you will get a chance to try a new virtual world every month, including a mall, a brothel, the Sistine Chapel, Paris during the Revolution of 1789, and even the fully navigable human brain. A 3D networked virtual world is waiting for you; all we need is your credit card number.

This advertisement is likely to appear on your computer screen quite soon, if it has not already. Thirteen years after William Gibson's fictional description of cyberspace[1] and several years after the first theoretical conferences on the subject,[2] cyberspace is finally becoming a reality. More than that, it promises to become a new standard in how we interact with computer — a new way to work, communicate and play.

Virtual Worlds: History and Recent Developments

Although a few networked multi-user graphical virtual environments had already been constructed in the 1980s, they were specialized projects involving custom hardware and designed for particular groups of users. In Lucasfilm's Habitat, described by its designers as a "many-player online virtual environment," a few dozen players used their home Commodore 64 computers to connect to a central computer running a simulation of a two-dimensional animated world. The players could interact with the objects in this world as well as with each other's graphical representations (avatars).[3] Conceptually similar to Habitat but much more upscale in its graphics was SIMNET (Simulation Network) developed by DARPA (U.S. Defense Advanced Research Projects Agency). SIMNET was probably the first working cyberspace — the first collaborative *three-dimensional* virtual environment. It consisted of a number of individual simulators linked to a high-speed network. Each simulator contained a copy of the same world database and the virtual representations of all the other simulators. In one of SIMNET's implementations, over two hundred M-1 tank crews, located in Germany, Washington D.C., Fort Knox, and other places around the world, were able to participate in the same virtual battle.[4]

I remember attending a panel at a SIGGRAPH conference where a programmer who worked for Atari in the early 1980s argued that the military stole the idea of cyberspace from the games industry, modeling SIMNET after already existing civilian multi-participant games. With the end of the Cold War, the influences are running in the opposite way. Many companies that yesterday supplied very expensive simulators to the military are busy converting them into location-based entertainment systems (LBE). In fact, one of the first such systems which opened in Chicago in 1990 — BattleTech Center from Virtual World Entertainment, Inc. — was directly modeled on SIMNET.[5] Like SIMNET, BattleTech Center comprised a networked collection of futuristic cockpit models with VR gear. For $7 each, a number of players could fight each other in a simulated 3D environment. By 1995, Virtual World was operating dozens of centers around the world that depended, as in SIMNET's case, on proprietary software and hardware.[6]

In contrast to such custom-built and expensive location-based entertainment systems, the Internet provides a structure for 3D cyberspace that can simultaneously accommodate millions of users, that is inherently modifiable by them, and runs on practically every computer. A number of researchers and companies are already working to turn this possibility into reality.

Among the attempts to spatialize the Net, the most important is VRML (Virtual Reality Modeling Language), which was conceived in the spring of 1994. According to the document defining Version 1.0 (May 26, 1995), VRML is "a language for describing multi-participant interactive simulations — virtual worlds networked via the global Internet and hyperlinked with the World Wide Web."[7] Using VRML, Internet users can construct 3D scenes hyperlinked to other scenes and to regular Web documents. In other words, 3D space becomes yet another media accessible via the Web, along with text, sounds, and moving images. But eventually a VRML universe may subsume the rest of the Web. So while currently the Web is dominated by pages of text, with other media elements (including VRML 3D scenes) linked to it, future users may experience it as one gigantic 3D world which will contain all other media, including text. This is certainly the vision of VRML designers who aim to "create a unified conceptualization of space spanning the entire Internet, a spatial equivalent of WWW."[8] They see VRML as a natural stage in the evolution of the Net from an abstract data network toward a "'perceptualized' Internet where the data has been sensualized,"[9] i.e., represented in three dimensions.

VRML 1.0 makes possible the creation of networked 3D worlds but it does not allow for the interaction between their users. Another direction in building cyberspace has been to add graphics to already popular Internet systems for interaction, such as chat lines and MUDs. Worlds Inc., which advertises itself as "a publisher of shared virtual environments"[10] has created WorldChat, a 3D chat environment which has been available on the Internet since April 1995. Users first choose their avatars and then enter the virtual world (a space station) where they can interact with other avatars. The company imagines "the creation of 3-D worlds, such as sports bars, where people can come together and talk about or watch sporting events online, or shopping malls."[11] Another company, Ubique[12], created technology called Virtual Places which also allows the users to see and communicate with other users' avatars and even take tours of the Web together.[13]

Currently, the most ambitious full-scale 3D virtual world on the Internet is AlphaWorld, sponsored by Worlds Inc. At the time of this writing, it featured 200,000 buildings, trees and other objects, created by 4,000 Internet users. The world includes a bar, a store which provides prefabricated housing, and news kiosks which take you to other Web pages.[14]

The movement toward spatialization of the Internet is not an accident. It is part of a larger trend in cyberculture — spatialization of *all* representations and experience. This trend manifests itself in a variety of ways.

The designers of human-computer interfaces are moving from 2D toward 3D — from flat desktops to rooms, cities, and other spatial constructs.[15] Web designers also often use pictures of buildings, aerial views of cities, and maps as front ends in their sites. Apple promotes QuickTime VR, a software-only system which allows the user of any personal computer to navigate a spatial environment and interact with 3D objects.

Another example is the emergence of a new field of scientific visualization devoted to spatialization of data sets and their relationships with the help of computer graphics. Like the designers of human-computer interfaces, the scientists assume that spatialization of data makes working with it more efficient, regardless of what this data is.

Finally, in many computer games, from the original "Zork" to the best-selling CD-ROM "Myst," narrative and time itself are equated with movement through space (i.e., going to new rooms or levels). In contrast to modern literature, theater, and cinema, which are built around the psychological tensions between characters, these computer games return us to the ancient forms of narrative where the plot is driven by the *spatial* movement of the main hero, traveling through distant lands to save the princess, to find the treasure, to defeat the Dragon, and so on.

A similar spatialization of narrative has defined the field of computer animation throughout its history. Numerous computer animations are organized around a single, uninterrupted camera move through a complex and extensive set. A camera flies over mountain terrain, moves through a series of rooms, maneuvers past geometric shapes, zooms out into open space, and so on. In contrast to ancient myths and computer games, this journey has no goal, no purpose. It is an ultimate "road movie" where the navigation through the space is sufficient in itself.

Aesthetics of Virtual Worlds

The computerization of culture leads to the spatialization of all information, narrative, and, even, time. Unless this overall trend is to reverse suddenly, the spatialization of cyberspace is next. In the words of the scientists at Sony's Virtual Society Project, "It is our belief that future online systems will be characterized by a high degree of interaction, support for multi-media and most importantly the ability to support shared 3D spaces. In our vision, users will not simply access textual based chat forums, but will enter into 3D worlds where they will be able to interact with the world and with other users in that world." What will be the visual aesthetics of spatialized cyberspace? What would these 3D worlds look like? In answering this question I will try to abstract the aesthetic features common to different virtual worlds already in existence: computer games; CD-ROM titles; virtual sets in Hollywood films; VR simulations; and, of course, virtual worlds on the Internet such as VRML scenes, WorldChat, and QuickTime VR movies. I will also consider the basic technologies and techniques used to construct virtual spaces: 3D computer graphics; digitized video; compositing; and the point and click metaphor. What follows are a few tentative propositions on the visual aesthetics of virtual worlds.

1. Realism as Commodity

Digit in Latin means number. Digital media reduces everything to numbers.

This basic property of digital media has a profound effect on the nature of visual realism. In a digital representation, all dimensions that affect the reality effect — detail, tone, color, shape, movement — are quantified. As a consequence, the reality effect produced by the representation can itself be related to a set of numbers.

For a 2D image, the crucial numbers are its spatial and color resolution: the number of pixels and the number of colors per pixel. For instance, a 640 x 480 image of an object contains more detail and therefore produces a stronger reality effect than a 120 x 160 image of the same object. For a 3D model, the level of detail, and consequently the reality effect, is specified by 3D resolution: the number of points the model is composed of.

Spatial, color, and 3D resolutions describe the realism of static representations: scanned photographs; painted backgrounds; renderings of 3D objects; and so on. Once the user begins to interact with a virtual world, navigating through a 3D space or inspecting the objects in it, other dimensions become crucial. One of them is temporal resolution. The more frames a computer can generate in a second, the smoother the resulting motion. Another is the speed of the system's response: if the user clicks on an image of a door to open it or asks a virtual character a question, a delay in response breaks the illusion. Yet another can be called consistency: if moving objects do not cast shadows (because the computer can't render them in real time) while the static background has them, the inconsistency affects the reality effect.

All these dimensions are quantifiable. The number of colors in an image, the temporal resolution the system is capable of, and so on can be specified in exact numbers.

Not surprisingly, the advertisements for graphics software and hardware prominently display these numbers. Even more importantly, those in the business of visual realism — the producers of special effects, military trainers, digital photographers, television designers — now have definite measures for what they are buying and selling. For instance, the Federal Aviation Administration, which creates the standards for simulators to be used in pilot training, specifies the required realism in terms of 3D resolution. In 1991 it required that for daylight, a simulator must be able to produce a minimum of 1,000 surfaces or 4,000 points.[16] Similarly, a description of the Compu-Scene IV simulator from GE Aerospace states that a pilot can fly over a geographically accurate 3D terrain that includes 6,000 features per square mile.[17]

The numbers which characterize digital realism simultaneously reflect something else: the cost involved. More bandwidth, higher resolution and faster processing result in a stronger reality effect — and cost more.

The bottom line: the reality effect of a digital representation can now be measured in dollars. Realism has became a commodity. It can be bought and sold like anything else.

This condition is likely to be explored by the designers of virtual worlds. If today users are charged for the connection time, in the future they can be charged for visual aesthetics and the quality of the overall experience: spatial resolution; number of colors; complexity of characters (both geometric and psychological); and so on. Since all these dimensions are specified in software, it becomes possible to automatically adjust the appearance of a virtual world on the fly, boosting it up if a customer is willing to pay more.

In this way, the logic of pornography will be extended to the culture at large. Peep shows and sex lines charge their customers by the minute, putting a precise cost on each bit of pleasure. In virtual worlds, all dimensions of reality will be quantified and priced separately.

Neal Stephenson's 1992 *Snow Crash* provides us with one possible scenario of such a future. Entering the Metaverse, the spatialized Net of the future, the hero sees "a liberal sprinkling of black-and-white people — persons who are accessing the Metaverse through cheap public terminals, and who are rendered in jerky, grainy black and white."[18] He also encounters couples who can't afford custom avatars and have to buy off-the-shelf models, poorly rendered and capable of just a few standard facial expressions — virtual world equivalents of Barbie dolls.[19]

This scenario is gradually becoming a reality. A number of online stock-photo services already provide their users with low-resolution photographs for a small cost, charging more for higher resolution copies. A company called Viewpoint Datalabs International is selling thousands of ready-to-use 3D geometric models widely used by computer animators and designers. For most popular models you can choose between different versions, with more detailed versions costing more than less detailed ones.[20]

2. Romanticism, Adorno, Photoshop Filters: From Creation to Selection

Viewpoint Datalabs' models exemplify another characteristic of virtual worlds: they are not created from scratch but assembled from ready-made parts. Put differently, in digital culture creation has been replaced by selection.

E. H. Gombrich's concept of a representational schema and Roland Barthes's "death of the author" helped to sway us from the romantic ideal of the artist creating totally from scratch, pulling images directly from his imagination.[21] As Barthes puts it, "[t]he Text is a tissue of quotations drawn from the innumerable centers of culture."[22] Yet, even though a modern artist may be only reproducing or, at best, combining in new ways pre-existing texts and idioms, the actual material process of art making supports the romantic ideal. An artist operates like God creating the universe — he starts with an empty canvas or a blank page. Gradually filling in the details, he brings a new world into existence.

Such a process of art making, manual and painstakingly slow, was appropriate for the age of pre-industrial artisan culture. In the twentieth century, as the rest of the culture moved to mass production and automation, literally becoming a "culture industry," art continued to insist on its artisan model. Only in the 1910s when some artists began to assemble collages and montages from already existing cultural "parts," was art introduced to the industrial method of production.

In contrast, electronic art from its very beginning was based on a new principle: modification of an already existing signal. The first electronic instrument designed in 1920 by the legendary Russian scientist and musician Leon Theremin contained a generator producing a sine wave; the performer simply modified its frequency and amplitude.[23] In the 1960s video artists began to build video synthesizers based on the same principle. The artist was no longer a romantic genius generating a new world purely out of his imagination; he became a technician turning a knob here, pressing a switch there — an accessory to the machine.

Substitute a simple sine wave by a more complex signal (sounds, rhythms, melodies) and add a whole bank of signal generators and you have a modern music synthesizer, the first instrument which embodies the logic of all new media: not creation but selection.

The first music synthesizers appeared in the 1950s. They were followed by video synthesizers in the 1960s, followed by DVE (Digital Video Effects) in the late 1970s (the banks of effects used by video editors), and followed, in turn, by computer software such as 1984's MacDraw that already come with a repertoire of basic shapes. The process of art making has finally caught up with modern times. It has become synchronized with the rest of modern society where everything is assembled from ready-made parts; from objects to people's identities. The modern subject proceeds through life by selecting from numerous menus and catalogs of items — be it assembling an outfit, decorating the apartment, choosing dishes from a restaurant menu, choosing which interest groups to join. With electronic and digital media, art-making similarly entails choosing from ready-made elements: textures and icons supplied by a paint program; 3D models which come with a 3D modeling program; melodies and rhythms built into a music program.

While previously the great text of culture from which the artist created his own unique "tissue of quotations" was bubbling and shimmering somewhere below consciousness, now it has become externalized (and greatly reduced in the process) — 2D objects, 3D models, textures, transitions, effects which are available as soon as the artist turns on the computer. The World Wide Web takes this process to the next level: it encourages the creation of texts that completely consist of pointers to other texts that are already on the Web. One does not have to add any new content; it is enough to select from what already exists.

This shift from creation to selection is particularly apparent in 3D computer graphics — the main technique for building virtual worlds. The amount of labor involved in constructing three-dimensional reality from scratch in a computer makes it hard to resist the temptation to utilize pre-assembled, standardized objects, characters, and behaviors readily provided by software manufacturers — fractal landscapes, checkerboard floors, complete characters and so on.[24] Every program comes with libraries of ready-to-use models, effects or even complete animations. For instance, a user of the Dynamation program (a part of the popular Wavefront 3D software) can access complete pre-assembled animations of moving hair, rain, a comet's tail or smoke, with a single click.

If even professional designers rely on ready-made objects and animations, the end users of virtual worlds, who usually don't have graphics or programming skills, have no other choice. Not surprisingly, Web chat-line operators and virtual world providers encourage users to choose from the libraries of pictures, 3D objects, and avatars they provide. Ubique's site features "Ubique Furniture Gallery" where one can choose images from such categories as "office furniture," "computers and electronics," and "people icons."[25] VR-SIG from the UK provides a VRML Object Supermarket while Aereal delivers the Virtual World Factory. The latter aims to make the creation of a custom virtual world particularly simple: "Create your personal world, without having to program! All you need to do is fill-in-the-blanks and out pops your world.[26] Quite soon we will see a whole market for detailed virtual sets, characters with programmable behaviors, and even complete worlds (a bar with customers, a city square, a famous historical episode, etc.) from which a user can put together his own "unique" virtual world.

While a hundred years ago the user of a Kodak camera was asked just to push a button, he still had the freedom to point the camera at anything. Now, "you push the button, we do the rest" has become "you push the button, we create your world."

3. Brecht as Hardware

Another aesthetic feature of virtual worlds lies in their peculiar temporal dynamic: constant, repetitive shifts between an illusion and its suspense. Virtual worlds keep reminding us of their artificiality, incompleteness, and constructedness. They present us with a perfect illusion only to reveal the underlying machinery.

Web surfing provides a perfect example. A typical user may be spending equal time looking at a page and waiting for the next page to download. During waiting periods, the act of communication itself — bits traveling through the network — becomes the message. The user keeps checking whether the connection is being made, glancing back and forth between the animated icon and the status bar. Using Roman Jakobson's model of communication functions, we can say that communication comes to be dominated by contact, or the phatic function — it is centered around the physical channel and the very act of connection between the addresser and the addressee.[27]

Jakobson writes about verbal communication between two people who, in order to check whether the channel works, address each other: "Do you hear me?" and "Do you understand me?" But in Web communication there is no human addresser, only a machine. So as the user keeps checking whether the information is coming, he actually addresses the machine itself. Or rather, the machine addresses the user. The machine reveals itself, it reminds the user of its existence — not only because the user is forced to wait but also because he is forced to witness how the message is being constructed over time. A page fills in part by part, top to bottom; text comes before images; images arrive in low resolution and are gradually refined. Finally, everything comes together in a smooth sleek image — the image which will be destroyed with the next click.

Will this temporal dynamic ever be eliminated? Will spatialized Net become a perfect Utopian city rather than remain a gigantic construction site?

An examination of already existing 3D virtual worlds suggests a negative answer to this question. Consider the technique called "distancing" or "level of detail" which for years has been used in VR simulations and is now being adapted to 3D games and VRML scenes. The idea is to render the models more crudely when the user is moving through virtual space; when the user stops, detail gradually fills in. Another variation of the same technique involves creating a number of models of the same object, each with progressively less detail. When the virtual camera is close to an object, a highly detailed model is used; if the object is far away, a lesser detailed version is substituted to save unnecessary computation.

A virtual world which incorporates these techniques has a fluid ontology that is affected by the actions of the user. As the user navigates through space the objects switch back and forth between pale blueprints and fully "fleshed-out" illusions. The immobility of a subject guarantees a complete illusion; the slightest movement destroys it.

Navigating a QuickTime VR movie is characterized by a similar dynamic. In contrast to the nineteenth-century panorama that it closely emulates, QuickTime VR continuously deconstructs its own illusion. The moment you begin to pan through the scene, the image becomes jagged. And, if you try to zoom into the image, all you get are oversized pixels. The representational machine keeps hiding and revealing itself.

Compare this dynamic to traditional cinema or realist theater which aims at all costs to maintain the continuity of the illusion for the duration of the performance. In contrast to such totalizing realism, digital aesthetics have a surprising affinity to twentieth century leftist avant-garde aesthetics. Bertolt Brecht's strategy to reveal the conditions of an illusion's production, echoed by countless other leftist artists, became embedded in hardware and software themselves. Similarly, Walter Benjamin's concept of "perception in the state of distraction"[28] found a perfect realization. The periodic reappearance of the machinery and the continuous presence of the communication channel in the message prevent the subject from falling into the dream world of illusion for very long, making him alternate between concentration and detachment.

While virtual machinery itself already acts as an avant-garde director, the designers of interactive media (games, CD-ROM titles, interactive cinema, and interactive television programs) often consciously attempt to structure the subject's temporal experience as a series of periodic shifts. The subject is forced to oscillate between the roles of viewer and user, shifting between perceiving and acting, between following the story and actively participating in it. During one segment the computer screen presents the viewer with an engaging cinematic narrative. Suddenly the image freezes, menus and icons appear and the viewer is forced to act: make choices; click; push buttons. (Moscow media theorist Anataly Prokhorov describes this process as the shift from transparency to opacity — from a window into a fictional 3D universe to a solid surface, full of menus, controls, text and icons.[29] Three-dimensional space becomes a surface; a photograph becomes a diagram; a character becomes an icon.)

Can Brecht and Hollywood be married? Is it possible to create a new temporal esthetic based on such cyclical shifts? So far, I can think of only one successful example — a military simulator, the only mature form of interactive media. It perfectly blends perception and action, cinematic realism and computer menus. The screen presents the subject with an illusionistic virtual world while periodically demanding quick actions: shooting at the enemy; changing the direction of a vehicle; and so on. In this art form, the roles of viewer and actant are blended perfectly — but there is a price to pay. The narrative is organized around a single and clearly defined goal: staying alive.

4. Riegl, Panofsky, and Computer Graphics: Regression in Virtual Worlds

The last aesthetic principle of virtual worlds that I will address can be summarized as follows: virtual spaces are not true spaces but collections of separate objects. Or: there is no space in cyberspace.

To explore this thesis further we can borrow the categories developed by art historians early in this century. The founders of modern art history (Alois Riegl, Heinrich Wolfflin, and Erwin Panofsky) defined their field as the history of the representation of space. Working within the paradigms of cyclic cultural development and racial topology, they related the representation of space in art to the spirit of entire epochs, civilizations, and races. In his 1901 "Die Sptrmische Kunstindustrie," Riegl characterized humankind's cultural development as the oscillation between two extreme poles, two ways to understand space, which he called "haptic" and "optic." Haptic perception isolates the object in the field as a discrete entity, while optic perception unifies objects in a spatial continuum. Riegl's contemporary, Heinrich Wolfflin, similarly proposed that the temperament of a period or a nation expresses itself in a particular mode of seeing and representing space. Wolfflin's "Principles of Art History" (1913) plotted the differences between Renaissance and Baroque on five dimensions: linear/painterly; plane/recession; closed form/open form; multiplicity/unity; and clearness/unclearness. Finally, another founder of modern art history, Erwin Panofsky, contrasted the "aggregate" space of the Greeks with the "systematic" space of the Italian Renaissance in a famous essay "Perspective as a Symbolic Form" (1924-1925). Panofsky established a parallel between the history of spatial representation and the evolution of abstract thought. The former moves from the space of individual objects in antiquity to the representation of space as continuous and systematic in modernity; in Panofsky's neologisms, from "aggregate" space to "systematic" space. Correspondingly, the evolution of abstract thought progresses from ancient philosophy's view of the physical universe as discontinuous to the post-Renaissance understanding of space as infinite, ontologically primal in relation to bodies, homogeneous, and isotropic — in short, as "systematic."

We don't have to believe in grand evolutionary schemes but we can retain the categories themselves. What kind of space is a virtual space? At first glance, 3D computer graphics, the main technology of creating virtual spaces, exemplify Panofsky's concept of Renaissance "systematic" space which exists prior to the objects. Indeed, the Cartesian coordinate system is hardwired into computer graphics software and often into the hardware itself.[30] When a designer launches a modeling program, he is typically presented with an empty space defined by a perspective grid, the space that will be gradually filled by the objects he will create. If the built-in message of a music synthesizer is a sine wave, the built-in world of computer graphics is an empty Renaissance space, the coordinate system itself.

Yet computer generated worlds are actually much more "haptic" and "aggregate" than "optic" and "systematic." The most commonly used 3D computer graphics technique to create 3D worlds is polygonal modeling. The virtual world created using this technique is a vacuum filled with separate objects defined by rigid boundaries. A perspective projection creates the illusion that these objects belong together but in fact they have no connection to each other. What is missing is space in the sense of space-environment or space-medium: the environment between objects; an atmosphere which unites everything together; the effects of objects on one another.

Another basic technique used in creating virtual worlds — compositing (superimposing, keying) — also leads to an "aggregate" space. It involves superimposing animated characters, still images, QuickTime movies, and other graphical elements over a separate background. A typical scenario may involve an avatar animated in real time in response to the user's commands. The avatar is superimposed over a picture of a room. An avatar is controlled by the user; a picture of a room is provided by a virtual world operator. Because the elements come from different sources and are put together in real time, the result is a series of 2D planes rather than a real 3D environment.

In summary, although computer-generated virtual worlds are usually rendered in linear perspective, they are really collections of separate objects, unrelated to one another. In view of this, commonly expressed arguments that 3D computer graphics send us back to Renaissance perspectivalism, and, therefore, from the viewpoint of twentieth-century abstraction, should be considered regressive, turn out to be groundless. If we are to apply the evolutionary paradigm of Panofsky to the history of virtual computer space, it has not even achieved its Renaissance yet. It is still on the level of Ancient Greece, which could not conceive of space as a totality.

And if the World Wide Web and VRML 1.0 are any indication, we are not moving any closer toward systematic space; instead, we are embracing "aggregate" space as a new norm, both metaphorically and literally. The "space" of the Web in principle can't be thought of as a coherent totality: it is a collection of numerous files, hyperlinked but without any overall "perspective" to unite them. The same holds for actual 3D spaces on the Internet. A VRML file which describes a 3D scene is a list of separate objects which may exist anywhere on the Internet, each created by a different person or a different program. The objects have no connection to each other. And since any user can add or delete objects, no one may even know the complete structure of the scene.

The Web has already been compared to the American Wild West. The spatialized Web as envisioned by VRML (itself a product of California) even more closely reflects the treatment of space in American culture: the lack of attention to space which is not functionally used. The territories that exist between privately owned houses and businesses are left to decay. The VRML universe simply does not contain space as such — only objects which belong to different individuals.

And what is an object in a virtual world? Something which can be acted upon: clicked; moved; opened — in short, used. It is tempting to interpret this as regression to the world view of an infant. A child does not think of the universe as existing separately from himself — it appears as a collection of unrelated objects with which he can enter in contact: touch; suck on; grab. Similarly, the user of a virtual world tries to click on whatever is in front of him; if the objects do not respond, he is disappointed. In the virtual universe, Descartes's maxim can be rewritten as follows: "I can be clicked on, therefore I exist."

5. The Whole Picture

I have discussed different aesthetic features of 3D virtual worlds. But what would a future full-blown virtual world feel like? What would be its overall gestalt?

One example of a highly detailed virtual world, complete with landscapes and human beings, is provided by Disney's 1995 "Toy Story," the first completely computer-animated feature length film. Frighteningly sterile, this is a world in which the toys and the humans look absolutely alike, the latter appearing as macabre automatons.

If you want to experience cyberspace of the future today, visit the place where "Toy Story" was made — Los Angeles. The city offers a precise model for the virtual world. There is no center, no hint of any kind of centralized organization, no traces of the hierarchy essential to traditional cities. One drives to particular locations defined strictly by their street addresses rather than by spatial landmarks. A trendy restaurant or club can be found in the middle of nowhere, among the miles of completely unremarkable buildings. The whole city feels like a set of particular points suspended in a vacuum, similar to a bookmark file of Web pages. You are immediately charged on arrival to any worthwhile location, again as on the Web (mandatory valet parking). There you discover the trendy inhabitants (actors, singers, models, producers) who look like some new race, a result of successful mutation: unbelievably beautiful skin and faces; fixed smiles; and bodies whose perfect shapes surely can't be the result of human evolution. They probably come from the Viewpoint catalog of 3D models. These are not people but avatars: beautifully rendered with no polygons spared; shaped to the latest fashion; their faces switching between a limited number of expressions. Given the potential importance of any communicative contact, subtlety is not tolerated: avatars are designed to release stimuli the moment you notice them, before you have time to click to the next scene.

The best place to experience the whole gestalt is in one of the outdoor cafés on Sunset Plaza in West Hollywood. The avatars sip cappuccino amidst the illusion of 3D space. The space is clearly the result of a quick compositing job: billboards and airbrushed café interior in the foreground against a detailed matte painting of Los Angeles with the perspective exaggerated by haze. The avatars strike poses, waiting for their agents (yes, just like in cyberspace) to bring valuable information. Older customers look even more computer generated, their faces bearing traces of extensive face-lifts. You can enjoy the scene while feeding the parking meter every twenty minutes. A virtual world is waiting for you; all we need is your credit card number.

Notes

1. William Gibson, *Neuromancer*. New York: Ace Books, 1984.
2. Michael Benedikt, ed., *Cyberspace:First Steps*. Cambridge, MA: The MIT Press, 1991
3. Chip Morningstar and F.Randall Farmer, "The Lessons of Lucasfilm's Habitat," in *Cyberspace:First Steps*, ed. Michael Benedict. Cambridge, MA: The MIT Press, 1991, 273-302.
4. Howard Rheingold, *Virtual Reality*. New York: Simon & Schuster, 1991, 360-361.
5. See Tony Reveaux, "Virtual Reality Gets Real," *New Media*, January 1993, 39.
6. Virtual World Entertainment, Inc., Press Release, SIGGRAPH '95. Los Angeles, August 6-11, 1995.
7. Gavin Bell, Anthony Parisi and Mark Pesce, "The Virtual Reality Modeling Language. Version 1.0 Specfication," May 26,1995. WWW document.
8. Mark Pesce, Peter Kennard and Anthony Parisi, "Cyberspace." WWW document.
9. Bell, Parisi and Pesce.
10. See http://www.worlds.net/info/aboutus.html.
11. Richard Karpinski, "Chat Comes to the Web," *Interactive Age*, July 3, 1995, 6.
12. See http://www.ubique.com/.
13. In September of 1995, Ubique was purchased by America Online — a significant development since America Online is already the most graphically oriented among the commercial networks based in the US.
14. See http://www.worlds.net/alphaworld/.
15. For instance, Silicon Graphics developed a 3D file system which was showcased in the movie Jurassic Park. The interface of Sony's MagicLink personal communicator is a picture of a room while Apple's EWorld greeted its users with a drawing of a city.
16. Barbara Robertson, "Those Amazing Flying Machines," *Computer Graphics World*, May 1992, 69.
17. Ibid.
18. Neal Stephenson, *Snow Crash*. New York: Bantam Books, 1992, 43.
19. Ibid., 37.
20. See http://www.viewpoint.com.
21. E.H. Gombrich, *Art and Illusion*. Princeton: Princeton University Press, 1960; Roland Barthes, "The Death of the Author," in *Image, Music, Text*, ed. Stephen Heath. New York: Farrar, Straus and Giroux, 1977.
22. Barthes, 142.
23. Bulat Galeyev, *Soviet Faust. Lev Theremin — Pioneer of Electronic Art*, (in Russian). Kazan, 1995, 19.
24. For a more detailed analysis of realism in 3D computer graphics, see Lev Manovich, "Assembling Reality: Myths of Computer Graphics," *Afterimage 20*, no. 2. September 1992, 12-14.
25. See http://www.ubique.com/places/gallery.html.
26. See http://www.virtpark.com/factinfo.htm.
27. See Roman Jakobson, "Closing Statement: Linguistics and Poetics," in *Style In Language*, ed. Thomas Sebeok. Cambridge, MA: The MIT Press, 1960.
28. Walter Benjamin, "The Work of Art in the Age of Mechanical Reproduction," in *Illuminations*, ed. Hannah Arendt. New York: Schochen Books, 1969.
29. Private communication, September 1995, St. Petersburg.
30. See Lev Manovich, "Mapping Space: Perspective, Radar and Computer Graphics," in *SIGGRAPH '93 Visual Proceedings*, ed. Simon Penny. New York: ACM, 1993.

Deregulation/Globalisation

The Loss of Cultural Diversity?

Bernhard Serexhe

Towards Another "Brave New World"?

Today, we are witnessing the rapid installation of the complex systems that will become the technological and commercial foundations of a "global information infrastructure." This new, interactive communication space will doubtlessly function as a powerful tool in the service of the economy, but it will also be at the centre of radical and far-reaching changes in our societies. From this point of view, the simple admiration of what are merely technical advances, coupled with present-day justifications of a primarily economic nature, threatens to prevail over the higher interests of the cultural life and the social functioning of the peoples of Europe. Among the undeniable responsibilities of public authorities are the protection of essential community functions against possible encroachment and the promotion of the enormous potential of these new technologies for the cultural and social development of all our societies.

Present-Day Monopolistic Trends in the Future Multimedia Market

Observation of the world's financial markets reveals transactions of vital importance in all sectors of the cultural industries. Economic experts already predict a planetary market of several thousand billion dollars by the year 2000. For the first time in human history, the cultural sector which, by its nature, is not preoccupied with the race for raw materials, is promising profit-earning capacities that will exceed those of the traditional material-based industries.

The market is developing exponentially and is marked by cutthroat competition between strategic alliances and mass buyers at the centre of a rapid convergence of three previously separate sectors: audio-visual, computer technology and telecommunications. Currently, a very small number of world-wide corporations are active in this market. They are all impatient to reap profits from their huge investments by setting up the technical, legal and commercial norms best suited to their own involvement in this future world market.

At the same time, in the movement towards the creation of ever more powerful trusts, these same groups manage to take advantage of the discrepancies between national legal frameworks. In the last several years, a handful of giants in the computer and communication world have acquired the status of "global players," dominating the activities of the other, weaker competitors in the market. The absence of international law in this field, coupled with the scale of the necessary financial investment encourages this tendency towards concentration.

In view of the imminent liberalisation and probable homogenisation of this world market, it is impossible not to see that the main objective pursued by these cultural industries is nothing other than the most profitable exploitation of their audio-visual products and future on-line services. The recommendations of the main representatives of the cultural industries of Europe, Japan and the United States at the February 1995 G7 conference, held in Brussels, gave clear warning of this single-minded interest. Alongside the demands for a speed-up in the deregulation of the markets and the conclusion of agreements as to certain technical norms, much concern was also expressed as to the public's confidence in this information society. Without this confidence, according to these recommendations, the extraordinary gains to be won from the information revolution could not be completely realised.

In the context of the multimedia industry's concern about public mistrust, it is worth quoting Gerald Levin, president of one of the world's leading multimedia giants, Time-Warner, who argues that "the consumer has never known what he wanted before the industry made him an offer" (*Der Spiegel* special, March 1995, p. 31).

Promoted, then, by an essentially economic discourse, the result of this crusade on a world-wide scale will be the undermining of all sorts of social and ethical norms and the rapid evolution towards a new society, already baptised the "information society."

Although no one can yet measure the scope of the impact of new technologies on cultural life and on the functioning of our societies, or predict the physiognomy of this "information society," by making us accept its purely technical logic, the promises associated with this illusory vision already outline its marvellous advantages. These are the creation of tens of millions of new jobs by the year 2000, the availability of an educational tool of tremendous significance, a more democratic society, the prospect of free access to information by anyone and everyone, both as consumers and producers. Also expected is the imminent arrival of a better standard of living for Europe, Japan, the United States and, subsequently, to quote the industry's own recommendations at the G7 Brussels conference, for "the other regions of the world."

The Information Highway Project

The investigation of the means of distribution that will bring about all these advantages reveals a multitude of different techniques, including cable transmission, fibre optics, and satellites. All of these, however, rely on the concept of a high bandwidth, inter-operational global network, generally termed the "information highway."

Constructed by the powerful partners of the telecommunications industries and, in order to obtain a return on the enormous investments required, the infrastructure of this new interactive communication space must serve the same investors, in their capacity as producers and distributors. This will occur through the practically unlimited transmission of information and the exploitation, on a planetary scale, of a multitude of new services, generally classed under the somewhat vague term of "multimedia": tele-working, tele-shopping, e-mail, instant video, access to administrative services, and even electronic voting.

This notion of the information highway, suggesting universal and free access for each and every one of us as consumers, has a prerequisite: the user must dispose of the adequate cultural capital and the financial means to acquire the technical devices involved and to access the different services offered, which can only be pay-services, and probably expensive ones at that.

It goes without saying that the essential applications foreseen by the technicians of the powerful industrial groups will go far beyond the present-day and often libertarian experiments in the use of the Internet. As a fantastic instrument of free and individualistic exchange in the fields of science and artistic creation, the Internet cannot really be considered as a precursor to the information highway projects, except in the limited sense of its acceptance by a specialised public and in its technical operating modes.

In the face of today's clear trend towards an oligopolistic market, it is necessary to distinguish between the "cyberspace" myth, a vision of a virtual, cosmopolitan and liberal universe, and the industrial project of the "information superhighway," a powerful instrument in the advanced marketing of audio-visual products and other pay services. Contrary to the democratic pretensions in which the information and image industries would have us believe, the "info-cracy" may also have an inherently totalitarian tendency. In the case of their progressive monopolisation, the new technologies may also turn out to be an instrument for the worst of totalitarianisms, that of a "brave new world" in which everyone will be content, well-informed about all he or she should know in order to play a useful role, but ignorant of the rest, which need not be known, and amused permanently, even to satiety.

Before leaving the field of action open to a purely economic discourse, it is necessary then to address some of the major issues in a more precise manner, associating cultural dynamics and the new interactive communication spaces in Europe.

Identities and Cultural Expressions

From whatever viewpoint, a fair appraisal of the reality of the European situation must consider the extraordinary cultural richness of the countries of Europe as the product both of an ancient and shared historical evolution and of an extraordinarily large range of regional traditions. The essential characteristic of this shared culture is its spirit of openness. There is no doubt that European culture has profited from the selection, interpretation and subsequent assimilation of external and older cultural evolutions, which cannot be dissociated from its own specific identity. Generally, this appropriation was the result of acts of conquest which led to domination and even the suppression of other cultures. By the same token, other cultures have evolved thanks to the intense enrichment brought to them by European cultural values.

Conscious of the composite and fragile nature of its own cultural identity, Europe must today show exemplary responsibility where its own cultural heritage is concerned, and with regards to its present-day and future cultural life. This responsibility must involve a greater sensitivity in its contacts with other cultures. Inescapably bound up in permanent exchanges with other evolving cultures, the dynamics of European culture can only be impoverished and compromised by misguided protectionism.

Yet, at the same time, faced with the enormous initiatives launched by the United States and by Japan, we also feel deep concern — and justifiably so — regarding the preservation of cultural expressions and identities in Europe. Waiting for the wave of multimedia products to unfurl, products of more or less limited value, designed, fabricated and homogenised to be easily sold on the world market, this concern anticipates the threat of a profound upheaval in the European media landscape; thanks to the powerful instrument which the information highway represents, this landscape could be submerged by an ocean of images of which only the smallest proportion has any redeeming artistic content.

The Specific Interest of the European Heritage in Multimedia Creation

Today, in the multimedia world, European backwardness is often bemoaned, from the perspective of the United States and Japan. But the main question here should not be the preoccupations of European industries, unable to profit fully from the vast potential of a future market. Everywhere in Europe the traditional cultural sectors are threatened by budgetary cuts, while at the same time there is a scramble to invest in the multimedia sector, in order to stand up against the gigantic economic investments of the Americans and the Japanese.

Thanks to its deep roots, enormous diversity and extraordinary richness, European heritage constitutes the cultural treasure at the centre of the specific interest of the multimedia industry. The new interactive communication space will enlarge our horizons: but the price to pay for this incredible mass of ever-updated information may also be a loss, a loss difficult to appreciate, in the direct and sensorial contact between ourselves and reality. The rapid evolution of the global multimedia market, pushing the traditional arts and media into the background, may compromise the values and contents of the European heritage, levelling them down to a lowest common denominator. In the long term, the result of this globalisation may be an irreversible loss of European cultural identity.

As the information revolution accelerates, calling on ever-greater financial investments, only a vast intensification of the creative approach, throughout Europe, can succeed in counterbalancing a total commercialisation of the cultural sector. Yet the creative participation of all the cultural actors can only be initiated by a cultural policy directed in common at the European level. And the European multimedia industry, by accepting a larger share of responsibility for multimedia artistic creation, can only profit from this engagement in its own field.

Mobilisation of the Cultural Actors

If public authorities in Europe leave the field open to the economic interests of the "global players" in the vital sectors of information and communication, they must, in the interests of preserving our societies' cultural identity, establish norms that will ensure the beneficial use of new technologies. In order to prevent an irreversible impoverishment of European culture, the control of content and of its communication cannot be left to the sole ambitions of the industrial and commercial parties.

At the risk of encouraging Euro-scepticism, it should be stated that a better promotion of the enormous potential of new technologies for the cultural and social life of all our societies can only come about through a concerted harmonisation of cultural and economic policies. These must take into account and respect the cultural richness and diversity of all the societies in Europe and encourage the creative participation of all its cultural actors.

This necessary mobilisation of creative resources could be based on a growing number of initiatives in the artistic domain. In anticipation of the promising results expected from the association between art and new technology, research centres and centres of artistic experimentation have emerged in art schools throughout Europe. For several years, there have been exhibitions and festivals in this same field. Along with these initiatives, which are often of an institutional nature and which denote a growing acceptance of these new media by the concerned public, we also see the emergence of a large number of "private" cultural initiatives in the field of electronic networks, such as the Internet.

The aim of these initiatives is the study of specific techniques and the realisation and presentation of total multimedia works of art. They aim to promote innovation and also to criticise blind enthusiasm for the new communication technologies. In order to preserve Europe's identity and cultural diversity, and bring new life to it, it is precisely in this direction that the concerted efforts of its cultural and economic policies should be oriented.

The Technology Of Uselessness

Critical Art Ensemble

I am useless, but God loves me.

Mike Kelly

The expectation that technology will one day exist as pure utility is an assumption that frequently surfaces in collective thought on the development of society and social relations. This prospect has typically suggested two opposite scenarios of the future. On one hand, there is the utopian millennium predicted by modern thinkers who were guided by belief in progress; this concept slowly began to supplant belief in the concept of providence during the 17th and 18th centuries. Both concepts were characterized by belief in the unilinear development of the human race, but providence was a force that was expected to result in spiritual, rather than in economic, autonomy. The engine of providence was considered the guiding hand of God (which was later amputated and stitched to the cyborg of capitalism by Adam Smith). In Early Modernity, when belief in providence began giving way to belief in progress, intellectuals and scholars were debating whether the social utopia of the future should be based on spiritual or on secular principles. Philosophers searched for an independent force in the universe that could save the earthly population from its economic shortcomings and its spiritual privation. Thomas More constructed a rather dubious literary utopia that marked the beginning of the shift from God/Christ to science/technology as savior. From More's perspective, neither of the two choices seemed particularly satisfying. Given the choice between El Dorado and the regime of Mahomet the Prophet, Voltaire found the former more tolerable. This type of thought which valued secular human advancement and cast doubt on spiritual systems began to tip the scales of judgment in favor of science and technology, but certainly no celebration accompanied this shift. With the coming of the industrial revolution, the scales tipped decisively in favor of science and technology once and for all. At last, a foreseeable end was imagined to the problem of production — soon there would be enough goods for everyone, and with such surplus, competition over scarce goods would cease. The idea of progress began to flourish from this point on. Both the left (Condorcet and Saint-Simon) and the right (Comte and Spencer) shared an optimism about the future in spite of the wildly divergent destinies predicted by each — for example, council socialism was anticipated by Saint-Simon, and the appearance of the bourgeois Übermensch was expected by Spencer.

Let us not forget Marx in this thumbnail sketch. Although Marx was not one to wax utopian very often, he did have his moments. Marx believed that the factory system would solve problems of production (i.e., scarcity); however, he foresaw a new problem, that of distribution. The crisis in distribution would in turn lead to revolution, by which means the victorious workers would restructure the exploitive routes of bourgeois distribution. Such speculation has continued to manifest itself even later, in utopian visions well exemplified by René Clair in the film *A Nous la Liberté*. The film depicts a time after the glorious revolution when the workers enjoy the fruits of zero work, and live only to celebrate, to drink, and to sing, while the machines work dutifully, producing the goods needed to carry this utopia into a shining future. One of the main currents in modern art (Futurism, Constructivism, and Bauhaus) illustrated this soon-to-come secular utopia. All the same, it would be quite unfair to hang the sometimes shameful optimism of the 20th century on Marx. Although he demonstrated how rationalized capitalist economy would end the problem of production, he also realized that people could not be satisfied by goods alone. Marx foresaw that in the epoch of capitalism, although production rates would rise, so would the degree of alienation from our own human nature, from economic process, from economic products, and from other social beings. In terms of individuals' psychic condition, things would not get better, but would grow tortuously worse. For Marx, once other variables besides production were examined, unilinear social advancement was not to be found.

This brings us to the second scenario — the pessimists' dystopia. This point of view seems to gain new proponents with each new mechanized and/or electronic war. Yet even when the idea of progress was at its apex, before the military catastrophes of the 20th century, some critics of the idea were already predicting that human "advancement" would end in disaster. First and foremost was Ferdinand Tönnies, who argued that advanced technology would only serve to increase the complexity of the division of labor (society), which in turn would strip people of all the institutions that are the basis of human community (family, friendship, public space, etc.). After World War I, Oswald Spengler was among the leaders of this line of thought. To his mind, advanced technology and sprawling cities were not indications of progress; rather, they were indicators of the final moments of civilization — one that has hit critical mass and is about to burn itself out. The great sociologist Pitirim Sorokin summed up this perspective in *The Crisis of Our Age* when he stated:

> Neither happiness, nor safety and security, nor even material comfort has been realized. In few periods of human history have so many millions of persons been so unhappy, so insecure, so hungry and destitute, as at the present time, all the way from China to Western Europe.

Here then are the two sides, forever in opposition. Today the two antithetical opinions continue to manifest themselves throughout culture. Corporate futurologists sing the praises of computerized information management, satellite communications, biotechnology, and cybernetics; such technological miracles, they assure us, will make life easier as new generations of technology are designed and produced to meet social and economic needs with ever-greater efficiency. On the other hand, the concerns of pessimists, neoluddites, retreatists, and technophobes ring out, warning that humanity will not control the machines, but that the machines will control humanity. In more fanciful (generally Hollywood) moments, the new dystopia is envisioned as a world where people are caught in the evil grip of a self-conscious intelligent machine, one that either forces them into slavery, or even worse, annihilates the human race.

These are the two most common narratives of social evolution in regard to technology. For the utopians, the goal of progress is similar to the vision of René Clair — technology should become a transparent backdrop that will liberate us from the forces of production, so that we might engage in free hedonistic pursuits. For the dystopians, technology represents a state apparatus that is out of control — the war machine has been turned on, no one knows how to turn it off, and it is running blindly toward the destruction of humanity.

Evidence can certainly be found to support both of these visions, but a third possibility exists, one that is seldom mentioned because it lacks the emotional intensity of the other two. To expand on the suggestion of Georges Bataille, could the end of technological progress be neither apocalypse nor utopia, but simply uselessness? Pure technology in this case would not be an active agent that benefits or hurts mankind: it could not be, as it has no function. Pure technology, as opposed to pure utility, is never turned on; it just sits, existing in and of itself. Unlike the machines of the utopians and dystopians, not only is it free of humanity, it is free of its own machine function — it serves no practical purpose for anyone or anything.

Where are these machines? They are everywhere — in the home, in the workplace, and even in places that can only be imagined. So many people have become so invested in seeing technology as a manifestation of value or anti-value, that they have failed to see that much of technology does nothing at all.

Recently, there has been considerable fascination with the perception that most people cannot learn to operate their video tape decks. As one comedian put it, "I just bought a VCR for $400, and can't figure out how to work it. $400 is just too much for a clock that only blinks 12:00." This situation is certainly exaggerated, but there is an interesting point of truth in it. To program many of the functions on a VCR require skills beyond those of the average consumer. When video first hit the consumer markets, the belief was that everyone would soon have a TV studio in h/er house (along with a jet pack). The home TV studio would mark the end of progress in video production. Instead, VCRs filled with useless computer chips now gather cobwebs in home entertainment centers. For example, consider the existence of a chip which allows a VCR to be programmed for a month in advance; this is actually nothing more than an homage to the useless. It simply exists in and of itself, having no real life function. Most programming information is not generally available a month in advance, and even if it were, why would someone need to tape a month's worth of television programs, and who would remember the appropriate times to insert new blank tapes?

Why such a chip was made in the first place falls into a web of possibility that is difficult to untangle. First, the perverse desires that consumers associate with utility should not be underestimated. Driven by spectacularized engines of desire, consumers want more for their money — even if what they get is something that will never be used. The corporate answer is to meet a cliché with a cliché: Give customers what they want. Consequently, the marketing departments of corporations, in their struggle for market share in the electronics industry, force their engineers and designers to create new products laden with extra features. One main selling point: Our machine has the most features for the money. The question for the consumer is: "Did I get a good deal [i.e., the most for the money]?" The question of "Can I actually use what I buy?" is never raised. The corporations know of the desire for the useless (a desire that can never be fulfilled), and comply by heaping on their products as much useless gadgetry as possible in order to seduce the bargain-hungry consumer. And so the cycle starts.

The cycle begins to spiral as new generations of technology are introduced — in this case depurified technology. The slogan of one electronics company — "so smart, it's simple" — is symbolic of depurification. The corporation is, in a sense, announcing that its technology actually has a use. Consumers can buy it not just for the sake of having it, but because they will be able to make it do something. The slogan also signals that consumers are buying the privilege of being stupid (the ultimate commodity in the realm of conspicuous consumption). There will be no manuals to read, no assembly, no understanding required. The manual is the TV commercial for the product. Having seen it, consumers can make the product function.

While the buying patterns of those seduced by pure technology are guided by a perverse consumer activism, thoroughly corrupted by the Veblenesque nightmare of conspicuous consumption, the patterns of those buying impure technology are guided by a need to keep the apparatus of use as invisible as possible, so as not to interrupt the trajectory of one's "lifestyle." This attempt to return to impure technology eventually backfires, and the spiral becomes a circle again. The consumer zeal for simple technology that will not distract from daily tasks is too easily rechanneled into specialized products that rarely deliver the convenience that is so desperately sought. Two types of products emerge from this variety of artificially generated desire. First there is the product that is a con, such as an electric martini shaker. This is one case where the old fashioned way works just as well if not better. The second type is exemplified by a consumer-grade pasta making machine. One evening at home with this gizmo will quickly teach a person the meaning of labor intensification. This is not a technology of convenience. Either way, these pieces of bourgeois wonder will take their rightful place in upper cabinets and in closets as useless pieces of bric-a-brac that did not even serve the function of delivering enriched consumer privation. Unlike the VCR chip, these pieces of technology require human contact before they achieve purity.

In all cases, the desire that consumer economy (the economy of surplus) has most successfully tapped is the need for excess, that is, the need to have so much that it is beyond human use. Pleasure is derived through negation — by not using a product. This form of excess is the privilege of those who enjoy the surplus of production. Although the bourgeoisie has never achieved the purity of uselessness of previous leisure classes, they still aspire with great fear, and with very little success, to total counter-production. This class typically falls short of the upper level of the hierarchy of master and slave so aptly articulated by Hegel. The products which members of this class consume transform themselves into stand-ins for the obscene debauchery of excess, in which, they, as chieftains, should personally participate. The cowardice of the bourgeoisie can never be underestimated. Confronted with the opportunity to test the limits of the possible, they instead let things take their place in the realm of the useless. Within this realm, the products of counter-production acquire a being analogous to that of the sacred in "primitive" cultures, and become the icons of secular transcendentalism, accumulating mana by controlling the lives of those around them.

The uncanny notion that technology which is out of sight and out of mind best defines human existence within the economy of desire is one that is typically resisted by commonsense thought. As William James and Alfred Schutz proposed in their own unique ways, the principle of practicality structures everyday life. Objects are perceived first and foremost in terms of their instrumental value. In constructing a model of individual existence centered around perception, there can be little doubt that the visible will be at the center and the invisible at the margins. Within the middle ground, utility is the primary governing factor. Hence, within this visible realm, the consumption of excess and excess consumption maintains an element of practicality. For example, a wealthy person buys a luxury car. Although it may have many useless elements, the main reason for its purchase is that it is a "nice ride." The modifying adjective "nice" refers to its useless components, while the center component, the noun "ride," refers to the product's function. The potential for the car to make an instrumental process pleasurable is what relegates it to the realm of desire and excess, and therefore makes it suitable as a product for conspicuous consumption.

Another example is the Magnetic Resonance Imaging (MRI) device. In many cases, the way this diagnostic tool is used in medical institutions may actually be abuse. The MRI is a very expensive piece of state of the art med-tech, so it is an investment that must be used to recoup the initial capital expenditure. The MRI can deliver on its corporate promise, as it is the perfect medical sight machine. In a manner far beyond any of its predecessors, the MRI can articulate the space of the body with such clarity that there can be no place for a biological body invader to hide. However, in many cases, the MRI is not needed. An X-ray is often all that is required to diagnose an illness. Excess enters this equation when the MRI is used abusively on the part of the doctor (simply as means to increase profit or to protect capital). Much the same can be said even when the machine is used as an extra precaution by the doctor or the patient. In any case, the MRI, like the luxury car, can only strive toward purity; it will never actually reach it. The MRI will always have the practical function of vision associated with it. Unlike these aforementioned examples, the useless is rarely noticed, because it is not a part of limited bourgeois excess. As consumers, we are not trained to witness uselessness or consciously value it — its psychic roots are buried much deeper in consciousness and in the economy.

Too often, excessive luxury in the center realm of the visible is mistaken for the limits of excess, but the limits of excess go far beyond the visible. To comprehend extreme excess, one must go beyond conspicuous consumption. Excess will never be seen, only imagined, and within this ideal space the margins can at least be understood. Whether it is a useless chip in the bowels of a machine, the technology that lives in people's closets, or an underground missile system, the purity of uselessness, the limits of excess, are not visible. The real deployment of power flows in absence, in the uncanny, nonrational margins of existence.

Sacrifices beyond the boundary between the visible and the invisible occasionally surface in everyday life. We all know that many people die on the roads and highways of the US every year (approximately 50,000 per year). These people are willingly and uselessly sacrificed to show the sincerity of our desire for transportation technology. No means to end this sacrifice exists, short of closing the roads, and yet no honor is paid to those who give their life for the excess of travel — it remains forever hidden. Philosopher and artist Gregory Ulmer proposed that an addendum be made to the Viet Nam war memorial in which the names of those killed on the highway would be spooled off on a printer beside the monument. Needless to say this monument was rejected, since such sacrifice and excess must remain hidden in modern societies. To monumentalize death and uselessness is simply too frightening.

Monuments to the sacrifices of the state are typical, but are only the beginning. Most of these monuments are abstracted bits of concrete, marble, bronze, or some other material that will signify the longevity of artificially created memory. But there are times when these monuments are brutally honest, and useless technology along with its slaves is put on public display. The USS Arizona, for example — a half sunken ship with the ship's full complement of corpses (officers included) rests silently in Pearl Harbor. This national monument, a functional item made useless through sacrifice, suggests the metaphysical moment of profound loss through its lack of function. (Woe to anyone who does not treat this sacred relic with proper respect, for it speaks of the will to excess, which is grounded in human uselessness in the face of death). But what is even more compelling about this monument is that the ship is carried on the active duty roster. This necropolis is more a symbol of the absent core of the war machine than a monument to the US soldiers who died in the battle of Pearl Harbor; it monumentalizes transcendental uselessness.

Utopian technology is that technology which has fallen from grace. It has been stripped of its purity and reendowed with utility. The fall is necessitated by a return to contact with humanity. Having once left the production table, the technology that lives the godly life of state-of-the-art uselessness has no further interaction with humans as users or as inventors; rather, humans serve only as a means to maintain its uselessness. The location of the most complex pure technology is of no mystery. Deep in the core of the war machine is the missile system. Ultimately, all research is centered around this invisible monument to uselessness. The bigger and more powerful it becomes, the greater its value. But should it ever be touched by utility — that is, should it ever be used — its value becomes naught. To be of value, it must be maintained, upgraded, and expanded, but it must never actually do anything. This idol of destruction is forever hungry, and is willing to eat all resources. In return, however, it excretes objects of utility. Consumer communications and transportation systems, for example, have dramatically improved due to the continuous research aimed at increasing the grandeur of the apparatus of uselessness.

There can be a stopping point to this process — a discovery made by the collapsing Soviet Union. For all the "patriots of democracy" who gave a collective sigh of relief and boasted that they were at last proven right — "communism doesn't work" — there still may be a need to worry. The fall of the USSR had little to do with ideology. The US and USSR were competitors in producing the best apparatus of uselessness in order to prove its own respective Hegelian mastery of the globe. Modern autocrats and oligarchs have long known that a standing army puts an undue strain on the economy. To be sure, standing armies were early monuments to uselessness, but in terms of both size and cost, they are dwarfed by the standing missile system of the electronic age. As with all things that are useless, there will be no return on the investment in it. The useless represents a 100% loss of capital. Although such investment seems to go against the utilitarian grain of visible bourgeois culture, whether in socialist or in constitutional republics, the compulsive desire for a useless master is much greater (Japan is an interesting exception to this rule). Unfortunately for the USSR, they were unable to indulge in pure excess expenditure at the same rate as the US. The soviet techno-idol was a little more constipated, and could not maintain the needed rate of excretion. Consequently, once the limits of uselessness were reached, that system imploded.

The US government, on the other hand, has to this day remained convinced that further progress can be made. Reagan and his Star Wars campaign issued a policy radically expanding the useless. Reagan, of course, was the perfect one to make the policy, since he was an idol to uselessness himself. He represents one of the few times that uselessness has taken an organic form in this century. (This is part of the reason he was considered such a bourgeois hero. He was willing to personally plunge into uselessness without apology. He did not let a thing stand in for him). Playing on yuppie paranoia (the fascists' friend), Reagan convinced the public loyal to him that a defensive monument (Star Wars) to uselessness was needed, just in case the offensive monument (the missile system) was not enough. He was successful enough in his plea to guarantee that years of useless research will ensue that no one will be able to stop, even if his original monumental vision (a net of laser armed satellites) should be erased. In this manner, Reagan made sure that the apparatus of uselessness would expand even if the cold war ended.

Indeed, this situation has come to pass. Currently, the US has no competitors in the race to uselessness, but the monument continues to be maintained and even to grow, which is particularly odd, since even the cynical argument of deterrence is now moot. Even though the offensive monument to uselessness seems to be shrinking — missiles are being defused and cut apart with the care and order of high ritual, and technology costing millions of dollars is being laid to rest, having never done anything but exist — thanks to Reagan's farsightedness, the general system continues to expand. Although many are still in denial, the desire of the bourgeois to subordinate themselves to the useless has become, for the moment, glaringly visible. The research is done, the system is upgraded, but for what reason? The missiles are now aimed at the ocean, so that even if they are "used," they will still be useless. The fragments of Star Wars technology have not been released in pure form from the experimental labs, and even if they were, no enemy exists against which Star Wars technology would protect US citizens. The American system has achieved utter transcendental uselessness. This techno-historical moment is the highest manifestation of technological purity.

In his rush to save the apparatus of the useless from stalling, Reagan may have made one error. When he put the idea of the defensive monument in the minds of Americans, he disrupted the primary sign of the war machine — mutually assured destruction. He restored hope in American consciousness that perhaps utility could save US citizens from the total annihilation certain to destroy the rest of the world. The disassociation of death and uselessness took previously sacred elements of war-tech out of the privileged realm. When these elements became depurified, their value in terms of the satisfaction of bourgeois desire plummeted. This is partly why Reagan's original Star Wars vision has been dismantled.

Thus far, however, most war-tech has not been depurified due to this ideological slippage, and the purity of offensive weapons of mass destruction continues to be enforced. Nations that do not understand the code of uselessness but that have state of the art military technology are a cause for great concern. Iraq, Libya, and North Korea are all good examples. The US government is willing to take hostile action based merely on the belief that North Korea and Libya might get weapons of mass destruction and actually use them. In the case of Iraq, the code was actually broken when that government used chemical weapons. Iraq has not done well economically or militarily since that time. The lesson to be learned is that nations that do not subordinate themselves to the bourgeois idols of uselessness will be sacrificed as heretics, and will be denied access to the icons of uselessness.

In spite of the common wisdom of using the variables of national interest and utility to explain the relationship between desire and power, it is just as fruitful to do so using the principles of the anti-economy — perversity and uselessness. The economy of unchanneled desire and perversity, as suggested by Bataille, penetrates the surface of utility in a most convincing way. Progress in the 20th century has primarily consisted of bourgeois culture looking for a new master. In the time of bourgeois revolution, the aristocracy was destroyed, as was the church with its spiritual hierarchies, but the primordial desire to serve the useless has never been affected. The "primitive" ritual of offering goods to an angry or potentially angry

God in order to appease it into a state of neutrality continues to replay itself in complex capitalist economy. All things must be subordinated to neutrality — to uselessness. One major difference between the age of the virtual and more primitive times is that the contemporary idols have no metaphysical referent. The ones that have been constructed are not the mediating points between person and spirit, or life and afterlife; rather, they are end-points, empty signs. To this paper master, sacrifice has no limit. The stairs of the temple flow with blood every day. How fitting for progress to come to this end in the empire of the useless. As this mythic narrative continues to play itself out, the suggestion of Arthur and Marilouise Kroker begins to make more and more sense. We are not witnessing the decline of late capital, but instead, its recline into its own delirious death trance.

Contributors

Arthur and Marilouise Kroker are writers and lecturers in the areas of technology and contemporary culture. Arthur Kroker is the author of *Spasm* and co-author of *Data Trash: The Theory of the Virtual Class*. Together, they edit both the CultureTexts Series and the electronic journal CTHEORY. Their most recent book was *Hacking the Future*, published by St. Martin's Press, New York, and in German translation by Passagen Verlag, Vienna.

Kathy Acker is a leading American writer. Among others, her books include *Empire of the Senseless, Don Quixote, My Mother: Demonology*, and *Blood and Guts in High School*. Her most recent novel is entitled *Pussy, King of the Pirates*. She is a member of the Editorial Board of CTHEORY.

Robert Adrian X is a Canadian artist who has lived in Europe since 1960 and in Vienna since 1972. As a visual artist working in most media — sculpture, painting, video, photography and electronic art — he has been particularly active in the field of "Art and Telecommunications." He is a member of the Editorial Board of CTHEORY.

Paolo Atzori and **Kirk Woolford** are writers and electronic artists based at the Academy of Media Arts, Cologne, Germany.

Jean Baudrillard is an internationally acclaimed theorist whose writings trace the rise and fall of symbolic exchange in the 20th century. Many of his books are available in English translation, among them *Seduction, Fatal Strategies, Forget Foucault*, and *The Perfect Crime*. He is a member of the Editorial Board of CTHEORY.

Caroline Bayard is a professor of French and an Associate member of the Department of Philosophy at McMaster University. Her works include *More Than Two Hundred Years of Solitudes* (Toronto: ECW Press, 1992); and *Transatlantiques postmodernites* (Montréal: Balzac, 1996).

Hakim Bey is best known for his zine-publications that were collected under the title *TAZ: The Temporary Autonomous Zone, Ontological Anarchy, Poetic Terrorism*, and more recently, *Immediatism*. His most recent book is entitled *Millennium* (Brooklyn, NY: Autonomedia; and Dublin: Garden of Delight, 1996).

Jace Clayton (/rupture) is a writer, installation artist, and cultural activist. **Sasha Costanza-Chock (Splice)** has been trying to grow something electro-organic (including experimental musicians, visual artists, assorted cyborgs, magicians, and freaks, called tone*burst) in the Boston area for the past couple of years.

David Cook is professor of Political Science at the University of Toronto, and author of *Northrop Frye: A Vision of the New World* (New York: St. Martin's Press, 1985), and *The Postmodern Scene* (New York: St. Martin's Press, 1986), with Arthur Kroker. He is a member of the Editorial Board of CTHEORY.

BC Crandall is the founder and director of Molecular Realities and the founder and president of Memetic Engineering. His most recent book is entitled, *Nanotechnology: Molecular Speculations on Global Abundance* (Cambridge, MA: MIT Press, 1996).

Critical Art Ensemble (CAE) is a collective of six artists of different specializations committed to the production of a new genre art that explores the intersections among critical theory, art and technology. Their most recent book is entitled *Electronic Civil Disobedience* (Brooklyn, NY: Autonomedia, 1997).

Michael Dartnell is a lecturer in Political Science at Concordia University, Montréal. He is the author of *Action Directe: Ultra-left Terrorism in France, 1979-1987*. He has published several articles on both French political violence and sexual identity.

Ricardo Dominguez is part of the editorial collective of Blast5 <http://interport.net/~xaf>, Managing Editor of The Thingnyc <http://www.thing.net/thingnyc>, a member of the New York Committee for Democracy in Mexico, and a former member of Critical Art Ensemble.

Alexander Galloway is Director of pressé media, and editorial assistant at RHIZOME INTERNET. He has written on Tel Quel and the French avant-garde.

Sue Golding is a political philosopher and theatre director, and is Reader at the University of Greenwich, London. Her latest book as author/editor is entitled *The 8 Technologies of Otherness* (London: Routledge 1997).

Lynn Hershman Leeson is a professor of electronic art at the University of California, Davis. In 1995 she received the Siemens Media Prize with Peter Greenaway and Jean Baudrillard. An artist in mixed media, including photography, film, installation and computers, she created the first interactive artwork, *Lorna*. Her most recent project is the feature film, *Conceiving Ada*. She is a member of the Editorial Board of CTHEORY.

Ken Hollings lives in London. He is the author of "Electronically Yours, Eternally Elvis" in *The Last Sex*, Arthur and Marilouise Kroker, eds. (New York: St. Martin's Press, 1993). He recently completed a manuscript entitled "Destroy All Monsters."

Graham Knight teaches sociology at McMaster University in Hamilton, Ontario, Canada. His interests lie primarily in the areas of contemporary social theory, mass communications and popular culture.

Knowbotics Research (KR+cF), Yvonne Wilhelm, Alexander Tuchacek and Christian Hübler, is based in Cologne, Germany, at the Academy of Media Arts. KR+cF has won many media art awards, including the Prix Ars Electronica 93.

Frank Lantz is a computer game designer from New York City. He also teaches game design at NYU and writes software reviews for ID (International Design) magazine.

Jon Lebkowsky was cofounder and former CEO of FringeWare, Inc. and is currently contributing editor for HotWired's Piazza, hosting the weekly Electronic Frontiers Forum <http://www.hotwired.com/eff>. He's hung out on the cyber* (*=punk, activist, foo, et al) fringes for over a decade.

Geert Lovink is a Dutch media theorist and a member of "Adilkno." He is involved with the Digital City project in Amsterdam and most recently has worked in Eastern Europe as an advisor for media art and independent media. He is a member of the Editorial Board of CTHEORY.

Lev Manovich is a theorist and critic of new media. He is currently working on two books: a collection of essays on digital realism and a history of the social and cultural origins of computer graphics technologies, entitled *The Engineering of Vision from Constructivism to Virtual Reality*. He is Assistant Professor in the Visual Arts Department at the University of California, San Diego.

Lorenzo Miglioli is an Italian media theorist. He has written three novels: *Hitler-Warhol Experience*; the first italian hypertext novel, entitled *Ra-Dio* and *Berlusconi is a Retrovirus*. His new novel, entitled *Natura Morta*, will be published soon.

When he isn't trout fishing or chasing elk, **Pat Munday** teaches in the Program in Society & Technology at Montana Tech of the University of Montana in Butte. His current research interest is "Trout as Modern Object/Postmodern Subject."

John Nòto is a writer who lives in San Francisco. A volume of his work entitled *Psycho-motor Breathscapes* was recently published by Vatic Hum Press, San Francisco. He is also the editor of *Orpheus Grid*, a magazine of poetry, poetic prose and essays.

Marcos Novak is an architect, artist, composer, and theorist investigating actual, virtual and mutant intelligent environments. He originated the study of liquid architectures in cyberspace, and is founding director of the RealityLab and the Advanced Design Research Program at the School of Architecture at the University of Texas at Austin.

Warren Padula is best known for his series, INFERNO: Shopping in America. Padula has exhibited internationally and is in numerous museum collections. Padula is a frequent contributor to the Krokers' projects, most recently *Hacking The Future*.

Stephen Pfohl is the author of the CultureTexts book, *Death at the Parasite Café*. A video-maker and performing artist, he is Professor of Sociology at Boston College and a member of the CTHEORY Editorial Board.

Bernhard Serexhe is Curator at the Media Museum, Center for Art and Media ZKM, in Karlsruhe, Germany. You can visit their World Wide Web site at <http://www.zkm.de/departments/medienmuseum/main.en.html>.

Alan Shapiro is a software developer who lives in Frankfurt, Germany. He also taught sociology for several years at New York University. He has published essays in *Semiotext(e)* and *And Then*. He is writing about the virtuality syndrome, the gambling boom in America, and fatal theory.

R.U. Sirius is best known as co-founder and original Editor-In-Chief of the first cyberculture magazine, *Mondo 2000*. He's co-author, with Timothy Leary, of *Design For Dying* (New York: Harper Edge, 1997). He's a regular columnist for *ARTFORUM International, 21C*, and *EYE-COM*, and a contributing writer for *Wired*. He is a member of the Editorial Board of CTHEORY.

Stelarc is an Australian performance artist who uses medical instruments, robots, virtual reality systems and the internet to explore alternate body possibilities. He has performed with a prosthetic hand, a virtual arm, robot manipulators and a mechanism inserted inside his body. He is a member of the Editorial Board of CTHEORY.

Bruce Sterling, science-fiction writer extraordinaire, is the author of, among others, *Islands in the Net* and *The Hacker Crackdown: Law and Disorder on the Electronic Frontier*. He is a member of the Editorial Board of CTHEORY.

Richard Thieme is a professional speaker, consultant, and writer. His focus is the impact of computer technology on people and organizations. He helps people understand the relationship of computer networks to their lives.

Paul Virilio is the emblematic French theorist of technology. His major works include: *Pure War, Speed and Politics*, and *War and Cinema: the Logistics of Perception*. Two of his most recent books are *Desert Screen* and *The Art of The Engine*.

Michael A. Weinstein is Professor of Political Science at Purdue University. **Deena Weinstein** is Professor of Sociology at DePaul University. Their most recent jointly-authored work is *Postmodern(ized) Simmel* (London: Routledge). Michael Weinstein is most recently the author of *Culture/Flesh: Explorations of Postcivilized Modernity* (London: Rowman & Littlefield Publishers, 1995). Deena Weinstein also authored *Heavy Metal: A Cultural Sociology* (Lexington MA: Lexington Books, 1991). They are members of the Editorial Board of CTHEORY.

Daniel R. White is an associate professor in the Department of Philosophy at the University of Central Florida, where he teaches critical theory and cultural studies. His recent works include *Postmodern Ecology: Communication, Evolution and Play* (forthcoming, SUNY Press, 1997), and *Labyrinths of the Mind* (forthcoming, SUNY, 1998).

Louise Wilson is a British artist whose work involves site specific installations and perfomance.

Siegfried Zielinski has written numerous books in the areas of art, philosophy and communications, including *Audiovisionen: Kino und Fernsehen als Zwischenspiele in der Geschichte*. He is director of the Academy of Media Arts in Cologne, Germany <http://www.khm.uni-koeln.de/>. He is a member of the Editorial Board of CTHEORY.

Slavoj Zizek, a leading intellectual in the new social movements of Eastern and Central Europe, is a researcher at the Institute of Sociology at the University of Ljubljana, Slovenia. He is the author of numerous books, including *Looking Awry: An Introduction to Jacques Lacan Through Popular Culture*.

www.ctheory.com

Kathy Acker
Robert Adrian X
Paolo Atzori &
   Kirk Woolford
Jean Baudrillard
Caroline Bayard
   & Graham Knight
Hakim Bey
Aleksandar Boskovic
David Cook
Sasha Costanza-Chock
   & Jace Clayton
BC Crandall
Critical Art Ensemble
Michael Dartnell
Ricardo Dominguez
Alexander Galloway
Sue Golding
Lynn Hershman Leeson
Ken Hollings
Knowbotics Research
Arthur Kroker
   & Marilouise Kroker
Frank Lantz
Jon Lebkowsky
Geert Lovink
Lev Manovich
Lorenzo Miglioli
Pat Munday
John Nòto
Marcos Novak
Stephen Pfohl
Bernhard Serexhe
Alan Shapiro
R.U. Sirius
Stelarc
Bruce Sterling
Richard Thieme
Paul Virilio
Deena Wein
   & Michael
Daniel R. White
Louise Wilson
Siegfried Zielinski
Slavoj Zizek

St. Martin's Press
175 Fifth Avenue, New York, NY 10010
Printed and Bound in Canada

DIGITAL DELIRIUM

**edited and introduced by
Arthur and Marilouise Kroker**

Digital Delirium writes the new horizon of electronic culture. The latest addition to the CultureTexts Series, *Digital Delirium* brings together some of the best minds involved in rethinking technoculture in the 90s.

30 Cyber-Days in San Francisco

Digital Delirium writes the streets of San Francisco as a way of talking about the ambiguous legacy of wired culture.

Digital Futures

Digital Delirium interviews R.U. Sirius, Paul Virilio, Jean Baudrillard, and Slavoj Zizek, and includes a state of the digital union address by Bruce Sterling.

Net Politics

The 90s began with a blast of techno-utopianism, but it will end with slow suicide in the surplus streets. Net Politics is the story of the 90s as a radically split reality: surplus class and virtual class, surplus flesh and virtual flesh, separate and digitally unequal.

The Global Algorithm

What is gained and what is lost by being digital? What do we see when we look in the ⎯⎯⎯⎯ mirror: Future-Fallout or Net-Utopia? ⎯⎯ s and diamond eyes or real blood

Cover photo: Paul Winternitz

ISBN 0-312-17237-0